EXPOSITION

OF THE

SERMON ON THE MOUNT

EXPOSITION

OF THE

SERMON ON THE MOUNT

DRAWN FROM THE

Writings of St. Augustine

WITH AN INTRODUCTORY ESSAY ON

AUGUSTINE AS AN INTERPRETER OF SCRIPTURE

BY

RICHARD CHENEVIX TRENCH, D.D.

ARCHBISHOP

FOURTH EDITION, REVISED

Wipf and Stock Publishers
199 W 8th Ave, Suite 3
Eugene, OR 97401

Exposition of the Sermon on the Mount
Drawn from the Writings of St. Augustine with an Introductory
Essay on Augustine as an Interpreter of Scripture
By Trench, Richard Chenevix
ISBN: 1-59752-639-8
Publication date 4/14/2006
Previously published by Kegan Paul, Trench, & Co., 1886

PREFACE

TO

THE FIRST EDITION.

THIS VOLUME is not, as a glance at any page will show, a translation of St. Augustine's *Commentary on the Sermon on the Mount*, but an attempt to draw from the whole circle of his writings (that one of course included), what of most valuable he has contributed for the elucidation, or for the turning to practical uses, of this portion of Holy Scripture.

Yet I am conscious, from the very plan upon which the book is written, that it may be open to a charge, at least from an unfriendly critic, of something like presumption. It may be urged that there is in it a continual passing of judgment,—an allowing and a disallowing,—a selecting and a putting aside,—an approving and a condemning; and this in regard of one whom the Church has ever and justly recognized among the very foremost and greatest of her teachers. A friend, to whom the manuscript, when nearly prepared for press, was shown,—and whose counsel and judgment that I am able so freely to profit by, is one of the chief happinesses of my life,—has warned me that it will hardly escape a charge of the kind. Yet I have not therefore been persuaded to alter my scheme, as indeed an attempt so to do could only have issued in a renouncing of the work altogether. For the plan which is now finding so much favour among us, of presenting in the mass, unsifted and untried, the old expositions of Scripture, often placing side by side explanations which, in their minor details at least, exclude one another, and this with no attempt to judge or discriminate between them,—with no endeavour to separate the accident of one age, the superfluous, it may be the injurious, excrescence from the eternal truth, which is of all and for all ages,—seems to me profitable for little, and not likely to lead us into any deeper or clearer and more intelligent knowledge of Scripture. Moreover, when we confine ourselves merely to giving back the old, and this with well-nigh a suspension of all judgment about it, what is this but saying, that the productive powers of the Church have ceased; that her power of educing from God's Word, by that Spirit which is ever with her, the truth in those forms wherein it will best meet our present needs, exists no longer; that henceforth the Scripture shall be for us a cistern, clear it may be, and full, but not any more a spring of water springing up as freshly and newly for our lips, as for the lips of any generation which has gone before; and that as her productive, so also that her discriminative power is gone; she may no longer discern that which is akin to, and will assimilate with, her true life, and claim that and that only for her own?

Neither seems there any genuine humility in foregoing or denying our advantages—they may be slight ones compared with those which other ages enjoyed—for entering into the meaning of God's Word; but, if slight, therefore

to be husbanded the more. And, not to speak of the
accumulation of merely critical and external helps, some
such advantages we plainly have. To deny this were to
deny to the Church,—to her who, according to her truest
idea, is ever teacher and ever taught,—that she has been
learning anything in the eighteen hundred years of her
troubled warfare with the evil within her and the evil
without. Yet some things surely she has found out: some
practices which promised well, which she anticipated would
further piety, her own life and history have taught her do
inevitably sooner or later run to seed, and hinder that
holiness which they were meant to set forward; that,
tolerably safe in the hands of the earnest few, they are
most unsafe when they descend, as by inevitable progress
they must descend, to the more careless many. Some
language which for a while she held, or did not at least
absolutely exclude, she has now discovered not to be the
most adequate expression of the doctrines which she has
always held, and therefore she will use no longer; and
will disclaim, though she find it used by the most honoured
of her teachers, even as she is sure that they would themselves disclaim it now. Before the false teaching of
Eutyches had compelled her clearly to represent to herself
the relation of the two natures in Christ, it impeached no
man's orthodoxy, though he spoke of our blessed Lord as
God *mingled with* man; but who that meant right would
have used this language after? Before the order of our
justification had been brought out with that distinctness,
wherewith a truth can be brought out only through an
earnest contending for it against some that would obscure
or deny it, men might put the first last, and speak of sins
' expiated with alms,' or ' washed out with tears.' In such

language we recognize a loss, as in all lack of distinctness there is such, but not a denial upon their parts who used this language *then*, that 'we are justified by faith only.' It would be quite another thing to seek to revive and return to that language now.

The consciousness, moreover, that we too, in our age, have our errors,—most of them, like some inner vest, worn so close, as to be invisible even to ourselves,—that we, too, have our mistaken tendencies, our superstitions, our faulty statements of the truth, which we are handing down to the Church of a later age, for her slowly to discern, painfully to get rid of,—this, while it may well hinder that boastful self-exalting spirit, which is more fatal than any thing beside to a profiting by the past, yet must not hinder from a respectful using, even as regards our great forefathers in the faith themselves, whatsoever since their time the Church has won. Such a freedom they used toward one another, such they demanded should be used toward themselves; and such we must use toward them, if we would obtain from their writings the large blessing which they are capable of yielding; if these are to help to lead us into liberty, and not into bondage; if they are to be indeed our riches, and not, under that name, in reality our poverty.

For myself, who would not willingly for this little volume's sake be exposed to this charge of presumption, I can only say that it was begun in a thankful admiration, which has gone on ever increasing and deepening, for the infinite spiritual and intellectual riches which are contained in the writings of St. Augustine. All added acquaintance with these has more and more explained to me the mighty influence, the wondrous spell which he has exerted over so many among the strongest spirits of all ages,—the great purposes which God in his providence has made him to fulfil for his Church.

For first, if one accurately regards the earlier theology of the Christian East, one is struck with this, that it was in the main a metaphysic of the Divine Being, a contemplation of the Divine attributes and perfections. It was with these, most needful indeed to be fixed and to be first fixed, that the Church was mainly occupied for more than the three earlier centuries of her existence. But in Augustine the theology of the West, and of the modern world,—the theology which relates not merely to God, but to the God of men,—first came out into its full importance. St. Paul had now his rights no less than St. John. Theology was no longer the science of God merely or mainly as He is in Himself, but in his relation to us. It is not any more the objective knowledge of God which is all, but with this the subjective knowledge of God's image in man, that image defaced, and that image restored; it is no longer predominantly a God revealing, but also a God communicating, Himself;—not Christ the God-man only, but Christ the Redeemer as well. And now, too, man first appears in his true worth and dignity. That which shows him to be nothing, shows him also to be much; for in him all these counsels of grace centre; round him these purposes of eternity revolve; he appears as the meeting-place of two worlds; the personal significance of every man comes out, and the free modern western world begins,—the germs of it at least are securely laid. And believing this, one cannot sufficiently admire the manner in which Augustine's appearance was timed; for it was the last moment, at which living he could have shared the fulness of the culture of the ancient world; for thenceforward that whole world was daily becoming more incoherent, and ever falling more rapidly into ruins. He in fact himself survived it in Italy: it hardly survived him a few months in Africa. At the same time he thus lived the nearest to, and in the most favourable position for influencing, that new world, in the forming and moulding of which he was so mightily to aid.

How much he did form it, how far he ruled the Middle Ages, either in his own name, or by fashioning the men who in their turn ruled their generation, is known to every student of Church History. Nor is it hard to understand how this should have been: for the two great tendencies of those ages, the mystic and scholastic, are both lying, in much more than their first elements, side by side in his writings. There is in them, on the one hand, a rare dialectic skill, with the keenest delight in its exercise, and in all speculative inquiry; a desire ever, where it is possible, to justify to the reason what has first been received by faith, with a confidence that what was humbly received by the one would in due time commend itself to the other. Yet with all this there is borne by him a continual witness against the excesses of the dialectic and speculative tendencies: he evermore summons to a more excellent way of knowing, one not mediate, but intuitive and immediate, a knowing which is first a loving; he evermore would have us remember that we shall sooner enter into the deepest mysteries of the faith by praying than disputing.

Nor did his dominion end with the Middle Ages. On the contrary, that work for which we owe him the greatest thanks was yet to be accomplished. The Reformers felt and found that he more than any other was their Doctor. The issue of their later controversy in the matter of justification lay in fact wrapped up in the issue of his controversy with the Pelagians. This last being won, that was implicitly won also, for it was only the same question at a later stage of development, the necessary carrying out of the truths which he then asserted. The contest concerning the extent of the corruption of human nature did most truly involve the question concerning the nature of the remedies which would be equal to meet that corruption, the conditions under which it was possible that the sick man could recover his health; whether aught, in short, could be the remedy, except that *faith* which should place him in immediate relation with Christ, and thus be the channel whereby the uninterrupted streams of a healing life should flow into his soul. And in the Roman Catholic Church itself, whensoever any of her children, a Baius or Jansenius, without being prepared absolutely to break with her, and to forsake her communion, have yet longed to adopt these doctrines of grace in all or nearly all their fulness, they have ever sheltered themselves under the authority of Augustine; they have ever pleaded that they were only holding and teaching what he had held and taught long before.

When we feel thus concerning him,—when we have this thankful recognition of the greatness of his work, which has extended through so many ages, which has indelibly stamped itself on the very form of our Catechism and our Articles,—there can be little reason why we should shrink from expressing, with exactly the confidence we feel in the matter, any occasional dissent from the details of his Scriptural interpretation: above all when in this matter also we know that after every drawback which the truth may require is made, our obligations to him, whether we regard scientific or popular exposition, the laws of interpretation, or the practical application of those laws, are probably larger than to any other single interpreter of God's Word. But because we owe to Augustine a debt of gratitude so large, shall we therefore count ourselves bound to affirm that, in his practical application of his principles, he is always true to his own laws? or that he had himself the same external helps at command as an Origen or a Jerome? or that his Latin Version or his Septuagint has not sometimes led him astray? or that his exposition is not occasionally warped by, and submitted to the influence of, his dogmatic system? or that his allegories and mystical numbers are worthy in every case to stand unquestioned, and may now be profitably reproduced to edify all that come after him? To demand this were to demand for him what he would not have demanded for himself; what can be withheld without abating one jot of genuine reverence and honour, the more valuable because rendered not blindly, but with discrimination and with knowledge.

I will add a few words more upon the plan on which this book has been composed. It resembles, to compare a very small matter with a great, that of the *Augustinus* of Jansenius, a book familiar to many. His purpose, as is well known, in his celebrated work, was to bring all which Augustine had written on one great matter, under review at once, to set it in order, and to present it thus ordered and arranged, with a quotation of the most material passages, before the eyes of his readers. He implied not, in so doing, that Augustine's own works wanted the highest order and method; that they were only as a rough quarry, from which others should dig and build. But the very circumstances of their production necessarily caused that what bears on any single subject should be scattered up and down in divers treatises, and that subject only to be fully discussed when these separated portions are united and brought together. For a large number of his polemical works will not be contemplated from a right point of view, till we see them as occasional tracts, drawn from him by the urgent necessities of the Church at the moment, in answer to the solicitation of friends, or the provocation of enemies; and this, while the controversy was ever shifting its aspect, and each party was more and more feeling its ground, completing and harmonizing its system, discerning little by little the ultimate results to which that would lead. This is the especial value of his writings in more than one conflict wherein he is the standard-bearer of the Church, that they are not one great carefully digested work, reviewing calmly, and in part with a literary interest, a finished controversy; not the history of a battle which the Church has fought and won, but themselves, so to speak, acts and exploits, often the decisive ones, in that battle. Yet while this is their value, it also leaves room for such a work as that with which the Bishop of Ypres so disturbed from his grave the Vatican, and all who wished to reconcile a professed veneration for the great Doctor of the West, with a real departure from the truths which he lived to maintain. This reconciliation, as I need hardly remind those acquainted with the subject, is one of the hardest tasks which the Church of Rome has found imposed upon her; one which signally perplexed her at Trent; which put her to her shiftiest world-wisdom then as since, and one by the *Augustinus* of Jansenius rendered far more difficult than ever.

Now there is room for a conspectus of the same kind, in which should be marshalled and arranged all of most important which Augustine has contributed to the illustration of various portions of Scripture. It is seldom we find in one place all that he has written upon one subject; and even though he should seem, when he returns to it, to be only repeating himself, his intellectual and spiritual resources are such that it rarely happens but that some further touch is added. Then too his convictions on some very important questions gradually underwent a change; thus Rom. vii. 7–25 he explained differently in his earlier and in his later years. These changes can only be profitably studied, when the passages which most distinctly mark them, are set side by side with one another. Take for example that portion of Scripture with which this volume has chiefly to do. His *Exposition of the Sermon on the Mount*, written while he was still a presbyter, contains comparatively little of what he has contributed for the elucidation of this, the longest connected discourse of our Lord. Thus he dismisses the promise, 'For they shall see God' (Matt. v. 8), in two or three lines, while yet this vision of God in other places occupied him greatly: he has dedicated a letter, so long, and in its kind so thorough, that it is often numbered among his treatises, to this single theme. The relation, again, of the new legislation of Christ to the law of Moses, the right apprehension of which can alone give us a key to this Discourse, is very slightly touched on there, as compared with the full and masterly handling which it finds in his writings directed against the Manichæans. Many other examples of the kind might easily be adduced. It is in his *Sermons*, in his *Letters*, in his *Exposition of the Psalms*, in his controversial Tracts, that what he has most precious as bearing on the Sermon on the Mount is to be found ; from these it must be gathered together. It has been my endeavour to concentrate these scattered rays.

I cannot indeed hope that I have brought to bear all or nearly all in his writings which helps to the interpretation of these Chapters, or is characteristic of him as their interpreter; nor that I have made the happiest use of the materials which I had at command. Yet I can truly say that I have been continually embarrassed, not by the scantness, but by the abundance of my materials ; perplexed how to work them up,—how, without exceeding the limits which I had set myself, not to leave out much of a deep interest. Often I have given only a single sentence, sometimes only a reference, when I would willingly have given a page : so that although the book is constructed throughout on the assumption that the reader will not have an *Augustine* at hand, or will not care to afford time for the following up the references, yet it also is arranged to yield much more to one who should be willing to undertake this labour.

Here too another observation may be necessary. It is well known that the Benedictine editors of Augustine, on very slight evidence, often on no evidence at all save their own inward conviction, have dismissed numerous sermons much too hastily, as since has been generally admitted, from the body of his accepted writings. Now there should be something to justify this dismissal, more than a general observation, with which they are often satisfied, that such or such a sermon is quite in the manner of Cæsarius,[1] or of some other. There should be phrases of a later Latin, allusion to Church rites and customs which had not in his time grown into use, inaccuracies in dogmatic statement, thoughts altogether unworthy of a great teacher. Such in many of these discarded sermons there are, entirely justifying what they have done; but in others these marks are altogether wanting, and without the presence of any such the Editors relegate, apparently at their caprice, a sermon to the *Appendix*. I have a few times quoted from these sermons, yet always giving notice of the quarter from whence the quotations are drawn, that the reader may know they are from writings which the Benedictine editors have adjudged not to be his. Of course those I have quoted I have believed to be genuine. On the other hand, I have refrained from making any use of the volume of sermons lately published as Augustine's at Paris,[2] and this, because in it there is a running into the opposite extreme. Doubtless several genuine discourses of his, valuable additions to those which we already possessed, are here published for the first time; but very much also, altogether unworthy of him, is boldly put forth under his name. There is not apparently much in these discourses which would directly bear upon the subject which I have in hand, and till a decision is arrived at about them, carrying with it more weight than any which this very uncritical edition can lend, I have thought it better to leave them altogether untouched.

Perhaps a still more difficult task than to know where

[1] Cæsarii stylum et mentem refert.
[2] *Sancti Aurelii Augustini Sermones inediti, curâ et studio* D. A. B, CAILLAU. Parisiis, 1842.

to stay one's hand in actual quotation, was to leave unnoticed the innumerable interesting subjects which the Sermon on the Mount of itself suggests, to refuse to follow down the avenues, which, as one advances, present themselves ever to the right hand and to the left. Yet this self-denial I have used, wherever a subject was not fairly in one way or another suggested by something which Augustine has said. There is indeed a disadvantage in this, a loss like his who undertakes to paint a picture with a single colour, and whose work is in danger of lacking liveliness and variety, yet a loss amply counterbalanced by the advantage of continuing true to the scheme of one's book; and this scheme in the present instance was not to bring together from all quarters all that I could for the elucidation of this all-important Discourse, but only what of best one great writer had contributed thereto, and thus to give the reader such an idea of him as a practical interpreter of Scripture, as would only have been disturbed and obscured by the introduction of alien matter.

ALVERSTOKE: *May*, 1844.

AUGUSTINE

AS

AN INTERPRETER OF SCRIPTURE.

CHAPTER I.

AUGUSTINE'S GENERAL VIEWS OF SCRIPTURE AND ITS INTERPRETATION.

It is not my intention to offer in the pages which follow any estimate of the worth and significance of St. Augustine's theology, regarded as a whole; but so far as possible to restrict myself to the subject indicated by the title of this Essay, and to consider him in a single light, that is, as an interpreter of Scripture. An essay undertaking this, unless closely watched in its growth, might easily, and almost unawares, pass into that, and thus diffusing and losing itself in an almost illimitable field, become quite another thing from that which it was originally intended to be. At the same time, an attempt to trace his leading characteristics as an expositor, to estimate his accomplishments, spiritual, moral and mental, for being a successful one, to set forth the rules and principles of exposition which he either expressly laid down or habitually acted on, and to give a few specimens of his actual manner of interpretation (which is all I propose to myself here), need not logically involve the necessity of going on to consider his whole scheme of theology. Between so vast and arduous an undertaking as that, and the comparatively humbler, and certainly more limited task which I am attempting here, a line of demarcation may very clearly be drawn, and, if due watchfulness is exercised, may without any serious difficulty be maintained.

In considering the merits of a theologian and interpreter of God's Holy Word, we naturally inquire first, what were his moral qualifications for the work which he undertook; for if goodness be so essential even to the orator, that one of old defined him as '*Vir bonus*, dicendi peritus,' how much more necessary will it be, and in its highest form of love towards God and towards all which is of God, to the true theologian. That old maxim, '*Pectus facit theologum*,' will always continue true, and, other things being equal or nearly equal, he will best explain Scripture, who most loves Scripture, and who has most lived Scripture: as was said long since concerning the interpretation of the Psalms, 'Davidica intelligit, qui Davidica patitur.' We may therefore very fairly commence our task by gathering from Augustine's own lips a few testimonies of the love with which *he* regarded Scripture, and the labour which he counted well bestowed upon its study: for herein lay the pledge and promise that it should yield up to him the hid treasures which it contained. And certainly no one came to the study of Scripture with a more entire confidence that in it were laid up all treasures of wisdom and knowledge, that in the investigation of it truer joys were to be found than anywhere besides.[1] Perhaps in no Christian writer of any

[1] *Enarr. in Ps.* xxxviii. 1.

age do we meet more, or more varied, expressions of a rapturous delight in the Word of God; none ever laid himself down in its green pastures with a deeper and a fuller joy; none more confidently felt that he might evermore draw water from these 'wells of salvation' without fear of drawing them dry;[1] that in these wells, to use his own image, there were first draughts, and second draughts, and third draughts, for those who would return to them again and again.[2]

Falling back on his own experience, he loved to contrast the Scriptures of truth not merely with the Manichæan falsehoods and figments, the 'husks,' with which he had once sought to fill himself, but even with the noblest and loftiest productions of the uninspired intellect of man. Thus in many places, and especially in an eloquent and affecting passage in his *Confessions*, he contrasts Scripture with the books which he had studied in the time of his addiction to the philosophy of Plato, and tells us what he found in it, which he did not find in them.[3] And as he had proved in his own case that love,

[1] *Ep.* cxxxvii. 1 : Tanta est enim Christianarum profunditas litterarum, ut in eis quotidie proficerem, si eas solas ab ineunte pueritiâ usque ad decrepitam senectutem maximo otio, summo studio, meliore ingenio conarer addiscere : non quod ad ea quæ necessaria sunt saluti, tantâ in eis perveniatur difficultate : sed cum quisque ibi fidem tenuerit, sine quâ pie recteque non vivitur, tam multa, tamque multiplicibus mysteriorum umbraculis opacata, intelligenda proficientibus restant, tantaque non solum in verbis quibus ista dicta sunt, verum etiam in rebus quæ intelligendæ sunt, latet altitudo sapientiæ, ut annosissimis, acutissimis, flagrantissimis cupiditate discendi hoc contingat, quod eadem Scriptura quodam loco habet, Cum consummaverit homo, tunc incipit.

[2] Habet Scriptura Sacra haustus primos, habet secundos, habet tertios.

[3] *Conf.* vii. 20, 21 : He concludes : Hoc illæ litteræ non habent. Non habent illæ paginæ vultum pietatis hujus, lacrymas confessionis,

and love only, had 'the key of knowledge,' so he continually presses this same truth upon all others. For indeed this was a fundamental principle with him, that Scripture, to be rightly understood, must be contemplated from within and not from without; so that in more than one place he has excellent remarks, of which the application has not now passed away, on the absurdity of taking the account of it—and not of it only, but of any book which had won a place in the world—not from its friends and admirers, but from its professed foes, from them who start with declaring their hostility to it, or their indifference about it.[1]

An especial glory which Holy Scripture had in his eyes was this, that it was not a book for the few learned, but quite as much for the many simple. He delighted to trace in its construction all which marked it out as such;

sacrificium tuum, spiritum contribulatum, cor contritum et humiliatum, populi salutem, sponsam, civitatem, arrham Spiritûs Sancti, poculum pretii nostri: nemo ibi cantat: Nonne Deo subdita erit anima mea? nemo ibi audit vocantem: Venite ad me, qui laboratis.

[1] *De Util. Cred.* 6: Nihil est profecto temeritatis plenius, quam quorumque librorum expositores deserere, qui eos se tenere ac discipulis tradere posse profitentur, et eorum sententiam requirere ab his qui conditoribus illorum atque auctoribus acerbissimum, nescio quâ cogente caussâ, bellum indixerunt. Quis enim sibi unquam libros Aristotelis reconditos et obscuros ab ejus inimico exponendos putavit? ut de his loquar disciplinis, in quibus lector fortasse sine sacrilegio labi potest. Quis denique geometricas litteras Archimedis legere, magistro Epicuro, aut discere voluit? contra quas ille multum pertinaciter, nihil earum, quantum arbitror, intelligens, disserebat. And again, *De Mor. Eccles.* 1: Quis enim mediocriter sanus non facile intelligat, Scripturarum expositionem ab iis petendam esse, qui earum doctores se esse profitentur; fierique posse, immo id semper accidere, ut multa indoctis videantur absurda, quæ cum a doctioribus exponuntur, eo laudanda videantur, et eo accipiantur aperta dulcius, quo clausa difficilius aperiebantur?

which here as in so many other arrangements of God's providence and grace, set a seal to that word of the Psalmist: 'Thou, O God, hast of thy goodness prepared for the poor' (Ps. lxviii. 10); and in this respect to trace the glorious prerogative which at once differenced this Book from, and exalted it above, all other books, even the greatest to which man's wisdom had given birth. These last were often so constructed as to repel all but a few; while this Book, of a wisdom far exceeding theirs, invited, welcomed, spread a table for all.[1] Small to the small, and large to the large, its words have been so tempered that they adapt themselves to the humblest capacities, while at the same time they enlarge themselves to the largest demands which the human intellect can make upon them.[2]

[1] Thus making spiritual application of the words, 'All beasts of the field drink thereof' (Ps. civ. 11), to the streams of Holy Scripture, as those from which *all* may thus quench their thirst, he exclaims (*Enarr. in Ps.* ciii.): Non dicit aqua, Lepori sufficio et repellit onagrum; neque hoc dicit, Onager accedat, lepus si accesserit, rapietur. Tam fideliter et temperate fluit, ut sic onagrum satiet ne leporem terreat. Sonat strepitus vocis Tullianæ, Cicero legitur, aliquis liber est, dialogus ejus est, sive ipsius, sive Platonis, seu cujuscumque talium; audiunt imperiti, infirmi minoris cordis, quis audet illuc aspirare? Strepitus aquæ, et forte turbatæ, certe tamen tam rapaciter fluentis, ut animal timidum non audeat accedere et bibere. Cui sonuit, In principio fecit Deus cælum et terram, et non ausus est bibere? Cui sonat Psalmus, et dicat, Multum est ad me? Augustine's comparison here may remind us of the beautiful, but now somewhat overworn comparison of Scripture to a river with depths where the elephant may swim, and shallows which the lamb may ford; an image belonging, I believe, originally to Gregory the Great. At least I have never met with it earlier than in the prefatory Epistle to his *Commentary on Job*, where he certainly seems to use it as his own: Divinus etenim sermo sicut mysteriis prudentes exercet, sic plerumque superficie simplices refovet. . . . Quasi quidam quippe est fluvius, ut ita dixerim, planus et altus, in quo et agnus ambulet, et elephas natet.

[2] *In Ev. Joh. Tract.* cvii. 6: Scriptura nos non levat nisi descendat

Nor did the manifold difficulties and obscurities in the Bible in the least deprive it in his sight of this its distinctive glory and character.[1] For in the first place, as he is strong to urge, there was nothing hard in one passage of Scripture, but, if it nearly concerned the salvation of men, the same was set down more plainly in another;[2] or if not so, then it was assuredly something of which simple men, those to whom the gift of an especial insight into mysteries was not granted, might safely remain ignorant; while these obscurer and harder passages, which only after frequent knocking yielded up their meaning, or, it might be, would not yield it up at all, served many important moral purposes, and could not

ad nos; sicut Verbum caro factum descendit ut levaret, non cecidit ut jaceret. Cf. *Confess*. xii. 26-28.

[1] *Ep*. cxxxvii. 5 (*ad Volus*.): Modus autem ipse dicendi quo sancta Scriptura contexitur, quam omnibus accessibilis, quamvis paucissimis penetrabilis. Ea quæ aperta continet, quasi amicus familiaris, sine fuco ad cor loquitur indoctorum atque doctorum. Ea vero quæ in mysteriis occultat, nec ipsa eloquio superbo erigit, quo non audeat accedere mens tardiuscula et inerudita, quasi pauper ad divitem; sed invitat omnes humili sermone, quos non solum manifestâ pascat, sed etiam secretâ exerceat veritate, hoc in promtis quod in reconditis habens. Sed ne aperta fastidirentur, eadem rursus operta desiderantur, desiderata quodam modo renovantur, renovata suaviter intimantur. His salubriter et prava corriguntur, et parva nutriuntur, et magna oblectantur ingenia. *De Doctr. Christ*. 29: Non enim, quia neque incedit ornata, neque armata, sed tanquam nuda congreditur, ideo, non adversarium nervis lacertisque collidit, et obsistentem subruit ac destruit membris fortissimis falsitatem.

[2] *De Doctr. Christ*. ii. 14: In iis quæ aperte in Scripturis posita sunt, inveniuntur omnia quæ continent fidem, moresque vivendi, spem scilicet atque caritatem. *Conf*. vi. 5: Excipiens omnes populari sinu. The Reformers, who affirmed the *perspicuitas* Scripturæ against the Romish exaggerations of its extreme obscurity, had, and were forward to urge that they had, Augustine on their side (see REISER, *Augustinus Veritatis Evangelico-Catholicæ Testis et Confessor*, Frankfort, 1678, pp. 37-41).

have been absent from a Book intended to serve such ends as those for which this Book was intended. By them it was proved and seen who were worthy to have mysteries revealed to them, and who not; who were content patiently and humbly to wait at the doors of the Eternal Wisdom, and even when these were not opened to them at their first knocking, to tarry there; to believe that all was well said, was best said, when to their limited faculties it might seem contradictory and confused.[1] It was seen, on the other hand, who were ready to go away in a rage; who, having come to Scripture with no due moral preparations for understanding it, were prepared to jump to the conclusion that that was without meaning, of which they could not grasp the meaning at the first[2]—no

[1] As in one place he says: Latere te æquitas potest; esse ibi iniquitas non potest. *Serm.* li. 4: In illo sunt omnes thesauri sapientiæ et scientiæ absconditi. Quos non propterea abscondit, ut neget; sed ut absconditis excitet desiderium. Hæc est utilitas secreti. Honora in eo quod nondum intelligis, et tanto magis honora, quanto plura vela cernis. Quanto enim quisque honoratior est, tanto plura vela pendent in domo ejus. Vela faciunt honorem secreti; sed honorantibus levantur vela. Irridentes autem vela, et a velorum vicinitate pelluntur. Quia ergo transimus ad Christum, aufertur velamen.

[2] For himself, there are not a few passages concerning which he is content to avow his own continued ignorance, or at least that he has nothing certain to propose for their interpretation. Nay, in respect of Scripture in general he exclaims, certainly with no mock modesty, but in entire sincerity (*Ep.* xcv.): Quid ipsa divina eloquia, nonne palpantur potius quam tractantur a nobis, dum in multis pluribus quærimus potius quid sentiendum sit, quam definitum aliquid fixumque sentimus? In respect of all these he lays down that golden rule (*De Gen. ad Litt.* viii. 5): Melius est dubitare de rebus occultis, quam litigare de incertis. Among the passages of which he thus confesses his ignorance is 2 Thess. ii. 7, being unable to say *who* is meant by ὁ κατέχων there, Ego prorsus quid dixerit me fateor ignorare (*De Civ. Dei*, xx. 19. 2); see too upon 1 Pet. iii. 18, his interesting letter on this hard question of the preaching to the spirits in prison (*Ep.* clxiv. *ad Euod.*). He does not fear to acknowledge at the close

righteousness in those dealings, whose righteousness they could not at once comprehend; forward to accuse Scripture of absurdity or immorality, rather than themselves of a dulness of mental, or, which was more probably the case, of spiritual vision.[1] No one, indeed, oftener or more earnestly urges humility as the one condition of so knock-

of his life that he has never been able to reconcile to his own perfect satisfaction the various statements of Christ and his Apostles, which bear on divorce and remarriage (*Retract.* ii. 57). Thus too on the question of the origin of souls, and whether they be ex traduce, or each one a new creation, though he must greatly have inclined to the former opinion as a strong confirmation of his dogmatic system, still, weighing the difficulty of the question, and acknowledging the silence in which Scripture has left it, he declares that he has come to no certain determination, observing (*Ep.* exc. 5): Ubi res naturaliter obscura nostrum modulum vincit, et aperta Divina Scriptura non subvenit, temere hinc aliquid definire humana conjectura præsumit. He satisfies himself with the consideration that after all it is not the birth, but the *new* birth, of the soul, which mainly concerns the Christian, making these beautiful remarks (*Ep.* cxc. 3, *ad Optat.*): Unde si origo animæ lateat, dum tamen redemptio clareat, periculum non est. Neque enim in Christum credimus, ut *nascamur*, sed ut *renascamur*. See his *Letter to Jerome* (*Ep.* clxvi.) on the same subject; and another in which he replies to a correspondent who had put various hard passages of Scripture before him, for him to explain them (*Ep.* cxcvii.): Mallem quidem eorum quæ a me quæsivisti habere scientiam quam ignorantiam; sed quia id nondum potui, magis eligo cautam ignorantiam confiteri, quam falsam scientiam profiteri.

[1] *De Util. Cred.* 7: Nullâ imbutus disciplinâ Terentianum Maurum sine magistro attingere non auderes; Asper, Cornutus, Donatus et alii innumerabiles requiruntur, ut quilibet poëta possit intelligi, cujus carmina et theatri plausus videntur captare: tu in eos libros, qui, quoquo modo se habeant, sancti tamen divinarumque rerum pleni, prope totius generis humani confessione diffamantur, sine duce irruis, et de his sine præceptore audes ferre sententiam; nec si tibi aliqua occurrunt quæ videantur absurda, tarditatem tuam et putrefactum tabe hujus mundi animum, qualis omnium stultorum est accusas potius, quam eos qui fortasse a talibus intelligi nequeunt. Cf. *In Joh. Tract.* xx.: Perversa corda perturbat, sicut pia corda exercet Verbum Dei.

ing at the door of divine mysteries, that it may be opened to us. He had himself known, as he is forward to confess, what it was to knock in quite another spirit, in a temper which inevitably entailed that he should knock in vain.[1]

But beside offering such exercises of humility, or supplying a touchstone of the absence of humility, these difficulties and obscurities are further profitable, in that they hinder men from growing weary of Scripture, as though it were a book which they had entirely mastered, of which they had so taken the length and breadth and height and depth, that it had now no further secrets to reveal to them, no new pastures into which to lead them.[2] Then, too, there is the delight of finding, which is so much the livelier after the labour of seeking.[3] And in

[1] Thus *Conf.* iii. 5: Institui animum intendere in Scripturas sanctas, ut viderem quales essent. Et ecce video rem non compertam superbis, neque nudatam pueris; sed incessu humilem, successu excelsam et velatam mysteriis; et non eram ego talis, ut intrare in eam possem, aut inclinare cervicem ad ejus gressus. Visa est mihi indigna quam Tullianæ dignitati compararem. And *Serm.* li. 5: Loquor vobis aliquando deceptus, cum primo puer ad divinas Scripturas ante vellem afferre acumen discutiendi quam pietatem quærendi; ego ipse perversis moribus claudebam januam Domini mei; quum pulsare deberem, ut aperiretur, addebam ut clauderetur. Superbus enim audebam quærere, quod nisi humilis non potest invenire. Ego miser, cum me ad volandum idoneum putarem reliqui nidum, et prius cecidi quam volarem. Sed Dominus misericors me, a transeuntibus ne conculcarer et morerer, levavit et in nido reposuit.

[2] *De Doctr. Christ.* ii. 6: Magnifice igitur et salubriter Spiritus S. ita Scripturas Sacras modificavit, ut locis apertioribus fami occurreret, obscurioribus autem fastidia detergeret. Cf. *De Div. Quæst.* qu. 53: Deus enim noster sic ad salutem animarum divinos libros Spiritu Sancto moderatus est, ut non solum manifestis pascere sed etiam obscuris exercere nos vellet.

[3] *Enarr. in Ps.* xxxviii. 1: Dulcedo inventionis, quam præcessit labor inquisitionis; and again (*Con. Mendac.* 10): Quæ propterea figuratis velut amictibus obteguntur, ut sensum pie quærentis exer-

the very claims which these harder portions of God's Word made on the powers and faculties of the mind, there was profit; since there is nothing that so dwarfs the powers and stunts the growth of the mind as the having always to do with that which is perfectly easy and at once comprehended; while, on the contrary, the mind gradually dilates and grows to the dimensions of that which it has to take in.[1] All this Augustine does not cease to urge.

ceant, et ne nuda ac prompta vilescant. Quamvis quæ aliis locis aperte ac manifeste dicta didicimus, cum ea ipsa de abditis eruuntur, in nostrâ quodam modo cognitione renovantur, et renovata dulcescunt. Nec invidentur discentibus, quod his modis obscurantur; sed commendantur magis, ut quasi subtracta desiderentur ardentius, et inveniantur desiderata jocundius.

[1] Thus on the words of the Psalmist, 'His eyelids try the children of men' (Ps. xi. 4), he says (*Enarr. in Ps.* x. 5) : Quippe quibusdam Scripturarum locis obscuris tanquam clausis oculis Dei exercentur [filii hominum], ut quærant: et rursus quibusdam locis manifestis, tanquam apertis oculis Dei, illuminantur, ut gaudeant. Et ista in sanctis libris crebra opertio atque adapertio tanquam palpebræ sunt Dei quæ interrogant, id est, quæ probant filios hominum, qui neque fatigantur rerum obscuritate, sed exercentur; neque inflantur cognitione, sed confirmantur. Cf. *Serm.* li. 4; and again, *Enarr. in Ps.* cxlvi. 6: Non intelligis, parum intelligis, non consequeris: honora Scripturam Dei, honora verbum Dei, etiam non apertum, differ pietate intelligentiam. Noli protervus esse accusare aut obscuritatem, aut quasi perversitatem Scripturæ. Perversum hic nihil est, obscurum autem aliquid est; non ut tibi negetur, sed ut exerceat accepturum. Ergo quando obscurum est, medicus illud fecit ut pulses. Voluit ut exercereris in pulsando; voluit, ut pulsanti aperiret. Pulsando exerceberis; exercitatus, latior efficieris; latior factus, capies quod donatur. Ergo noli indignari quod clausum est: mitis esto, mansuetus esto. Noli recalcitrare adversus obscura et dicere, Melius diceretur si sic diceretur. Quando enim potes tu sic dicere aut judicare, quomodo dici expediat? Sic dictum est, quomodo dici debuit. Non corrigat æger medicamenta sua, novit ea medicus modificare; ei crede, qui te curat. And again: Si nusquam aperta esset Scriptura, non te pasceret; si nusquam occulta, non te exerceret. *Serm.* lxxi. 7: In omni quippe copiâ Scripturarum sanctarum pascimur apertis; exercemur obscuris. Illic fames pellitur, hic fastidium.

An element, or rather a result, of this humility, will be a right understanding of the relations in which reason and faith stand to one another; and the light in which Augustine regards the submission in the Christian man of the former to the latter, is peculiarly interesting. We see here how it came to pass that he was the Doctor to whom Schoolman and Mystic alike appealed. He does demand this submission; he does evermore affirm that the true order is not, as proud man would have it, Know and believe, but rather, Believe and know.[1] Yet at the same time reason, in the very submission which it makes, does homage to its own dignity; since it is by an act of its own that it recognizes the reasonableness of putting itself into a higher school, of *postponing* its own exercise. For this he very much dwells on, that it is on the part of reason a *postponing*, not a *renouncing*, of its own exercise. Reason is subjected indeed, but ' subjected in hope,' in the hope that, partly in this world, and altogether in the world to come, any seeming oppositions between its own conclusions and faith's mandates shall be removed, and these two for ever reconciled with one another. This shall be the reward of faith, that what the faithful man now believes, he shall by and by entirely understand. He knows that the intellectual eye of his soul is now, not indeed extinguished, but diseased, and is therefore liable to see things distorted, not because they are so, but because *it* has lost in part its healthy capacity of vision. Under the treatment of the Great Physician it hopes to recover

[1] *Serm.* xliii. 3: Dicet mihi homo, Intelligam ut credam. Ego ei respondeam, Immo crede ut intelligas. Intellectus enim merces est fidei. And again: Credat in Christum, ut possit intelligere Christum. And in this sense he expounds the words of our Lord, John vii. 17. (*In Ev. Joh. Tract.* xxix. 6.)

perfect healthiness of vision ; which recovered, it does not doubt that there will be an entire identity between what it then shall see and what faith now receives and believes.[1] Understanding, while it is not the way to faith, shall yet be the reward of faith. It is only what he somewhere calls the immaturus amor rationis, which he condemns. The sick man's wisdom, so long as he is sick, is to take his medicines, not to modify or change them.

As was to be expected from one who perceived so clearly that God was not to be found out by searching, but was known to them, and to them only, unto whom He was pleased to reveal Himself, Augustine speaks often of prayer as that to which alone the shut doors of Scripture mysteries would open; and in his writings are many devoutest prayers of his own, in which he turns to God as to the one fountain of light and understanding, as to the One who alone can show him the hidden things which are contained in his law; seeking insight and illumination from Him, and desiring above all that he may neither be himself deceived therein, nor deceive others therefrom.[2]

---

[1] *Ep.* cxx. 1 : Ut ergo in quibusdam rebus ad doctrinam salutarem pertinentibus quas ratione nondum percipere valeamus, sed aliquando valebimus, fides præcedat rationem, quâ cor mundetur, ut magnæ rationis capiat et perferat lucem, hoc utique rationis est. Et ideo rationabiliter dictum est per prophetam, Nisi credideritis, non intelligetis (Isai. vii. 9). Ubi procul dubio discrevit hæc duo, deditque consilium quo prius credamus, ut id quod credimus, intelligere valeamus. . . . Si igitur rationabile est, ut ad magna quædam quæ capi nondum possunt, fides præcedat rationem, procul dubio quantulacunque ratio quæ hoc persuadet, etiam ipsa antecedit fidem.

[2] This is only a fragment of one of them (*Conf.* xi. 2) : Domine Deus meus, circumcide ab omni temeritate omnique mendacio interiora et exteriora labia mea. Sint castæ deliciæ meæ Scripturæ tuæ ; nec fallar in eis, nec fallam ex eis. Domine attende, et miserere, Domine Deus meus, lux cæcorum et virtus infirmorum, statimque lux videntium

et virtus fortium, attende animam meam, et audi clamantem de profundo. Largire spatium meditationibus nostris in abdita Legis tuæ, neque adversus pulsantes claudas eas. Neque enim frustra scribi voluisti tot paginarum opaca secreta.—It would, I think, help us a little to appreciate the extent to which Augustine modified and moulded the thoughts and feelings, and even the very expressions, of the most eminent Church writers who came after him, if we were to compare, on subjects of moral and theological interest, some of their chiefest utterances with his ; as, for example, with some of these his sayings in regard of Scripture, a very beautiful passage on the same subject in Gregory the Great, which in every line shows the influence of his great teacher (*Moral.* xx. 1) : Quamvis omnem scientiam atque doctrinam Scriptura sacra sine aliquâ comparatione transcendat ; ut taceam quod vera prædicat, quod ad cælestem patriam vocat, quod a terrenis desideriis ad superna amplectenda cor legentis immutat, quod dictis obscurioribus exercet fortes, et parvulis humili sermone blanditur ; quod nec sic clausa est, ut pavesci debeat ; nec sic patet ut vilescat ; quod usu fastidium tollit, et tanto amplius diligitur quanto amplius meditatur ; quod legentis animum humilibus verbis adjuvat, sublimibus sensibus levat : quod aliquo modo cum legentibus crescit : quod a rudibus lectoribus quasi recognoscitur, et tamen doctis semper nova reperitur ; ut ergo de rerum pondere taceam, scientias tamen omnes atque doctrinas ipso etiam locutionis suæ more transcendit, quia uno eodemque sermone dum narrat textum prodit mysterium, et sic scit præterita dicere, ut eo ipso noverit futura prædicare, et non immutato dicendi ordine, eisdem ipsis sermonibus novit et anteacta describere, et agenda nuntiare ; sicut hæc eadem beati Jobi verba sunt, qui dum sua dicit, nostra prædicit, dumque lamenta propria per sermonem indicat, sanctæ Ecclesiæ causam per intellectum sonat.

CHAPTER II.

THE EXTERNAL HELPS FOR THE INTERPRETATION OF SCRIPTURE POSSESSED BY AUGUSTINE.

WHILE Augustine does not set too high a value on external helps, on the outward furniture and accomplishment of the interpreter, but recognizes to the full that spiritual things can only be spiritually discerned, that only the Spirit can interpret what was given by the Spirit; he is as far removed as can be from that conceited enthusiasm which would despise these helps, as though they were not also gifts of God, capable in their place of doing excellent service to the cause of His truth. Nor did he sparingly or reluctantly acknowledge the value of those subsidiary aids, which he did not himself possess, or which he only imperfectly possessed; but attached to them their full honour and importance. In his valuable treatise, *De Doctrinâ Christianâ*, he images forth the perfect interpreter, such as he ought to be; and gives suggestions which may help to form him, even while he confesses how far off he knows himself from fulfilling his own ideal. Thus he urges the great advantage which he may derive from recurring to the Hebrew and Greek originals,[1] and where this is not possible, from the use of many translations, as checking, throwing light on, and com-

[1] ii. 11. 16.

pleting, one another.¹ He will have his ideal and perfect interpreter well acquainted with natural history,² with music,³ with history,⁴ with chronology,⁵ with logic,⁶ and with philosophy;⁷ for not one of these but will come into play; some of them will be most important for the great work which he has undertaken.⁸ If he has been in the spiritual Egypt, let him come forth from it as richly furnished with its stuffs as he may, with its silver and its gold, which may afterwards be worked up for the very service of the tabernacle itself (Exod. xii. 35 ; xxxv. 22).⁹

Here then may very fitly be considered what was the

---

[1] ii. 12. 17.   [2] ii. 16. 24; cf. *Enarr. in Ps.* lviii. *Serm.* i. 10.
[3] ii. 16. 26.   [4] ii. 28. 43.   [5] ii. 28. 42.
[6] ii. 31. 48.   [7] ii. 40. 60.

[8] For the sake of others who may not possess this whole circle of knowledge, he proposes (ii. 39. 59) that some one who does, should undertake a *Dictionary of the Bible*, such as since has often been done: Ut non sit necesse Christiano in multis propter pauca laborare, sic video posse fieri, si quem eorum qui possunt, benignam sane operam fraternæ utilitati delectet impendere, ut quoscumque terrarum locos quæve animalia vel herbas atque arbores, sive lapides vel metalla incognita, speciesque quaslibet Scriptura commemorat, ea generatim digerens, sola exposita litteris mandet.

[9] ii. 40. 60 : Philosophi autem qui vocantur, si qua forte vera et fidei nostræ accommodata dixerunt, maxime Platonici, non solum formidanda non sunt, sed ab eis etiam tanquam injustis possessoribus in usum nostrum vindicanda. Sicut enim Ægyptii non solum idola habebant et onera gravia, quæ populus Israël detestaretur et fugeret, sed etiam vasa atque ornamenta de auro et argento, et vestem, quæ ille populus exiens de Ægypto sibi potius tanquam ad usum meliorem clanculo vindicavit, non auctoritate propriâ, sed præcepto Dei, ipsis Ægyptiis nescienter commodantibus ea, quibus non bene utebantur, sic doctrinæ omnes Gentilium non solum simulata et superstitiosa figmenta gravesque sarcinas supervacui laboris habent, sed etiam liberales disciplinas usui veritatis aptiores; quod eorum tanquam aurum et argentum, quod non ipsi instituerunt, sed de quibusdam quasi metallis divinæ providentiæ, quæ ubique infusa sunt, eruerunt, debet ab eis auferre Christianus ad usum justum prædicandi Evangelii.

actual extent of Augustine's own outward equipment for the work of an interpreter. It is superfluous to observe that he possessed no knowledge whatever of Hebrew. Indeed there were but two of the early Fathers, Origen in the Greek Church, and he but slightly,[1] and Jerome in the Latin, who did so. It is, as Augustine declares, a *lingua incognita* to him, he everywhere proclaiming his entire unacquaintance with it.[2] His knowledge of Punic, (for that he knew it we may certainly conclude)[3] would no doubt materially have helped him, had he been inclined seriously to grapple with the difficulties of the Hebrew tongue. Bochart, Gesenius, and others who have studied the few fragments of this tongue which remain, so express their regret at the almost entire perishing of all its monuments, and at our deprivation thus of all the helps that might have been derived from it, as to show that the resemblance between the languages could not have been slight; even as we might conclude, *a priori*, that the Punic, brought from Phœnicia to the northern coasts of Africa, must have retained a considerable resemblance to its mother, or, rather, its sister dialect. The

---

[1] See Huet's *Origeniana*, ii. 2, for proofs how slight and inaccurate his acquaintance with Hebrew was (Judaicis litteris leviter tinctus).

[2] *De Doctr. Christ.* ii. 23; *Conf.* xi. 3; *Enarr. in Ps.* cxxxvi. 7; et passim.

[3] It seems implied in such language as this (*Serm.* clxvii. 3): Proverbium notum est Punicum, quod quidem Latine vobis dicam, quia Punice non omnes nostis; cf. *Exp. Inchoat. in Rom.* § 13; *De Magistro*, 44; *Ep.* xvii. 2 (*ad Max. Madaur.*); and see *Conf.* i. 14. Yet it would not seem a very common knowledge among the provincials, for he complains more than once (thus *Enarr. in Ps.* cxxiii. 8) of the difficulty of obtaining presbyters who were acquainted with the language for some churches in country districts, where no other tongue was understood by the population.

fact of this connexion between the languages Augustine several times notes, and not unfrequently adduces words which the two had in common.[1] Yet with the exception of such slight assistances to his exposition as those indicated below, it did not afford him any effectual service in his work.

Being thus ignorant of Hebrew, Augustine's nearest approach to the original text of the Old Testament was through the Septuagint Version. There was a serious misfortune here. This Version, as all would now admit, with a multitude of isolated felicities of translation, and resting evidently on a true tradition in regard of many difficult words and passages, having, too, had signal honour put upon it in the use which the Apostles made of it, our Lord Himself setting his seal on one memorable occasion to its development of the original text (cf. Matt. xix. 5 with Gen. ii. 24), is still infinitely faulty, full of intentional and unintentional departures from the original. But of this Augustine was nearly or quite unaware, sharing as he did with well-nigh the whole early Church in an extravagant estimate of its merits, and yielding himself to this untrustworthy guide with the most unquestioning confidence.[2] He was not disinclined[3] to give credit to

---

[1] *Serm.* cxiii. 2 : Istæ enim linguæ sibi significationis quâdam vicinitate sociantur ; cf. *In Joh. Tract.* xv. 27. Thus he notices that Baal, which appears in so many of the Carthaginian names, Hanni*bal*, Asdru*bal*, meant 'lord' in Punic no less than in Hebrew (*Quæst. in Jud.* qu. 16) ; that Edom was Punic for *blood*, as in Hebrew it is applied to aught that is blood-*red* (*Enarr. in Ps.* cxxxvi. 7); he mentions Messiah and Mammon as being Punic as well as Hebrew words : and notes (*Loc. in Gen.* i. 24) the similarity between the languages as not merely one of word but of idiom.

[2] On the whole question of Augustine's relation to the two Latin Versions, and on the several merits of these, see Kaulen's *Gesch. d. Vulgata*, Mainz, 1868.

[3] *De Doctr. Christ.* ii. 15 ; *Ep.* xxviii. 2 (*ad Hieron.*); *Qu. in Gen.* qu. 169 ; *De Civ. Dei*, xviii. 42, 43.

the legend told by Aristeas, and repeated with various modifications by Philo, Josephus, Justin Martyr,[1] and others, of the miraculous consent of its seventy-two interpreters shut up in their seventy-two separate cells, a fiction which St. Jerome characterized in the language which it deserved.[2] Nay further, he appears to have recognized a prophetic spirit in them; and not to have doubted that the same Spirit which dictated the original, did also guide them and preserve them from all error: so that he will not allow any such in their Version, and is in nothing offended by some plain deviations of theirs from the original text. Thus when they make Jonah to proclaim, 'Yet *three* days and Nineveh shall be overthrown,' he persuades himself that they did not this without authority, and that there is a meaning in their *three*, as well as in the *forty* of the Hebrew text.[3] It was this belief in the faultlessness of the Septuagint, this confident persuasion that there was nothing in the Hebrew Scriptures which was not contained in it, and through it in the version (or versions) already in use, which caused him at first altogether to disapprove of, and for a long time to look coldly on, Jerome's correction and revision of this earlier Version, or rather on what was to a great extent a new translation from the Hebrew.[4] He seems to have counted

---

[1] *Coh. ad Græc.* 13.
[2] *Præf. in Pent.*: Nescio quis primus auctor cellulas Alexandriæ mendacio suo extruxerit.
[3] *De Cons. Evang.* ii. 66; *De Doctr. Christ.* iv. 15; *Qu. in Gen.* qu. 169; *De Civ. Dei*, xv. 14. 2; and 23. 3.
[4] *Ep.* xxviii. 2; lxxxii. 5; lxxi. 2, 3 (*ad Hieron.*): in which last Epistle he gives a curious account of the uproar which followed in some African church, when a bishop attempted to introduce Jerome's translation directly from the Hebrew instead of that from the Septuagint, to which the people had hitherto been accustomed.

the Septuagint too sacred to be touched, or at any rate that the danger of unsettling men's minds through altering anything in so time-honoured a version exceeded the advantages which might be derived from the removal of any incorrectnesses in it, if such were indeed there. Besides the Septuagint he has the Versions of Symmachus, of Theodotion, and of Aquila within reach, and from time to time makes use of them.[1]

Augustine's own knowledge of Greek did not go very far, nor yet, so far as it went, was it very accurate. Still there has been a fashion among those who in later times have estimated his merits, or demerits rather (for many have had no eye except for these), as an expositor of Scripture, to exaggerate his deficiencies herein. It is quite true that his Greek was irregularly gotten; that he did not in his earlier years lay strong and sure foundations on which to build later acquisitions; that he speaks of an early distaste which he had for the language; though from his own account this seems to have been no more than a boy's distaste for the labour needful to overcome the first difficulties in a foreign tongue.[2] It is true too that he himself often speaks slightingly of his own acquaintance with the original language of the New Testament, and confesses that, where he had to do with abstruse and recondite matters in theology or philosophy, a Plato or a Plotinus, he preferred to read a Latin translation to a Greek original;[3] yet when one and another speak of him as 'unacquainted alike with the Greek and Hebrew

[1] *Quæst. in Num.* qu. 52. [2] *Conf.* i. 13, 14.
[3] *De Trin.* iii. 1; cf. *Conf.* vii. 9; *Con. Lit. Petil.* ii. 38: Et ego quidem Græcæ linguæ perparum assecutus sum, et prope nihil.

tongues,'[1] and a third of his 'everywhere betraying a shameful ignorance of Greek,'[2] or again when Gibbon declares 'the superficial learning of Augustine was confined to the Latin language,' in this there is undoubted exaggeration and injustice. We have so many examples of a tact and skill very far from contemptible with which he draws the distinction between words that in their meaning border on one another, and of other acquaintance with the language, as would quite justify and indeed require a serious modification of any such judgments as these.[3]

[1] WALCH (*Bib. Patrist.* p. 352): Augustinus extitit, ut alii, Ebrææ et Græcæ linguæ ignarus; ROSENMÜLLER, *Hist. Intt. S. Ss.* vol. iii. 404: Imperitus non tantum Hebrææ, sed etiam Græcæ linguæ. Compare RICH, SIMON, *Hist. Crit. du V. T.* vol. iii. 9.

[2] Turpem litterarum Græcarum inscitiam passim prodidit (WINER, *Annott. in Ep. ad Gal.* p. 22). But single mistakes ought not to go for much: Winer himself not many pages from the place where he expresses this judgment, writes *inurerit* for *inusserit*! yet is he in the main not merely a correct but an elegant writer of Latin; and Reiche, the author of a commentary far from unlearned on the Romans, deliberately derives ἀποθώμεθα (Rom. xiii. 12) from ἀπωθεῖν (p. 458). For a juster, and not too favourable, estimate of Augustine's attainments in Greek, see his *Life*, in the last volume of the Benedictine edition of his works, p. 5.

[3] A few examples in proof. Thus he draws an important distinction between πνεῦμα and πνοή, with reference to John xx. 22 and Gen. ii. 7, and the attempt of some to make the first act of insufflation, 'He breathed into his nostrils the breath of life, and man became a living soul,' equivalent to the second, 'He breathed on them and saith, Receive ye the Holy Ghost' (*De Civ. Dei*, xiii. 24). The distinction drawn by Döderlein (*Synon.* v. 95), between spirare and flare, spiritus and flatus, supplies an interesting parallel and confirmation. He has a fine discussion on the relations between λατρεία, θρησκεία, εὐσέβεια, θεοσέβεια, and their Latin equivalents (*De Civ. Dei*, x. 1). He handles certainly not ill the difficult synonyms at 1 Tim. ii. 1; προσευχαί, δεήσεις, ἐντεύξεις, εὐχαριστίαι (*Ep.* cxlix. 2). He distinguishes between πρεσβύτης and γέρων, the elder and the old man (*Enarr. in Ps.* lxx. 18; cf. *Quæst. sup. Gen.* i. qu. 70); between πλεονεξία and φιλαργυρία, showin how much larger the former is in its

CHAP. II.]   INTERPRETER OF SCRIPTURE.   21

Thus Augustine used his Latin text with frequent, if not continual, reference to the original, oftentimes rectifying significance than the latter (*Enarr. in Ps.* cxviii. 36); again, between ἄμωμος and ἄσπιλος (*Qu. in Lev.* iii. qu. 40); between ἐπένδυμα, superindumentum, and ἐπωμίς, superhumerale (*Qu. in Jud.* vii. qu. 41); between πρωτότοκος, πρωτογενής, and μονογενής (*Qu. in Deut.* v. qu. 23); between ἀλλογενής and ἀλλόφυλος (*Qu. in Num.* qu. 3); between ἀντιλογία and λοιδορία (*Qu. in Num.* qu. 39), ἄγαν and σφόδρα (*Enarr. in Psalm.* cxviii. *Serm.* iv.); between ἀπαρχαί and πρωτογεννήματα (*Qu. in Num.* iv. qu. 32); between αὐτοῦ and ἑαυτοῦ (*Quæst. in Gen.* i. 62); between σχίσμα and αἵρεσις (*Con. Crescen. Don.* ii. 7); between δῶρον and δόμα (*Loc. de Num.* iv.); ἐνταφιάζειν and θάπτειν (*Loc. de Gen.* i.); ἄλογος and ἀμαθής (*Loc. de Gen.* ii.); καιρός and χρόνος (*Ep.* cxcvii. 2, 3); βίος and ζωή (*De Trin.* xii. 11); ἕξις and σχῆμα (*De Div. Quæst.* lxxiii.); ἁμαρτία and ἁμάρτημα (*Con. Jul. Pel.* vi. 2); μοιχεία and πορνεία (*Qu. in Exod.* qu. 71); ὄχλος, δῆμος and λαός (*Loc. de Gen.* i. 198); θυμός and ὀργή (*Enarr. in Ps.* lxxxvii. 8); σκεῦος and ἀγγεῖον (*Quæst. in Lev.* iii. qu. 51); λατρεύειν and δουλεύειν (*Qu. in Lev.* iii. qu. 66); δικαιοσύνη and δικαίωμα (*Enarr. in Ps.* cxviii. 56); ἐλπίς and πίστις (*Enchirid.* viii.). Not a few of these points are excellently handled by him. So, too, he notes that ἔκστασις may mean more than fear or great astonishment; it may be as much as mentis alienatio (ἐξίστημι), and is therefore a word eminently fit for expressing that condition of mind in which men receive communications from a higher world (*Qu. in Gen.* i. qu. 80; *Enarr. in Ps.* ciii. 11); that ἀδολεσχεῖν, though used in the Septuagint in a good, is oftener used in classic Greek in a bad, sense. He gives (*Qu. in Exod.* ii. qu. 177) the right explanation of πλάγια, that it means the flanks, and cannot mean the front and rear, and so too of κλίτη (*Qu. in Exod.* ii. qu. 131). He notices the usage of παιδεία in the Greek Scriptures as different from the classical, that it is not instruction generally, as in other Greek, but always *per molestias* eruditio (*Enarr. in Ps.* cxviii. 66). He takes note of a difficulty in the use of ὀρθρίζω at Judg. ix. 33, LXX., ὄρθρος being the morning *before* sunrise, and not, as it seems to be used there, *after* (*Qu. in Jud.* qu. 46); of a double use of παράκλησις, and the verb from which it is derived, that it is both exhortation and consolation (*Enarr. in Ps.* cxviii. 52). His Greek etymologies are in general correct: thus of τραγέλαφος (*Annot. in Job.* 39); of ἄτομος (*Serm.* ccclxii. 17); of παράπτωμα (*Qu. in Lev.* iii. qu. 20); he shows the popular derivation of πάσχα from πάσχειν to be impossible (*Enarr. in Ps.* cxl. 10; *in Johan. Tract.* lv. 3). He is acquainted with the force of the middle

ing the errors of the former by an appeal to the latter. In one place[1] he silences a Manichæan objection, showing that it merely rested on a carelessness of the Latin interpreter. Nor was he an uncritical taker up of the first text of the original which came in his way, but laboured earnestly after the most accurate that was attainable, and with this end spared no labour in the comparison of manuscripts. It is well known that of the various readings which exist in the manuscripts of the New Testament which have come down to us, all or nearly all of any importance must have found their way very early into the text, certainly before the middle of the third century.[2] Augustine often refers to the weightiest of these, and

future as distinguished from the active (*Qu. in Exod.* 78). He corrects the Latin Version, which had rendered αὐλαῖαι (Exod. xxvi. 3) as if it had been αὐλαί, vestibula, instead of cortinæ. So too he notes that γνωστῶς (Exod. xxxiii. 13) should not have been rendered as though it had been φανερῶς. He states truly that in rendering the ethical terminology of Greece into Latin, πάθη should be rather rendered passiones than perturbationes (*De Civ. Dei*, ix. 4). He observes how inadequate a rendering of ἀορασία (Gen. xix. 11) cæcitas is, and that the Latin has in fact no word exactly corresponding (*De Civ. Dei*, xxii. 19). He explains how compeditos had found its way into the Latin text, Ps. lxxxix. (xc.) 12, seemingly as the rendering of πεπαιδευμένους, namely, that the translator must have had in his copy πεπεδημένους. I am far from saying that all which he affirms on these and other like matters can always be maintained without modification ; or that the knowledge here displayed is very profound ; or that he does not commit curious blunders ; see for instance his derivation of συκομωραία as ficus *fatua* (*Serm.* clxxiv. 3): he errs too in πλημμέλεια, not making it a violation of μέλος, a disharmony or discord, but deriving it from μέλει, curæ est (*Quæst. in Levit.* qu. 20); yet in this handful of notices, gathered almost at random, there are evidences of something better than 'a disgraceful ignorance of Greek.'

[1] *Con. Faust.* xi. 4.

[2] *Con. Faust.* xi. 2 : Paucæ, et sacrarum literarum studiosis notissimæ sententiarum varietates.

draws them and their external authority and internal probability into consideration when explaining the passages in which they occur.[1]

And generally he is well acquainted with the primary rules of textual criticism, however the scientific elaboration and full development of these rules may have been, and naturally was, the work of a later age. Thus he lays down a canon which all who in modern times have laboured at fixing the text have duly recognized; namely, that a reading which involves an apparent doctrinal or other difficulty is to be preferred, other things being equal, to one which will make everything easy and smooth.[2] In obedience to this canon he will not evade the difficulty of a reference of the thirty pieces of silver to ‘ *Jeremy* the

---

[1] Thus he refers (*Ep.* cxciii. 10) to the various readings of 1 Cor. xv. 31, with the view of considering how far there may be help in these for removing any difficulty which the passage may possess. Again he refers (*Ep.* cxlix. 28) to the remarkable omission in some MSS. of the μή at Col. ii. 18; an omission which enhances the difficulties of the passage, but which no doubt is correct; as is now generally admitted. He enters on the question, one of the hardest in textual criticism, whether εἰκῇ should be admitted or not into the text at Matt. v. 22: in his *Exposition of the Sermon on the Mount* he has given it room; but afterwards (*Retract.* i. 19) withdraws it, because, as he says, the Greek MSS. have it not. He takes no notice of the *palam* found in many Latin copies of his time, at Matt. vi. 4, inasmuch, he says, as he finds nothing to correspond to it in the Greek : I need not observe that the modern critical editions omit the corresponding ἐν τῷ φανερῷ of the received text. He prefers Θεοῦ to Θεῷ at Phil. iii. 3, because, as he says, a majority of Greek copies so read (*Serm.* clxix. 1); it is the reading of *all* uncial MSS. save one which have reached us. At the same time it must be allowed that not unfrequently he takes up with a plainly faulty Latin translation, and grounds some teaching on this, or discusses at length a difficulty, which would at once have disappeared, had he turned to the Greek original.

[2] Difficilior lectio præstat procliviori.

prophet' (Matt. xxvii. 9), by urging the fact, of which yet he is entirely aware, that for 'Jeremy' in some manuscripts 'Zechariah' was found written; since, quite apart from the preponderance of diplomatic authority in favour of the former reading, it is altogether inexplicable how 'Jeremy,' if not the true reading, should have found its way into the text; while, on the contrary, nothing is so easy as to explain how, albeit the true reading, some should have omitted, or exchanged it for 'Zechariah.'[1]

Having spoken thus much of his knowledge, or his ignorance, of those foreign languages which were, or might have been to him, subsidiary aids in his exposition of Scripture, a few remarks may fitly follow on his use and command of that language, in which he has deposited all the rich stores and treasures of his mind. If it be true, as has been sometimes said, that the style is the man, we might assume beforehand that where the man was so genuine and so true, there would be nothing, as certainly there is nothing, unreal or affected in the style. It would have been in many ways affectation for a Christian writer of the fourth or fifth century to aim at writing the Latin of the Augustan age. He knows nothing of this affectation. So far as a large acquaintance with the best writers in the language would have carried him in such an attempt, had he been inclined to make it, he was not unprovided; nor can his departure from the standard of classical Latinity be laid to any ignorance of the best models. Amid all the tumults and disorders of his youth, his classical studies were never intermitted.[2] That mighty

[1] *De Cons. Evang.* iii. 7.
[2] On the extent of these studies and the diligence with which he pursued them, see his *Confessions,* iv. 16.

longing which always possessed him, drove him as eagerly into these studies, so long as he believed that from such sources he could draw that which would slake the thirst of his soul, as afterwards to those fountains which indeed could slake it. And remembering that he professed rhetoric and grammar, or more properly literature, not at Tagaste only, but at Carthage, at Milan, and at Rome, we may confidently presume that his familiarity with those authors who alone could furnish him with the needful preparation was not superficial nor inaccurate; for he certainly was not the man to undertake to teach others that which he did not adequately possess himself. But indeed we have more immediate evidence of the fact. His writings bear abundant testimony to the extent of his acquaintance with the literature of Rome, and not seldom to his just and subtle estimate of the several merits of her principal writers. His chief familiarity is perhaps with Varro, with Cicero, and with Virgil. Many important fragments of the first of these, especially of his *Divine Antiquities*, have come down to us only through their incorporation into his great prose epic and apology for the Christian Church, *The City of God*.[1] But his range of authors is

[1] Ille undecumque doctissimus Marcus Varro, as he calls him in one place (*De Civ. Dei*, xviii. 2. 2); and see a larger and admirable estimate of him in the same work, vi. 2. What he owed to the *Hortensius* of Cicero, and what nobler cravings it woke up in him, he has told us in one of the most interesting passages in his *Confessions*, iii. 4. Provokingly enough this book, having managed to live on till the twelfth century, has since disappeared. How happily, too, he seizes one side at least of the literary merits of Cicero—verborum vigilantissimus appensor et mensor, as he calls him (*Con. adv. Leg. et Proph.* 54); nor has Lucan, with whom he is evidently familiar, for he quotes him several times, ever been more felicitously designated in his merits and in his defects, than as magnus in carmine declamator (*De Cons. Evang.* i. 30. 46); while Sallust, with many demerits,

not a narrow one ; he quotes or makes allusion to almost the whole circle of Latin classics ; thus to Ennius,[1] to Terence,[2] to Horace,[3] to Statius,[4] to Juvenal,[5] to Persius,[6] to Pliny the Elder,[7] to Apuleius,[8] to Claudian,[9] and draws his illustrations freely from them all.

Yet for all this, his own Latin is not the attempted bringing back of something gone by, but the language as it had been modified and moulded in the course of the four centuries which had elapsed since the time of its greatest perfection, and by the new, most of all by the Christian, influences which had been brought meanwhile to bear upon it.[10] Nor does his diction want signs of that

yet deserves the praise which he gives him, as lectissimus pensator verborum (*De Beatâ Vitâ*, 31); and again, as Romanæ linguæ disertissimus (*Ep.* 167, § 6). None who have read will forget the account in his *Confessions* (i. 13) of his early passion for Virgil.
  [1] *De Civ. Dei*, vii. 27.   [2] *Ibid.* xiv. 8.   [3] *Ibid.* v. 13.
  [4] *Ibid.* ii. 12.   [5] *Ep.* 138.   [6] *Ibid.* 118.
  [7] *De Civ. Dei*, xv. 9.   [8] *Ibid.* viii. 19.
  [9] *Ibid.* v. 26. I can well remember the immense enthusiasm with which my tutor at Harrow, Henry Drury, was wont to cite the lines from Claudian, as the finest in the Latin language. They refer to the fighting of winds and waves in favour of Theodosius the Great when he was engaged in mortal conflict with one of the competitors for his throne, and are as follows:

O nimium dilecte Deo, cui militat æther,
Et conjurati veniunt ad classica venti.

Noble lines, beyond all doubt, but the best in the language is another question.
  [10] Thus he boldly employs Salvator, about which there had been some hesitation before; the Latin of the golden age having salus and salvus, but not salvare or salvator. He, however, will not refrain from their use, disposing of all objections to them with the pertinent remark, that a new thing demanded a new word; that salvator might not have been good Latin before Christ came, but that it was so now (*Serm.* ccxcix. 6): Christus Jesus, id est Christus Salvator; hoc est enim Latine Jesus. Nec quærant grammatici, quam sit Latinum, sed Christiani, quam verum. Salus enim Latinum nomen est; salvare

further transformation which the language should presently undergo.¹ The words that figure in the glossaries of later Latinity already begin to appear in his pages, although in no very large number, and chiefly in his familiar Epistles, or discourses addressed to the multitude; and then very often they are wilfully introduced that his hearers may understand him the better.² His classical

et salvator non fuerunt hæc Latina, antequam veniret Salvator; quando ad Latinos venit, et hæc Latina fecit. Compare on this matter Pearson, *On the Creed, Art.* 2.

¹ A slight but very curious anticipation of the great changes in store for the Latin language, of the new capabilities which it was about to display, is the frequent occurrence of rhymes in the Latin of Augustine, and these evidently not unsought, or at any rate not unwelcomed when they offered themselves; such for instance as the following, in all of which there is an evident intention of giving point to the sentence by their aid: thus a definition of faith: Quid est enim *fides*, nisi credere quæ non *vides?* (*In Joh. Tract.* xl.); the relation of the two Testaments to one another: In Novo Testamento *patent*, quæ in Vetere *latent* (*Qu. in Exod.* qu. 73); the mystical meaning of John xxi. 9, 13: Piscis *assus* Christus est *passus* (*In Joh. Tract.* cxxiii.); on Stephen's keenest rebuke of his countrymen, whom he prayed for notwithstanding (Acts xii. 51, 60); Lingua *clamat*, cor *amat*; or exhortations such as the following: Hoc agamus *bene*, ut illud habeamus *plene* (*Serm.* civ. 3); Noli amare *impedimentum*, si non vis invenire *tormentum* (*Serm.* cccxi. 4); or once more, of the Heavenly Jerusalem, Ibi nullus *oritur*, quia nullus *moritur* (*De Civ. Dei*, v. 16); or again, on what the world calls joy, Seculi *lætitia* est impunita *nequitia* (*Serm.* clxxi. 4); or on the freedom of God, which prophecy does not restrict or limit, Prædixi, non fixi; thus, too, on the motive, as that which truly constitutes the act, Lupus venit fremens, lupus redit tremens; lupus est tamen et tremens et fremens (*Serm.* 178).

² *Enarr. in Ps.* cxxiii. 8: Sæpe enim verba non Latina pono, ut vos intelligatis. Thus the African provincials knew but of one os, *i.e.* os, oris, the countenance, while for os, a bone, they used the more vulgar ossum; which usage he falls into, *Enarr. in Ps.* cxxxviii. 15; and elsewhere defends on the ground that, speaking more elegantly, he would certainly have been misunderstood by them; by this example justifying in popular discourses that diligens negligentia, which chooses rather the solecism or barbarism that will convey the mean-

culture preserves him for the most from phrases and idioms of a needless offence, and in the main from the harsher Africanisms of Tertullian and Arnobius. Nor are there any tokens of that *reluctancy* in the language to yield itself freely to all the uses whereto he would put it, of which we are so often painfully conscious in reading the former of those writers. On the contrary, it shows itself ever as a handmaid at once willing and able to accomplish whatever task, even the hardest, he would impose upon it.[1] Full and free, it is a garment in the

ing of the speaker, than the more correct expression that will not; for, as he observes (*De Doct. Christ.* iii. 3): Plerumque loquendi consuetudo vulgaris utilior est significandis rebus quam antiquitas literata; and again (iv. 10): Melius est reprehendant nos grammatici, quam non intelligant populi. On the character of Augustine's Latin see Rönsch, *Itala und Vulgata*, pp. 8, 481.

[1] One great test of mastery over a language is familiarity with its synonyms, and power of distinguishing accurately between them. In this Augustine excels, having an evident pleasure in tracing such finer distinctions, which he does often with no common subtlety and skill. Thus he distinguishes between flagitium and facinus: Quod agit indomita cupiditas ad corrumpendum animum et corpus suum, flagitium vocatur; quod autem agit ut alteri noceat, facinus dicitur (*De Doctr. Christ.* iii. 10, 14; *Conf.* iii. 8; cf. DÖDERLEIN, *Latein. Synon.* vol. ii. 145); again, between delictum and peccatum (*Qu. in Lev.* qu. 20), keeping clear of the common error, which makes one the sin of omission, the other of commission (see DÖDERLEIN, vol. ii. 139); rather the delictum is the *desertio* boni; peccatum, *perpetratio* mali. So too, between æmulatio and invidia ($\zeta\hat{\eta}\lambda os$ and $\phi\theta\acute{o}\nu os$, *Expos. ad Gal.* v. 20): æmulatio est dolor animi, cum alius pervenit ad rem, quam duo pluresve appetebant, et nisi ab uno haberi non potest: invidia vero dolor animi est, cum indignus videtur aliquis assequi etiam quod tu non appetebas. He discriminates well between arrha and pignus (*Serm.* xxiii. 8, 9; and *Serm.* ccclxxviii.); curiosus and studiosus (*De Util. Cred.* 9); lætitia and gaudium, cautio and metus, volo and cupio (*De Civ. Dei*, xiv. 8); astutus, prudens, and sapiens (*De Gen. ad Lit.* ix. 2); precor, imprecor, deprecor (*Ep.* cxlix. 2). In several instances it is true that he only follows the lead of Cicero and others; but this is something. His etymologies too are

flowing and stately folds of which his thoughts are amply yet not redundantly arrayed. He knows what the language can effect, and oftentimes tests its powers to the uttermost; his works, indeed, are full of passages of an almost unequalled eloquence.[1] Now and then, it is true, almost always correct: as, prodigia, quod porro dicant (*De Civ. Dei*, xxviii. 8); or if they are such as some would call in question, such as his derivation of religio from religare, rather than relegere (*Retract.* i. 13), yet here, if he has many against him, some also are with him, and he is aware of, and had once inclined to, the preferable etymology (*De Civ. Dei*, x. 3). His derivation of abominor as though it was abhominor, so to hate one as not to esteem him a man (*Serm.* ix. 9), might seem indeed in more ways than one to militate against his Latin scholarship; but elsewhere he rightly derives it from omen (*Retract.* i. 13); and doubtless the other, like so many of the ancient etymologies, which are quite misunderstood when taken in any other spirit, was intended for a *calembourg* and no more. In like manner when he says, Est enim severitas, quasi sæva veritas, Dei (*Serm.* clxxi. 5), he doubtless offers this as a *moral* rather than *verbal* etymology. I gather from the following passages (*Solil.* ii. 7. 14) that soliloquium was a word of his own coining; though we now find it hard to understand how the language could have done without it so long: Sermocinationes, quæ, quoniam cum solis nobis loquimur *soliloquia* vocari et inscribi volo, novo quidem et fortasse duro nomine, sed ad rem demonstrandam satis idoneo.

[1] As for instance this passage, upon the Church and her teaching (*De Mor. Eccles.* 30): Tu pueriliter pueros, fortiter juvenes, quiete senes, prout cujusque non corporis tantum sed et animi ætas est, exerces et doces. Tu feminas viris suis non ad explendam libidinem sed at propagandam prolem, et ad rei familiaris societatem, castâ et fideli obedientiâ subjicis. Tu viros conjugibus, non ad illudendum imbecilliorem sensum sed sinceri amoris legibus subjicis. Tu parentibus filios liberâ quâdam servitute subjungis, parentes filiis piâ dominatione præponis. Tu fratribus fratres religionis vinculo firmiore atque artiore quam sanguinis nectis. Tu omnis generis propinquitatem et affinitatis necessitudinem, servatis naturæ voluntatisque nexibus, mutuâ caritate constringis. Tu dominis servos non tam conditionis necessitate, quam officii delectatione doces adhærere. Tu dominos servis, summi Dei communis Domini consideratione placabiles, et ad consulendum quam coërcendum propensiores facis. Tu cives civibus, gentes gentibus, et prorsus homines primorum parentum

in the pointed antithesis of his sentences, though the
antithesis never perils, but is made alway to subserve, the
sense, or again in the sustained balance of some long-
drawn periods, we are just reminded that he had once
taught rhetoric in the capitals of Africa and of Italy, at
Carthage and Milan.

recordatione, non societate tantum sed quâdam etiam fraternitate
conjungis. Doces reges prospicere populis, mones populos se sub-
dere regibus. Quibus honor debeatur, quibus affectus, quibus reve-
rentia, quibus timor, quibus consolatio, quibus admonitio, quibus
cohortatio, quibus disciplina, quibus objurgatio, quibus supplicium,
sedulo doces, ostendens quemadmodum et non omnibus omnia, et
omnibus caritas, et nulli debeatur injuria.

CHAPTER III.

AUGUSTINE'S PRINCIPLES AND CANONS OF INTERPRETATION.

HAVING said thus much in my first chapter on the tone and temper in which Augustine approached, and would fain see others to approach, the Word of God; and, in my second, on the extent to which he was himself furnished with external helps for the interpretation of it, I shall now proceed to gather from his writings some of those principles and canons of interpretation, which, either adopting from others, or generalizing from his own experience, he has laid down, as needful to be observed, if the interpretation is not to be abandoned to merest hazard and caprice. This I shall do, not thereby implying that he was himself always faithful to these canons which he recognized. I shall at the same time endeavour to trace those circumstances of his own position which may have wrought most effectually in the forming and further unfolding of his system of interpretation.

And first, Augustine often presses excellently well the duty of interpreting Scripture according to the analogy of faith; in other words, that no single saying there shall receive such an explanation as shall put it in contradiction with the whole body and complex of doctrinal truth drawn from other Scriptures; that the explanation which does place any single passage in this opposition must, however plausible it may seem, at once be rejected; since all Scripture, as coming from one and the same Spirit of truth, must be, so to speak, *panharmonic*. Thus he is refuting those who were fain to find in 1 Cor. iii. 15, a declaration that evil livers should yet, if only they were members of the Catholic Church, after passing through certain purgatorial fires, attain to final salvation; and who said that the Apostle had these in his eye, when he spoke of some who should be saved, 'yet so as by fire.' This cannot be his meaning, Augustine answers, because the entire testimony of Scripture in a multitude of plainest passages avouches the contrary to this; which passages it would be absurd to override and overrule by an interpretation, which would be doubtful at the best, of one obscure passage, even if there were not those other to prove that it is a *false* one.[1] And he well lays down this as a general canon, that the obscurer passages are ever to receive their interpretation from the clearer, and not the contrary.[2]

In dealing with the tropical language of Scripture, Augustine often calls to notice that in it certain figures are not indissolubly tied to corresponding realities of the

---

[1] *De Octo Dulcit. Quæst.* qu. 1; *De Fide et Oper.* 15; *De Fide, Spe, et Carit.* 57: Quidam ita intelligendum putant, ut qui, quum fidem habeant, male operantur, per quasdam ignis pœnas possint purgari ad salutem percipiendam. ... Si ergo innumerabilia quæ per omnes Scripturas sine ambiguitate dicta reperiri possunt [de necessitate bonorum operum] falsa erunt, poterit verus esse ille intellectus. Sed quia hæc apostolica manifestissima et apertissima testimonia falsa esse non possunt, illud quod obscure dictum est sic intelligendum est, ut his manifestis non inveniatur esse contrarium.

[2] *De Doctr. Christ.* ii. 14: Ad obscuras locutiones illustrandas de manifestioribus sumantur exempla, et quædam certarum sententiarum testimonia dubitationem incertis auferant.

kingdom of heaven, that any assumption that they are so would often lead us altogether astray. He recognizes the freedom with which the inspired writers and the Lord Himself appropriated from the vast storehouse of imagery in nature and in art, what was best adapted for the setting forth of that truth which at the moment they had in hand, yet not forbidding thereby that the very same image, contemplated indeed on some other side, should presently set forth an altogether different, nay opposite, truth. Thus Christ is a lion (Rev. v. 5), and Satan is a lion (1 Pet. v. 8); the truth is leaven (Matt. xiii. 33), and malice, wickedness, and hypocrisy are leaven (1 Cor. v. 8; Luke xii. 1); for, to use a modern illustration, the imagery of Scripture is not so much stereotype, never to be shifted any more from the place which it once has occupied, but rather like those moveable types which may continually be brought into new combinations; or, to cite Augustine's own comparison, it resembles the letters of the alphabet, which, still the same, yet help now to compose words expressive of what is best, and then presently, it may be, of what is worst. Yet no one would affirm that because D has done duty in diabolus, it is therefore an impiety to use it also in Deus.[1]

---

[1] Thus *Serm.* xxxii. 6: Non enim semper in Scripturis eadem significantur rebus certis. Non semper mons Dominum significat, non semper lapis Dominum significat, non semper leo Dominum significat, non semper bonum, non semper malum: sed pro locis Scripturarum, quo pertinent cætera circumstantia ipsius lectionis. Quemadmodum litteræ in tot millibus verborum atque sermonum ipsæ repetuntur, non augentur; . . . quum una littera variis in locis ponitur, et pro loco valet, non unam rem valet. This last thought he further unfolds, *Enarr. in Ps.* ciii. 21: Si audieris litteram primam in nomine Dei, et putaveris eam semper ibi ponendam, delebis eam in nomine diaboli, ab eâdem enim litterâ incipit

Again, he insists strongly on the futility of appealing to any but to plain and literal passages of Scripture for the laying of first foundations of doctrines, most of all when in controversy with gainsayers and opposers. Afterwards, when these foundations are securely laid, the confirmations of the truth, which may be superinduced from the allegorical and figurative, will fitly find their place; but to begin with these is like painting on a cloud or building in the air. Moreover, it is idle for us to expect that adversaries will be convinced by these passages, which, if they are capable of our meaning, are also capable of another; which those of the other side may refuse to admit to have any deeper meaning at all. Proofs, therefore, of this character should be laid aside for the time, not because they are worthless, but because they do not belong to this stage of the argument, inasmuch as they do not of necessity carry conviction with them;[1] afterwards they will be good for the delight and yet further confirmation of friends, though not for the conviction or the putting to silence of foes. They must be regarded as the ornamental fringe, never as the main woof or texture, of the argument. The thrice repeated 'Holy' of the seraphim in Isaiah's vision (Isai. vi. 3) is good for us, who already, and on other grounds, have received the doctrine of the Ever Blessed Trinity; but it would be idle to seek to convince a denier of that doctrine thereby.

nomen Dei a quâ incipit nomen diaboli; et nihil tam disjunctum quam Deus et diabolus. And again, *Enarr. in Ps.* viii. 8: Hæc regula in omni allegoriâ retinenda est, ut pro sententiâ præsentis loci consideretur quod per similitudinem dicitur.

[1] *De Unit. Eccl.* 5: Illa interim seponenda sunt, quæ obscure posita et figurarum velaminibus involuta, et secundum nos et secundum illos possunt interpretari. . . . Aperta veritas clamet, luceat, in obturatas aures irrumpat, dissimulantium oculos feriat.

How well, again, he warns against that exaggeration of one side of a truth, which, with the overlooking or slighting of the other—of that which should at once counterpoise and complete it, has been the fruitful occasion of so many heresies that have afflicted the Church; for the half truth is very often no truth at all, at least to them who hold it with the ignoring of the other half.[1] Thus was it, as he often observes, with the Sabellian and the Arian. Each had his array of texts to appeal to; but neither had taken in the whole circle of Catholic teaching concerning the relation of the Son to the Father, and therefore neither had the truth. Their errors he likens to Scylla and Charybdis; sailing between which, he that would avoid making perilous shipwreck of the faith, must give all diligence that, in his eagerness to keep as far as possible aloof from the one, he do not entangle himself in the dangers of the other.[2] It is not sufficient for his safety that he avoid *one*; he must at the same time avoid the other. But the conflict with these particular forms of error had been already fought, and the battle gained, before his time. He has indeed oftentimes instructive matter on them both,[3] as one and the other the partial exaggeration of certain Scriptures with the overlooking of others; yet

---

[1] *De Fide et Oper.* 5, 7 : Errant homines, non servantes modum : et quum in unam partem procliviter ire cœperint, non respiciunt divinæ auctoritatis alia testimonia, quibus possint ab illâ intentione revocari, et in eâ quæ ex utrisque temperata est veritate et moderatione consistere. . . . Nos vero ad sanam doctrinam pertinere arbitramur ex utrisque testimoniis vitam sententiamque moderari.

[2] Elsewhere, thus *Con. Adimant.* xiv. 2, he denounces the fraud of them, qui particulas quasdam e Scripturis eligunt, quibus decipiant imperitos, non connectentes quæ supra et infra scripta sunt, ex quibus voluntas et intentio scriptoris possint intelligi.

[3] See, for instance, *In Ev. Joh. Tract.* xxxvi. 9.

not being compelled to these discussions by present and urgent needs of the Church; for he himself speaks of these heresies, the first as altogether of the past, the other as just alive and no more.[1]

But with other forms of opposition to the truth it was otherwise. It was this same accusation of overlooking and slighting one half of the truth of Scripture in their blind and passionate urging of the other, which he brought especially against the Donatists. Those of that schism refused, as is well known, to hold communion with the Catholic Church; and it was exactly in this way that they justified their schism. They laid hold on all passages in Scripture which spoke of the holiness of the Church, its freedom from impurities; overlooking all those others which characterized that holiness in the present time as imperfect even in the faithful themselves; disregarding too all those which declared or implied that, until the end of the present æon, sinners would be mingled with the faithful; and because they did not find that entire immunity from evil in the Church Catholic, they would not admit it to be the Church at all. Augustine had here to show that what they advanced was not so much untrue as one-sided. Yet we can scarcely affirm that his controversy with these fierce and fanatic separatists, seriously as it occupied him (for Donatism was the running sore of the African Church, and one which never entirely ceased till the body, and the disease which afflicted the body, perished together), we can scarcely, I say, affirm that this controversy contributed in any important measure to the forming of his system of interpretation. Its influence is felt to a certain degree in his exegesis, as in the manner

[1] *In Ev. Joh. Tract.* xl. 7.

in which it causes him to *weight* certain statements of Scripture ; but Donatism, so far as argument was concerned (for practically the case was very different), was more easily disposed of than that it could have seriously moulded or affected him.

The wandering rabble of that faction was indeed formidable enough, when, in some remote district, men and women, rudely but terribly armed, at first with clubs only, 'Israels' as they called them,[1] but afterwards with slings and hatchets, lances and swords,[2] and with their cry of *Deo Laudes,* more dreaded than a lion's roar,[3] they exacted extreme penalties from some unfortunate creditor, who had claimed his own, notwithstanding their threatening letters, forbidding him this. Nor were they less formidable when they laid wait in the way for some member, some priest or bishop, if it might be, of the Catholic Church,—more than once they set ambushes for Augustine himself,—or surrounding his house by night, pulled it down or burned it over his head, and forcing him thence, or from the altar itself,[4] so wounded that he presently expired ; or after having thus maltreated, dragged him till nearly dead through filthy pools ;[5] or pouring quick lime, and when they found that of that their victims sometimes recovered, lime mingled with vinegar, into his eyes, deprived him amid excruciating torments, of sight ;[6] or in their milder mood, having clothed in some masquerade dress of scorn, paraded him through the neighbouring villages, and hardly after many

---

[1] *Enarr. in Ps.* x. 3.
[2] *Con. Lit. Petil.* ii. 88, 96.
[3] *Enarr. in Ps.* cxxxii. 1.
[4] *Con. Cresc.* iii. 43.
[5] *Con. Cresc.* iii. 48 ; *Ep.* lxxxviii. 6.
[6] *Ep.* cxi. 1 ; *Con. Cresc.* iii. 42.

days let him go;[1] or harnessing in a mill, compelled him with many stripes to turn it.[2] Nor were they less to be dreaded, when, in that insane spirit of self-destruction which possessed them,[3] meeting a Catholic they insisted on his killing them, under threat of his own instant death if he refused.[4] But those who bore the word for this schism, wielded the weapons of their warfare in no such effectual manner. It is not a little curious in the many debates carried on either in writing or by word of mouth between Augustine and various Donatist bishops or theologians, some of these evidently sincere and earnest men, to note the rapidity with which he turns their position, and puts himself almost at once within their lines of defence. After a while they discover that thus it will inevitably prove; and the Ithacan mendicant not more reluctantly advanced to make proof of the thews and sinews of Ulysses, than do these to a calm discussion with him of the differences between themselves and the Catholic Church; for to this method of settling the points at issue between them, and, if possible, healing this miserable schism, Augustine continually invites them, while they avoid it by every subterfuge they can.[5]

But it was not altogether thus with the Manichæans. They were no such weaklings in his hands. In them he encountered adversaries, not indeed intellectually his peers; for where could he have met such? yet crafty, dexterous, and eloquent; by no means unpractised in the

---

[1] *Ep.* lxxxviii. 6; *Con. Cresc.* iii. 48.   [2] *Ep.* clxxxv. 4.
[3] *In Evang. Joh. Tract.* xi. 17; *Con. Gaudent.* 30; *Hæret.* 69.
[4] *Ep.* clxxxv. 4; for other outrages see *Ep.* cxxxiii. and cxxxiv.; and WITSIUS, *Miscell. Sacra,* vol. i. 762.
[5] *Ep.* xxxiv. 6.

logical fence, and wielding the weapons of a destructive criticism with a skill which it is impossible not sometimes to admire. And in other ways, also, the contest was a more serious one. He had not against them to vindicate a few passages of Scripture from perverse and partial interpretation, but to defend and to secure the very foundations of the faith; which they assailed, and which their triumph would have utterly overthrown. The question at issue was not here one of doctrine; and as little how this or that Scripture should be understood, and whether it could only be rightly understood, when controlled and tempered by other passages. It was a question far more serious; namely, whether there was a Scripture at all, such a Scripture, that is, as men might securely commit themselves to, the very Word of God, containing all truth in it, and nothing but the truth; and if so, whether those writings which were in the keeping of the Catholic Church, and which she could show to have been in her keeping in an unbroken succession from the times of the Apostles indeed constituted this Book. This when the Manichæans denied on evidence which professed to be drawn from the writings themselves, it became his task to trace the perfect harmony existing between the different portions of this Book; to show that one part, the New Testament, did not, as those affirmed, go counter to and thus condemn another, that is, the Old; that the several portions of the New were not repugnant to one another, and did not thus (since in that case it could only be partially true) leave each man at liberty to select for himself such sections of it as he was willing to receive and believe.

The Manichæans could not but feel that if the controversy between them and the Church Catholic, as to what was the genuine doctrine which Christ had delivered, should be decided by an appeal to the canonical Scriptures, the decision must inevitably be given against them, and in favour of the Church. There remained therefore nothing for them but either entirely to refuse to accept this appeal, as they did in the matter of the Old Testament, or, where such absolute refusal would have at once put them out of court, and left them without even a nominal profession of the Christian faith, to seek to weaken as far as they might the authority of this judge, and so to take away from the force of his decisions. They began, as is ever the course with those who would be quit of the Bible, with an assault upon the Old Testament; and from the authority of this they sought to release themselves altogether. It was from the vantage-ground of the New that they made their assault upon the Old, maintaining that it was full of statements irreconcileable with the doctrines delivered there. Adimantus, an immediate scholar of Mani, wrote a book full of these so-called 'contradictions,' of which it may be instructive to adduce a few. Thus the very first verse of Genesis, that 'God created the heaven and the earth,' is contrary to the opening of St. John, where it is declared that the world was made by Christ.[1] The words of Genesis, 'God rested on the seventh day,' do not agree with those of the Lord, 'My Father worketh hitherto' (John v. 17).[2] The declaration, 'It is not good that the man should be alone; I will make him an help meet for him' (Gen. ii. 18), contradicts the blessing which the Lord pronounced on every one who should leave (among other things) wife for his

[1] *Con. Adimant. Man.* 1.   [2] *Ibid.* 2.

sake (Matt. xix. 29).[1] That God made man in his own image (Gen. i. 26) is against that word of Christ to the Pharisees, 'Ye are of your father the devil' (John viii. 44).[2] God's declaration in the Old Testament that He is a jealous God, visiting the sins of the fathers upon the children, is in contradiction to the word of Christ, 'He maketh his sun to rise on the evil and on the good' (Matt. v. 45).[3] All passages in the Old Testament in which God is set forth as speaking or appearing to man are convinced of falsehood by that one word of Christ's Apostle: 'No man hath seen God at any time' (John i. 18); as indeed by the Lord Himself (John v. 37).[4] In the Old Testament certain meats are declared to be unclean; but Christ declared that there is nothing that entering into a man can defile him (Mark vii. 18).[5]

It will be observed of the larger number of these very characteristic 'antitheses' that they are merely ridiculous, although some of them not too ridiculous to have done duty anew in later times. Others rest on an ignoring of the *progressive* character of Revelation, of the fact that it has been a *gradual* education of men into the knowledge of God, they moving up from the more elementary and imperfect into the higher and more perfect, as they were able to bear it; this consideration is indeed one which will have to be recognized by theologians much more freely than has hitherto been the case, if they would not find themselves sometimes, when engaged with the adversaries of revealed truth, in all the grievous embarrassments which a false position will inevitably entail. This fact of the progressive education of men, of their gradual training

[1] *Con. Adimant. Man.* 3. [2] *Ibid.* 5. [3] *Ibid.* 7.
[4] *Ibid.* 9. [5] *Ibid.* 15.

into the knowledge of the truth, and of the consequent use and fitness, at one stage of the teaching, of helps which were laid aside and would have been inapplicable, where not injurious, at a later,[1] is one of which Augustine had a very firm grasp, and on which he often expresses himself with remarkable clearness and force;[2] for this probably he was in part indebted to these very gainsayers themselves.[3] With the setting forth of this law of progress in

[1] He has many illustrations drawn from our daily life. Thus *Enarr. in Ps.* lxxiii. 1 : Tu ipse dedisti filio tuo, et nuces parvulo, et codicem grandi. *De Verâ Rel.* 17 : Quis perturbatur si unus medicus alia per ministros suos imbecillioribus, alia per se ipsum valentioribus præcipiat ad reparandam vel obtinendam salutem? We have here an eminent illustration of what St. Paul calls the πολυποίκιλος σοφία of God (Ephes. iii. 10), varying its treatment according to the varying needs of different men in different ages.

[2] *Conf.* iii. 7 : Tanquam si in uno die indicto a pomeridianis horis justitio, quisquam stomachetur non sibi concedi quid venale proponere, quia mane concessum est: aut in unâ domo videat aliquid tractari manibus a quoquam servo, quod facere non sinatur qui pocula ministrat: aut aliquid post præsepia fieri, quod ante mensam prohibeatur; et indignetur, cum sit unum habitaculum et una familia, non ubique atque omnibus idem tribui. Sic sunt isti qui indignantur, cum audierint illo sæculo licuisse justis aliquid, quod isto non licet justis; et quia illis aliud præcepit Deus, istis aliud pro temporalibus causis, cum eidem justitiæ utrique servierint: cum in uno homine et in uno die et in unis ædibus videant aliud alii membro congruere, et aliud jamdudum licuisse, post horam non licere : quiddam in illo angulo permitti aut juberi quod in isto juste vetetur et vindicetur. Numquid justitia varia est et mutabilis? Sed tempora quibus præsidet, non pariter eunt; tempora enim sunt. Cf. *Con. Faust.* xxii. 47 ; *De Doctr. Christ.* iii. 10.

[3] For, as he himself says in an interesting passage on the profit which comes to the Church from such gainsayings (*Serm.* li. 7): Negligentius veritas quæreretur, si mendaces adversarios non haberet. And again, *Enarr. in Ps.* liv. 22 : Numquid enim perfecte de Trinitate tractatum est antequam oblatrarent Ariani? numquid perfecte de pœnitentibus tractatum est antequam obsisterent Novatiani? Sic non perfecte de baptismate tractatum est antequam contradicerent foris positi rebaptizatores. In reference to this fact, which all Church

the divine economy, he at once disposes of a multitude of the so-called contradictions which they had found between the earlier revelation of God and the later, as the distinction of meats, ordained in the Old Dispensation, abolished in the New,—the retaliation of injuries allowed in the Old, their forgiveness enjoined in the New,—circumcision appointed in the one, forbidden in the other.

But the Manichæans did not and could not stop here. The experience of all past controversies, and a very little consideration of the actual relations in which the Old and New Testament stand to one another, attest the certainty of the fact that they will stand or fall together. None can give up the authority of the Old, and hope to retain that of the New. None who attack the Old will ever pause there; they will find themselves irresistibly and necessarily carried on to assail the New. Whatever victories they may seem to themselves to have won over that, they will themselves feel to be nothing worth, unless they can overthrow the authority of this also; for the Old may all be established again by the aid and authority of the New, which everywhere presupposes and sets the seal of a divine character upon it; in the same way as the Old prophesies of and contains the New enfolded up in itself,[1]—that being, according to Augustine's own image, the closed hand, and this the open, but one and the other the same hand still. They were conscious, therefore, that nothing was really won, unless they could thus overthrow the absolute authority of the New Testament no less than that of the Old,[2]

history confirms, he quotes often 1 Cor. xi. 19; cf. *Conf.* vii. 19; *Enarr. in Ps.* lxvii. 31 ; *De Gen. con. Man.* i. 1.

[1] As in one place he says: Vetus Testamentum est occultatio Novi, et Novum manifestatio Veteris.

[2] The process of first setting the New Testament against the Old,

and this in various ways they set themselves to effect. They affirmed in the first place, that the books of Canonical Scripture which the Catholic Church received, were in whole or in part the composition of others than those whose names they bore; having been either interpolated by some who would fain mingle Jewish error with Christian truth [1] (and that there should be such corruption they declared foreannounced in the parable of the tares [2]), or else, as was the case with the Acts of the Apostles, being altogether supposititious.[3] Even where they were driven from this position, they had another to which they retired. Granting that the ascription of authorship was correct, that St. Matthew, St. Paul, and the others did write the books that went by their names, still at the time when they wrote them, they were themselves only partially disengaged from the Jewish superstitions and errors among which they had been reared. From all this, as they urged, it followed that in every case a test was needed, whereby it should be judged whether this portion of Scripture or that should be received as authoritative or

and when this antagonism has done its work, then the several parts of the New against one another, was exactly that which the German assailants of Holy Scripture in the last century pursued, who did not venture to lay profane hands on the New Testament for long after they had renounced their faith in the Old. We have seen exactly the same process repeat itself in England.

[1] *Conf.* v. 11; *Ep.* lxxxii. 2. 6. How poor this escape of theirs, Augustine tells us that he felt even while he was still entangled in their snares (*De Util. Cred.* 3). His acquaintance with classical literature must have taught him how worthless objections to the genuineness of a passage are, drawn merely from the subjective sense of the reader, and with no wavering and uncertainty in the external evidence to back them.

[2] *Con. Faust.* xviii. 3, 7.

[3] *De Util. Cred.* 3; *Ep.* ccxxxvii. 2.

not.[1] This test was of course, practically, whether they could turn it into a plausible support of their dogmas, in which case it was allowed; or whether it went plainly contrary to them, when it was rejected.

They agreed with the modern rationalists, in trying Holy Scripture by the subjective standard of their own likings and dislikings, accepting that which fell in with their own preconceived opinions, disallowing that which did not.[2] Like them, too, they proceeded to find motives for this disallowance in some contradiction or discrepancy which they professed to detect in the Scripture they dismissed, making difficulties where there were none, exaggerating them where such there really were; and under cover of differences which they had discovered between one Scripture and another, or on some similar plea, excusing themselves from yielding credit to either. Thus they left no choice to the defenders of the truth but

---

[1] Thus Faustus (*Con. Faust.* xxxii. 1): Ego de Testamento Novo purissima quæque legens et meæ saluti convenientia, prætermitto quæ a vestris majoribus inducta fallaciter, et majestatem illius et gratiam decolorant. Cf. xxxiii. 3: Nec immerito nos ad hujuscemodi Scripturas tam inconsonantes et varias, nunquam sane sine judicio ac ratione aures afferimus; sed contemplantes omnia, et cum aliis alia conferentes, perpendimus utrum eorum quidque a Christo dici potuerit, necne.

[2] *Con. Faust.* xi. 2; cf. xxii. 15: Inde probas hoc illius esse, illud non esse, quia hoc pro te sonat, illud contra te. Tu es ergo regula veritatis? quidquid contra te fuerit, non est verum? And when they in their turn adduced such portions of Scripture as they did profess to receive in proof of doctrines of their own, he admirably brings out the absurdity of this (*Ibid.* xxxii. 16): Ex Evangelio probatis. Ex quo Evangelio? Quod non totum accipitis, quod falsatum esse vos dicitis. Quis ergo testem suum prius ipse dicat falsitate esse corruptum, et tunc producat ad testimonium? Si enim quod vultis ei credimus, et quod non vultis ei non credimus, jam non illi sed vobis credimus.

to enter on discussions, not a few of which have an interest which can never grow old; for studying the cavils and objections of Faustus the Manichæan, one seems transported into the present age, so marvellously have he and others, in almost all essential matters, and curiously often in minutest details,[1] anticipated the destructive criticism which has been brought to bear against Scripture in the last seventy or eighty years. And certainly it is encouraging to observe that this whole battery of assault has been once already directed against the Word of God with at least the same confidence of success as now, with exactly the same boastful announcements that all truth and reason were with the assailants,[2] and that the Church was hopelessly clinging to the antiquated or the exploded; and this by men of as keen dialectic skill, of as subtle intellectual power as any who have inherited their mantle;[3]

---

[1] Thus Faustus has anticipated the trivial objection drawn from the titles of the several Gospels, κατὰ Ματθαῖον, κατὰ Μάρκον, namely, that on their fronts these Gospels do not profess to be what the Church affirms them—namely, the writing of these Apostles or apostolic men, but only of some who claimed to write according to accounts received severally from these four. Thus, as he describes them, in words quoted *Con. Faust.* xxxii. 2, the Evangelists were— incerti nominis viri, qui ne sibi non haberetur fides, scribentibus quæ nescirent, partim Apostolorum nomina, partim eorum qui Apostolos secuti viderentur, scriptorum suorum frontibus indiderunt, *asseverantes secundum eos se scripsisse quæ scripserint.*

[2] *De Mon. Manich.* 17: Magni pollicitatores rationis atque veritatis. *Conf.* iii. 6: Dicebant veritas et veritas; et multum eam dicebant mihi, et nusquam erat in eis.

[3] For the chief characteristics of Faustus the Manichæan, that 'great snare of the devil' (magnus laqueus diaboli), as Augustine calls him, a man who hardly finds his peer among the modern assailants of Scripture, see *Conf.* v. 3, 6, 7, 8; and at 13, a comparison between his eloquence and that of St. Ambrose. Cf. *Con. Faust.* i. 1.

and yet that all has been brought against it in vain. The whole fury of the assault passed away like a noise, like a flood that foams and frets for a brief season round some everlasting foundations, but which presently subsides, and shows that it has been unable to displace one stone from its position.

Compelled by these assaults of theirs, Augustine has many most instructive discussions on matters, which but for them he might have only slightly and superficially handled, if indeed he had handled at all. Thus, one of the subjects on which these gainsayers forced him to express himself often and distinctly, was the authority and evidence with which the canonical books come down to later generations in the Church, as indeed the works of those whose names they bear; and he not less excellently shows how impossible it is to designate or even to imagine any moment in the Church's history when the interpolation or serious corruption of them could have been accomplished.[1]

So, too, he treats often on the relation between various records of the same event, and the differences, which yet are not contradictions, that sometimes exist between them.[2] Thus, the miracle of the healing of the centurion's servant (Matt. viii. 5–13; Luke vii. 1–10) was peculiarly unwelcome to the Manichæans, and they greatly desired to get rid of it on account of those concluding words, in which the Lord gives such signal honour to Jewish patriarchs, ascribing to them foremost places in the future kingdom

[1] The following are among the most important passages, *De Mor. Eccles.* 29; *Con. Faust.* xi. 2; xxviii. 2; xxxii. 16.

[2] Diversa multa, adversa nulla esse possunt; and *De Cons. Evang.* ii. 66: Ubi utrumque factum potest intelligi, nulla repugnantia est, si alius aliud, et aliud alius commemorat.

of heaven. The adversaries sought to undermine the authority of the whole narrative, by urging the well-known difference between the two Evangelists, that in the first the centurion comes himself, in the second sends others to be the bearers of his petition. To such unworthy objections he replies with a just indignation, and in words which abundantly deserve to be quoted.[1]

Refusing as he does to be embarrassed by these slight variations, he is free from the temptation to adopt unnatural, or at best improbable, devices and combinations in order to get rid of these. The fact that, according to St. Matthew, the disciples wakened their Lord in the storm with the words, 'Lord, save us; we perish' (viii. 25); according to St. Mark, exclaiming, 'Master, carest Thou not that we perish?' (iv. 38); while in St. Luke their cry is, 'Master, master, we perish' (viii. 24); does not trouble him at all. He readily admits that all these words *may have been* uttered, some by one, and some by another, disciple; but he does not require this of necessity. If the inspired narratives have truly expressed the exact

---

[1] Having shown how futile their objections in this particular instance, he more generally adds (*Con. Faust.* xxxiii. 8): Vellem sane ut aliquis istorum vanorum, qui hujusmodi quæstiunculas quasi magnas calumniose objiciunt Evangelio, narraret aliquid idem ipse bis numero, non falsum nec fallaciter, sed omnino id volens intimare et exponere, et stilo exciperentur verba ejus eique recitarentur: utrum non aliquid plus minusve diceret, aut præpostero ordine, non verborum tantum, sed etiam rerum; aut utrum non aliquid ex suâ sententiâ diceret, tamquam alius dixerit, quod eum dixisse non audierit, sed voluisse atque sensisse plane cognoverit; aut utrum non alicujus breviter complecteretur sententiæ veritatem, cujus rei antea quasi expressius articulos explicâsset: et si quid est aliud quod fortasse possit certis regulis comprehendi, quomodo fiat ut vel in duorum singulis ejusdem rei narrationibus, vel in duabus unius ex unâ eâdemque re, multa diversa inveniantur, nulla tamen adversa; et multa varia, nulla contraria.

intention of the words uttered by the disciples at that moment, this is enough for him, and all that he demands from them.¹ In other statements to the same effect, and in statements yet stronger than these, there is on Augustine's part a freedom and boldness in recognizing the *human* element in Scripture, which has perplexed some.² But that he himself did not in the least believe that he was thus trenching on the divine inspiration of Scripture, is manifest from innumerable passages that might be quoted, in which he claims for it immunity from all error, styles its authors 'the pen of the Holy Ghost,' and the like.³

¹ *De Cons. Evang.* ii. 24: Nec opus est quærere quid horum potius Christo dictum sit. Sive enim aliquid horum trium dixerint, sive alia verba quæ nullus Evangelistarum commemoravit, tantumdem tamen valentia ad eandem sententiæ veritatem, quid ad rem interest? Quanquam et hoc fieri potuit, ut pluribus eum simul excitantibus, omnia hæc, aliud ab alio, dicerentur. (Cf. *Qu. in Gen.* x. qu. 64.) Thus again on the concordant diversity of the four Evangelists (66): Quâ nobis ostenditur non esse mendacium, si quisquam ita diverso modo aliquid narret, ut ab ejus voluntate cui consonandum et consentiendum est, non recedat. Quod nosse et moribus utile est, propter cavenda et judicanda mendacia; et ipsi fidei, ne putemus, quasi consecratis sonis, ita muniri veritatem, tanquam Deus nobis quemadmodum ipsam rem, sic verba quæ propter illam sunt dicenda, commendet; cum potius ita res quæ dicenda est, sermonibus per quos dicenda est, præferatur, ut istos omnino quærere non deberemus, si eam sine his nosse possemus, sicut illam novit Deus, et in ipso angeli ejus.

² As when, accounting for the different order in which the Evangelists narrate events, and the greater fulness of one than another, he says (*De Cons. Evang.* ii. 12): Ut enim quisque meminerat, et ut cuique cordi erat vel brevius vel prolixius eandem tamen explicare sententiam, ita eos explicâsse manifestum est. See RICH. SIMON, *Hist. Crit. du N. T.* xviii. 262.

³ *De Cons. Evang.* ii. 12: Omnem falsitatem abesse ab Evangelistis decet, non solum eam quæ mentiendo promitur, sed etiam eam quæ obliviscendo. Cf. *Ep.* xix. (*ad Hier.*): Si aliquid in eis offendero litteris quod videatur contrarium veritati: nihil aliud quam men-

dosum esse codicem, vel interpretem non assecutum esse quod dictum est, vel me minime intellexisse non ambigam. So too *Conf.* vii. 21 : Arripui venerabilem *stilum Spiritûs S. tui*, et præ cæteris apostolum Paulum, et perierunt illæ quæstiones, in quibus mihi aliquando visus est adversari sibi, et non congruere testimoniis legis et prophetarum, et apparuit mihi una facies eloquiorum castorum. Cf. *De Gen. ad Litt.* v. 8.

CHAPTER IV.

AUGUSTINE'S ALLEGORICAL INTERPRETATION OF SCRIPTURE.

IN a faithful portrait the lights and shadows ought both to find their place.[1] Such a faithful portrait it is my desire here to present; the excesses therefore of Augustine's allegorical interpretation of the Old Testament cannot be passed over altogether. Keeping these out of sight, one might present him in an aspect more exclusively favourable as an expositor, but certainly not in an aspect at all so true. He never indeed pushes this scheme of interpretation so far as to cast a slight, as Origen did, on the historic letter of the earlier Instrument. He may believe and teach of some portions of this that they borrow all, or nearly all, their value from the higher spiritual truth of which they are the vehicle; but he never teaches or implies that anything which is there told as history, was indeed not history at all, had no objective reality, being only the clothing of some moral or spiritual truth. On the contrary, he witnesses often and earnestly against all extenuations of the historic letter of Scripture; which letter must needs stand firm, whatever superstructure may afterwards be built thereon. This later

[1] On some shadows in the portrait which I am tracing here see DIESTEL, *Gesch. d. Alten Testamentes*, 1869, p. 86 sqq.

superstructure is ever to be reared on the establishment of the literal sense, not upon its ruins.[1] The allegory which Augustine urges must always be taken with a salvâ rerum gestarum fide,—often expressed, always understood.[2]

Of course it can be only with this scheme of interpretation driven into excess, and further than the hints which Scripture itself supplies for its due limitation will warrant, that any fault can be found. There is in all Scripture, and naturally most of all in the Old Testament Scripture, an allegorical element which has a right to claim recognition from the Christian interpreter. Few, if any, would deny this. Indeed there are large portions of God's Word, as the delineation of Ezekiel's temple (chap. 40-48), as the Song of Songs, which only come to their full rights

---

[1] *Serm.* ii. 6: Ante omnia, fratres, hoc in nomine Domini et admonemus quantum possumus et præcipimus, ut quando auditis exponi sacramentum Scripturæ narrantis quæ gesta sunt, prius illud quod lectum est credatur sic gestum quomodo lectum est; ne, subtracto fundamento rei gestæ, quasi in aëre quæratis ædificare.

[2] On this matter he has an important chapter in the *De Civ. Dei*, xiii. 21: he is speaking of the paradise of Gen. i-iii., to which the allegorists denied any historic reality, and probably has ORIGEN (*De Princip.* iv. 16) especially in his eye: Nonnulli totum illum Paradisum ubi primi homines S. Scripturæ veritate fuisse narrantur, ad intelligibilia referunt, arboresque illas et ligna fructifera in virtutes vitæ moresque convertunt: tanquam visibilia et corporalia illa non fuerint, sed intelligibilium significandorum caussâ eo modo dicta vel scripta sint. Quasi propterea non potuerit esse Paradisus corporalis, quia potest etiam spiritalis intelligi: tanquam ideo non fuerint duæ mulieres, Agar et Sara, et ex illis duo filii Abrahæ, unus de ancillâ, unus de liberâ, quia duo Testamenta in eis figurata dicit apostolus; aut ideo de nullâ petrâ, Moyse percutiente, aqua defluxerit, quia potest illic figuratâ significatione etiam Christus intelligi, eodem apostolo dicente, Petra autem erat Christus. Cf. xvii. 3: Audeant sensum intelligentiæ spiritalis exsculpere, servatâ primitus duntaxat historiæ veritate. *De Gen. ad Litt.* viii. 4. 7.

when regarded from this point of view, and which, regarded from any other, must inevitably receive an unworthy explanation. And as the thing is recognized in Scripture, so also the word by which it is usually designated (Gal. iv. 24). The allegory is that which ἄλλο ἀγορεύει: in it the words signify something more, in general something deeper and higher, than that which they offer upon the surface;[1] they invite the reader to look beyond themselves into altogether another sphere of thought and feeling, and need to be translated into that, before they attain to their full rights, and fulfil the intention with which they were uttered.

The extent, indeed, to which the Old Testament is in this sense prefigurative of the New, and exactly how far its personages are prophetic, its institutions typical, and its actions allegorical, is a matter very hard satisfactorily to determine.[2] I believe it can only be approximately determined, that, after all rules have been laid down, much must still be left to the tact and religious instinct of the interpreter. We indeed feel entirely confident that the comparatively few types and prophecies which are directly claimed in the New Testament, the brazen serpent

[1] In the allegory, as he himself explains it (*De Doctr. Christ.* iii. 37), Aliud dicitur, ut aliud intelligatur.

[2] On the extent of this the *real*, as distinguished from the *verbal*, prophecy of the Old Testament, Augustine expresses himself often. Thus *Serm.* ii. 6: Tales ergo illos viros habebat Deus, et illo tempore tales fecerat præcones Filio venturo, ut non solum in his quæ dicebant, sed etiam in his quæ faciebant, vel in his quæ illis accidebant, Christus quæratur, Christus inveniatur. *Con. Faust.* xxii. 24: Hoc primum dico, illorum hominum non tantum linguam, verum etiam vitam fuisse propheticam, totumque illud regnum gentis Hebræorum, magnum quendam, quia et Magni cujusdam, fuisse prophetam. Cf. *De Div. Quæst.* qu. lviii. 2; *De Civ. Dei*, vii. 32.

(John iii. 14), the manna (John vi. 48–51), the Paschal lamb (John xix. 36), Jacob's ladder (John i. 51), Agar and Sarah (Gal. iv. 22–31), Melchisedek (Heb. vii.), the High Priest entering into the holiest (Heb. ix. 11–28) and such other as the Lord and his Apostles and Evangelists may expressly declare to be such, do not at all exhaust the typical element therein, but should rather serve as examples of something which is true to a much larger extent; the earlier history being everywhere full of stirrings of that divine life which ultimately took form and bodily shape in Christ, of outline sketches only to be filled up by Him,[1] of attestations of all kinds, embedded deep in that earlier economy, that one and the same God was the author of it and of the later. It is only when we come to consider how far we may proceed in this direction, and where we should pause, that our perplexities begin.

Better indeed, far better to find Christ everywhere in the Old Testament than to find Him nowhere: and to address ourselves to the prophetic books in any other expectation than that of everywhere finding Him, or to expect that under any other conditions they will render up to us their secret, is wilfully to cast away 'the key of knowledge,' and yet to expect that the door will be opened to us notwithstanding.[2] But with the historic

---

[1] On the partial fulfilment of prophecies in personages of the Old Testament, with the exhaustive fulfilment which was yet reserved for Christ, Augustine has excellent observations, speaking of Solomon and the prophecies that went before of him, *De Civ. Dei*, xvii. 8.

[2] With a beautiful application of the miracle of the turning of the water into wine, Augustine exclaims (*In Ev. Joh. Tract.* 9): Tollitur insipientia cum transieris ad Dominum; et quod aqua erat, vinum tibi fit. Lege libros omnes propheticos; non intellecto Christo, quid tam insipidum et fatuum invenies? Intellige ibi Christum, non solum sapit quod legis, sed etiam inebriat.

books it is otherwise. Even granting that the events recorded in them only found place for the sake of those higher ulterior meanings, of which the lower and actual were an allegory; granting that they were all as a great acted parable and nothing more; yet to insist on making every portion of this parable significant is to forget a primary canon of parabolic interpretation,—that parts in the parable exist merely for the holding other and more important parts of it together; as there must be passages in the most splendid and best arranged house, as there is in the knife a handle which is not for cutting, and portions not a few of the lyre which yield no sound. Augustine admits all this; he very often himself places this limit on the seeking for a secondary and, as he would count it, a higher meaning in all parts of the Old Testament: he allows that such connecting parts must be looked for there, and that it would be idle to demand of these an ulterior and higher meaning.[1] And sometimes he makes a stand in a still more advanced position against the allegorists, altogether refusing to go along with them

---

[1] *Con. Faust.* xxii. 94: Christum igitur sonant hæc omnia; nec esse quidquam credendum est librorum propheticorum contextione narratum, quod non significet aliquid futurorum; nisi quæ ideo posita sunt ut ex eis quodam modo religentur ea, quæ illum Regem populumque ejus, sive propriis sive figuratis locutionibus rebusve prænuntient. Sicut enim in citharis et hujuscemodi organis musicis, non quidem omnia quæ tanguntur canorum aliquid resonant, sed tantum chordæ; cætera tamen in toto citharæ corpore ideo fabricata sunt, ut esset ubi vincirentur, unde et quo tenderentur illæ, quæ ad cantilenæ suavitatem modulaturus et purcussurus est artifex; ita in his propheticis narrationibus quæ de rebus gestis hominum prophetico spiritu deliguntur, aut aliquid jam sonant significatione futurorum; aut si nihil tale significant, ad hoc interponuntur, ut sit unde illa significantia tanquam sonantia connectantur. Cf. *De Civ. Dei*, xvi. 2.

in their extremes,[1] and recognizing the literal interpreter as worthy by comparison of superior honour.[2] But at other times he expresses himself with a certain wavering and uncertainty; nay, seems himself prepared to go all lengths with them, to make the entire Old Testament history, and this not in its grand outline and plan, but in all its details, prophetic,[3] to allow nothing to have been there set down simply for its own sake, to account as though it had been unworthy of the Holy Ghost to occupy Himself in the record of such matters as fill up very many pages of the Book, unless this second and New Testament meaning could be shown everywhere to underlie the plainer and the earlier.[4]

---

[1] *De Civ. Dei*, xvii. 3: Quibusdam visum est, nihil esse in eisdem libris vel prænuntiatum et effectum, vel effectum quamvis non prænuntiatum, quod non insinuat aliquid ad supernam Civitatem Dei ejusque filios in hâc vitâ peregrinos figuratâ significatione referendum. Mihi autem sicut multum videntur errare qui nullas res gestas in eo genere litterarum aliquid aliud præter id quod eo modo gestæ sunt significare arbitrantur; ita multum audere qui prorsus ibi omnia significationibus allegoricis involuta esse contendunt. Hoc enim existimo, non tamen culpans eos, qui potuerint illic de quâcunque re gestâ sensum spiritalis intelligentiæ exsculpere, servatâ primitus duntaxat historiæ veritate.

[2] *De Gen. con. Manich.* ii. 2: Sane quisquis voluerit omnia quæ dicta sunt, secundum litteram accipere, id est non aliter intelligere, quam littera sonat, et potuerit evitare blasphemias, et omnia congruentia fidei catholicæ prædicare, non solum ei non est invidendum, sed præcipuus multumque laudabilis intellector habendus est. Si autem nullus exitus datur ut pie et digne Deo quæ scripta sunt intelligantur, nisi figurate atque in ænigmatis proposita ista credamus, habentes auctoritatem apostolicam, a quibus tam multa de libris Veteris Testamenti solvuntur ænigmata, modum quem intendimus teneamus, adjuvante Illo qui nos petere quærere pulsare adhortatur.

[3] *Enarr. in Ps.* cxxxvi. 3: Diximus omnia quæ secundum litteram in illa Civitate contingebant figuras nostras fuisse. Cf. *De Catech. Rud.* 6.

[4] This seems to me to speak out in such words as the following

The result is oftentimes that in the endeavour to wring from Scripture more than it was intended to yield, less is indeed obtained. A shadow is snatched at, which is not grasped; but in the snatching at it a substance has been let go and lost. We may illustrate this from Augustine's own exposition of the 103rd Psalm (according to our reckoning the 104th). Instead of that fresh healthy feeling which would read in this Psalm a setting forth of the glories of God in creation, with a drawing of strength and encouragement for the faithful from a contemplation of these, he will not be content, unless he has allegorized it throughout. The sun that 'knoweth his going down' (ver. 19) is the 'Sun of righteousness' who *knew* of his own death, and (with an urging of the *agnovit* of the Latin) was well pleased to lay down his life. The beasts that 'get them away together' and hide in their

(*De Civ. Dei*, xvii. 1): Ipsa Scriptura, quæ per ordinem reges eorumque facta et eventa digerens, videtur tanquam historicâ diligentiâ rebus gestis occupata esse narrandis, si adjuvante Dei Spiritu considerata tractetur, vel magis vel certe non minus prænuntiandis futuris, quam præteritis enuntiandis invenietur intenta. Cf. *Enarr. in Ps.* cxiii. 1. Thus too after a rapid and masterly oversight of the whole Jewish history, with a tracing of the Christian element which he everywhere found therein, a sketch occupying a great part of his twelfth book against Faustus, he sums up all in such language as this (37): Hæc omnia figuræ nostræ fuerunt [1 Cor. x. 11]. Nam si Ismael et Isaac homines nati, duo Testamenta significant, quid credendum est de tot factis, quæ nullo naturali usu, nullâ negotii necessitate facta sunt? nihilne significant? Si quis nostrûm qui Hebræas litteras ignoramus, videret eas in pariete conscriptas, honorato aliquo loco, quis esset tam excors, ut eo modo pictum parietem putaret? an non potius intelligeret scriptum, ut si legere non valeret, non tamen illos apices aliquid significare dubitaret? At the same time he is obliged to acknowledge that in the Jewish history, so far at least as relates to the history of the kings, the typical character after Solomon's time almost altogether disappears (*De Civ. Dei*, xvii. 21).

dens at the rising of this sun, are the persecutors in heart, who yet do not dare to show themselves openly as such in the bright day of the Church's prosperity; with much more in the same fashion.[1] It may be said that here is no slight on the historic facts of the Old Testament; and this is perfectly true; but there is a slight on God's revelation of Himself in nature, as though that had no glory of its own, which a sweet and inspired singer in his Church might fitly occupy himself in proclaiming.[2] Scripture, it is true, is not mainly idyllic, but epic; its primary theme and argument is not nature but man; yet as all worthy forms of human composition find their prototypes or their consummation therein, so even the idyl will not be wholly wanting there.

And the *historic* element in the Old Testament oftentimes does not fare better. It is never, as has been already observed, in the least denied; but something else is everywhere superinduced upon it, as though without this addition the facts of the history would not have worth and significance enough to justify the place which they

---

[1] *Enarr. in Ps.* ciii. Thus too on the words of the Psalmist, 'I laid me down and slept; I awaked, for the Lord sustained me' (Ps. iii. 5), he asks (*De Civ. Dei*, xvii. 18): An forte quisquam ita desipit, ut credat velut aliquid magnum nobis indicare voluisse prophetam, quod dormierit et exsurrexerit, nisi somnus iste mors esset, et evigilatio resurrectio, quam de Christo sic oportuit prophetari? But why not? for entirely granting that these words look on to our Lord's resurrection, yet is not the wondrous mystery of our sleeping and waking, and the mercies which evermore attend it, one well worthy of being ascribed to God? might it not, even without that higher meaning, have found its place in a Psalm?

[2] How deficient an eye for this is indicated in such interpretations as Hilary's, when he makes 'the lilies of the field,' which we are bidden to 'consider' (Matt. vi. 28), not to be lilies, but angels (*Comm. in Matt. in loc.*). Augustine protests against this.

occupy in the Scriptures of God. Thus the Ark is pitched within and without (Gen. vi. 14) in sign that the Church shall be so joined and knit together, that neither heresies nor scandals from within, nor open assaults from without, shall dissolve its framework, or make it pervious to the waters of the world.[1] Jacob's deception of his father, with all the profound lessons to be drawn from the conduct and after fortunes of the four principal actors in that transaction, none of them without fault, and none without punishment, is passed slightly over, while Augustine hunts after a higher mystical meaning in the transaction, to which he unsuccessfully adjusts it.[2] Assuredly there was meaning enough in it already; and the divine character of the family and of the nation, and of all those human relationships which spring from them, abundantly justify a teaching, which in minutest detail and in a thousand forms should show us what is the blessing of maintaining God's order in the family and the State, what the penalties which attend the violation of this order. A Holy Scripture does not demean itself, nor exhaust itself on matters alien to its very highest purpose, when it largely occupies itself with these.

And in other ways no less he betrays the want of an historic sense. How inconceivable a lack of such, for instance, is shown in his assumption that *all* the Psalms were composed by David;[3] that so, when in one Psalm we

---

[1] *Con. Faust.* xii. 14.   [2] *Serm.* iv. 11-33.
[3] *De Civ. Dei,* xvii. 14: Mihi autem credibilius videntur existimare, qui omnes illos centum et quinquaginta Psalmos ejus operi tribuunt, eumque aliquos prænotâsse etiam nominibus aliorum, aliquid quod ad rem pertineat figurantibus; ceteros autem nullius hominis nomen in titulis habere voluisse; sicut ei varietatis hujus dispositionem, quamvis latebrosam, non tamen inanem, Dominus inspiravit.

read, 'By the waters of Babylon there we sat down, yea, we wept when we remembered Zion' (cxxxvii. 1), and in another, 'When the Lord turned again the captivity of Zion, we were like them that dream' (cxxvi. 1), we are to hear not some inspired singer from the children of the Captivity mourning over a present woe, or rejoicing in a present redemption, but David and still David, artificially adapting spiritual songs which he had composed to conditions altogether remote and different from his own.

I will not leave this subject without a few general observations in conclusion. The whole scheme of allegorical and mystical interpretations is one manifesting itself in too many quarters, and finding far too much favour with hearers and readers, to be referred to the caprice or idiosyncrasies of particular teachers in the Church; even as it is absurd to trace it up to Philo or to any foreign source, and to suppose that we have in this way accounted for it. We do it, its authors and favourers, most right, not when we seek to defend it throughout, because we find it allowed or zealously furthered by men to whom the Church owes so immense a debt;—but rather when we seek to explain it, and how it should have cast its roots so widely, and grown up to so extraordinary a height. It was then, as I believe, not merely the excusable, but the inevitable, consequence of that great wrench and shock whereby the Church forcibly detached itself from Judaism (the writings of Justin Martyr mark the moment), and by God's grace was for ever delivered from the danger of merely knowing a Christ, the Son of Abraham, the Son of David, the King of Israel. This shock was one with results that were felt for centuries; during all which the controversies which most occupied the minds and hearts of men led the Church to an almost exclusive contemplation of the *divine* nature and person of her Lord. But it belongs to the limitation of human faculties and powers, that when mighty truths are mightily felt and witnessed for by men, there will go along with this a partial throwing into the background, and thus a present obscuration, of other truths, especially of such as are the balancing counterweight to these. In this way it came to pass that when the Church passed over to, and rooted itself in a Gentile soil, and became virtually a Church of the Gentiles, having just fulfilled its protest against Ebionite and all other forms of Judaizing error, the protestors found it hard to recognize at its full worth this preparatory history of the kingdom of God; to see in Jewish story and Levitical institutions the periphery of a circle whereof Christ was the centre, the womb in which the Christ after the flesh had been gradually forming and taking shape,[1] and coming to the birth. This inability to recognize the worth of the preparatory history shows itself in its worst excess and caricature in the various forms of Gnostic heresy; all of these having this in common, that they brought down their Christ direct from heaven, and would know of no human preparation for his appearing, no earthly root and stalk out of which He, as the perfect flower, was unfolded at the last: they all as a consequence of this taking up a position of more or less fanatical hostility to the Old Testament.

Nor were there wanting even among them who were within the Church, and who would have been shocked at

[1] Augustine himself expresses this truth, though in words somewhat obscure (*De Civ. Dei*, xvii. 11): Ipse Jesus intelligitur, substantia populi ejus, ex quo natura est carnis ejus.

such blasphemous exaggerations as those of the Gnostics, some who drove this tendency into positive error. Origen at once presents himself as the most notable example of this. It is plain, however, that in those endeavours of his to take the veil from off Moses' face, for so he calls it, he found opposition even in his own day;[1] for he complains that when he, like Isaac, has opened the wells of spiritual understanding, others come like the Philistines, and stop them again (Gen. xxvi. 14, 15).[2] In this resistance which he everywhere encountered, we have a remarkable evidence of the divine leading of the Church. Those very teachers who resisted Origen were themselves, as I cannot doubt, giving too large an allowance to this same system of allegorical interpretation; yet so soon as he or any other put in actual peril the truth of God, and threatened seriously to impugn the historic basis on which the truth rested, and on which alone it could rest,[3] so soon as ever he overpassed the bounds within which this tendency was safe—the comparatively harmless, if not always the edifying, play of the fancy—they at once and earnestly protested against it, affirmed with all clearness the importance of setting determinate limits to it, such as it should on no account be permitted to overpass.

With all this, it was only the excesses and perilous extravagances of this school of interpretation which for the most part they resisted. So long as these were avoided,

---

[1] See HUET, *Origeniana*, ii. 13; DE LA RUE, *Preface* to the second volume of his works.

[2] *In Gen. Hom.* xiii. 3. The position of these 'friends of the letter' is plain from his own account of them. They resisted him on the right ground, veritatem negantes stare posse nisi super terram.

[3] In proof that Origen does so see the remarkable passage, *De Princip.* iv. 15; one of many that might be referred to.

they felt no misgiving about it; and this scheme of capricious allegorical interpretation continued in full force, and abode in highest honour during all the Middle Ages, with indeed the same protests on the part of the great teachers of those ages, when it seemed to threaten vital truth, as we meet in the earlier Church.[1] It was not till the Reformation, asserting as this did the dignity of the family and the nation against the Papacy which made war upon them both, that the letter of the Old Testament, with its record of an elect family and a chosen nation, came to its full rights and honour, or that men understood all which was contained for them therein. Doubtless it was in Luther his reverence for the fundamental institutes of family and national life, for the relations of husbands and wives, parents and children, masters and servants, kings and subjects, which moved him to such exceeding and oftentimes extravagantly expressed indignation against

[1] Thus the great medieval scholar of Augustine, Hugh of St. Victor, alter Augustinus, lingua Augustini, as in his own time he was called, treading in his master's footsteps (*Erud. Didasc.* vi. 3) : Sicut vides, quod omnis ædificatio fundamento carens, stabilis esse non potest, sic est etiam in doctrinâ. Fundamentum autem et principium doctrinæ sacræ historia est, de quâ, quasi mel de favo, veritas allegoriæ exprimitur. Ædificaturus ergo primum fundamentum historiæ pone; deinde per significationem typicam in arcem fidei fabricam mentis erige; ad extremum ergo per moralitatis gratiam quasi pulcherrimo superducto colore ædificium pinge. Yet the same illustrious writer gives curious evidence of the upper hand which the allegorical interpretation had acquired, even in their minds who felt most bound to vindicate the worth also of the historic letter, when even in the very act of protesting against the excesses of the allegorists he counts it necessary to use such humble apologies for the letter of Scripture as the following (*Prænott. Elucid.* 5) : Quasi lutum tibi videtur totum hoc quod verbum Dei foris habet, et ideo forte pedibus conculcas quia lutum est, et contemnis quod corporaliter et visibiliter gestum littera narrat. Sed audi: luto isto quod pedibus tuis concalcatur, cæci oculus ad videndum illuminatur.

the allegorizers of the early Church. He felt that a record which was concerned with these relations as seen in the light of God, must possess the very highest worth, and be full of the most important instruction; but that all this was called in question and virtually denied by those who were so eager to find another, and as they vaunted it, a higher and deeper meaning in those portions of Scripture which were mainly occupied with the setting forth of these relations. Certainly his own great work on Genesis, upon which he laboured with a peculiar care and love, and which employed him during eight years of his life, is a glorious monument of the simpler historic interpretation. In this his dislike to the allegorizers often finds the most passionate utterance.[1] Augustine indeed had too many other titles to the respect and reverence of Luther to allow him ever to speak slightingly of him; though, in this matter, if others are counted faulty, he cannot be altogether acquitted of all share in the fault.

[1] In the following passage he expresses himself with more than usual moderation: Hæc est historia et simplex sententia hujus loci, quæ utcunque a nobis tractata est, et aliis etiam spero satis planam fore. Tam et allegoria attingenda erat. Sed sæpe dixi, allegorias esse periculosas in explicandâ Scripturâ sanctâ, quia alius aliud sequitur, alii aliud fundamentum ponunt, et alius aurum, alius stipulas ædificant. Ac pulchre dixit Augustinus, Figura nihil probat. Ideo in asserendis et confirmandis dogmatibus fidei nostræ non valent allegoriæ aut aliæ figuræ, sed probationibus et testimoniis opus est, quæ ex ipsis fontibus Scripturæ sanctæ sumuntur. Figuras enim et allegorias quilibet suo arbitrio aut interpretari, aut fingere ipse potest. Ideo nihil firmi et certi habent. Possunt tamen adhiberi tanquam lumina et ornamenta ad ornandam et illustrandam doctrinam, vel sensum literalem. Sicut Paulus, Gal. iv. (22), adducit exemplum Abrahæ, Hagar et Saræ, ut ornet et illustret doctrinam de justitiâ fidei et de duobus Testamentis. Et quando allegoria congruit cum doctrinâ et ejus assertione, est pulcherrimum ornamentum et quasi condimentum doctrinæ.

CHAPTER V.

ILLUSTRATIONS OF AUGUSTINE'S SKILL AS AN INTERPRETER OF SCRIPTURE.

WHAT has been thus far said of Augustine's fitnesses for being an able expositor of the Word of God, and also of the spirit in which he approached so serious and solemn a work, I shall now endeavour to illustrate by examples selected from his writings. Here indeed we are solicited and drawn different ways by an abundance, which, if it does not make poor, yet continually perplexes as to what we shall choose; for certainly there was never charge more unfounded than that which Père Simon brings against the exegetical writings of Augustine—namely, that one must read a vast deal in them to light on anything which is good. This charge, were it true, would involve almost every other in itself; but is so far from truth, that it is impossible not to say that he who made it did therein pronounce sentence against himself, and declare his own incapacity to recognize the highest gifts of the Spirit brought to bear on the deepest truths of revelation, even when these gifts in their actual exercise were presented to him.[1]

[1] Rosenmüller's judgment is harsher and unjuster still (*Hist. Interp. Lib. Sac.* vol. iii. p. 502) : Nobis quidem *sine omni suo merito* consecutus esse videtur eam nominis celebritatem et auctoritatem quâ per omnia deinceps secula floruit.

In seeking to make good what I have just affirmed, I shall draw my materials not merely from those writings avowedly dedicated to the exposition of Scripture, but indifferently from the whole circle of Augustine's writings. For it is a consequence of the immense digressions in which he so freely allows himself, that oftentimes the secondary gains from his exposition are larger than the primary. Thus he is expounding a Psalm, and we suddenly find him explaining a parable or unfolding at large a miracle of our Lord's—eagerly following the game which starts up before him on his path. These digressions, sometimes untimely, as keeping too long out of sight the subject which he professes to be handling, affecting too, and not favourably, the *form* of his exposition, must be regarded as in some sort a blemish, and do in their degree detract from its merits; while yet on another side they may be contemplated as a portion of his wealth, of that inexhaustible fulness which on all occasions is seeking to pour itself forth,—so that we should be very much poorer if these were withdrawn.

And first, we may consider his skill in the reconciliation of Scripture; I do not mean merely in the removal of apparent discrepancies, lying on the surface of the several narratives, between one and another record of the same fact; but in the removal of those seeming oppositions, ethical or doctrinal, which lie much deeper, and can only be reconciled in some higher unity, wherein the differences are atoned. Let serve as an example of his skill herein the way in which he justifies, as not contradicting one another, the very different manners in which at different times St. Paul bore himself toward the Jewish ceremonial law; which law he appears sometimes himself to observe

(Acts xxi. 23–26); while at other times he forbids, under peril of their salvation, his converts to do the like (Gal. v. 3, 4). There are some very interesting letters between him and St. Jerome, in which these and some like passages, with all the difficulties that beset them, are fully and most profitably discussed.[1] The discussion has its rise in an offence which Augustine had not unreasonably taken at a passage in Jerome's *Commentary on the Galatians*. In this, out of a mistaken zeal to clear the character of a saint and Apostle from every speck and blemish, he implies that the scene referred to at Gal. ii. 14 was, so to say, got up between the two great Apostles, St. Paul and St. Peter, for the better maintaining of peace in the Church at Antioch; that the Apostle of the Gentiles did not really blame the Apostle of the Circumcision, but that each sustained a part in a transaction arranged beforehand—St. Peter, who had indeed done well in preserving the peace of the Church, having by his withdrawal satisfied the Jewish converts, and St. Paul by his blame of him having vindicated the liberty in Christ, which else that withdrawal might have perilled.[2] Augustine, too straightforward a lover of the truth to tolerate *economies* of this kind, protests with a righteous earnestness against this explanation, which he invites Jerome to

[1] Augustine's are the 28th, 40th, and 82nd; Jerome's, the 68th, 72nd, and 75th in the Benedictine edition of Augustine's works. Bishop Lightfoot in his *Commentary on the Epistle to the Galatians* deals very thoroughly with the contention between the two great fathers of the Church.

[2] In the same way he speaks (*Ad Philem.* 7) of the contention between Paul and Barnabas (Acts xv. 39) as *ædificatorium* Ecclesiæ jurgium—which in a sense is most true; but the contention was not a make-believe, but truly meant all that it said.

defend or to withdraw.[1] The latter defends it, and mainly on the following grounds—However the one Apostle may have seemed to find fault with the other for conforming to the prejudices of the Jewish converts, yet he could not really have blamed him; since, if such conformity was sinful, he too was in the same condemnation; for he also made the Jews, or rather the judaizing Christians, to believe that he kept the law; and, in proof of this, Jerome urges his circumcising of Timothy (Acts xvi. 3), his shaving of his head at Cenchrea (Acts xviii. 18), his purifying of himself in the temple (Acts xxi. 26), and his general admission that to the Jews he became a Jew.[2]

But Augustine will not allow this defence, and planting himself in the true position from which to judge the conduct

---

[1] *Ep.* xxviii. 3, he communicates his grief; and again *Ep.* xl. 3, 4. In this last epistle he unfortunately bids St. Jerome to sing his recantation (παλινῳδίαν cane). The phrase was not a happy one, coming from the younger to the older man; and Jerome, whom none can deny, with the amplest recognition of the Church's immense obligations to him, to have been somewhat tetchy and prompt to take offence, was exceedingly hurt at this exhortation; and his part of the correspondence is full of characteristic touches, as indeed the noble character of Augustine appears very clearly in his. There is an interesting analysis of this correspondence, bringing out the *personal* in it, which I have not thought it needful to touch on, by Möhler (*Verm. Schrift.* vol. i. p. 1-18); in which, very noticeably for one of the Roman communion, he gives the entire right to Paul as against Peter, to Augustine as against Jerome. Indeed Jerome himself must be considered ultimately to have done the same; seeing that in his *Dialogue against the Pelagians* (i. 8), written very shortly after, he adduces this which Peter here did in proof that not merely ordinary Christians, but Apostles themselves, were not free from sin. Augustine (*Ep.* clx. 5, *ad Oceanum*) at a later day notes that they are now both of one mind on this matter.

[2] Jerome (*Ep.* lxxv. 3): Quâ igitur fronte, quâ audaciâ Paulus in altero reprehendat, quod ipse commisit?

of St. Paul, he shows what the rule of that conduct was—
not, that is, to make the faithful who still clung to the
law to believe that he also kept it throughout; a pretence
of this kind would have made his whole life a lie; but to
prove to them that he did not, as some charged him,
account those Jewish customs abominable, and for a
Christian man sinful and sacrilegious; that he had none
of that enthusiasm *against* the Law, which afterwards
declared itself in what we may call the ultra-Pauline
sects, in Gnostics and Manichæans : but, on the contrary,
saw in it shadows and prophetic outlines of good things
which had their body and substance in Christ. Those
who had grown up in the law, those to whom it had become a second nature, were perfectly at liberty to retain
it,[1] provided only they did not impose it as a necessity on
others, or suppose that their own salvation in any way
depended on it. He did not blame Peter for observing,
nor for countenancing Jewish Christians in observing,
those customs; but for compelling Gentiles to judaize,
and so implicitly saying that these observances were
necessary for salvation.[2] So far from abhorring the
ceremonial law, he would himself willingly come under it
from time to time, in this way stopping their mouths who
affirmed that he set the rites and customs of Judaism on
a level with heathen superstitions and idolatries, and
taught that they were to be renounced in the same spirit

[1] *Con. Faust.* xix. 17.
[2] *Ep.* ix. 4: Non ideo Petrum emendavit, quod paternas tradi-
tiones observaret : quod si facere vellet, nec mendaciter nec incongrue
faceret : quamvis enim jam superflua, tamen solita non nocerent ; sed
quoniam gentes cogebat judaïzare : quod nullo modo posset, nisi ea
sic ageret, tanquam adhuc etiam post Domini adventum necessaria
saluti forent: quod vehementer per apostolatum Pauli Veritas dissuasit.

as were those. But this doing, he never acted a falsehood, nor sought to persuade any that he was a constant observer of that law. Only by occasional compliance with its enactments he paid it the honour due to that which had been, though for a temporary purpose, framed by God Himself, and honoured of Him as a preparatory discipline of men, until the coming in of that which was perfect.

St. Paul had no desire that the Christian Church, least of all where it was formed out of Jewish elements, should with violence and revolutionary haste rend itself away from that economy, in which and out of which it had grown. His wish was rather that it should gently detach itself therefrom, as does the ripe fruit from the husk which protected it once, but whose protection it now needs no more, nay rather finds an encumbrance.[1] Such a process he would not have sought to hasten, being perfectly content to let time accomplish what it would inevitably bring about at last. But it was altogether another thing when some thought to submit to these practices, legal and ceremonial, the converts from the heathen world, who had never known them before. This he resisted to the uttermost; as he would have resisted the reintroduction of these customs, and their reimposition, under any pretext whatever, even upon converts of a Jewish stock, after they had once fallen into desuetude. That which Paul countenanced and allowed might be regarded as a burying of the body of the synagogue leisurely and with due honours; this would have been the disinterring of its corpse, after it had lain long in the grave.[2]

[1] *Con. Faust.* xxxii. 13.
[2] *Ep.* lxxxii. 2: Sicut defuncta corpora, necessariorum officiis de-

Augustine gives here the true reconciliation of all the apparent contradictions in St. Paul's conduct, as his circumcising of Timothy, and at the same time saying, 'If ye be circumcised Christ shall profit you nothing' (Gal. v. 2); the explanation, too, of still weightier moral perplexities; as of that most difficult case of all, namely, his undertaking at his last visit to Jerusalem of a Nazarite vow in the temple (Acts xxi.). Was this with the hypocritical intention of leading Jews or Jewish Christians to believe that he was a constant observer of the whole ceremonial law, nay more, one who went beyond the letter of its requirements, and took freewill vows upon himself? Nothing of the kind;[1] but only in the more emphatical way to disprove that which the Judaizers asserted about him, with the view of making him hateful at Jerusalem, and of marring his work everywhere—namely, that he obliged his converts from among the Jews of the dispersion to forsake Moses, that he absolutely *forbade* any longer adherence on their parts to legal ordinances

---

ducenda erant quodammodo ad sepulturam [vetera sacramenta]; nec simulate, sed religiose; non autem deserenda continuo, vel inimicorum obtrectationibus tanquam canum morsibus projicienda. Proinde nunc quisquis Christianorum, quamvis sit ex Judæis, similiter ea celebrare voluerit, tanquam sopitos cineres eruens, non erit pius deductor vel bajulus corporis, sed impius sepulturæ violator.

[1] *Ep.* lxxxii. 2: Tanquam inimicum legis, mandatorumque divinorum criminabantur; cujus falsæ criminationis invidiam congruentius devitare non posset, quam ut ea ipse celebraret, quæ damnare tanquam sacrilega putabatur: atque ita ostenderet, nec Judæos tunc ab eis tanquam a nefariis prohibendos, nec Gentiles ad ea tanquam ad necessaria compellendos. This too, he goes on to say, was the principle of St. Paul's dealing in the cases of Timothy and Titus; he circumcised the first, that none might say he esteemed circumcision an execrable thing; he would not circumcise Titus, that the liberty of the Gospel might stand fast.

(Acts xxi. 21); while all, in fact, that he did forbid, was their supposing that a man was justified by these; or their laying of the yoke of these on heathen converts (Acts xv. 1): which could only have been done on an implicit assumption that such was the case. Here indeed he did speak out, and proclaim that, if they so preached circumcision or practised it, Christ would profit them nothing (Gal. v. 4); they were fallen from grace. Otherwise it was for him a thing indifferent, which neither helped nor hindered. No doubt he desired to see even this outward mark of separation between the different members of the new family in Christ Jesus disappear; but he was willing to wait till it should fall away of itself, as he knew that in the second or third generation of Jewish converts it inevitably must.[1]

Another slighter example of Augustine's skill in setting Scriptures at one may follow. He takes the words of St. Paul, 'Bear ye one another's burdens' (Gal. vi. 2), and then, with an interval only of two verses, 'Every man shall bear his own burden' (ver. 5), statements at first sight seeming to contradict one another, and this while they stand in closest neighbourhood the one to the other;

---

[1] *Con. Mendac.* 12 : Id autem quod Paulus fecit, ut quasdam observationes legitimas Judaicâ consuetudine retinendo et agendo non se inimicum Legi Prophetisque monstraret, absit ut mendaciter eum fecisse credamus. De hâc quippe re satis est ejus nota sententia, quâ fuerat constitutum, nec Judæos qui tunc in Christum credebant prohibendos esse a paternis traditionibus, nec ad eas Gentiles, cum Christiani fierent, esse cogendos; ut illa sacramenta quæ divinitus præcepta esse constaret, non tanquam sacrilegia fugerentur; nec tamen putarentur sic necessaria jam Novo Testamento revelato, tanquam sine illis quicunque converterentur ad Deum salvi esse non possent. Hoc error quorundam putabat, hoc timor Petri simulabat, hoc libertas Pauli redarguebat; cf. *De Mendacio*, 8.

and he shows their reconciliation to lie in a recognition of the twofold use of the word 'burden.' The 'burden' of one another's infirmities, the 'burden' even of one another's sins, in so far as they are the occasion to ourselves of annoyance, of pain, of labour, of loss, we can and we ought to bear; even while there is another 'burden,' the solemn answer of each man for his own life to God, which every one must bear for himself, and which none can bear for a brother.[1]

Once more: on the words of St. Paul, 'We must all appear before the judgment seat of Christ' (2 Cor. v. 10); What is this? he exclaims; what does St. Paul say here? Has not the Lord Himself promised, that he who heareth his word and believeth on Him that sent Him, shall not come into judgment, but is passed from death unto life? (John v. 24); and now the servant appears to unsay the Master's word, and to bring us all before the judgment-seat anew. The reconciliation of the several statements lies in a right seizing of the different uses of the word 'judgment' ($\kappa\rho\iota\sigma\iota\varsigma$), which signifies sometimes condemnation, and sometimes discrimination. Only in the second sense is it true that we must all appear before the judgment-seat—namely, that to each may be severally

---

[1] *De Cons. Evang.* ii. 30: Alia sunt onera portandæ infirmitatis, alia reddendæ rationis Deo de actibus nostris; illa cum fratribus sustentanda communicantur, hæc propria ab unoquoque portantur. See an admirable sermon (*Serm.* clxiv.) on these two texts, in their relation to one another; and on the first of them some beautiful observations, *Div. Quæst.* 71. The seeming contradiction between the two declarations comes out more strongly in the Latin, which has *onus* in both places, as the English has 'burden,' than in the Greek, which in the first has $\beta\acute{\alpha}\rho\eta$, in the second $\phi o\rho\tau\acute{\iota}o\nu$, a variation which Augustine has not used as a help to his explanation, but whereby it is abundantly justified.

distributed things suitable to his condition, good to the good, evil to the evil.[1] Augustine's interpretation of this passage goes altogether counter to their doctrine who teach that for the faithful man also there will be a judgment according to works. His faith has saved him; however afterwards, according to the measure of his holiness, of Christ formed in him, will be the measure of his capacity for receiving the divine reward, and his place, higher or lower, in the future kingdom.

So far as the relation of St. Paul to the law is concerned, Augustine had but to set right the error of a friend: but at other times his task is to deal with the cavils of a foe. It may be well to show by two or three examples how he disposes of the objections of the Manichæans and other adversaries, who, rejecting the whole Old Testament, yet naturally made some which seemed to them the more exposed and indefensible positions there, the chief points of their attack. One of these was with them, as it notoriously was with the English Deists of the last century, the destruction of the Canaanites root and branch, and at the express command of God: another, such an enveloping of the (comparatively) innocent in a common doom with the guilty, and making of the innocent to suffer for the sin of the guilty, as found place when for Achan's as yet undiscovered sin not a few of the children of Israel perished in battle with their enemies (Josh. vii. 5).

In the matter of the destruction of the Canaanites Augustine betakes himself to none of those poor evasions, which some in conflict with modern Deism have sought out,—as, for instance, that the land of Canaan had

[1] *In Ev. Joh. Tract.* xxii.: Ut bonis bona, malis mala distribuantur.

originally belonged to the children of Israel through the occupation of it by the patriarchs, who therefore, under Joshua, did but reclaim and recover their own;[1] but Augustine sees in the excision of those wicked nations an act of the divine righteousness, which those only will misunderstand, but which they will certainly misunderstand, who are ignorant of what sin is, and what sin deserves.[2] The Canaanites were the 'carcase;' and it is the everlasting law of God's moral government, that 'where the carcase is, there shall the eagles be gathered together;' a law indeed as loving as it is righteous, that this carcase shall not for ever be permitted to pollute the moral atmosphere of his world. The 'eagles' that on this occasion were gathered together for its removal out of the way, were the children of Israel. If any among them did his appointed work in the bitterness of his spirit, out of a mere lust after the possessions of those whom he destroyed, having pleasure in the sufferings which he inflicted, and leaving out of sight that he was a minister and executor of the righteousness of God, this was his sin; he was indeed a robber and a murderer; but nothing of

---

[1] Michaëlis, *Mos. Recht.* (vol. i. p. 125-203), is very earnest in seeking to prove this, and to justify on these grounds the forcible occupation of the land by the children of Israel; but the facts of the case do not bear out this claim. Moreover, nothing would be gained, if it could be made out. God gave this land to the Canaanites, and when their iniquity was full, He took it away from them and gave it to the children of Israel; and in this gift, and not in anything else, was the title-deed of their possession; see this matter handled excellently well by Hengstenberg, *Authen. d. Pent.* vol. ii. p. 171-99.

[2] *Quæst. in Jos.* 16: Qui propter hoc Veteris Testamenti verum Deum fuisse nolunt credere, tam perverse de operibus Dei quam de peccatis hominum judicant, nescientes quid quisque pati dignus sit, et magnum putantes malum cum casura dejiciuntur, mortalesque moriuntur.

this lay in his commission; nay, he contradicted his mission, so far as in the fulfilling of it he gave room to any such evil passions as these.[1] In what manner Augustine disposed of the other objection, his words quoted below will sufficiently declare.[2]

The blots and blemishes in the lives of the faithful were a frequent and favourite subject of malignant comment on the part of some, Manichæans especially, with whom Augustine had to contend. He does not, of course, deny the existence of such blots, some of them very dark ones, in their lives; which being there, the Scripture is too faithful a mirror not to give them back.[3] At the

---

[1] *Con. Adimant. Man.* 17: Displicet istis miseris quod Deus populo suo interficiendos tradidit inimicos. Intelligant sine odio esse posse vindictam, quam pauci intelligunt; et tamen quamdiu non intelligitur, tamdiu necesse est ut lector in libris utriusque Testamenti magno labore aut errore jactetur, et putet contrarias sibi esse Scripturas.

[2] *Quæst. in Jos.* 8: Non enim aliquid dirum, quantum attinet ad universi mundi administrationem, contingit mortalibus, cum moriuntur quandoque morituri: et tamen apud eos qui talia metuunt, disciplina sancitur, ut non se solum quisque curet in populo, sed invicem sibi adhibeant diligentiam, et tanquam unius corporis et unius hominis alia pro aliis sint membra solicita. Nec tamen credendum est, etiam pœnis quæ post mortem irrogantur, alium pro alio posse damnari; sed in his tantum pœnis hanc irrogari pœnam, quæ finem fuerant habituræ, etiamsi non eo modo finirentur. Simul etiam ostenditur, quantam connexa sit in populi societate ipsa universitas, ut non in se ipsis singuli, sed et tanquam partes in toto existimentur. He carries so far his view of the merely corrective character which temporal death may often have, as to assume that Ananias and Sapphira were thus judged temporally, that they might not be condemned eternally (*Serm.* cxlviii.). Much very noteworthy he has (*De Serm. Dom. in Monte,* 1 § 64) on the deaths of men, so often intended to be disciplinary and corrective for other men, and thus not thrown away.

[3] *Con. Faust.* xxii. 60: [Scriptura] tanquam speculi fidelis nitor, admotarum sibi personarum non solum quæ pulcra atque integra,

same time he shows how a malignant misinterpretation oftentimes made sins out of actions of theirs, which indeed were innocent or laudable; while other works of theirs, confessedly sinful, were yet hatefully exaggerated by these adversaries; to whom Noah was a drunkard, Moses, for the killing of the Egyptian, a murderer,[1] and the unhappy daughters of Lot, who, it is plain, believed themselves and their father the sole survivors in the world of the catastrophe of Sodom (Gen. xix. 31), monsters of lust and impurity.[2] But let the sin have been what it might, Holy Scripture was in no wise committed or compromised by it; and as little the righteousness of God, whose voice and utterance that Scripture is. It recorded these sinful actions of theirs, but did not praise them; very often expressed the strongest moral disappro-

verum etiam quæ deformia vitiosaque sint, indicat; and 65: Nullius accipit adulandam personam, sed et laudanda et vituperanda hominum facta vel ipsa judicat, vel legentibus judicanda proponit; nec solum homines ipsos vel vituperabiles vel laudabiles intimans, verum etiam quædam in vituperabilibus laudanda et in laudabilibus vituperanda non tacens.

[1] He sees in this energetic act of Moses on behalf of a suffering brother, carnal and unlawful as it was, the promise and prophecy of the man that should afterwards redeem Israel, and has a striking comparison on the subject (*Con. Faust.* xxii. 70): Verumtamen animæ virtutis capaces ac fertiles, præmittunt sæpe vitia, quibus hoc ipsum indicant, cui virtuti sint potissimum accommodatæ, si fuerint præceptis excultæ. Sicut enim et agricolæ quam terram viderint, quamvis inutiles, tamen ingentes herbas progignere, frumentis aptam esse pronuntiant; et ubi filicem aspexerint, licet eradicandam sciant, validis vitibus habilem intelligunt, et quem montem oleastris silvescere aspexerint, oleis esse utilem culturâ accedente non dubitant, sic ille animi motus, quo Moyses, peregrinum fratrem a cive improbo injuriam perpetientem, non observato ordine potestatis, inultum esse non pertulit, non virtutum fructibus inutilis erat, sed adhuc incultus vitiosa quidem sed magnæ fertilitatis signa fundebat.

[2] *Con. Faust.* xxii. 43.

bation of them (2 Sam. xiii. 27); or where it kept silence, this silence was itself for the better exercise of the moral sense of the faithful; that, applying the rules drawn from other parts of the Word of God, and from the immutable principles of morality graven in all hearts, they might pass their own judgment on the deed, excusing or accusing; which that they should sometimes be thus invited to do was far more profitable, and involved far more of instruction, than that they should always find judgments of praise or blame ready made to their hand, and, so to speak, cut and dried in the Scriptures themselves.[1]

Nor yet, he adds, was the existence of these faults and failings, yea of these great and grievous sins on the part of good men, inconsistent with their position as the bearers in their time of the promises of God, the witnesses for his truth. Such bearers of his word, such witnesses for his truth they were; as such, having a treasure; yet having it in earthen vessels, so that it was nothing strange if the earthen vessel should sometimes appear. There was only ONE whose sin, if such the Scripture had been obliged to record, would have set that Scripture at contradiction with itself, and shaken the everlasting foundations upon which the faith of the Church reposes.[2]

---

[1] *Con. Faust.* xxii. 45 : Narrata ista sunt, non laudata. Quædam vero enunciato judicio Dei, quædam tacito narrari oportuit; ut quando promitur quid inde judicaverit Deus, instruatur nostra imperitia; quando autem tacetur, vel exerceatur peritia ut quod alibi didicimus recolamus, vel excutiatur pigritia ut quod nondum novimus, inquiramus. Cf. *Con. Mendac.* 14.

[2] On the different ways in which we may contemplate the sins of God's saints, how we may get from them all harm, but how they were recorded for our good, he has many most useful observations, commenting on the 50th (51st, *A. V.*) Psalm (*Enarr. in Ps.* 1. 1, 2): Multi cadere volunt cum David, et nolunt surgere cum David. Non

Very excellent, again, is his reply to some of these same cavillers, whose nice ears were offended at the occasional plainness of speech which Scripture claims for itself in speaking of certain sins and their consequences, such plainness of speech as Moses has sometimes used; as St. Paul, and eminently on one occasion (Rom. i. 26, 27), does not shrink from employing. How well he defends this needful outspokenness of Scripture against the affected, or where not affected, untimely, delicacy of men, who could bear that such things should be done, but not that they should be spoken about ; nay, who fain would have silence kept about them, when by the speaking the doing might perhaps be prevented.[1]

ergo cadendi exemplum propositum est, sed si cecideris, resurgendi. Non sit delectatio minorum, lapsus majorum; sed sit casus majorum, tremor minorum. Ad hoc propositum est, ad hoc scriptum est, ad hoc in Ecclesiâ sæpe lectum et cantatum ; audiant qui non ceciderunt ne cadant; audiant qui ceciderunt ut surgant. Tanti viri peccatum non tacetur, prædicatur in Ecclesiâ. Audiunt male audientes, et quærunt sibi patrocinia peccandi; attendunt unde defendant quod committere paraverunt, non unde caveant quod non commiserunt, et dicunt sibi, Si David, cur non et ego. Alii vero audientes salubriter, in casu fortis metiuntur infirmitatem suam, ab adspectu securo abstinent oculos, non eos defigunt in pulcritudine carnis alienæ. Proponunt enim sibi casum David, et ad hoc illum magnum vident cecidisse ut parvi nolint videre unde cadere possint. And for an interesting estimate of David's character with its one shadow, a dark and deep one indeed, but also its many brightest lights, see *Con. Faust.* xxii. 66.

[1] *Con. adv. Leg. et Proph.* i. 24: [Cicero] cum doceret, in translatione verborum obscœnitatem esse vitandam, Nolo, inquit, dici, morte Africani *castratam* esse republicam. Sed si hoc verbum ipse quod vitari volebat, ut vitandum ostenderet, non vitavit, et quod dici noluit, coactus est dicere, quanto magis res quæ verbo eodem recte significatur, ut ab audiente possit intelligi, suo verbo enuntiatur? Atque ut ad illud redeamus, quod iste reprehendit: si Cicero vir eloquentissimus et verborum vigilantissimus appensor et mensor, quod dici noluit, dixit, ne diceretur: quanto melius Deus magis morum quam

There are passages, and those of high importance, the interpretation of which Augustine was the first to set upon its right basis. Such a passage is John v. 25–29; for the true explanation of which a large debt of gratitude is owing to him. The earlier expositors were driven, apparently by their antagonism to the Gnostics, who denied a resurrection of the body, and consequently spiritualized the whole passage, into an opposite extreme, understanding it throughout as having reference, and that exclusively, to the bodily resurrection at the end of the world.[1] They get over the difficulty of the words, 'The hour is coming *and now is*,' by referring this 'now is' to such foretastes of the resurrection as found place in the raising of Lazarus, of the daughter of Jairus, and of the widow's son. Nor did the succeeding expositors either of the Greek or Latin Church, Chrysostom, or Jerome, or Ambrose, extricate themselves from this erroneous track. Augustine was the first to show plainly that a literal construction of the whole passage is as much an error, though the error is more venial, as one which spiritualises it wholly; that the Lord in fact is here speaking of *two* resurrections; in ver. 25, 26, of a spiritual resurrection already present, the quickening of the spirits of as many as hear and obey his voice; and then in ver. 28, 29, of that universal bodily resurrection which shall be at the end of the world. Nilus, a scholar of Chrysostom, had just indicated this right exposition,[2] but

verborum pulcritudinem quærens atque munditiam, turpe aliquid non turpiter sed minaciter dixit, ut hoc horreretur, ne illud committeretur. Compare *Enarr. in Ps.* l. 1: Cum dolore quidem dicimus et tremore; sed tamen Deus noluit taceri quod voluit scribi.

[1] So TERTULLIAN, *De Res. Car.* 37.
[2] *Ep.* iii. 135.

it was Augustine who first set it upon secure foundations;[1] nor would it be easy anywhere to find a more admirable specimen of Biblical interpretation, at once popular and profound, than his vindication in more places than one, of this explanation of these words.

Dealing first with ver. 25, 26, he clears his way by showing that it is in perfect consistency with the general language of Scripture to set forth the state of sin as one of death, and the quickening of the spirits of men through Christ's life-giving word as a resurrection. He quotes in proof such obvious texts as these, Ephes. v. 14; Isai. ix. 2; Col. iii. 1; Rom. viii. 10, 11. He then proceeds to justify an exposition in this sense of the passage before him, tracing the admirable fitness, even to the minutest details, of every part when this key is applied; while very much does not fit at all, or only fits badly and with much forcing, when these two verses are explained of the final resurrection, or, again, when ver. 28, 29, of the present spiritual quickening of souls. Christ begins, 'The hour is coming,' and then, lest his hearers should understand Him to speak of an absolute future and of the end of the world, He adds 'and now is'—marking in this way a grace at once already present, and in part also future; even as He could say to his disciples during the days of his flesh and before his ascension, 'Now ye are clean' (John xv. 3), although the fulness of sanctifying grace did not descend till after Pentecost. He proceeds, 'when the dead,' that is, the spiritually dead,—He does not say 'all,' as when speaking of the final resurrection,—'shall hear the voice of the Son of God, and they that hear shall live.' The words 'they

---

[1] Yet not so secure but that Hengstenberg has sought again to shake them; though in my judgment he has utterly failed in so doing.

that hear,' imply that some will hear and some will not, even as it lies in every man's will to open or to close his ear to *this* voice of the Son of God; but the words would be altogether inappropriate to that other voice of his, which, sounding through all the chambers of death, all must hear, whether they will or no. Nor yet would He have said, ' all that hear *shall live,*' had He been looking on to the rising at the last day of good and bad alike; for only the good 'live;' and 'life' in Scripture is evermore synonymous with blessedness.[1] When the Lord would express the fact of the rising again of the wicked, He uses quite another language; that is not life, but a second death. And indeed the change of language is most marked throughout, when He begins to speak, as at ver. 28, 29 He does, of the bodily resurrection of all at the end of the world. Then the hour ' is coming,' but no longer ' now is,' for He is treating of an event altogether in the future,—' in the which *all* that are in the graves '— there was no mention before of all, nor yet of graves— ' shall hear his voice ' ('the voice of the Archangel and the trump of God,' 1 Thess. iv. 16), ' and shall come forth,' the word implying a bodily action; with not now any single word expressing what the portion shall be of those whom this voice calls forth; but, as this is a resurrection which embraces all men, the Lord assigning severally to these, according as they have done good or evil, a 'resurrection of life' or a ' resurrection of damnation ' (cf. Matt. xxv. 31–46).[2]

[1] *Serm.* cccvi. 6: Sola intelligitur vita, quæ beata; quæ autem non beata, nec vita.

[2] Having reached ver. 28, 29, and starting from them, he thus sums up the whole of his argument (*Serm.* ccclxii. 23, 24): Superius cum dixisset, Venit hora, adjecit, et nunc est: ne illa hora prænuntiata

CHAP. V.] INTERPRETER OF SCRIPTURE. 83

Thus far I am persuaded that Augustine has right; though not when he co-ordinates, or indentifies rather, these two resurrections of John v. 25–29, the spiritual and the bodily, severally with the first and second resurrection of the Apocalypse (Rev. xx. 4–6).[1] This is part and parcel of an interpretation almost everywhere beside the mark, as I must needs esteem it, of this book; upon the exposition of which in the after Church for many hundred years Augustine's influence was very far from favourable.[2] Yet

putaretur, quâ in fine sæculi futura est corporum resurrectio. Hic ergo quia ipsam volebat intelligi, cum dixisset, Venit hora, non adjecit, et nunc est. Item superius mortuos dixit audire vocem Filii Dei, monumentorum autem nullam commemorationem fecit, ut distingueremus mortuos per mentis errorem qui resurgunt modo per fidem, ab eis mortuis quorum cadavera in monumentis sunt resurrectura in ultimo sæculi. Hic ergo, ut illa in fine speraretur corporum resurrectio, Omnes, ait, qui in monumentis sunt, audient vocem ejus et procedent. Item superius, Audient, inquit, vocem Filii Dei, et qui audierint, vivent. Quid opus erat addere, Qui audierint, nisi quia de his dicebat qui secundum mentis errorem mortui sunt, quorum multi audiunt et non audiunt, id est, non obtemperant, non credunt. Hic autem ubi secundum corpora resurrecturos pronuntiat, non ait, Audient vocem ejus, et qui audierint, procedent. Omnes enim novissimam tubam audient, et procedent, quia omnes resurgemus. Superius, ubi per fidem secundum Spiritum reviviscitur, ad eandem sortem omnes reviviscunt; ut vita eorum non distribuatur in beatitudinem et miseriam, sed ad bonam partem omnes pertineant. Et ideo cum dixisset, Qui audierint, vivent; non adjecit, Qui bona egerunt, in vitam æternam, qui vero mala egerunt, in pœnam æternam. Hoc enim ipsum quod dictum est, vivent, in bono tantummodo accipi voluit. Hic autem dixit, Audient et procedent, quo verbo significavit corporalem motum corporum de locis sepulturarum suarum. Sed quia procedere de monumentis non omnibus ad bonum erit: Qui bona, inquit, fecerunt, in resurrectionem vitæ; etiam hic vitam in bono tantum intelligi voluit: qui vero mala egerunt in resurrectionem judicii, judicium scilicet pro pœnâ posuit. Cf. *In Ev. Joh. Tract.* 19; *De Civ. Dei*, xx. 6.

[1] *De Civ. Dei*, xx. 6, 7.

[2] The great passage in which he unfolds his view of the Apocalypse is *De Civ. Dei*, xx. 7–17.

one important principle bearing on its interpretation he affirms, and one which, overlooked or denied, breeds infinite confusion, namely, that we are not to read it as one continuous series of events, stretching onward in unbroken succession to the consummation of all things; but rather that there are in it many new beginnings,—thus chapter xii. is such,—and often when it seems at first sight to be narrating different events, it is indeed only narrating the same in different ways and from different points of view.[1]

Augustine was not always so successful an innovator. I shall here profit by that liberty which he, using in respect of the writings of those who went before him, desired also should be used in respect of his own,[2] to adduce two or three examples of what seem to me errors more or less serious, which he committed in the interpretation of Scripture. Thus he did serious wrong to the Christology of the Old Testament, through his lowering to the rank of created angels, of the Angel of Jehovah; who appears, and ever in his own name, and not in that of any other, at so many grand crises of the theocracy, and to whom divine

---

[1] *De Civ. Dei*, xx. 17: In hoc quidem libro obscure multa dicuntur, ... maxime quia sic eadem multis modis repetit, ut alia atque alia dicere videatur; cum aliter atque aliter hæc ipsa dicere vestigetur.

[2] *Ep.* cxlviii. 4: Neque enim quorumlibet disputationes, quamvis Catholicorum et laudatorum hominum, velut Scripturas canonicas habere debemus, ut nobis non liceat salvâ honorificentiâ quæ illis debetur hominibus, aliquid in eorum scriptis improbare atque respuere, si forte invenerimus quod aliter senserint quam Veritas habet, divino adjutorio vel ab aliis intellecta, vel a nobis. Talis ego sum in scriptis aliorum, tales volo esse intellectores meorum. *De Trin.* i. 3: Quisquis hæc legit, ubi pariter certus est, pergat mecum; ubi pariter hæsitat, quærat mecum; ubi errorem suum cognoscit, redeat ad me; ubi meum, revocet me. Ita ingrediamur simul caritatis viam, tendentes ad eum, de quo dictum est, Quærite faciem ejus semper.

titles, honour, and attributes, are constantly ascribed (Gen. xxxii. 28, 30; xlviii. 16; Exod. iii. 5; Josh. v. 14, 15; Judg. xiii. 18).[1] Not seeing in this angel the Son of God, the Word as yet unincarnate, Augustine deprived these his epiphanies of the most of their significance, manifestly of all which they possessed as preludes and figures of the coming incarnation.[2] Jansenius, and as many as seek to glorify Augustine at the expense of all the other illustrious doctors of the early Church, even of an Athanasius himself (indeed one might suppose from Jansenius that he first had discovered in Scripture the doctrines of grace), these all very highly extol his departure here from the unanimous exegetical tradition of as many as had gone before him. They do not scruple to attribute to him the honour of having hereby given the finishing stroke and death-blow to Arianism; which, as they affirm, found one of its main supports—and when in the course of the controversy all other had been removed from it, its only support—in the admission which the Church had incautiously and erroneously made, that this intermediate angel was the Word of God.[3] The steps of the Arian argument, put in its barest

[1] The chief passage on this subject is *De Trin.* iii. 11. Later favourers of this interpretation have added nothing to the arguments which he there adduces. Cf. *De Civ. Dei,* xvi. 29; *Con. Maxim. Arian.* ii. 26.

[2] Præludia et figuræ incarnationis, as Bull (*Def. Fid. Nic.* iv. 3. 14) calls them, who quotes the remarkable passages from Hilary, *De Trin.* iv. 23, 42, in which the elder faith of the Church on this subject is maintained. For a full collection of testimonies from the early Fathers, see Bull, i. 1. 2–8; and Petavius, *De Trin.* viii. 2.

[3] Thus in his *Augustinus* JANSENIUS: Augustinus adversus constantem præcedentium sententiam magno ausu, majore conscientiâ subnixus scripturarum pondere, et rationum gravissimarum acumine ac texturâ primus pansis velis in libris de Trinitate demonstravit omnes apparitiones illas Veteris Testamenti, non Deo sed angelo

form, were these: God is invisible (1 Tim. i. 17); but this angel, whom the whole Church has ever recognized as the Word not as yet incarnate, was visible: therefore this angel, that is, the Word, is not God. Many have shown, Bishop Bull perhaps best of all, that there was no need of going back from the Church's original faith in this matter, for the purpose of avoiding such a conclusion ; and the eagerness of all modern Arians to maintain Augustine's position is evidence sufficient that they anticipate more gain than loss from such an interpretation of the passages in which the Angel of the Lord appears. Nor indeed is it with them alone that it has found favour; but with others also, from a very different, though not a worthier, theological interest; for, not to speak of the Socinians, who indeed are but the Arians at a little later stage of their development, to whom it was welcome as depriving the doctrine of the Trinity of an important support, it has been favourably received by Roman Catholics as well, promising to supply them with a scriptural authority for their worship of angels.

The Epistle to the Romans, the interpretation of which owes so much to Augustine (some part of its gains from him I shall desire presently to recount), yet is not everywhere a gainer by him. Here and there he has gone astray; and as it was not given to so great a man to go astray alone, has drawn many after him, and this during long ages, to be sharers of his error. Thus I take his exposition of the latter clause of the fifth verse of the fifth

tribuendas esse. So too Rivius (*Vita Augustini*, Antverp, 1646, p. 587): Non dubitavit ire contra totam Patrum vetustorum scholam, melioribusque auspiciis fontem hæreseos [Arianæ] occludere. Com pare Rich. Simon, *Hist. Crit. du N. T.* 19.

chapter to be altogether erroneous. The history of the exposition of the verse is curious. To Augustine's influence we mainly owe the almost entire loss for many centuries of its true interpretation. This interpretation Origen, Chrysostom, and Ambrose, men every one of them less penetrated with the spirit of St. Paul than Augustine was, had yet rightly seized; while for all this, by his influence and frequent use of this passage in another sense, its proper meaning was so far put out of sight, as not to be recovered till the time of the Reformation. He read in his Latin, Caritas Dei *diffusa* est in cordibus nostris per Spiritum Sanctum, qui datus est nobis. Had he read, as Ambrose reads it,[1] and as it should be, *effusa*,[2] he might have been saved from his mistake: for the comparison thus suggested with such passages as Acts ii. 17; Isai. xxxii. 15; Ezek. xxxvi. 25; Joel ii. 28, in all of which God's large and free communication of Himself to men is set forth under the image of a stream from heaven to earth, would have led him to see that this 'love of God' which is poured out in our hearts, and is here declared to be our ground of confidence in Him, is *his love to us*, and not, as Augustine will have it, our love to Him;[3] as from a comparison with ver. 8, is plain. The passage is of considerable dogmatic importance. The perverse interpreta-

---

[1] *De Spir. Sanct.* i. 8. 88. [2] Ἐκκέχυται in the original.

[3] The caritas Dei *diligentis*, not the caritas Dei *dilecti*. In several other passages where ἀγάπη Θεοῦ occurs, Θεοῦ is the genitive of the subject, not of the object (Rom. viii. 39; 2 Cor. v. 14, and elsewhere).—It is by no oversight that Augustine so interprets the passage. On the contrary, he distinctly rejects the correcter explanation (*De Spir. et Litt.* 32): Caritas Dei dicta est diffundi in cordibus nostris, non quâ nos ipse diligit, sed quâ nos facit dilectores suos: sicut justitia Dei, quâ nos justi ejus munere efficimur; et Domini salus, quâ nos salvos facit; et fides Jesu Christi, quâ nos fideles facit.

tion became in after times one of the main stays, indeed by far the chiefest one, of the Roman theory of an *infused* righteousness constituting the ground of our confidence toward God. This the true explanation excludes, yet at the same time affirms this great truth, that God's justification of the sinner is not, as Roman controversialists affirm we hold it, an act merely *declaratory*, leaving the sinner as to his real state where it found him, but a *transitive* act, being not merely negatively a forgiveness of sin, but positively an imparting of the spirit of adoption, with the *sense* of reconciliation, and of all else into which God's love received and believed in the heart will unfold itself.

Of far slighter importance is his departure from the hitherto received interpretation of Gen. vi. 2; although here, too, I must needs believe that he forsook, and caused others to forsake, the true explanation of the words. Most, if not all, of the Fathers who had gone before him, certainly Justin, Clement of Alexandria, Tertullian, Cyprian, and Ambrose, had understood 'the sons of God,' of whom Moses speaks, as angels; for 'sons of God' is a standing title of the angels in the Old Testament (Job i.6; ii. 1; xxxviii. 7; Ps. xxix. 1; lxxxix. 7; Dan. iii. 25); and never, till under the New Testament there had come forth a Son of God, is it given to mortal men (John i. 12). He, however, saw in them, and was among the first who so did, the descendants of Seth,[1] and understood the inspired historian by this notice to indicate a breaking down of the distinction which up to this time had been maintained between the two lines, running hitherto parallel but apart,

---

[1] *De Civ. Dei*, xv. 22 : in the following chapter he seeks to refute at length the contrary explanation ; but see what may be said, convincingly as it seems to me, on the other side by Delitzsch, *Genesis, in loco*.

of Cain and of Seth. The question is full of difficulty; yet there is much to lead us to the conclusion that the earlier expositors were in the right, who beheld in these unions, which were the crowning wickedness of the old world, and from whence the giants sprung, something more mysterious than marriages contracted between the Cainites and the Sethites—some 'spiritual wickednesses,' which rendered the flood an inevitable moral necessity.

In his fear of giving so much room to the human side of the Saviour's work as should imperil the divine, Augustine occasionally brings a certain unreality into words of his which were indeed the deepest and truest utterance of his soul. It is impossible to free him from such a charge as this, when dealing with our Lord's words, 'Let this cup pass from Me' (Matt. xxvi. 39). He does not scruple to affirm that Christ only spake them as the representative of our infirmity, of our fear of death; that they are no proper voice of his own, but only the voice of his body, of the Church; which assuredly cannot for an instant be admitted.[1]

He sometimes lays upon a Scripture a greater weight than it can bear. He does so, certainly, on Rom. xiv. 23, 'Whatever is not of faith is sin.' Without calling in question the great truth that only the good tree, or the tree made good, can bring forth good fruit (Matt. vii. 16–20), one cannot doubt that Augustine gives a larger meaning to St. Paul's words than the Apostle intended, when he makes them as large as those other words in the Epistle to the

---

[1] *Enarr.* 2ª *in Ps.* xxi. : Dixit utique de me, de te, de illo. Corpus enim suum gerebat, id est Ecclesiam. Paulus optat mortem ut sit cum Christo [Phil. i. 25], et Christus timet mortem ? Sed quid nisi infirmitatem nostram portabat, et pro his qui adhuc timent mortem in corpore suo constitutis, ista dicebat ? Inde erat illa vox ; membrorum ipsius vox erat, non capitis.

Hebrews which declare that without faith it is impossible to please God (Heb. xi. 6).[1] No one accurately weighing the context can doubt that 'faith' is here a man's moral conviction of the rightfulness of that which he is doing; and all which St. Paul asserts (itself indeed a most important assertion), is that whosoever willingly does any act contrary to his own moral conviction, sins. The thing which he does may be intrinsically indifferent, or even intrinsically right; but for him, doing it against his conscience, it is sin.

While we are thus noting spots upon the sun, it may be well to indicate one or two more passages, where Augustine's usual skill seems to have failed him. Thus, quoting the words of St. John, 'His head and his hairs were white like wool, as white as snow' (Rev. i. 14), he singularly enough sees in this whiteness of Christ's hair, the *hoary* head of old age; an outward expression of the inward fact, that He whom the seer beheld was 'the Ancient of Days.'[2] A little reflection justifies the instinctive dissent from such an explanation, which all I think must feel; for the blanching of the hair being one of the signs and consequences of life receding before death, of commencing weakness and decay, it is impossible that the hair 'white as snow' could ever in this sense be attributed to the everliving, to Him whose days are from everlasting to everlasting. Rather the '*white*' here is to be explained, as in all the divine apparitions in which it is mentioned,[3] by the

---

[1] *De Gest. Pelag.* 14: Quantumlibet autem opera infidelium prædicentur, Apostoli sententiam veram novimus et invictam, Omne quod non est ex fide, peccatum est. Cf. *Con. Jul. Pelag.* iv. 3.

[2] *Exp. in Gal.* iv. 21: Dominus non nisi ob antiquitatem Veritatis in Apocalypsi albo capite apparuit.

[3] Matt. xvii. 2; xxviii. 3; Mark ix. 3; xvi. 5; Luke ix. 29; cf.

fact that brightness in its utmost excess attains to be absolutely white: iron reaches at last a *white* heat. The hair 'white like wool, as white as snow,' is here only another manifestation of the unutterable brightness, with which from head to foot the Lord was invested.[1]

Even in little details in which one might suppose his exegetical tact would certainly have shown him the right way, he sometimes misses his point. Thus, in one place, he suggests a reason why the Lord promised a reward to one who should give even a cup of *cold* water to a disciple of his (Matt. x. 42), namely, that thus not even the poorest, not one so poor as to be unable to heat it, should be excluded from the power of showing this mercy, and so of inheriting this reward.[2] Writing under an African sky, he should have better interpreted these words; the '*cold*' is added to imply a certain zeal on the part of the offerer of this cup, which makes him careful to offer one of real refreshment; and this only the *cold* water, that which therefore had been freshly drawn, would be to the weary traveller (Prov. xxv. 25; Jer. xviii. 14). But why further enumerate the little spots upon the sun?

Luke xxiv. 4 with John xx. 12. The θρόνος λευκός, Rev. xx. 11, is = θρόνος δόξης, Matt. xxv. 31; the νεφέλη λευκή, Rev. xiv. 14 = νεφέλη φωτεινή, Matt. xvii. 5.

[1] See on this passage my *Commentary on the Epistles to the Seven Churches*, 4th edit. p. 34.

[2] *Enarr. in Ps.* cxxv. 5: Calicem aquæ *frigidæ* addidit, ne quis vel inde caussaretur, quod lignum non habuerit unde calefaceret aquam.

CHAPTER VI.

AUGUSTINE ON JOHN THE BAPTIST, AND ON ST. STEPHEN.

IT would not be difficult to compose a commentary, at once interesting and instructive, on the whole life of John the Baptist as recorded in Scripture, drawing the materials exclusively from the writings of Augustine, so abundant and so excellent would those materials be found. Such I cannot attempt, but must satisfy myself with rapidly touching on a few points in his life which Augustine has dwelt on with a peculiar care, or expounded with more than ordinary success; not forbearing, at the same time, to express my sense of one or two faulty explanations into which he has fallen. What indeed I must first note is an inaccuracy. Of this he is not the author, for we find it already in St. Ambrose, even as it maintained its ground during all the Middle Ages—I mean the making of Zacharias, the father of the Baptist, to have been *High* Priest, when indeed he exercised no other functions than those of an ordinary priest. This error sprung from a misapprehension of Luke i. 9, where Zacharias is described as going in to burn incense in the temple of the Lord.[1] This was understood as the entrance on one day in the

---

[1] *In Ev. Joh. Tract.* xlix. 27 : Nam incensum non licebat ponere nisi summo sacerdoti. Cf. *De Perfect. Just.* 17 ; *Serm.* ccxci. 3. For an ample refutation of an error so patent as not to need one, see WITSIUS, *Vita Joh. Bapt.* p. 475.

year into the Holy of Holies, which was permitted to the High Priest alone. It is needless to observe that the Evangelist refers not to this, but to the daily burning of incense, morning and evening, which was not the High Priest's exclusive prerogative, but devolved on other priests as well (Exod. xxx. 7, 8), who in the order of their course executed the priest's office before God.

Augustine, having in view such births as the Baptist's, where the parents have remained childless long, and now, it may be, are stricken in years, and have overlived the hope and expectation of children, notes well that, however remotely, they are yet approximations to the one Virgin birth. The relation is not merely that those as well as this are out of the usual order; it does not lie only in the *wonder* that belongs, though in very different measures, to both; but also in the fact that in those also who are born as the Baptist was, there is, we may venture to say, less of the will of the flesh, and more of the will of God, than in more ordinary births (John i. 13). In those births according to promise and by the special grace of God, that disturbing element which mingles with the very foundations of our natural life even at the very moment when they are first laid, is not indeed altogether wanting, as in *his* birth who was virgin-born; yet it has fallen into the background. It was therefore most meet that He who was born of a pure Virgin should have as his herald one born by virtue of a promise, born too of those that, like Abraham and Sarah, had overlived their youth, and renounced the expectation of children.[1] In this aspect it

---

[1] *Serm.* ccxc. 1 : Ambo mirabiliter nati, præco et Judex, lucerna et Dies, vox et Verbum, servus et Dominus. De sterili servus, de Virgine Dominus. *Serm.* ccxci. 1 : Quia enim venturus erat per

is not without its significance that, among all the saints of God, John is the only one the day of whose Nativity is celebrated by the Church.[1]

The distinction between John's baptism and Christ's, and the immeasurable superiority of the latter over the former, Augustine everywhere asserts or assumes.[2] I have no passage at hand in which he draws out *what* the essential prerogatives of the baptism of the Master, as compared with that of the servant, were.[3] He probably considered, though in this he was mistaken, that no one could confound that preparatory washing with the Christian sacrament of baptism, and that the difference was expressed with sufficient clearness in the words of the Baptist himself: 'I indeed baptize you with water unto repentance; but He that cometh after me shall baptize you with the Holy Ghost and with fire' (Matt. iii. 11); John's the baptismus *fluminis*, the Lord's not *fluminis* alone, but

Virginem Deus homo, præcessit eum de sterili mirabilis homo. *Serm.* ccxciii. 1: Johannem parit sterilitas, Christum integritas.

[1] *Serm.* ccxc. 2: Denique quia in magno sacramento natus est Johannes, ipsius solius justi natalem diem celebrat Ecclesia. Et natalis Domini celebratur, sed tanquam Domini. Date mihi alium servum præter Johannem inter patriarchas, inter prophetas, inter Apostolos, cujus natalem diem celebret Ecclesia Christi. Passionum diem servis plurimis celebramus, nativitatis diem nemini nisi Johanni.

[2] *Serm.* ccx. 2: Baptismus Johannis a baptismo Christi discernendus est. *In Ev. Joh. Tract.* v. 5: Qui baptizati sunt a Johanne non eis suffecit; baptizati sunt enim baptismo Christi: Augustine has probably especially in his thought the disciples of John baptized by Paul at Ephesus (Acts xix. 1–5); cf. *Con. Litt. Petil.* ii. 37. For the humiliating evasions by which the maintainers of the identity of the two baptisms seek to get rid of this decisive statement, see GERHARD, *Loc. Theoll.* loc. xxi. 4. 63.

[3] They are best stated by Tertullian in a remarkable passage, *De Baptismo*, 10.

flaminis as well. The attempt to identify the two is found for the most part in connexion with a poor and unworthy apprehension of the benefits of Christian baptism. John's baptism is not raised to a level with it, but it is reduced to a level with John's. One who, like Augustine, held that it was of the essence of a New Testament sacrament, not merely to promise, but actually to impart, grace,[1] was not likely to confound them; for this none would affirm of the baptism of John.

Augustine has altogether a right insight into the words of the Baptist, John i. 15; the exact meaning of which not all or nearly all interpreters have seized. It would be long to follow them in their several deviations from the right way. This right way is, to take the words as declaring first a fact, 'He that cometh after me is preferred before me;' and then the ground on which this fact reposes, 'for He *was* before me;' and they only escape the appearance of a tautology, when we seize rightly, as Augustine has done, the distinction between the verb of time and of *becoming* ($\gamma \acute{\epsilon} \gamma o \nu \epsilon$) in the first clause of the sentence, and that of eternity and of *being* ($\mathring{\eta} \nu$) in the second. John is here declaring, first, that Christ, although coming into the world later than himself, had yet, as one might say, overtaken and passed him by, had got beyond him; so that the glory and fame of John, however it had an earlier beginning, was yet fading and waning now before the greater glory of his Lord: and then, in the second clause of the verse, he announces that this was only fitting, since He who thus came into the world after him, yet *was* before him, being even from eternity. It was

[1] *Enarr. in Ps.* lxxiii. 1: Sacramenta Novi Testamenti dant salutem, sacramenta Veteris Testamenti promiserunt Salvatorem.

only just, then, that the Sun should extinguish the lamp, the King cause the herald to be forgotten, He whose goings forth had been from everlasting should surpass in glory and honour him who belonged only to time.[1]

These relations between John and his Lord Augustine loved to find expressed in the titles, severally, of the voice (φωνή), which is all John claimed for himself (John i. 23); and of the Word (Λόγος), which is claimed for his Lord (John i. 1); and not less in that of the lamp, burning and shining indeed (John v. 35), but with a derived light, and one quenched after a season, which was John, as compared with the Light, 'the true light which lighteth every man that cometh into the world,' which was Christ (John i. 9; viii. 12).[2] This last antithesis has taken strong hold upon

[1] *Serm.* ccclxxx. 5 : Quomodo si duo ambulant in itinere, et unus sit tardior, alter velocior, et præcedat tardior aliquantum, post paululum autem sequatur velocior; respicit tardior præcedens velociorem, sequentem, et dicit, Post me venit. Et ecce accelerante illo, et propinquante, et adhærente, et transeunte, videt ille anteriorem quem respiciebat posteriorem ; certe si celeritatem ejus expavescat quodam modo et admiretur, nonne poterunt esse ista verba ejus, Ecce homo post me erat, et ante me factus est? And again : Præcessit honore Johannem. Sed vide utrum merito. Interroga ipsum Johannem. Qui te sequebatur, quare tibi prælatus est? Sequitur, Quia prior me erat. Prior Johanne, prior Abraham, prior quam Adam, prior quam cælum et terra, prior quam Angeli, Sedes, Dominationes, Principatus, et Potestates.

[2] This antithesis between John the lamp, and Christ the Light, we have obscured in our Version : where ἐκεῖνος ἦν ὁ λύχνος ὁ καιόμενος καὶ φαίνων, is rendered, 'he was a burning and a shining *light*;' which would have been better rendered, 'He was the Lamp that burneth and shineth;' and so Augustine : Ille erat *lucerna* ardens et lucens. Lucerna threw him back, as it had done Tertullian before him, on the words of the Psalmist, Paravi lucernam Christo meo (Ps. cxxxi. 17), where they both saw a third distinct prophecy of John, besides the two which the Old Testament undoubtedly contains. Thus *Serm.* ccxciii. 4 : Deus Pater in prophetiâ loquens, Paravi lucernam Christo meo, Johannem Salvatori præconem, Judici præcursorem venturo, futuro amicum Sponso.

him, and he recurs to it again and again. Nor is it only as a play in which his fancy has found pleasure; for under what might seem at first no better than this, there was expressed a truth, than which none was dearer to his heart, a truth which Pelagian gainsayings had more and more made him to feel was central in all theology—this, namely, that God is the one fountain-source of all wisdom, light, and knowledge, 'the Father of lights;' while all that man has is derived. He *receives* light, he *transmits* light, he never *originates* it. If he is light, he is 'light *in the Lord*:' even as the eyes at their healthiest and best have but the capacity of vision; another light than their own can alone enable them actually to see. Thus Christ was *the* Light, the true light that lighteth every man; the chiefest, highest, holiest beside Him, a John himself, was but a lamp kindled from his beams,[1] but which, as it was kindled, might also be quenched in darkness again.[2] He remarks too, by the way, although this is a very subordinate thought with him, that it was part of

---

[1] On the noble humility of John, and the freedom with which he abases himself, that he may give all glory to his Lord, Augustine exclaims (*Serm.* cclxxxvii. 2): Lucerna enim erat, et vento superbiæ timebat exstingui.

[2] *Serm.* lxvii. 5: Tu tibi lumen non es. Ut multum, oculus es; lumen non es. Quid prodest patens et sanus oculus, si lumen desit? Sic et Johannes lumen putabatur. And then with reference to John v. 33: Ille lucerna, hoc est, res illuminata, accensa ut luceret. Quæ accendi potest, potest et exstingui. Cf. *Serm.* cccxli. 2: *In Ev. Joh. Tract.* xiv. 1: Potest quidem dici lumen Johannes, et bene dicitur et ipse lumen; sed illuminatum, non illuminans. Aliud est enim lumen quod illuminat, et aliud lumen quod illuminatur. Nam et oculi nostri *lumina* dicuntur, et tamen in tenebris patent et non vident. Lumen autem illuminans a seipso lumen est, et sibi lumen est, et non indiget alio lumine ut lucere possit, sed ipso indigent cætera ut luceant. Cf. *Ibid.* xxiii. 3, 4.

God's gracious discipline and training of men that the lamp should precede the Light. The weak and diseased eyes that could not at once have endured the brightness of this were thus trained to bear it by the feebler splendour of the other.[1]

But, as Christ was the Light and John only the lamp, in the same way Christ was the Word and John only the voice. In drawing out the relations of the two as expressed by these titles, Augustine traces with a singular subtlety the manifold and profound fitnesses which lie in them for the setting forth of those relations. A word, he observes, is something even without a voice, for a word in the heart is as truly such before it is outspoken as after; while a voice is nothing, a mere unmeaning sound, an empty cry, unless it be also the vehicle of a word. But when they are thus united, the voice in a manner goes before the word, for the sound strikes the ear before the sense is conveyed to the mind : yet while it thus *goes* before it in this act of communication, it *is not* really before it, but the contrary. Thus, when we speak, the word in our hearts must precede the voice on our lips, which yet is the vehicle by whose aid the word in us is transferred to and becomes

---

[1] *Serm.* lxvii. 5 : Propter cæcos lucerna diei testimonium perhibebat—which thought he expresses in another image elsewhere (*In Ev. Joh. Tract.* ii. 7) : Quomodo plerumque fit ut in aliquo corpore radiato cognoscatur ortus esse sol, quem oculis videre non possumus. Quia et qui saucios habent oculos, idonei sunt videre parietem illuminatum et illustratum a sole, vel montem, vel arborem, aut aliquid hujuscemodi idonei sunt videre : et in alio illustrato demonstratur ortus ille, cui videndo adhuc minus idoneam aciem gerunt. Sic ergo illi omnes, ad quos Christus venerat minus idonei erant eum videre : radiavit Johannem, et per illum confitentem se radiatum ac se illuminatum esse, non qui radiaret et illuminaret, cognitus est ille qui illuminat, cognitus est ille qui illustrat.

also a word in another; but this being accomplished, or rather in the very accomplishing of this, the voice has passed away, exists no more; but the word which is planted now in another's heart, as well as in ours, remains. All this Augustine transfers to the Lord and to his forerunner. John is nothing without Jesus : Jesus just what He was before without John, however to men the knowledge of Him may have come through John. John the first in time, and yet He who *came* after him most truly having *been* before him. John, so soon as he had fulfilled his mission, passing away, ceasing, having no continuous significance for the Church of God; but Jesus, of whom he had told, and to whom he witnessed, abiding for ever.[1]

To many no doubt it must have appeared strange, that even after the Lord had commenced his ministry, John still went forward with his; that John's baptism did not cease when Christ's had begun (John iii. 22, 23); that John, so far from dissolving the company of his disciples, or handing them all over to the more perfect Teacher who now was

[1] *Serm.* ccxciii. 3: Johannes Vox ad tempus, Christus Verbum in principio æternum. Tolle verbum, quid est vox ? Ubi nullus est intellectus, inanis est strepitus. Vox sine verbo aurem pulsat, cor non ædificat. Verumtamen in ipso corde nostro ædificando advertamus ordinem rerum. Si cogito quid dicam, jam verbum est in corde meo : sed loqui ad te volens, quæro quemadmodum sit etiam in corde tuo, quod jam est in meo. Hoc quærens quomodo ad te perveniat, et in corde tuo insideat verbum quod jam est in corde meo, assumo vocem, et assumtâ voce loquor tibi : sonus vocis ducit ad te intellectum verbi, et cum ad te duxit sonus vocis intellectum verbi, sonus quidem ipse pertransit, verbum autem quod ad te sonus perduxit, jam est in corde tuo, nec recessit a meo. Cf. *Serm.* cclxxxviii. 3: an admirable specimen of Augustine's skill in making the hard comparatively easy, and uniting at once the deep and the popular; and *Serm.* cclxxxix. 3. It may be well to mention that this distinction between the voice and the word, and the application of the distinction to John and the Lord, is anticipated by Origen, *In Joan.* ii. 26.

come, not only retained those whom he had made already (Matt. ix. 14), but also gathered round him others beside (John iv. 1).[1] Augustine gives the true explanation of the fact; namely, that a certain independence and aloofness on his part was necessary to his function as a witness to the Lord. If his witness was to go far with his countrymen, it needed to be that, not of a mere disciple of Jesus, who could do no more than reproduce the impressions received from Him, and whose witness consequently would only be a poorer repetition of the Lord's witness to Himself.[2] As it was, the testimony of John came with quite another force, being that of one who, while he did fullest and freest homage to the superior greatness of the Lord, yet retained, for so God had willed it, a position, in a certain degree an independent position, of his own. The fact that this position was one exactly the best fitted to rouse feelings of jealousy in his mind at the glory which was fast eclipsing his own, feelings which there wanted not those who attempted to stir up (John iii. 26), must have caused his testimony to the character and mission of the Son of God to come with a weight and conviction which under no other circumstances it could have possessed.[3]

At the same time John's aloofness from Jesus reaches deeper than this, grounds itself on a fact which Augustine

[1] *Serm.* ccxcii. 2: Hic ergo Johannes non invenitur inter discipulos Domini, sed potius invenitur discipulos habuisse cum Domino; . . . . absit ut dicam, contra Dominum, sed tamen quasi extra Dominum. Discipulos habebat Christus, discipulos habebat Johannes; docebat Christus, docebat Johannes.

[2] *Serm.* ccxciii. 6: Laudatis quem sequimini, prædicatis cui adhæretis.

[3] *Serm.* ccxciii. 6: Hoc erat procul dubio necessarium præcursori fideli, ab eo Christum prædicari qui posset æmulus credi.

often urges—namely, that the Baptist was, so to speak, the impersonation of the whole preparatory discipline for men's reception of a Saviour:[1] that whole preparation culminating in him; 'the law and the prophets were until John.' Yet though standing thus at the threshold, he did not himself move in the sphere, of New-Testament and Evangelical life, but in that of the Old; and thus it would have been a confounding of things which it was the intention of God should be kept distinct, the law and the gospel, prophecy and its fulfilment, it would have troubled and marred the representative character of John, personifying, as in a manner he did, Law and Prophecy, had he entered into closer personal relation with Him who was the end of the law and the fulfilment of prophecy.

The somewhat startling character of John's message to Jesus, 'Art Thou He that should come, or do we look for another' (Matt. xi. 3)? of such a message from such a man, the strange surprise which it has for us that he who had borne the first and most authentic witness to Jesus as the Christ, should now himself seem to doubt whether He were the promised One or not, Augustine well brings out;[2] while at the same time he keeps clear of, indeed he seems expressly to contradict, Tertullian's error,[3] who will have

[1] *De Div. Quæst.* 58: Johannes Baptista multis probabilibus documentis non absurde creditur prophetiæ gestare personam. . . . . Totius prophetiæ, quæ ab exordio generis humani usque ad adventum Domini de Domino facta est, imaginem gestat.
[2] *Serm.* lxvi. 3: Illa laudatio facta est dubitatio? Tu digitum intendisti, tu eum ostendisti; tu dixisti, Ecce agnus Dei, Ecce qui tollit peccata mundi. Tu dixisti, Nos omnes de plenitudine ejus accepimus. Tu dixisti, Non sum dignus corrigiam calceamenti ejus solvere. Et modo tu dicis, Tu es qui venis, an alium expectamus?
[3] TERTULLIAN, *De Bapt.* 10; *Adv. Marcion.* iv. 18: Ipso jam Domino operanti in terram necesse erat portionem Spiritus S. quæ

the Baptist to have sent not for his disciples' satisfaction and establishment in the faith, or certainly not merely for theirs, but also for his own; as though in that dungeon of Machærus, he too had been assailed with doubts by the Tempter, and now needed for himself a word of re-assurance. This explanation of the message attracts at first sight, and Olshausen has done for it all which is possible to commend it to the Christian sense of the reader, and to remove from it what it has of strange and perplexing: yet I cannot believe with him that there was any such shaking in the Baptist's faith. Rather in sending his disciples with this question to the Lord, he did but continue to do what he had done from the first, namely, turn all eyes so far as might be *from* himself, the waning lamp, *to* Jesus, the risen Sun. His disciples had heard *his* testimony that Jesus was the Christ, and they might have been tempted to believe this, mainly because their master said it, instead of because the Lord Himself declared it, to make even their very affiance on the Lord itself an act of homage done to their own master, and not to Him. How few would have resisted, nay, how few would have detected, the flattery offered to them in a shape so subtle as this. But John did resist it. Their faith in Christ shall rest not on their faith in him, that is, on man's word, as its ultimate ground, but rather on the word of God, on the Lord's own testimony that He is the Christ. John desired, as Augus-

ex formâ prophetici moduli in Johanne egerat præparaturam viarum Dominicarum abscedere jam ab Johanne, redactam scilicet in Dominum, ut in massalem suam summam. This statement Augustine, I think, meant pointedly to contradict, when he explains the reason of the Lord's testimony to John (ver. 7–15), as being, Ne fortis aliquis dicat; Bonus erat primo Johannes, et Spiritus Dei deseruit illum.

tine well expresses it, that his disciples should dig down to the rock, and set their foundations there, and would not be satisfied until they had so done; and this was the meaning of his sending them with that question to the Lord.[1]

He further adds that the Lord's honourable testimony to John, which directly follows (ver. 7–11), was in all likelihood especially timed to hinder on the part of those present, or of others to whom the notice of this message should come, any such misinterpretation of it, or misapplication of his own warning words, 'Blessed is he whosoever shall not be offended in Me,'[2] as should derogate in the least from the just esteem and honour in which the Baptist deserved ever to be holden. The Lord reminds those present of what the Baptist was, of what they themselves in times past had seen and found him—no reed shaken by every wind, but a cedar-tree braving the shock of storms—no server of the time, ready to say soft things to kings, that he might wear the soft clothing of those that are in kings' palaces,—no such shaper therefore of his doctrines to the shifting moods of the times as would now seek for fear or for favour to go back from his former testimony to Christ. But what had they found him? a lineal successor in outward manner of life, and in inner spirit, of the old prophets—himself a prophet—'yea,' the Lord adds out of his own deeper insight into the signifi-

---

[1] *Serm.* lxvi. 4: Ite dicite illi; non quia ego dubito, sed ut vos instruamini. Ite, dicite illi: quod ego soleo dicere, ab illo audite: audistis præconem, confirmamini a judice.

[2] *Serm.* lxvi. 4: Nam ut sciremus quia non de Johanne dixit: Illis abeuntibus cœpit dicere ad turbas de Johanne: dixit laudes ejus veras verax, Veritas.

cance of John's appearance, for this the multitude had not apprehended—' and more than a prophet.'

But in what way 'more than a prophet'? To this Augustine replies that he was more, and had higher honour, than any other prophet, first, in that he was the only prophet who was himself prophesied of and announced by others; his coming having indeed a double announcement (Isai. xl. 3; Mal. iv. 5, 6);[1] and secondly, as the connecting link between the Old Dispensation and the New (Luke xvi. 16); and himself, though not perfectly belonging to, yet partaking of the prerogatives of, the New;[2] and thirdly, which was indeed but another aspect of this second, he was more than any other prophet, in that he bore testimony, not as all others had done, to a Saviour yet future, but to one already present; and *that*, not in dark figures, but in plainest words, seeing with his eyes what many prophets and kings of the elder Covenant had desired to see and had not seen—they telling at most of a Sun which should one day rise up above the horizon, he actually gilded by the brightness of his risen beams.[3]

But the further words, 'For this is he, whom it is written, Behold, I send my messenger before thy face'

[1] Thus *Serm.* cclxxxviii. 2: Hic propheta, immo amplius quam propheta, prænuntiari meruit per prophetam.

[2] *Serm.* ccxciii. 2: Videtur Johannes interjectus quidam limes Testamentorum duorum, Veteris et Novi. . . . . Sustinet ergo personam vetustatis, et præconium novitatis. And in a sermon which the Benedictine editors reject, he is called legis et gratiæ fibula.

[3] *Con. duas Epp. Pelag.* iii. 4: Quasi præteritæ dispensationis limes quidam, qui mediatorem ipsum non aliquâ umbrâ futuri, vel allegoricâ significatione, vel ullâ propheticâ prænuntiatione venturum esse significans, sed digito demonstrans ait, Ecce agnus Dei, Ecce qui tollit peccatum mundi. *Con. Litt. Petil.* ii. 37: Prioribus justis prænuntiare tantum Christum concessum est, huic autem et prænuntiare absentem, et videre præsentem. Cf. *Serm.* cclxxxviii. 2.

(Matt. xi. 10), with the explanation, 'This is Elias, which was for to come' (ver. 14), added to that later declaration which all admit to have reference to John, 'Elias is come already' (Matt. xvii. 11, 13), how, it may be asked, shall these be reconciled with John's own distinct denial of his being Elias (John i. 21)? The solution of the apparent contradiction is of course not difficult, the key to it lying, as Augustine rightly remarks, in the words of Gabriel that John should go before the Lord 'in the spirit and power of Elias' (Luke i. 17): so that in one sense, that is literally, John the Baptist was not Elias; in another, that is, in a figure, he was.[1] But at the same time Augustine does not believe that this coming of John the Baptist was the exhaustive fulfilment of the prophecy of Malachi, or more than a partial and initial one. There is yet in reserve an actual and personal coming of the great Reformer of the Old Testament, who, in contemplation of this, was withdrawn from the earth without having tasted death.[2] In this I must believe he was right, and it is hard to perceive how the Lord could have been at more pains to declare to his disciples that so it should be, or to prevent their confounding these two cognate

[1] *In Ev. Joh. Tract.* 4: Si figuram præcursionis advertas, Johannes ipse est Elias, quod enim ille ad primum adventum, hoc ille ad secundum. Si proprietatem personæ interroges, Johannes Johannes, Elias Elias.

[2] *In Ev. Joh. Tract.* 4: Quod erat Johannes ad primum adventum, hoc erit Elias ad secundum adventum. Quomodo duo adventus Judicis, sic duo præcones. *De Civ. Dei*, xx. 29: Ipse quippe ante adventum Salvatoris judicis non immerito speratur esse venturus; quia etiam nunc vivere non immerito creditur. Curru namque igneo raptus est de rebus humanis. With this connects itself his faith (*Serm.* ccxcix. 11), as that of so many in the early Church, that Elijah and Enoch are the two witnesses of Rev. xi. 7, so that of him it should be true, mortem distulit, non evasit.

but distinct events, than at Matt. xvii. 11, He is; not to say that the same is more lightly indicated in his, 'If ye will receive it,' here (ver. 14).

The words that follow are more difficult: 'Verily I say unto you, among them that are born of woman there hath not risen a greater than John the Baptist; notwithstanding he that is least in the kingdom of heaven is greater than he' (Matt. xi. 11); nor has Augustine planted himself at the true point of view from which to explain them. Indeed he himself wavers between two expositions; sometimes he makes 'the kingdom of heaven' to signify the future heavenly world, and thus the Lord to affirm that the lowest angel is greater than the greatest that is still compassed with infirmities here; but he does not lay much stress on this exposition, and only once or twice has suggested it.[1] He prefers to make the point of the declaration to lie in that 'born of woman,' finding a tacit antithesis between this and 'born of a Virgin,' as was only He who uttered these words, who will then Himself be that 'least,' or rather, lesser, 'in the kingdom of heaven,' who is greater than John.[2] But this interpretation is in every way unsatisfying. How

---

[1] *Con. Adv. Leg. et Proph.* ii. 5: Aut enim regnum cælorum appellavit eo loco Dominus, quod nondum accepimus et in quo nondum sumus; et quia ibi sunt sancti angeli, quilibet in eis minor major est utique quolibet sancto et justo, portante corpus quod corrumpitur et aggravat animam. Aut si regnum cælorum in eâ sententiâ illic intelligi voluit, quâ et in hoc tempore significatur Ecclesia, profecto se ipsum Dominus significavit, quia nascendi tempore minor erat Johanne, major autem divinitatis æternitate, et Dominicâ potestate. In like manner he suggests the two explanations, *Serm.* lxvi. 2.

[2] *In Ev. Joh. Tract.* 14: Minor nativitate, major potestate, major divinitate, majestate, claritate.

can we imagine the Lord counting it needful to say with such emphasis that He was greater than John? Moreover He too is expressly declared to have been 'made of a *woman*' (Gal. iv. 4), which language therefore fails to express that antithesis to Virgin born (cf. also John ii. 4; xix. 26), necessary for this explanation. Then further, and the most decisive objection of all to making the Lord to mean Himself by this 'least in the kingdom of heaven,' He was not *in* the kingdom of heaven, the kingdom of heaven being rather in Him, and unfolding itself from Him. But assuredly the opposition here is not between 'born of woman' and 'born of a Virgin;' but between 'born of woman' and 'born of the Spirit;' which last they all are that are in the new 'kingdom of heaven,' in that kingdom of the Spirit which dates from Pentecost, when the Holy Ghost was given as He never had been given before (John vii. 39); our Lord declaring here that the mystery of regeneration, whereof all the faithful down to the very least in the New Covenant are partakers, is a higher gift than any whereof the chiefest saints and servants of God, even a John himself, were partakers in the Old. The words say nothing as to the place which shall be vouchsafed to this saint or that, to him of the Old Covenant or to him of the New, in that kingdom of glory which shall be revealed.

There is a certain fitness, Augustine observes, such as we may trace running though the whole of the Baptist's history, in the fact, that the immediate occasion of his martyrdom was not his witness for Jesus as the Christ, or aught in immediate connexion with his Lord; but rather his assertion of the holiness of the Law: 'It is not *lawful* for thee to have thy brother's wife' (Mark vi. 18). He who was the last and noblest personification of the Law fitly sealed with his own blood his zeal for its holiness.[1] At the same time he, and others who like him resisted unto blood, inasmuch as they died for the truth, did in fact die for Christ, who *is* the Truth; they were his martyrs as really as those who were called by his name, and shed their blood more immediately for his testimony. This is a point which Augustine oftentimes presses; thus a sermon on the Maccabæan martyrs[2] is dedicated entirely to an assertion of the identity of the people of God before and after Christ, out of which identity and oneness of the two, it was only fitting that the Christian Church should celebrate those martyrs who died before their King had died, no less than those who died after.

And on deaths like this of the Baptist, when the servants of God seem given into the hands of the wicked, who do unto them whatsoever they list (Matt. xvii. 12), he often takes occasion to remark how different to the eye of sense the dealings of God with some of his servants, from his dealings with others. Those He gloriously delivers; these He appears to abandon to their foes; the Three Children are brought forth altogether unscathed from the fiery furnace (Dan. iii. 27); the Maccabæan martyrs perish in the flames (2 Macc. vi. 11; vii. 5); Peter is delivered from the sword of Herod, from that sword which had just been stained with James's blood (Acts xii. 2, 11); one John the malice of an emperor fails to hurt, and he is plunged unharmed into the burning oil; another falls a victim to a wicked woman's spite, and his life is given away at a wanton dancing-girl's request. But shall we therefore conclude that those God delivered,

---

[1] *Enarr. in Ps.* cxl. 10.   [2] *Serm.* ccc.

and these He did not deliver? Would such language rightly express the facts of the case? Should we not rather say, those were delivered openly, and in the face of the world—these as really delivered; however their deliverance did not as manifestly appear, but like so much besides, is at present seen and apprehended only by the eye of faith.[1]

Augustine's very conceits and fancies are oftentimes instructive. They at any rate are never puerile, or in other ways unworthy plays with things sacred. He allows himself in more than one of these conceits while he is commenting on the life and death of the Baptist. Thus he claims for the Church that it has embodied in a concrete form, in a visible symbol, those memorable words of the Baptist referred to already, 'He must increase, but I decrease,' selecting as it has done for the day of the servant's nativity June 24, being the turning-point in our Church-Year, from which the decrease in our days begins, but Dec. 25 for the day of the Nativity of the Lord, being the day when the increase of the year commences. Nor does he fail to call attention to the significance of the several manners of deaths of servant and Lord, one a cutting short, the other an exalting.[2]

Let us consider next Augustine's handling of the life of

[1] *Serm.* ccci. 3: Ergo illis Deus aderat, hos deseruerat? Absit. Immo utrisque adfuit, illis in aperto, istis in occulto. Illos visibiliter liberabat: istos invisibiliter coronabat. *Enarr.* 2ᵃ *in Ps.* xxxiii. 18: Ille qui tulit de flammâ tres pueros, numquid tulit de flammâ Machabæos? Nonne illi in ignibus hymnizabant, illi in ignibus exspirabant? Deus trium puerorum, nonne ipse est et Machabæorum? Illos eruit et illos non eruit? Immo utrosque eruit, sed tres pueros sic eruit, ut et carnales confunderentur.

[2] *Serm.* cclxxxvii. 3: Johannes in passione capite est deminutus, Christus in ligno est exaltatus.

another. The life, it is true, or say rather the death, of Stephen naturally does not yield such varied and abundant matter for comment as that of the Baptist: for the whole of the protomartyr's history, profoundly suggestive as in manifold ways it is, is yet shut up within the limits of two chapters. All that we certainly know of him is contained in these. He starts suddenly as from the ranks into the very foremost place of peril and of honour, a standard-bearer of the truth, and there nobly does and dies;[1] he rises above the horizon, a bright luminary of the Church, but sets for us almost as soon as risen; leaving to us one great discourse, one mighty deed. On this, however, Augustine has much. In the African Church the memory of the martyrs was especially dear. Some of the noblest of that noble army were children of her own; hers was Cyprian, and hers too Felicitas and Vivia Perpetua, women who out of weakness were made strong; with many more; and though now the days of the martyrs were over, the spirit that inspired them, and that pervades, though not without the admixture of some turbid elements, the writings of Tertullian, had not passed away. And thus some of Augustine's noblest discourses were delivered on the days dedicated to the memory of one or other of these. On St. Stephen he has several, and from these and other sources in his writings I select a few notices of one who in so many aspects was the forerunner of St. Paul.

Augustine does not enter with any fulness into the scheme of Stephen's discourse, which is certainly difficult to understand—why, namely, it should have so long an

[1] Augustine himself observes, with reference to this fact, that it was the deacons and not the Apostles who furnished the first martyr (*Serm.* cccxv. 19): Prior victima de agnis quam arietibus.

exordium, why he should dwell in such detail on the patriarchal history, which was as familiarly known to his hearers as to himself, and bore only remotely on the matters of which he was accused;—but without professing to explain all this,[1] he yet makes an important suggestion, namely, that this long introduction was, in the nobler sense of the term, a *captatio benevolentiæ*. Having much to say, before he concluded, that must be most distasteful to his hearers, he would fain conciliate them so far as he might, and especially would impress on them, by dwelling so fully on the early privileges and election of the Abrahamic family, that these privileges were most precious to himself, even while he was asserting that in Christ Jesus they had now become the common property of all the families of the earth.[2]

The sharp severity of speech and tone which appears in some parts of Stephen's address to his fellow-countrymen Augustine is fond of contrasting with the truest love to them which broke forth in his dying prayer. And he bids us note how much of tenderest love will often lie hid under

---

[1] He has however a brief but valuable analysis of the earlier parts of the discourse, though one would fain have had the connexion traced also between these and the latter (*Serm.* cccxv. 2): Hic prius exposuit illis ab initio legem Dei, ab Abraham usque ad Moÿsem, usque ad datam legem, usque ad introitum in terram promissionis; ut commendaret quia non erat verum testimonium unde illi calumniam commovebant [Acts vi. 13]. Deinde de Moÿse dedit eis magnam similitudinem ad Christum. Reprobatus ab eis Moÿses, et ipse eos liberavit; reprobatus liberavit. Sic et Dominus Christus reprobatus a Judæis, ipse illos est postea liberaturus.

[2] *Serm.* cccxix. 1: Conciliabat auditorem, ut commendaret Salvatorem. Blande cœpit, ut diu audiretur. Et quia hinc fuerat accusatus quod verba dixerat contra Deum et Legem, ipsam Legem iis exposuit; ut ejus Legis esset prædicator, cujus accusabatur esse vastator.

words that almost sound like words of bitterness and hate. Where could Stephen have found keener words than these —'Ye stiffnecked and uncircumcised in heart and ears, ye do always resist the Holy Ghost' (Acts vii. 51–53)? One who knew not the mysteries of love might suppose that he hated them whom he addressed in language like this; while yet presently, when they added to 'all their former resistance to the truth those further utterances of their enmity, gnashing upon him with their teeth, yea, even under the shower of their cruel stones, he could pray for these same, and did pray for them, even in the agonies of a painful death.[1]

And this example of Stephen's dying love Augustine, in his homiletic instruction, urges often on his hearers from another point of view. Many, when exhorted by the example of Christ their Lord to bless them that curse them, and to pray for them that despitefully use them, might perhaps make answer, '*He* could do this, *He* could say, even as they nailed Him to the cross, "Father, forgive them, for they know not what they do." This was not difficult for Him, for He was God; but it is impossible for us.' Augustine in reply bids them look not at their Master only, but also at their fellow-servant, one of like passions with themselves, by nature a sinful man—to look

---

[1] *Serm.* cccxvii. 4: Lingua clamat, cor amat; and in a beautiful passage, *In Ev. Joh. Tract.* vi. 3: Magnus impetus, sed columba sine felle sævit. *Serm.* cccxv. 2: Sævire videtur: lingua ferox, cor lene. Clamabat et amabat. Sæviebat, et salvos fieri volebat. Quis non crederet iratum, quis non crederet odiorum facibus inflammatum? Hoc dicat, qui cor non videt. Latebat cor ejus; sed audita sunt novissima verba ejus, et patuerunt occulta ejus cum lapidaretur: Domine, ne statuas illis hoc peccatum. Ubi est, Durâ cervice? Hoc est totum quod clamabas? hoc est totum quod sæviebas? foris clamabas, et intus orabas. Cf. *Enarr. in Ps.* cxxxii. 2.

at Stephen, who in that hour of agony prayed for his murderers; and with his example before them Augustine bids them to acknowledge that this same was possible for them, who had the same fountain of grace to draw from, the same Saviour to turn to as he had,—a Saviour in whose strength they too might overcome hate and revenge, and all sinful passions of the mind.[1]

It is singular that Augustine has not indicated with more clearness the meaning of St. Stephen's beholding in that hour of agony his Lord *standing* at the right hand of God, for it is exactly such a point as he seldom suffers to escape him. He often indeed notes that this is the only instance in which Christ is described as standing, that on every other occasion He is *sitting*, at the right hand of the Majesty on high; but he does not proceed to explain or to account for this exceptional case.[2] The right explanation we owe, as I believe, to Gregory the Great[3]—namely, that it

---

[1] *Serm.* cccxv. 6; cccxvii. 2: Quando audiunt: Pater, ignosce illis, quia nesciunt quid faciunt; dicunt sibi, Ipse hoc potuit tamquam Filius Dei, tamquam unicus Patris. Caro enim pendebat, sed Deus intus latebat. Nos autem quid sumus, qui ista faciamus? Fefellit qui jussit? Absit: non fefellit. Si multum ad te putas imitari Dominum tuum; adtende Stephanum conservum tuum. Dominus Christus, unicus Dei filius: numquid hoc Stephanus? Dominus Christus, de incorruptâ virgine natus: numquid hoc Stephanus? Dominus Christus venit, non in carne peccati, sed in similitudine carnis peccati: numquid hoc Stephanus? Sic natus est ut tu; inde natus est, unde et tu; ab eo renatus est, a quo et tu.

[2] He connects, indeed, Stephen's own standing or steadfastness in that hour with his Lord's (*Serm.* cccxiv. 1): Jesum stantem videbat; ideo stabat et non cadebat, quia stans sursum et deorsum certantem desuper spectans invictas militi suo vires, ne caderet, suggerebat.

[3] *Hom.* xxix. *in Evang.*: Sedere judicantis [adde, imperantis] est, stare vero pugnantis vel adjuvantis. Stephanus in labore certaminis positus stantem vidit, quem adjutorem habuit.

belongs to the passion of the moment that the dying martyr, filled with confidence in his Saviour's present help, should behold Him not *sitting* in majestic calmness, but uprisen from his throne, and thus *standing* at the right hand of the Father, as in act to come forth to the help of his suffering servant,—all which we have embodied in the opening of our Collect on St. Stephen's day : ' O blessed Jesus, who *standest* at the right hand of God *to succour* all those that suffer for Thee.'

It is at least a pardonable play upon words, even if it be no more, in which Augustine indulges when he urges the *nomen et omen* of Stephen's name. He who first, being steadfast unto death, received the *crown* of life, had borne long since the prophecy of this his martyr's crown in the name of Stephen ($\sigma\tau\acute{\epsilon}\phi\alpha\nu os$) which he bore.[1]

The connexion between a prayer and the answer to that prayer is not always distinctly traced in Scripture. Like so much else in Scripture, this is left for us to trace for ourselves from slight and scattered hints, rather than forcibly obtruded on our notice. Thus we are not told that there was any connexion between Peter's deliverance from the dungeon of Herod, and the prayer that ' was made without ceasing of the Church unto God for him ' (Acts xii. 5); yet who can doubt that such connexion

---

[1] *Serm.* cccxiv. 2; *Enarr. in Ps.* lviii. 3: Stephanus lapidatus est, et quod vocabatur accepit; Stephanus enim *corona* dicitur. So Adam of St. Victor :—

> Nomen habes *Coronati*,
> Te tormenta decet pati
> Pro coronâ gloriæ.

Less tolerable is another play upon words in which he allows himself on this same occasion (*Serm.* cccxvii. 4): *Petris* lapidabatur qui pro *Petrâ* moriebatur, dicente apostolo, Petra autem erat Christus.

there was; and, his attention once called to it, that it was the intention of the sacred historian to intimate as much? As little can we hesitate to recognize a deep inner connexion between St. Stephen's prayer and St. Paul's conversion. The great Apostle of the Gentiles, he whom John of Damascus has so grandly called νυμφαγωγὸς τῆς οἰκουμένης, was probably the direct fruit of the prayer which the dying martyr uttered for his enemies; of which enemies the 'young man whose name was Saul' was so far the bitterest, that he was not content with having a *single* hand in the protomartyr's death, but by keeping the clothes of the witnesses, of those therefore who flung the first stones, and by disencumbering them for their work, had as it were many hands in the slaughter.[1]

At the same time it is very noticeable that Augustine, who, as we have just seen, has so much to say about Stephen, yet never even suggests the probable influence which he must have had, first by the character of his teaching, and then by the martyrdom with which he set his seal to that teaching, on St. Paul; the extent to which Stephen must have been the πρόδρομος of Paul. And yet, so far as Paul was taught of men and not directly of God, every thing points to Stephen as having been his teacher, as having opened to him those larger aspects of the object and purpose of the death of Christ; which the other chief disciples, though they had been in Christ before

---

[1] *Serm.* cccxvi. 7 : Quantum sæviebat in illâ cæde, vultis audire? Vestimenta lapidantium servabat, ut omnium manibus lapidaret. *Serm.* cclxxix. 1 : Sic aderat lapidantibus ut non ei sufficeret si tantum suis manibus lapidaret. Ut enim esset in omnium lapidantium manibus, ipse omnium vestimenta servabat, magis sæviens omnes adjuvando quam suis manibus lapidando. Cf. *Ad Rom. Expos. inchoata*, 15.

Stephen or Paul was, had not as yet made their own. And yet there is much in Scripture to indicate how closely Paul trod here in the footsteps of Stephen. Thus it is very noteworthy that the accusations brought against Paul, at a later day, namely that he would not tie the Christian religion to the Jewish temple (Acts xxi. 28 ; xxv. 8), are exactly those which had been already brought against Stephen (Acts vi. 14), while such we nowhere find brought against any other of the Apostles. While St. James is held in highest honour among the Jews, the mere presence of St. Paul is sufficient to rouse the Jews to displays of the wildest hate.

The scattering abroad of the disciples in the persecution that followed, which disciples yet 'went everywhere, preaching the word' (Acts viii. 4), Augustine triumphantly compares to the scattering of sparks of fire, which before were heaped upon a single hearth, but are now flung far and wide, to kindle wheresoever they alight. The Jews, shortsighted in their hate, had thought to quench those live coals ; but indeed only succeeded in so spreading them everywhere that presently they set the world in a blaze.[1]

[1] *Serm.* cccxvi. 4: Fugati sunt fratres, sed tanquam ardentes faces, quocunque veniebant, accendebant. Stulti Judæi, quando illos de Hierosolymis fugabant, carbones ignis in silvam mittebant. And elsewhere (*Serm.* cxvi. 6) he compares the Church of Jerusalem to a heap of burning brands : Lapidato Stephano passa est illa congeries persecutionem ; sparsa sunt ligna, et accensus est mundus.

CHAPTER VII.

AUGUSTINE ON THE EPISTLE TO THE ROMANS.

It is a matter of regret that Augustine did not, among his other exegetical works, give to the Church a commentary on the Epistle to the Romans, seeing that for such a work the character of his mind, and the whole training of his life, eminently fitted him. He was of a spirit more akin to the great Apostle of the Gentiles than any other Father of the early Church. Not until Luther did there rise another capable of grasping its truths as he had grasped them. He, too, like St. Paul, had been brought by wonderful ways, and after many fearful struggles, there where he had found rest for his soul; his story a living commentary on the words, 'Where sin abounded, grace did much more abound.' It was a word from this Epistle which gave the last decisive impulse to his conversion.[1] Out of the long and terrible struggle which preceded this, he did not bring merely his wounds and his scars, but also a deep acquaintance with the devices of the enemy, with the weaknesses and treacheries of the human heart, with the mighty power of Him that had stood beside him to help and to save. But Augustine has not bequeathed to the Church any such work. The existence of brief *Scholia* on this Epistle, and of an *Inchoata Expositio*, which, though it occupies sixteen columns, only handles

[1] *Conf.* viii. 12.

the first five verses of the first chapter, and in which he did not proceed further, justly fearing the enormous size to which a commentary on that scale would grow, only slightly qualifies this statement. His work on the Epistle to the Galatians, which might be accepted as in part a substitute, belongs to an earlier period of his life, and, with very much of valuable, does not possess all the depth and fulness of his later exposition. For though there is, no doubt, a certain exaggeration in what Luther says of him, namely, that 'he was first roused up and made a man by the Pelagians when he strove against them,'[1] yet to his controversy with them he did certainly owe much. In conflict with these gainsayers he learned to possess his truth as he had never possessed it before, as but for this perhaps he never would have possessed it at all, and not to possess only, but to enlarge and to deepen it.

But although we have not such a work from his pen, there is largest material for the exposition of this Epistle to be drawn, if one would bring it together, from almost all parts of his writings, and more especially from his treatises having reference to that Pelagian controversy, and from his *Letters*. Modern interpreters of this scripture have too often left these rich and abundant mines well-nigh

---

[1] *Table Talk*, 29. Augustine himself often, with reference to 1 Cor. ii. 19, recognizes the service of which heresies may prove to the Church in stirring up the faithful to a deeper investigation of Scripture, and in causing them to attain to a firmer grasp of the truth. St. Paul he believes, in that passage, to have affirmed the same ; though it may very well be doubted whether this was his intention there. Thus *De Gen. con. Manich.* i. 1 : Ideo divina providentia multos diversi erroris hæreticos esse permittit, ut cum insultant nobis, et interrogant nos ea quæ nescimus, vel sic excutiamus pigritiam, et divinas scripturas nosse cupiamus. Cf. *Enarr. in Ps.* lxvii. 31 ; *Conf.* vii. 19 ; *in Joh. Evang. Tract.* 51, § 2.

unwrought. What they would yield, I should like by one or two specimens to show; and this, although it would be impossible in the compass of this present essay to do more than from two or three prominent passages to illustrate the manner in which he has addressed himself to the exposition of this theologically central portion of God's word.[1]

And, first, in regard of Rom. v. 12-21. This is Augustine's stronghold and citadel in all his long controversy with the Pelagians.[2] Of these it needs hardly to observe that they occupied the extreme opposite pole of error to the Manichæans. As the Manichæans implicitly denied the *possibility*, so the Pelagians the *necessity*, of a redemption. Augustine felt, and rightly, that in the relations in this chapter set out, of Adam and Christ to one another, and of the progeny of one to its natural Head, and of the other to its spiritual, the whole dispute between the Church and these deniers of her truth lay implicitly wrapped up. Indeed this chapter is the rock upon which all Pelagian schemes of theology, which rest on an extenuation of the Fall, on a denial of the significancy of Adam's sin (save in the way of evil example), to any but himself,—which break up the race of mankind into a multitude of isolated atoms, touching, but not really connected with, one another, instead of contemplating it as one great organic whole,—must for ever shiver and come to nothing. In the light of this chapter

---

[1] See an interesting passage in his book *De Spir. et Litt.* 7, in which he expresses himself on the subject-matter of this Epistle, and generally on the fitness of St. Paul to be eminently the preacher of the grace of God.

[2] It is a passage, ubi vel maxime fides Christiana consistit (*Ep.* cxc. 3).

such schemes appear as contrary to the revealed Word of God, as indeed they are to all deeper apprehensions which have been attained quite apart from Scripture, of the awful bands, physical, psychical and spiritual, which knit the members of the human family to one another. And to Augustine it was given, if not to feel this more strongly than any had done before, yet certainly to bring it out to the consciousness of the Church as no other hitherto had done.

The meaning of the latter part of this chapter, as he loves to draw it out, is as follows:—In what went before the Apostle had spoken of Christ's death, and the fruits of that death; but the question might well present itself: *How* should the death of one have such significance for all? Saint Paul answers the question. This One is not merely one; He stands in a relation to all men, which can only find its analogy in the relation wherein Adam stood to all. He may be rightly called a 'second Adam.' In Adam the whole natural development of man was included; the entire human race is but the unfolding of that first, that one man. Exactly so Christ is a spiritual Head. The whole race of regenerate men was shut up in Him, is unfolded from Him. They are but the one grain of gold beaten out, and extended into an infinite breadth. As the huge oak with its trunk and all its spreading branches is rudimentally wrapped up in the single acorn; so the world, or mankind natural, in Adam, and the Church, or mankind spiritual, in Christ.[1] What Adam and Christ were *in*

[1] *Op. Imp. con. Jul.* ii. 163: Unde fit ut totum genus humanum quodam modo sint homines duo, primus et secundus. Cf. ii. 69; and again, *Serm.* xc.: Venit unus contra unum: contra unum qui sparsit unus qui collegit. *In Ev. Joh. Tract.* iii. 12: Homo, et homo: homo ad mortem, et homo ad vitam.

intenso, they are *in extenso*. He often adduces, as a scriptural confirmation of this aspect of the matter, the language and argument of the Apostle to the Hebrews (vii. 5), who concludes that it was not Abraham alone who paid tithes to Melchisedek, but that in Abraham all the future Levites paid tithes as well.[1] The whole moral and spiritual history of the world oscillates between two persons. They are the centres round which everything revolves—the two poles of humanity—the two successive champions and representatives of the race. One is defeated, and the lot of the whole race for thousands of years is servitude and shame; one is victorious, and vast and enduring as were the issues of the other's defeat, those of his victory are vaster and more enduring still.

Only from this point of view, of the race, namely, as included in Adam, do we attain any right apprehension of the significance of Adam's sin. It was not so much *a* sin, differing from all other sins only in that it was the first, and when compared with many that followed perhaps a slight sin,—which is the Pelagian position;—it was not this so much as *the* sin, the head and front of the world's offending, not the first only, but the greatest, the mother sin in which every after sin was enfolded.[2] The injury which by that sin Adam inflicted on himself, he did not inflict on himself alone. It was, so to speak, a bruising and injuring of the seed, and thus more or less a marring and distorting of every single branch and fibre and leaf which should evolve itself therefrom. It was a casting of poison into the fountain head, and thus an infecting lower down of every drop of the stream.[3] And only so do we

---

[1] *Op. Imperf. con. Jul.* vi. 22. [2] *Ibid.* vi. 21, 27.
[3] In a minor detail of his interpretation of this passage, but one

attain any right apprehension of the significance of Christ's righteousness; for that other is but one side, the sadder and the darker side, of the same truth. That which held good for death, held good also for life. The same law of intimate union between the members of the race and their head, which made one man's sin so diffusive of death, has

on which he lays considerable stress, it is now acknowledged by all that he was at fault. He found at Rom. v. 12, in his Italic Version, as it is now in the Vulgate, *In quo* omnes peccaverunt; which *in quo* he referred to Adam, as though St. Paul would say, ' *In whom* all sinned.' The words of the original are ἐφ' ᾧ πάντες ἥμαρτον, and are rightly rendered in our Version '*for that* all have sinned' (ἐφ ᾧ = ὅτι, as 2 Cor. v. 4 = quatenus), the Apostle in those words affirming that no following man was capable of arresting the tide of evil, and so proving a new head of life, an ἀρχηγὸς ζωῆς for the race, inasmuch as each in his turn and by his own act, not merely by succession from Adam, came under the law of sin, and thus under the law of death. So far as these words went Julian the Pelagian had entire right on his side, explaining them thus (*Op. Imperf. con. Jul.* ii. 174): *In quo* omnes peccaverunt, nihil aliud indicat quam, *quia* omnes peccaverunt. Considering how much turned on the words, and how often they came into debate between them (see again vi. 23), it is strange that Augustine should not have turned to the original. The error does not seriously, or indeed at all, affect his position. That Adam's sin was the fontal sin of all other which followed, that also it reacted on the moral, and through that on the physical, condition not of one man, but of all who in that one were wrapped up, this is quite strongly enough stated in the passage, to bear the subtraction of the further proof of it which Augustine drew from a mistaken interpretation of these words. Such assertions as the following still remain true, though they may not be found in these words (*Con. duas Ep. Pel.* iv. 4): In illo primo homine peccâsse omnes intelligantur, quia in illo fuerunt omnes, quando ille peccavit: cf. *De Pecc. Mer. et Rem.* iii. 7: In Adam omnes tunc peccaverunt, quando in ejus naturâ, illâ insitâ vi, quâ eos gignere poterat, adhuc omnes ille unus fuerunt; *De Civ. Dei*, xiii. 14: Omnes fuimus in illo uno, quando omnes fuimus ille unus: nondum erat nobis sigillatim creata et distributa forma, in quâ singuli viveremus, sed jam natura erat seminalis, ex quâ propagaremur.

made one man's obedience or righteousness so diffusive of life. Christ shall diffuse Himself no less effectually than Adam, as the one by generation, so the other by regeneration. Nay there shall be, as there ever must be, a mightier power in the good than in the evil; for while the one sin was sufficient to ruin the world, the righteousness of one did not merely do away with that one sin, but with all the innumerable others which had unfolded themselves from it.[1]

But the Epistle to the Romans, before it describes the bringing in of Him, the restorer of all which Adam had forfeited and lost, sets forth the preparatory discipline of the law under which man was being trained for welcoming that Saviour, when at length in the fulness of time He should be revealed; and among the ends to which the law thus given should serve, the Apostle declares that it 'entered that the offence might abound' (Rom. v. 20). Two questions present themselves here, and, as carrying us into the heart of Augustine's exposition of this Epistle, and with it of his whole theology, we may consider severally his answer to each. And first, In what way did the entrance of the law cause the offence or sin to abound?

[1] Thus in his important letter, *Ad Hilarium* (*Ep.* clvii. 12): In hâc caussâ quo constituuntur homines, Adam, ex quo consistit generatio carnalis, et Christus, ex quo regeneratio spiritalis. Sed quia tantum ille homo, iste autem et Deus et homo, non quomodo illa generatio uno delicto obligat, quod est ex Adam, ita ista regeneratio unum delictum solum solvit, quod est ex Adam. Sed illi quidem generationi sufficit ad condemnationem unius delicti connexio, quidquid enim postea homines ex malis suis operibus addunt, non pertinet ad illam generationem, sed ad humanam conversationem: huic autem regenerationi non sufficit illud delictum tantummodo solvere, quod ex Adam trahitur, sed quidquid etiam postea ex iniquis operibus humanæ conversationis accedit. Ideo judicium ex uno in condemnationem, gratia autem ex multis delictis in justificationem.

To this he has a double answer. The law caused sin to abound, in that sin was more sinful now, being committed against the *express* commandment of God, the *lex manifesta*,[1] than when done only against the *lex occulta*, that commandment written at the beginning on the hearts of men, but which now through long neglect had become more or less illegible and obliterated there. Where there is no law, there indeed is sin, but not transgression.[2]

But this was not all; not in this way only did the entrance of the law cause the offence to abound. The law had also in a deeper sense, and one which fearfully revealed the evil of man's heart, an *irritating* power. Man craves to be αὐτόνομος, to be a law to himself, and the very fact of a law imposed by another and from without, does of itself suggest resistance to and defiance of that law. The prohibited comes by the mere fact of the prohibition to be also the desired. The stream of man's corruptions fretted and raged more furiously for the

---

[1] *Serm.* clxx. 2.

[2] *Enarr. in Ps.* cii.: Quare lege subintrante abundavit peccatum? Quia nolebant se confiteri homines peccatores, additâ lege facti sunt et *prævaricatores*. Prævaricator enim non est quisque, nisi cum legem transgressus fuerit. Cf. *Con. Faust.* xix. 7; *Serm.* clxx. 2; and my *Synonyms of the New Testament*, § 66. Yet Augustine at the same time is very earnest in not allowing the giving of a written law to call into question that there went another eternal law before that, however man may have refused, and through refusing become unable distinctly, to read it. Thus *Enarr. in Ps.* lvii. 1: Hoc et antequam Lex daretur, nemo ignorare permissus est, ut esset unde judicarentur et quibus Lex non esset data. Sed ne sibi homines aliquid defuisse quererentur, scriptum est et in tabulis, quod in cordibus non legebant; non enim scriptum non habebant, sed legere nolebant. Oppositum est oculis eorum quod in conscientiâ videre cogerentur, et quasi forinsecus admotâ voce Dei, ad interiora sua homo compulsus est.

obstacles placed in its way; as some mountain torrent foams round a rock that has fallen in its bed; which, not sufficing to dam it up, only rouses it to a fiercer tumult than before.[1] Confessions on the part of the heathen to the same truth are too familiar to need citation.

But the yet deeper question still remained. How was this giving of a law which made the guilty guiltier, and at the same time thus stirred up and roused the evil that might else have remained dormant in man's heart, reconcilable with the love and righteousness of God? Augustine answers, The physician does nothing contrary to or unworthy of his art, whereof the end is the healing of men, when he causes the floating sickness which pervaded the whole frame to concentrate itself into some fixed shape of disease, which then and only then he can encounter and overcome.[2] The sick man would not perhaps have acknowledged himself as sick before, and therefore might have refused to submit himself to the tedious and painful processes of cure.[3] It was so dealt with

---

[1] *De Spir. et Litt.* 4: Lex quamvis bona, auget prohibendo desiderium malum: sicut aquæ impetus si in eam partem non cesset influere, vehementior fit obice opposito, cujus molem cum evicerit majore cumulo præcipitatus violentius per prona devolvitur; nescio quo enim modo hoc ipsum quod concupiscitur, fit jucundius, dum vetatur. And again *Serm.* cliii. 5: Minor erat concupiscentia, quando ante Legem securus peccabas; nunc autem oppositis tibi obicibus Legis, fluvius concupiscentiæ quasi frenatus est paululum, non siccatus: sed increscente impetu qui te ducebat obicibus nullis, obruit te obicibus ruptis. Cf. *De Div. Quæst.* 66; *De Civ. Dei*, xiii. 5.

[2] A heathen moralist, Seneca, has confessed as much (*Ep.* 56): Omnia enim vitia in aperto leviora sunt: morbi quoque tunc ad sanitatem inclinant, cum ex abdito erumpunt, ac vim suam proferunt.

[3] The following quotations will enable us to understand the

mankind by the great Physician of souls. The law, demanding and threatening, revealed man to himself, who was hitherto in good part hidden from himself. It made him see his hurt, and thus sent him to his Healer,[1] to Him too who should enable him by assisting grace to do those things which the law indeed had required of him, but had never been able to bring about in him;[2] so that the wondrous circle ends in the establishing of that law which seemed at first about to be utterly overthrown

position which Augustine took, justifying the righteousness of God (*Enarr. in Ps.* cii. 7): Non crudeliter hoc fecit Deus, sed consilio medicinæ; aliquando enim videtur sibi homo sanus et ægrotat, et in eo quod ægrotat et non sentit, medicum non quærit; augetur morbus, crescit molestia, quæritur medicus, et totum sanatur. And again (*In Ev. Joh. Tract.* iii. 11, 14): Lex minabatur, non opitulabatur; jubebat, non sanabat; languorem ostendebat, non auferebat: sed illi præparabat medico venturo cum gratiâ et veritate: tanquam ad aliquem quem curare vult medicus, mittat primo servum suum, ut ligatum illum inveniat. Cf. *Ep.* cxlv. 3: Lex itaque docendo et jubendo quod sine gratiâ impleri non potest, homini demonstrat suam infirmitatem, ut quærat demonstrata infirmitas Salvatorem, a quo sancta voluntas possit, quod infirma non posset. Lex igitur adducit ad fidem, fides impetrat Spiritum largiorem, diffundit Spiritus caritatem, implet caritas legem. . . . Ita bona est lex illi, qui eâ legitime utitur; utitur autem legitime, qui intelligens quare sit data, per ejus comminationem confugit ad gratiam liberantem. Cf. *Serm.* clv. 4; clxx. 2; *Ad Simplic.* i. 1; *Ep.* cxcvi. 2.

[1] Augustine brings often out the force of συνέκλεισε, Rom. xi. 32; thus *Serm.* clxiii. 11: Conclusit Scriptura omnia sub peccato. Quomodo conclusit? Ne vagareris, ne præcipitareris, ne mergereris. Cancellos tibi fecit lex, ut non inveniendo quâ exires, ad gratiam convolares.

[2] *De Fide et Oper.* 14: Sequuntur enim bona opera justificatum, non præcedunt justificandum—'a golden sentence,' as one of the greatest of our old English divines has termed it. *Enarr. in Ps.* cx. 3: Justitiam enim homo non operatur, nisi justificatus. Credens autem in eum qui justificat impium, a fide incipit; ut bona opera non præcedentia quod meruit, sed consequentia quod accepit, ostendant.

(Rom. iii. 31). Augustine loves to liken the five porches (John v. 2, 3), to which the sick were brought from their unseen chambers of suffering, and wherein they lay exposed to the sight of all men, without being for all this a whit nearer to a recovery of their health hereby, to liken, I say, these, and the operation of these, to the operation of the law: for that in a manner not dissimilar drew sin and sinners from their hiding places, but all the while accomplished nothing for the effectual healing of the hurts and diseases of men's souls.[1]

On one more passage in this Epistle, and one that eminently brings out what is characteristic in Augustine's exposition, some further words may be added. It is well known that there have been in the Church two different expositions of Rom. vii. 7–25. Is the Apostle there describing the conflicts and struggles of the regenerate man *inter renovandum?* or is he describing those of the man as yet not partaker of Christ, but only brought by the law under strong convictions of sin and of the demands which that holy law makes on his obedience? Augustine, in the early part of his Christian life, and in conformity with the interpretation of the passage which had been prevalent in all the times before him, understood St. Paul to be here setting forth the struggles of the man not actually partaker as yet of the redemption which is by Christ Jesus. Thus in such writings of his as were composed and published at this period, we have an exposition of the passage according to this earlier scheme;[2] while at the close of his life he states, what indeed his treatment

---

[1] *Serm.* cxx. 3. These porches he describes as portantes ægrotos, non sanantes; prodentes, non curantes.

[2] As *De Div. Quæst.* 66; *Ad Simplicianum*, i. 1.

of this passage in many of his later writings would without this statement make sufficiently manifest, namely, that he had seen cause to change his view, giving at the same time the reasons which had moved him to this.[1] In this matter also we may doubtless trace the influence which that same contest with the Pelagians exercised upon his whole habit of thought, and on the form of his theology. These, as is well known, magnified the natural powers of man, gave all to nature, which they did not consider now to be otherwise than in its original integrity and as it came from God; and however *in word* they might attribute something to grace, yet in fact that grace, when more closely inspected, was but nature in disguise. And it seemed to him that the passage, understood as he had once understood it, putting as it did language like the following into the mouth of the man not as yet under grace, 'I delight in the law of God after the inward man' (ver. 22), favoured too much that erroneous estimate of the powers of our unrenewed nature, which was by those heretics entertained, cast a certain slight on that sanctifying and renewing grace of the Spirit whereby alone we either will or do that which is well pleasing to God.[2]

I may be allowed without presumption here to observe that I do not believe Augustine to have been right in

---

[1] *Retract.* i. 23 : Propter hanc itaque concupiscentiam motusque ipsos quibus ita resistitur, ut tamen sint in nobis, potest quisque sanctus, jam sub gratiâ positus, dicere ista omnia. Cf. *Con. duas Ep. Pel.* i. 10. 22.

[2] Non video, quomodo diceret homo sub lege : Condelector legi secundum interiorem hominem, cum ipsa delectatio boni quâ etiam non consentit ad malum non timore poenæ sed amore justitiæ (hoc est enim condelectari), non nisi gratiæ deputanda sit.

thus going back from the Church's and from his own earlier exposition of this chapter. There would be much more in his objection, if there were only the alternatives of accepting these words as the voice of the natural man, or else of the man renewed in the spirit of his mind. But a third course is possible, namely, to contemplate them as the utterance of the man convinced, and that by the Spirit of God, of sin and of righteousness, on the way to, but not having yet arrived at, the blessed freedom of the spirit in Christ Jesus, seeing it afar off, and struggling toward, though not grasping it as yet.

To Augustine himself it was abundantly clear that while he was escaping from one danger, he was, by the new interpretation which he favoured, running into another. If that which he abandoned might seem to play into the hands of the Pelagians, ascribing too much to the natural powers of man, did not that which he now supported, and which his influence caused to be received without a question in the Western Church for more than a thousand years, ascribe too little to the regenerate man? did it not set the standard of his obedience too low? He is quite aware that this charge might be brought against it, and is very earnest in vindicating his exposition of this 'difficult and perilous passage,' for so he calls it himself,[1] from all Antinomian abuse; in giving all care lest the evil of men should turn that which in itself was wholesome food into poison.[2] It is plain that to such abuse it would be much more exposed according to his later exposition than according to that of the earlier Church,

[1] Difficilis et periculosus locus (*Serm.* cliv. 1).
[2] *Serm.* cli. 1: Ne homines male sumentes salubrem cibum, vertant in venenum.

though of course this in itself was not sufficient reason to reject it.

The words which yield themselves the most readily to such an abuse, which might be and have been the most eagerly seized by the false-hearted, by all who are seeking in Christ's Gospel not strength to deliver them from sin, but excuses for remaining in sin, are the concluding ones of the chapter, 'So then with the mind I myself serve the law of God, but with the flesh the law of sin' (vii. 25). Augustine does not fail to urge that all this impotence for good whereof the regenerate man here or elsewhere complains has solely to do with the interior region of his heart, does but express his inability to bring the thoughts and desires of his heart into a perfect conformity to the will of God, and has nothing at all to do with the exterior sphere of his acts.[1] So long as we bear about this body of sin, we shall not altogether be delivered from the first; for the promise is not, even to those who walk in the Spirit, 'Ye shall not *have* the lust of the flesh;' but it is most truly, 'Ye shall not *fulfil* the lust of the flesh' (Gal. v. 16).[2] And he distinguishes between the *inhabitatio*

---

[1] It is one thing, as he observes, concupiscere; another, post concupiscentias ire. *De Nupt. et Concup.* ii. 31: Quod sic intelligendum est, mente servio legi Dei, non consentiendo legi peccati, carne autem servio legi peccati, habendo desideria peccati, quibus etsi non consentio, nondum tamen penitus careo. See the four preceding chapters, which have all an important bearing on this subject. Cf. *Enarr. in Ps.* lxxv. 3. Thus too on the confession of the Apostle (for he naturally rejects altogether the unworthy evasion that St. Paul is speaking of another, not of himself), 'The good that I would I do not; but the evil which I would not that I do' (ver. 19), he asks (*Serm.* cliv.): Itane Apostolus Paulus nolebat facere adulterium, et faciebat adulterium? nolebat esse avarus, et erat avarus? Cf. *Con. duas Ep. Pel.* i. 10. 18.

[2] *Ep.* cxcvi. 2.

peccati, over which the faithful man still mourns, and the *regnum peccati*, which in him has been destroyed (Rom. vi. 12). The Canaanite *will* dwell in the land, but he is under tribute.[1] The soldier of Christ is not in these words complaining of defeat, but grudges to be always at war, never to be able to lay aside his weapons, even while he thankfully owns that in Christ Jesus he is evermore a conqueror.[2]

Augustine brings into closest connexion with this passage in the Romans, and gives a right interpretation of, those other words of the same Apostle, so often misapplied in his own time, and so often misapplied still, ' The letter killeth, but the Spirit giveth life' (2 Cor. iii. 6). They are frequently taken as though 'the letter' meant the letter of Scripture, which profited nothing, which might often even be so misused as to ' kill,' at any rate would not make alive, unless the inner spiritual meaning, or ' the spirit,' were discovered and drawn out. This assertion, which of course has its truth,—indeed Augustine tells us that, used in this sense, the passage was one of his great teacher St. Ambrose's favourite sayings,[3]—has yet nothing to do with what the Apostle is stating here; and the fact of this explanation having both in old times and new acquired so

[1] See an important passage for his teaching on all this subject, *Exp. Ep. ad Gal.* v. 17, 18. He draws a distinction perhaps verbally hardly to be justified, but of which the attention is plain: Aliud est peccare, aliud habere peccatum.

[2] Thus in affecting words (*Serm.* cli. 8): Nolo semper vincere; sed volo aliquando ad pacem venire. And again, on the present conflict with indwelling sin: Quamdiu vitiis repugnatur, plena pax non est, quia et illa quæ resistunt periculoso debellantur prælio, et illa quæ victa sunt nondum securo triumphantur otio, sed adhuc solicito premuntur imperio.

[3] *Conf.* vi. 4.

wide a currency is a notable example of the tendency to isolate statements of Scripture, and to interpret them independently of the context which can alone rightly explain them. 'The letter' here, according to all the necessities of the context, is the law, called 'the letter' because *written* on tables of stone; the whole dispensation, commanding and threatening, yet not quickening, of the Old Testament. This, as the Apostle, in harmony with all his other teaching, declares, 'killeth,' not merely negatively, in that it does not make alive, but positively; for, as Augustine admirably brings out, the true parallel and interpretation of the words is to be found in those other words of St. Paul, 'I was alive without the law once, &c.;' while 'the Spirit' here is that dispensation of the Spirit of which he speaks Rom. viii. 1–11, as that in which, and in which only, resides the power of making men alive unto God.[1]

[1] *De Spir. et Litt.* 4: Doctrina quippe illa, quâ mandatum accipimus continenter recteque vivendi, littera est occidens, nisi adsit vivificans Spiritus. Neque enim solo illo modo intelligendum est quod legimus, Littera occidit, Spiritus autem vivificat; ut aliquid figurate scriptum, cujus est absurda proprietas, non accipiamus sicut littera sonat, sed aliud quod significat intuentes interiorem hominem spirituali intelligentiâ nutriamus; . . . . sed etiam illo, eoque vel maxime, quo apertissime alio loco dicit, Concupiscentiam nesciebam, nisi lex diceret: Non concupisces. And 5: Volo demonstrare illud quod ait Apostolus: Littera occidit, Spiritus autem vivificat, non de figuratis locutionibus dictum, quamvis et illinc congruenter accipiatur, sed potius de lege aperte quod est malum prohibente; and 19: Lex enim sine adjuvante Spiritu procul dubio est littera occidens; cum vero adest vivificans Spiritus, hoc ipsum intus conscriptum facit diligi, quod foris scriptum lex faciebat timeri. Yet Augustine is not himself uniformly true to the right explanation, clearly as he has stated it here, for see *De Doctr. Christ.* iii. 5.

CHAPTER VIII.

MISCELLANEOUS EXAMPLES OF AUGUSTINE'S INTERPRETATION OF SCRIPTURE.

I ADD one chapter more, that so I may produce a few miscellaneous specimens of Augustine's insight into the Word of God, and of the tact and skill with which he unfolded to others the riches which that Word contained.

Matt. ii. 1, 2. While angels announce Christ to the shepherds, a star announces Him to the Magi. There was a special fitness, as Augustine loves to bring out, in each of these announcements; in each case the channel by which the announcement is made has its own and its special fitness. He is full of what we may call the poetry of the Nativity, and returns to it again and again.[1]

Matt. xix. 23-26. His explanation of this passage furnishes an excellent example of the manner in which he

[1] Thus *Serm.* cxcix.: Pastoribus angeli, Magis stella Christum demonstrat; utrisque loquitur lingua cælorum, quia lingua cessaverat prophetarum. And again on the Magi in particular: Illi Magi primi ex gentibus Christum Dominum cognoverunt, et nondum ejus sermone commoti stellam sibi apparentem, et pro infante Verbo visibiliter loquentem velut linguam cæli secuti sunt. And again, *Serm.* cci. : Quid erat illa stella quæ nec unquam antea inter sidera apparuit, nec postea demonstranda permansit? Quid erat nisi magnifica lingua cæli, quæ narraret gloriam cæli, quæ inusitatum Virginis partum inusitato splendore clamaret; cui postea non apparenti Evangelium toto orbe succederet.

sometimes clears away a difficulty by penetrating further into the meaning of the words which present it, so setting himself at their moral centre, and from that centre unfolding them. The disciples had seen the rich young man go sorrowing away, and heard the Lord's comment on his withdrawal, 'How hardly shall they that have riches enter into the kingdom of God;' whereupon they exclaim, 'Who then can be saved?' This question of theirs, Augustine observes, showed how deeply they had entered into the meaning of their Lord's words. To those who had not so done, the difficulty of a *rich man's* entering into the kingdom would not have appeared to involve a difficulty for *all*; nay, from the very exceptional character of the assertion, many might have drawn an assurance that for the poor it was not difficult, but easy. Whence then this question, implying a misgiving, and one generated by that very saying of their Lord, whether any man could be saved? It arose from this, as he admirably brings out, namely, that the disciples saw into the deeper significance of what their Lord had just uttered; they understood that the 'rich'[1] of whom He spake were not merely the rich in possessions, but the rich in desires, the lovers of riches, whether they had them, or had them not. And thus out of a profoundly painful sense of the difficulty

[1] After much that is admirable, he goes on to say (*Enarr. in Ps.* li. 9): Illi apud se dicentes, Quinam poterit salvari, quid attenderunt? Non facultates, sed cupiditates. Viderunt enim etiam ipsos pauperes, etsi non habentes pecuniam tamen habere avaritiam. And again (*Quæst. Evang.* ii. 47): Eo manifestatur omnes cupidos, etiam si facultatibus hujus mundi careant, ad hoc genus divitum quod est reprehensum pertinere; quia postea dixerunt qui audiebant: Et quis poterit salvus fieri? cum incomparabiliter major turba sit pauperum: videlicet intelligentes in eo numero deputari etiam illos, qui quanquam talia non habeant, tamen habendi cupiditate rapiuntur.

of being really poor, that is, poor in spirit, of detaching the soul from the love of the creature, and from trusting in the world, 'they were exceedingly amazed, saying, Who then can be saved?' And how well he unfolds the Lord's further declaration, 'With men this is impossible, but with God all things are possible;' showing that these words do not mean that God will dispense with this law of his kingdom, since otherwise so many would be excluded from it, that He will widen the eye of the needle till it is large enough for the man of worldly lusts (actually rich or not makes no difference), to pass through it with all his baggage; but rather, 'With God all things are possible,' is the same as saying, 'All things are possible to him that believeth.' This, which it is impossible for man to accomplish in his own strength, namely, such a making of himself poor in spirit, such a loosening of himself from the bands which bind him so fast to the world and to the creature, shall yet be possible for him in the strength of God. The impossible thing, which yet is possible with God, is not the saving of the rich man in and with his riches, but the making of the rich man poor, one of God's poor, and so an inheritor of his kingdom.[1]

Matt. xxvi. 60. The question has been often asked, and not always sufficiently answered, wherein were the witnesses that witnessed against the Lord *false* witnesses,

---

[1] *Quæst. Ev.* ii. 47: Quod autem ait, Quæ impossibilia sunt apud homines, possibilia sunt apud Deum, non ita accipiendum est, quod cupidi et superbi, qui nomine illius divitis significati sunt, in regnum cælorum sint intraturi cum suis cupiditatibus et superbiâ, sed possibile est Deo ut per verbum ejus . . . . a cupiditate temporalium ad caritatem æternorum, et a perniciosâ superbiâ ad humilitatem saluberrimam convertantur. He has discussed all the questions which grow out of the Lord's interview with this rich young man *most* fully, *Ep.* clvii. 23-39.

as by St. Matthew, and by St. Mark as well (xiv. 57), they are styled? The Lord *had* said, 'Destroy this temple, and in three days I will raise it up' (John ii. 19). Wherein then did they witness untruly? Not, certainly, as some will have it, in taking literally what He had spoken figuratively. This might have been dulness of apprehension; it would not have constituted falsehood. But, as Augustine rightly urges, a very small turn which they gave to his words in reporting them, entirely altered their character. He had said, 'If you destroy, I will rebuild;' He had never proposed, nor even seemed to propose, as in the wantonness of power, Himself to destroy and throw down the holy temple of God, that so He might have the opportunity of displaying his might in the building up of it anew ; He had but presented Himself as the repairer of the ruin which they might effect ; and the slight alteration of his *Solvite* into the *Solvam* which they, whether intentionally or otherwise, put into his mouth, quite altered the character of the saying; while at the same time the falsehood, to secure a readier acceptance, preserved certain features of the truth.[1]

Luke iv. 13. How much of practical and edifying Augustine often draws from single words in the Scripture. Thus, on the hint which the third Evangelist furnishes in his record of the Temptation, that when the devil departed from our Lord, it was only 'for a season,' he takes occasion to bring this first Temptation, which signalized the opening of Christ's ministry, into relation with the second, which signalized its close, compares and contrasts the Temptation of the wilderness and that of the garden (Matt. xxvi. 36-42). The enemy in the first tries to

---

[1] *Serm.* cccxv. 1: Vicina voluit esse falsitas veritati.

overcome his constancy by bringing to bear against it all *pleasurable* things, in the last all *painful* things. He knocked first at the door of desire, and, when that proved shut against him, at the door of fear. And as it fared with the Master, so shall it fare with each one of the servants; they, too, shall have to tread both on the lion and the adder, to resist now a threatening, now a flattering, world.[1]

Luke xxiii. 39–43. Augustine magnifies often the heroic character of the faith of the penitent malefactor, how far it exceeded all ordinary faith, how far it exceeded in some respects even the faith of Apostles themselves.[2]

---

[1] *Enarr.* 3ᵃ *in Ps.* xxx. 5: Hujusmodi pugnæ exemplum ipse tibi Imperator tuus, qui propter te etiam tentari dignatus est, in se demonstravit. Et primo tentatus est illecebris; quia tentata est in illo janua cupiditatis, quando eum tentavit diabolus, dicens, Dic lapidibus istis ut panes fiant; Adora me, et dabo tibi regna ista; Mitte te deorsum quia scriptum est, Quia Angelis suis mandavit de te, et in manibus tollent te. Omnis hæc illecebra cupiditatem tentat. At ubi clausam januam invenit cupiditatis in eo qui tentabatur pro nobis, convertit se ad tentandam januam timoris, et præparavit illi passionem. Denique hoc dicit Evangelista, Et consummatâ tentatione diabolus recessit ab eo ad tempus. Quid est, ad tempus? Tanquam rediturus, et tentaturus januam timoris, quia clausum invenit januam cupiditatis. Cf. *Serm.* cclxxxiv.: Quid ait Evangelista? Postquam perfecit diabolus omnem tentationem; omnem, sed ad illecebras pertinentem. Restabat alia tentatio in asperis et duris, in sævis, in atrocibus atque immitibus restabat alia tentatio. Hoc sciens Evangelista, quid peractum esset, quid restaret, ait, Postquam complevit diabolus omnem tentationem, recessit ab eo ad tempus. Discessit ab eo, id est, insidians serpens, venturus est rugiens leo, sed vincet eum qui conculcabit leonem et draconem.

[2] *Serm.* ccxxxii. 6: Magna fides: huic fidei quid addi possit, ignoro. Titubaverunt ipsi qui viderunt Christum mortuos suscitantem; credidit ille qui videbat secum in ligno pendentem. Quando illi titubaverunt, tunc ille credidit. Qualem fructum Christus de arido ligno percepit? . . . . Non solum credebat resurrecturum, sed etiam regnaturum. Pendenti, crucifixo, cruento, hærenti, Cum veneris, inquit,

Nor does he fail to take note of the symbolic character of the whole wondrous transaction, and the prophecy that was embodied in the penitent and obdurate malefactor, and in the bearing severally of the one and the other to Christ, of all the after relations of men to the crucified Lord; one portion of the sinful race turning to Him, looking and living; the other turning away, and abiding in death.[1]

John xviii. 1. St. John alone mentions that it was in a 'garden' that the Lord's last and decisive conflict with all the powers of darkness found place. Augustine brings beautifully together, and notes as one of the minor harmonies of Scripture, that as it was in a garden that all was lost, so it was only meet that in a garden all should be won back again.[2]

John xix. 34. Augustine's commentary on this verse is a happy illustration of the rich typical allusiveness which he traces in Scripture, of the way in which he links the far and the near, and brings many passages, apparently the most remote from one another, to bear upon some one, and to light it up. At the same time what he here has written does not less notably illustrate what we sometimes have to complain of in him, namely, the

in regnum tuum: Et illi, Nos sperabamus. Ubi spem latro invenit, discipulus perdidit. Cf. *Serm.* xxxii. 2; and my *Studies in the New Testament*, 4th edit. p. 312.

[1] *Serm.* cclxxxv. 2: Ita factæ sunt tres cruces, tres caussæ. Unus latronum Christo insultabat, alter sua mala confessus Christi se misericordiæ commendabat. Crux Christi in medio non fuit supplicium, sed tribunal: de cruce quippe insultantem damnavit, credentem liberavit. Timete, insultantes; gaudete, credentes: hoc faciet in claritate, quod fecit in humilitate.

[2] Conveniens erat ut ibi funderetur sanguis medici, ubi primum cœperat morbus ægroti.

pressing of an emphasis which belongs only to his Latin translation, and which disappears so soon as ever reference is made to the original. Such an emphasis he here finds in the 'aperuit' of his Latin Version; marking, as he says the word does, that a door was opened in the sacred side, by which streams of life flowed freely forth; while 'percussit,' which he observes that the Evangelist of a purpose did *not* use, would be the exact equivalent, which 'aperuit' is very far from being, of the ἔνυξεν of the original.[1]

Acts ii. 1–4. The giving of the law from Mount Sinai has been often compared, especially in modern times, with the giving of the new law, or rather of the Gospel, from that other Mount, where the Lord sat down with his disciples (Matt. v. 1); and the circumstances which attended the speaking of that word of God and this, were severally very characteristic of the dispensations which they severally ushered in. But of old the parallel and the contrast were rather drawn between Sinai and that upper chamber where the disciples were assem-

---

[1] *In Joh.* xix. 34, *Tract.* cxx.: Vigilanti verbo Evangelista usus est, ut non diceret, latus ejus percussit aut vulneravit aut quid aliud, sed aperuit: ut illuc quodammodo vitæ ostium panderetur, unde sacramenta Ecclesiæ manaverunt sine quibus ad vitam quæ vera vita est, non intratur. Ille sanguis in remissionem fusus est peccatorum: aqua illa salutare temperat poculum: hæc et lavacrum præstat et potum. Hoc prænuntiabat quod Noë in latere arcæ ostium facere jussus est quâ intrarent animalia, quæ non erant diluvio peritura, quibus præfigurabatur Ecclesia. Propter hoc prima mulier facta est de latere viri dormientis, et appellata est vita materque vivorum. And *Serm.* cccxi. 3, he brings this passage very beautifully into connexion with John x. 7 : Christus est janua. Et tibi est ostium apertum quando est latus ejuslanceâ perforatum. Quid inde manavit recole, et elige quâ possis intrare. De latere Domini aqua sanguisque profluxit. In uno est mundatio tua, in altero redemtio tua.

bled, waiting the promise of the Father; and how strikingly Augustine draws out the parallel of likeness and opposition between the two, may be seen in the passage given below; one out of many similar passages that might be quoted.[1] Nor does he miss the relation which this day (wherein, for one prophetic moment at least, the distinction of languages disappeared) bore to that earlier day in which the tongues of mankind were divided; this outward division being, of course, but the sign and consequence of an inward division of spirits (Gen. xi. 1–9). Here was a pledge and a promise, that the one language and one speech which had then been lost, should yet through the Church be given back, that a day should arrive when all should be again of 'one lip' as at the first.[2]

[1] *Serm.* clv. 6: Sed videte ibi quomodo, et hic quomodo. Ibi plebs longe stabat, timor erat, amor non erat; nam usque adeo timuerunt, ut dicerent ad Moÿsem, Loquere tu ad nos, et non nobis loquatur Dominus, ne moriamur. Descendit ergo, sicut scriptum est, Deus in Sinâ in igne, sed plebem longe stantem territans, et digito suo scribens in lapide, non in corde. Huc autem quando venit Spiritus Sanctus, congregati erant fideles in unum; nec in monte terruit, sed intravit in domum. De cælo quidem factus est subito sonus, quasi ferretur flatus vehemens: sonuit, sed nullus expavit. Audisti sonum, vide et ignem, quia et in monte utrumque erat, et ignis et sonitus; sed illic etiam fumus, hic vero ignis serenus. Visæ sunt enim illis linguæ divisæ, velut ignis. Numquid de longinquo territans? Absit, nam insedit super unumquemque eorum, et cœperunt linguis loqui, sicut Spiritus dabat eis pronuntiare. A student who wished to realize to himself the infinite *productiveness* of Augustine during the Middle Ages, and the extent to which those ages lived on him, could do no better than compare this passage, or other similar ones which it would be easy to adduce, with some of Adam of St. Victor's hymns, as for instance with his sublime hymn on the giving of the Holy Ghost, quoted in my *Sacred Latin Poetry*, 3rd edit. p. 179, or again, on the same subject, p. 192.

[2] *Serm.* cclxxi.: Sicut enim post diluvium superba impietas homi-

Acts ix. 4. 'Why persecutest thou Me?' Many have noted before and since the common cause which the Lord in his heavenly glory makes with his suffering members upon earth, so that the wrong done to them He feels and resents as a wrong done to Himself; but few, if any, with such emphasis, with such frequent recurrence to it, with illustrations so happily drawn from the common speech of men; for they in like manner exclaim that *they* are hurt, when indeed it is foot or hand or some other member that is injured, the head, alike in things natural and things spiritual, suffering with the body; and refusing, alike in word and in act, to be separated from it.[1]

num turrim contra Dominum ædificavit excelsam, quando per linguas diversas dividi meruit genus humanum, ut unaquæque gens linguâ propriâ loqueretur, ne ab aliis intelligeretur; sic humilis fidelium pietas earum linguarum diversitatem Ecclesiæ contulit unitati, ut quod discordia dissipaverat, colligeret caritas, et humani generis tanquam unius corporis membra dispersa ad unum caput Christum compaginata redigerentur, et in sancti corporis unitatem dilectionis igne conflarentur. Cf. *Enarr. in Ps.* liv. 10: Spiritus superbiæ dispersit linguas, Spiritus Sanctus congregavit linguas; *De Civ. Dei,* xviii. 49; *Enarr.* 2ª *in Ps.* xviii. 10.

[1] *Enarr.* 2ª *in Ps.* xxx. 1: Hoc autem corpus [Ecclesiæ] nisi connexione caritatis adhæreret capiti suo, ut unus fieret ex capite et corpore, non de cælo quendam persecutorem corripiens diceret, Saule, Saule, quid me persequeris? Quando eum jam in cælo sedentem nullus homo tangebat, quomodo eum Saulus in terrâ sæviens adversus Christianos aliquo modo injuriâ percellebat? Non ait, Quid sanctos meos, quid servos meos; sed, Quid me persequeris, hoc est, quid membra mea? Caput pro membris clamabat, et membra in se caput transfigurabat. Vocem namque pedis suscipit lingua. Quando forte in turbâ contritus pes dolet, clamat lingua, Calcas me, non enim ait, Calcas pedem meum; sed se dixit calcari, quam nemo tetigit. Sed pes qui calcatus est, a linguâ non separatus est. He loves to quote Ephes. v. 31, 'And they two shall be one flesh,' in illustration; cf. *Enarr. in Ps.* lxxxvi. 2; cxl. 1. And so too with reference to 1 Cor. xii. 26 and the mutual care which the members of Christ's mystical body should have one of another, the very highest being prompt

Acts x. 9-16. There are two ways in which the vision of the sheet, full of 'all manner of four-footed beasts of the earth, and wild beasts, and creeping things, and fowls of the air,' and the command addressed to Peter, 'Kill and eat,' may be understood. Either Peter was thus taught that the Levitical distinction between clean and unclean meats had ceased, that this fixed line of practical demarcation between Jew and Gentile was taken away, and left to draw his own conclusion that the separation itself, which this distinction so much helped to maintain, was not intended to subsist any longer; or else, which seems to me the better, though the rarer interpretation of the vision, to say with Augustine, that all these unclean things in the vessel *represented the heathen*. This is more agreeable to ver. 16: 'What God has cleansed, that call not thou common;' for assuredly it was not the hitherto forbidden meats, but the heathen, and more particularly Cornelius, whom God had cleansed, and whom Peter declares (ver. 28) that he, through this vision, had learned not to call common or unclean. The only difficulty here is what the commandment, 'Kill and eat,' will then mean; but this, seeming at first sight the weak point of this interpretation, is in reality very far from so being. It only needs that we keep in mind the higher sacramental uses which eating has in almost all religions, emi-

---

to serve the lowest, he has another lively comparison, *Enarr. in Ps.* cxxx. 1 : Numquid quia in corpore pes quasi longe videtur ab oculis (illi enim sunt locati in sublimitate, illi autem infra positi), quando forte pes spinam calcaverit, deserunt oculi; et non, sicut videmus, totum corpus contrahitur, et sedet homo, curvatur spina dorsi, ut quæratur spina quæ hæsit in plantâ ? Omnia membra quidquid possunt faciunt, ut de infimo et exiguo loco spina, quæ inhæserat, educatur.

nently in the Christian, to discover the key to the meaning of these words. That which is eaten is entirely incorporated into and assimilated with the eater: there is thus the innermost identification of the one and the other. The command then to Peter is, in fact, that he should boldly incorporate the heathen into that body of which he is here, and for the moment, contemplated as the organ and the mouth.[1] Augustine explains further, and no doubt rightly, the exceptional case of the baptism of Cornelius, who, with those that belonged to him, received the Holy Spirit, not as others, in baptism or after, but before; of which, he observes, there is no other example in all Scripture [2]—namely, that it was for the entire removing of Peter's doubts whether the Gentile converts should be admitted into the fellowship of the Church at once, and without the intermediate step of first becoming Jews. It was the Lord Himself deciding the question, and saying to his Apostle, 'Why doubtest thou about water? Behold, *I* already am here.'[3]

---

[1] *Serm.* cxxv. 9: Petro dictum est, Macta et manduca, ut ostenderentur gentes crediturae et intraturae in corpus Ecclesiae, sicut quod manducamus in corpus nostrum intrat. Cf. *Serm.* cxlix. 5–7: Occidendi ergo erant et manducandi, id est ut interficeretur in eis vita praeterita, quâ non noverant Christum, et transierent in corpus ejus, tanquam in novam vitam . . . . societatis Ecclesiae. Cf. *Serm.* cclxvi. 6; and *Enarr. in Ps.* ciii. 11. Grotius, who is much readier to accept Scripture mysteries than he is commonly esteemed, follows him here, though without allusion to his predecessor: Linteum de caelo delapsum intellexit esse Ecclesiam caelitus collectam (Apoc. xxi. 2). Nec in Ecclesiam involvuntur, nisi jam mundati. Occidere, est tollere in eis quod restat de veteri homine; *manducare, sibi adunare.*

[2] *Serm.* cclxix. 2 : Singulare occurrit exemplum.

[3] *Serm.* xcix. 12: Quid de aquâ dubitas ? jam *Ego* hic sum. Cf. *Serm.* cclxvi. 7.

Rom. xi. 2-4. On that 'I only am left,' of Elijah (1 Kin. xix. 10, 14), quoted here, with the rebuke of God which follows, 'I have reserved to Myself' not thee only, as thou supposest, but 'seven thousand men who have not bowed the knee to the image of Baal,' Augustine makes many profitable remarks; likening the present aspect of the Church to a barn floor, where there shows to the eye at first sight little else but a heap of chaff. Yet if one look more narrowly, if, stretching out his hand, he grasp a portion of what is there, and then make a separation with the breath of his mouth as with a purging blast, there will be revealed to him precious grains which were concealed from him before. And as with that handful on which he has made this experiment, so will it be through the whole mass. The chaff indeed first meets the eye, yet among it and beneath it many golden grains lie hidden; separated, it may be, by intervening chaff, and not touching one another; and each one hardly knowing of more than itself; yet not therefore to give way to the temptation of exclaiming with the impatient prophet of old, 'I only am left.'[1]

1 Cor. xv. 22. Much, as is well known, has been

---

[1] Thus *Enarr. in Ps.* xxv.: Grana cum cœperint triturari, inter paleas jam se non tangunt; ita quasi se non noverunt, quia intercedit palea. Et quicunque longius attendit aream, paleam solam putat; nisi diligentius intueatur, nisi manum porrigat, nisi spiritu oris, id est, flatu purgante discernat, difficile pervenit ad discretionem granorum. Ergo aliquando et ipsa grana ita sunt quasi sejuncta ab invicem, et non se tangentia, ut putet unusquisque cum profecerit, quod solus sit. Hæc cogitatio, fratres, Eliam tentavit, tantum virum. Cf. *in Ps.* xlvii. § 10; *Serm.* cccxi. 10: Absit ut de areâ tanti Patrisfamilias desperem. Qui longe aream videt, solam paleam putat: invenit grana, qui novit inspicere. Ubi te offendit palea, ibi latet granorum massa.

made of the '*all*' and '*all*' in the words of St. Paul: 'For as in Adam *all* die, even so in Christ shall *all* be made alive,' as though the second 'all' must needs extend as far as the first; and since the first 'all' embraces the whole race of men, for there is no one who has not through Adam's sin come under sentence of natural death, so some have concluded that the second 'all' must have as wide a reach; and that a co-extensive 'all' will through Christ's righteousness be partakers of life eternal. But Augustine shows what is the true antithesis between these 'alls;' that Paul does but say, 'All who die, die in Adam; all who live, live through Christ.' In this respect indeed they are co-extensive, that none die, except as involved in Adam's sin; none live, except as justified through Christ's righteousness—in this sense, but no other.[1]

1 Cor. xv. 56. 'The sting of death is sin.' St. Paul is often understood to say that what gives to death its bitterness, and so imparts to it a 'sting,' is sin and the sense of sin. The words, however, as Augustine urges, cohere much more intimately with all which the Apostle teaches of death as the fruit and consequence of sin; and their true parallel and explanation is to be found in Rom. v. 12, 'Sin entered into the world, and death by sin' Sin is that weapon of mortal temper which kills those that otherwise would have lived for ever. 'The sting of death' ($\kappa\acute{\epsilon}\nu\tau\rho o\nu$ $\theta a\nu\acute{a}\tau o\nu$) in fact is equivalent to 'the deadly sting' ($\kappa\acute{\epsilon}\nu\tau\rho o\nu$ $\theta a\nu\acute{a}\sigma\iota\mu o\nu$), though the personifi-

---

[1] *De Civ. Dei*, xiii. 23 : Non quia omnes qui in Adam moriuntur, membra erunt Christi : sed ideo dictum est, *omnes* atque *omnes*, quia sicut nemo corpore animali nisi in Adam moritur, ita nemo corpore spiritali nisi in Christo vivificatur. Cf. *Serm.* ccxciii. 9; and on Rom. v. 18, exposed to like abuse, his words, *Ep.* clvii. 13 ; *Op. Imp. con. Jul.* i. 135.

cation of death which goes immediately before causes a little difficulty in precisely seizing the force of the words. And exactly in the same way, when the Apostle presently before demands, 'O death, where is thy sting?' he does not mean, 'Where is thy bitterness for him that believes?' He might very fitly have asked this, but he does not so here; and the precise meaning of this triumphant question is rather, Where is that sin, by which as by a deadly weapon thou didst once make such havoc and extend such ravages among the children of men? It is abolished by the free justification of the sinner, and therefore thou, who art nothing without it, and wouldest not have been at all except for it, shalt, in the kingdom of the Son of God, and for the children of the resurrection, be also abolished.[1]

2 Cor. xii. 2. There are certain passages in Scripture to which Augustine returns again and again; from which he seems never weary of drawing out the lessons wherewith they are fraught for him. This is one of them; so wonderfully instructive does it seem to him that a Paul, after all his experience, should need an antidote to pride; that this should have been vouchsafed to him in the shape of 'a messenger from Satan' (what exactly this was he does not attempt to define, but suggests that it may have been some sharp pain or sickness of body); that he, ask-

---

[1] *Pecc. Mer. et Rem.* iii. 11: Aculeus mortis peccatum; aculeus autem quâ mors facta est, non quem mors fecit; peccato enim morimur, non morte peccamus. Sic itaque dictum est, aculeus mortis, quomodo lignum vitæ, non quod hominis vita faceret, sed quo vita hominis fieret. Sic enim dicimus et poculum mortis, quo aliquis mortuus sit vel mori possit, non quod moriens mortuusve confecerit. Aculeus itaque mortis peccatum est, peccati punctu mortificatum est genus humanum. Cf. *Con. duas Epp. Pel.* iv. 4; *Serm.* ccxcix. 10.

ing to have this thorn in the flesh removed, should have had his prayer at once refused and granted; the actual boon he asked, which would have profited him nothing, but rather the contrary, withheld from him, while at the same time a better boon, one which should effectually promote his highest spiritual life, was through this very denial imparted to him. None that I know have dwelt with such peculiar affection on the teaching of this Scripture, or drawn from it lessons so profound as he has continually done.[1]

Gal. v. 19. In proof that charity is the first and the chief of all graces, Augustine does not fail to urge that in this catalogue of ' the fruit of the Spirit,' which St. Paul sets over against ' the works of the flesh,' it is with this charity he commences, that on this, so to speak, the whole beautiful cluster depends.[2]

Phil. ii. 12, 13. Augustine's explanation of this passage is directly opposed to that of the modern Roman

---

[1] *Enarr. in Ps.* xcviii. 13 : Tam perfectus erat, ut tamen timendum esset ne extolleretur ; nam non poneret Deus medicamentum, ubi vulnus non esset. Et rogavit ut tolleretur æger ille rogavit ut auferretur medicamentum : Propter quod ter Dominum rogavi, inquit, ut auferret eum a me, et dixit mihi, Sufficit tibi gratia mea, nam virtus in infirmitate perficitur. Ego novi quem curo ; non mihi det qui ægrotat consilium. Tanquam emplastrum mordax urit te, sed sanat te. Rogat medicum ut tollat emplastrum, et non tollit, nisi cum fuerit sanatum quo posuerat. *Serm.* clxiii. 8: O venenum quod non curatur nisi veneno—a magnificent passage, but too long to quote ; cf. *Enarr. in Ps.* cxxx. 7 ; and *in Ps.* xc. *Serm.* ii. 6.

[2] *Serm.* xxxvii. 28 : Vide ipsum botrum, unde incipiat. Enumeratis omnibus spinis in ignem mittendis, fructus autem Spiritûs est, inquit, caritas. Et ab hoc capite, ab hâc tanquam radice cetera contexuntur : gaudium, pax, longanimitas, benignitas, bonitas, fides, mansuetudo, continentia. Unde iste botrus pulcher? Quia pendet a caritate.

Catholic Church. This, as a necessary consequence of its doctrine that the measure of a man's holiness is the measure of his justification, teaches a constant insecurity on the part of every man concerning his state of grace; and, since in no man that holiness can be perfect, it could not teach otherwise; and this passage, with another from the Old Testament,[1] is mainly relied on in proof.[2] It would be out of place to show here that the other has nothing to do with this matter; but the present is as little in point. What 'fear' is here urged Augustine tells us—not the fear, or rather doubt, whether ours is a state of grace, but the fear of falling from that state, the ' metus vigilantiæ,' not the ' timor diffidentiæ;'[3] or, as sometimes with reference to the verse following he brings out, the fear of humility. You are to ' work out your own salvation;' but at the same time with an awful sense that it is not your work, but God's work in you and through you, ' with fear and trembling,' being mindful how solemn a thing it is to be brought into immediate contact with ' the powers of the world to come,' to have God working in you; who may cease working, if you hinder his godly motions, attributing in your pride any part of the work to yourselves; and then, when He ceases, all will be at a stand.[4] It may well be supposed that

---

[1] Eccles. ix. 1, which appears in the Vulgate: Nescit homo, utrum amore an odio dignus sit.

[2] See ESTIUS, *in loc.*, or any other Roman Catholic expositor.

[3] *Enarr. in Ps.* li.: Quare cum timore? Quapropter qui se putat stare, videat ne cadat. Quare cum tremore? Intendens te ipsum, ne et tu tenteris.

[4] *Serm.* cxxxi. 3: Depressa implentur, alta siccantur. Gratia pluvia est. Ideo cum timore et tremore, id est, cum humilitate. Noli altum sapere, sed time. Time, ut implearis: noli altum sapere, ne sicceris. *Enarr. in Ps.* ciii. 32: Ideo ergo cum timore, quia Deus

he, engaged in a struggle with the Pelagians, cites often, and often draws out the force of this verse. I quote a single passage.[1]

Phil. ii. 15. 'Among whom ye shine *as lights in the world.*' These 'lights' ($\phi\omega\sigma\tau\hat{\eta}\rho\epsilon\varsigma$) to which the faithful are compared, Augustine explains rightly as the heavenly luminaries, and mainly the sun and moon.[2] They have been variously interpreted. Some have understood them as torches, and the faithful to be exhorted to shine like these in the midst of a dark world; for others, the 'lights' are lighthouses, and the faithful bidden to a like office to theirs, namely, to the guiding of wanderers over the world's sea; while others find a reference to the golden candlestick in the sanctuary: but all erroneously; the word which stands here for 'lights' is never used in the Septuagint or New Testament to signify aught but the heavenly luminaries.[3]

operatur. Quia ipse dedit, non ex te est quod habes, cum timore et tremore operaberis; nam si non tremueris eum, auferet quod dedit. Cf. *De Grat. et Lib. Arbit.* c. 9.

[1] *De Don. Persev.* 33 : Nos ergo volumus, sed Deus in nobis operatur et velle ; nos ergo operamur, sed Deus in nobis operatur et operari.

[2] Thus he brings this passage into connexion with the creation of the fourth day (*Enarr. in Ps.* xciii. 1): Quomodo luminaria in cælo per diem et per noctem procedunt, peragunt itinera sua, cursus suos certos habent; . . . sic debent sancti, &c.; cf. ver. 23; and *Enarr. in Ps.* cxlvii. 4.

[3] Thus Gen. i. 14, 16; Ecclus. xliii. 7; Wisd. xiii. 2; and compare Dan. xii. 3, where the redeemed are likened to $\phi\omega\sigma\tau\hat{\eta}\rho\epsilon\varsigma$ $\tauο\hat{v}$ $ο\hat{v}\rho\alpha\nuο\hat{v}$, and in the only other passage in the New Testament where the word occurs (Rev. xxi. 11), ὁ $\phi\omega\sigma\tau\hat{\eta}\rho$ $α\hat{v}\tau\hat{\eta}\varsigma$ is that which to the heavenly City is in place of sun and moon (see ver. 23). It is worth noting, though this is not his merit, but that of the early Latin Version which he used, that he has the right translation of $\phi\alpha\acute{\iota}\nu\epsilon\sigma\theta\epsilon$: *apparetis*, and not *lucetis* as the Vulgate. To justify *lucetis*, or our

Col. i. 13. It is plain that Augustine would not have been content with resolving 'Son of his love' here, as our Version has done, into 'dear Son.'[1] It is this, but it is also much more than this. In his great work, *De Trinitate*, which contains his profoundest speculations on the being and nature of God, and which, though appealing to a more limited circle of readers than most of his writings, may perhaps be considered the loftiest work of his genius, a work which he began a young man and ended an old,[2] he urges that love being no mere attribute of God, but his essence and substance, 'Son of his love' is in fact equivalent with 'only begotten.' The oneness in the substance of the Father and the Son is involved, not it may be for the conviction of the Arian, but yet most really, in the words; for the 'Son of God's love' must in fact share, is in that very phrase declared to share, with Him in his own essential being.[3]

Heb. xii. 3–11. This too is a passage which Augustine delights to recur to again and again; drawing out the disciplinary and fatherly character of the afflictions which come upon the faithful,[4] the divine intention of

own 'Ye shine,' an error which reappears Matt. xxiv. 27; Rev. xviii. 23, it should have been φαίνετε: φαίνειν is to shine (Gen. i. 17; Exod. xiii. 22; John v. 35; Rev. i. 16; 2 Pet. i. 19); φαίνεσθαι, to appear or to be seen (Prov. xxi. 2; Matt. ii. 7; Jam. iv. 14; 1 Pet. iv. 18).

[1] Υἱὸς τῆς ἀγάπης, as though it were no more than υἱὸς ἀγαπητός. It is a fault in the Authorized Version of frequent recurrence.

[2] *Ep.* clxxiv.

[3] *De Trin.* xv. 19: Caritas quippe Patris quæ in naturâ ejus est ineffabiliter simplici nihil est aliud quam ejus ipsa natura atque substantia. Ac per hoc Filius caritatis ejus nullus est alius, quam qui de substantiâ ejus est genitus. And presently before, Filius caritatis suæ Filius substantiæ suæ.

[4] *Enarr. in Ps.* cii. 20: Jam sæviat quantum vult, pater est. Sed

making by aid of these as many as are holy to be holier still. On this matter he has more comparisons than one of very singular beauty. Thus, what, he asks, shall we say that God is doing when He takes the earthly joy out of men's lives, and instead of this mingles with those lives some utterly distasteful thing? What indeed, he replies, but even the same which nurses or mothers do, who willing to wean an infant that clings overlong to the breast, anoint this with bitter aloes or some other bitter thing, that so it may repel rather than invite. In ways not different God weans us from the world and the things of the world, to which He saw us addicting ourselves overmuch. With the same intent, as Augustine reminds his hearers, it is the grape after it is crushed in the wine-press, which yields the sweetness that except for this pressure would have there been looked for in vain.[1] So, too, he meets the wonder which we so often feel, when one or another, who seemed to us thoroughly purged of his dross, is yet left in his furnace of trial; or who having been withdrawn from this for a little is flung back into it again and again. What is this, he demands, but the carrying out of the word of the promise of the heavenly Husband-

---

flagellavit nos et afflixit nos, et contrivit nos: pater est. Fili, si ploras, sub patre plora. Quod pateris, unde plangis, medicina est, non pœna; castigatio est, non damnatio. Noli repellere flagellum, si non vis repelli ab hæreditate. Noli attendere quam pœnam habeas in flagello, sed quem locum in testamento. And again, *Serm.* xlvi.: Flagellat, inquit, omnem filium quem recipit. Et tu forte exceptus eris? Si exceptus a passione flagellorum exceptus a numero filiorum. Other beautiful passages to the same effect may be found *Enarr. in Ps.* xxxi. 11; xl. 6; xciii. 14; cxiv. 5.

[1] *Enarr. in Ps.* xxx. ; *Serm.* iii. 14 : Faciunt enim hoc nutrices mammothreptis, ut aliqua ponant in papillis suis, quibus offensi parvuli ab ubere resiliant.

man that He will prune the fruit-bearing branches, to the end that they may bring forth more fruit (John xv. 2). Elsewhere he uses another image; but it is the same truth which he is urging still. We stand, he says, before some exquisite work of painter's or sculptor's hand; and it seems to us so perfect that it is almost a wrong to touch it further. But the artist is not of this mind; he will not withdraw his hand. Again and again he returns to his work. There is still something to add or something to take away. And why, but because there floats before him an ideal perfection which only he can perceive.[1] So, too, on the other hand, as he urges often, there is nothing so miserable as prosperous wickedness; there can be no surer sign of ultimate reprobation than when sinful men are let alone; when it seems to have been said to them in the counsels of God, 'Why should ye be smitten any more?'

Rev. xx. 12. Such language as the giving of the white stone (Rev. ii. 17), the standing on the sea of glass (Rev. xv. 2), the opening of the books and the judging of men out of these (Rev. xx. 12), and all other in which the things of heaven, not otherwise intelligible to us, are

[1] *Enarr. in Ps.* xcviii. 12 : Pleraque faciunt artifices, et ostendunt imperitis; et cum jam judicaverunt imperiti esse perfecta, expoliunt illa artifices, qui noverunt adhuc quod illis desit, ut mirentur homines tantam expolitionem rebus accidisse, quas jam perfectas pronunciaverant. Fit hoc et in ædificiis et in picturis et in vestibus et prope in omni genere artium. Primo judicant illud jam quasi perfectum esse, ut oculi eorum amplius nihil desiderent; sed aliud judicat oculus imperitus, aliud judicat artis regula. Sic et illi sancti versabantur ante oculos Dei, tanquam sine culpâ, tanquam perfecti, tanquam angeli. Noverat autem quid illis deesset, qui vindicabat in omnes affectiones eorum. Vindicabat autem non irascens, sed propitius; ad hoc vindicabat, ut perficeret cœptum, non ut damnaret ejectum.

translated into the dialect of earth, is of course accommodation and condescension, but still with most real truth for its groundwork, and for a justification of the uses to which it is turned; and it is the task of the skilful interpreter to bring out the essential truth of which each of these images is the vehicle. This Augustine does very happily, as for instance in his very solemn explanation, quoted below, of what this 'opening of the books' at the last day may mean.[1]

With one or two concluding observations, I will draw these specimens of Augustine's exegetical skill to an end. With all his dialectic dexterity, and all his delight in subtlest speculations, which indeed he snuffs afar off, with something of the same exultation as the war-horse in Job 'the thunder of the captains and the shouting,' plunging into the thickest of them with an eager joy, with all his fondness for tracing up everything to its ultimate ground,[2] he abides still the man of the people, uniting in a remarkable degree with his metaphysical subtlety a broad practical common sense. Indeed without such a union he never could have exercised a dominion wide as that which he owns. So much will be allowed even by those who possess no larger acquaintance with his writings than these pages have already afforded. The inexhaustible

[1] *De Civ. Dei*, xx. 14: Quædam vis est intelligenda divina, quâ fiet ut cuique opera sua, vel bona vel mala, cuncta in memoriam revocentur, et mentis intuitu mirâ celeritate cernantur; ut accuset vel excuset scientia conscientiam, atque ita simul et omnes et singuli judicentur. Quæ nimirum vis divina, libri nomen accepit. In eâ quippe quodam modo legitur quidquid ea faciente recolitur.

[2] See, for instance, his interesting discussion on the origin of slavery, *De Civ. Dei*, xix. 15; and again, on the relation of thought to speech, his essay *De Magistro*.

treasure-house of our common life was open to him. Familiarity and use had not worn out its significance, nor robbed it of its mystery for him. He abounds in happiest illustration, the homeliest as the highest, appeals in his popular exegesis to proverbs in every day use, to familiar turns of language,[1] draws out from these the lesson which they contain, tracks those vestiges or foot-prints of the truth which are everywhere dispersed,[2] and compels men's most ordinary words and ways to throw light *on* Scripture, to receive light *from* Scripture, and oftentimes unconsciously to witness for truths the very highest of all.

It must be acknowledged too that in brief and felicitous antithesis Augustine is without a peer. More than any other of the great teachers of the Church he abounds in short and memorable, and, if I might so call them, epigrammatic sayings, concentrating with a forceful brevity the whole truth which he desires to impart into some single phrase, forging it into a polished shaft, at once pointed to pierce, and barbed that it shall not lightly drop from the mind and memory. And thus it has come to pass that as no theological writer lends himself so happily to quotation, none assuredly has been so often quoted.[3] And then with what a genial tact does he know how to plant himself at the central point of the truth which he desires to explain, and from thence securely to unfold it. How often does he in a single phrase gather up the whole significance of some Scripture history,

---

[1] As in one place he says himself: Ipsa lingua popularis plerumque est doctrina salutaris.

[2] *Enarr. in Ps.* cxviii. 36 : Vestigia veritatis, quæ ubique dispersa est.

[3] The Spaniards have a proverb: No hay sermon sin Agostino ; or better, Sermon sin Agostino olla sin tocino.

CHAP. VIII.]   INTERPRETER OF SCRIPTURE.   155

summon up before our eyes some Scripture scene, draw out and make application of it to the hearts and consciences of men in short and never-to-be-forgotten words; how often does he illuminate as with a flash of lightning some dark passage, or trace with a single word some delicate yet important distinction, which, once traced, can never be confounded again.[1] I know not how better

[1] I will instance a few examples of the fulness which is to be often found in his single sentences and phrases. Thus he gathers up in a single phrase the sin of Simon Magus (Acts viii. 16), who would have bought with money a share in the spiritual powers exercised by the Apostles : Voluit talia facere, non talis esse. Coming on those words, which describe how the whole crowd of the Lord's captors 'went backward and fell to the ground,' at that word of his, ' I am He' (John xviii. 6), he exclaims: Quid faciet judicaturus, qui judicandus hoc fecit ? Quid regnaturus poterit, qui moriturus hoc potuit ? even as on that earlier trouble of Herod (Matt. ii. 3) : Quid erit tribunal judicantis, cum superbos reges cunæ terrebant infantis ? He gives the purpose of the Lord in suffering Himself to be tempted: Ad hoc pugnat imperator, ut milites discant (*Serm.* cxxiii. 2). On the indignation of the ruler of the synagogue at the healing of the woman who had been bowed together (Luke xiii. 14), he exclaims: Bene scandalizati sunt de illâ erectâ ipsi curvi (*Enarr.* 2ª *in Ps.* lxviii. 24). On Christ left alone with the woman taken in adultery (John viii. 9) : Remansit adultera et Dominus, remansit vulnerata et medicus, remansit magna miseria et magna misericordia (*Enarr. in Ps.* l. 8). On the doubt of Thomas, doubtful of his Lord's resurrection: Dubitatio Thomæ, confirmatio Ecclesiæ ; with which we may compare the Church collect for St. Thomas's day. On the three days' blindness of Paul which followed his meeting of his Lord on the way to Damascus, he exclaims, Excæcatio Pauli, illuminatio mundi. He explains why the Lord, after the resurrection, should have three time over repeated his question to Peter, 'Lovest thou Me ? ' (John xxi. 15-17): Donec trinâ voce amoris solveret trinam vocem negationis (*Enarr. in Ps.* xxxvii. 13). The whole question at issue between the Church and the Donatists in respect of the true and the false separation from sinners, he expresses in these words : Fugio paleam ne hoc sim, non aream ne nihil sim. He sets forth the manifold relations of Christ to his Church in the matter of prayer (*Enarr. in Ps.* lxxxv. 1) Orat pro nobis, orat in nobis, et oratur a nobis: He prays for us, as

I can record my own sense of his excellences as an interpreter of Scripture, than in the words of one whose work as a whole has yielded me, as I am obliged to say, singularly little, but who on this matter has expressed himself excellently well:[1] Mira Augustini erat ingenii profunditas, ardens et cordata pietas; ut animum ad ea, quæ our High Priest; He prays in us, as our Head; He is prayed to by us, as our God. We may set beside this his exposition of the words, 'I am the way, the truth, and the life' (John xiv. 6): Hoc est, per me venitur; ad me pervenitur; in me permanetur (*De Doct. Christ.* i). On the words of our Lord, misunderstood and misapplied so often, 'My kingdom is not of this world' (John xviii. 36), he comments rightly : Non negat *hic* esse, sed *hinc.* Again, how profound is his commentary on the words of St. Paul (Rom. xii. 2), 'Be ye transformed by the renewing of your minds, *that ye may prove* what is that good and perfect and acceptable will of God:' Tantum videmus, quantum morimur huic seculo; quantum autem huic vivimus, non videmus. How conscience-searching his remark on the unprofitable servant, who is cast into outer darkness, not because he has *wasted*, but only because he has not multiplied, his Lord's money : Intelligitur pœna interversoris ex pœnâ pigri. Not less conscience-searching some other words, *Enarr. in Ps.* cxlvii. 12: Res alienæ possidentur cum superflua possidentur. Thus too on Peter's presumptuous word (Matt. xxvi. 33), Quid festinas, Petre? Nondum te suo spiritu solidavit Petra. With what a felicitous analogy he illustrates the fact that regenerate men do not beget regenerate, but natural and needing regeneration (*De Pec. Mer. et Rem.* iii. 8): Palea, quæ opere humano tantâ diligentiâ separatur, manet in fructu qui de purgato tritico nascitur. The profound spiritual truth of Matt. x. 39 is shown to have truest analogies in the world of nature (*Serm.* cccxxxi. 1): Agricola triticum si non perdit in semine, non amat in messe. How happily he has seized the central point of the type of the brazen serpent, which they who take it to represent the Lord, and not *the death* of the Lord, in part miss (*In Ev. Joh. Tract.* xiii.) : Quid est serpens exaltatus ? Mors Domini in cruce. Adtenditur serpens, ut nihil valeat serpens; adtenditur mors, ut nihil valeat mors; and again (*Enarr. in Is.* lxxiii. 2): Sanari a serpente, magnum sacramentum. Quid est, intuendo serpentem sanari a serpente ? Credendo in Mortuum salvari a morte.

[1] CLAUSEN, *Augustinus Sacræ Scripturæ Interpres*, p. 267. Berol. 1828.

intus quæque in sublimi sunt, totum conversum haberet: satis egisse se non prius arbitratus quam sibi usibusque suis religiosis satisfactum esset; veritates ex sacro idearum fonte elicere, ad interna conscientiæ oracula revocare studio generoso annisus est. Hinc egregiæ multæ interpretationis virtutes ortæ sunt: sollicitudo religiosa, gravitas verecunda, pia sinceritas: quum litteras sacras fidei regulam, lucem pietatis, vitæ magistram positas esse sciret, neque igitur, nisi ad doctrinam et vitam usus redundaret, docto labori laudem pretiumque constare. Et quanta Nostri in vestigiis ad metam hancce dirigendis constantia erat! quanta in sententiis multis dogmaticis vel ethicis efferendis construendisque diligentia, sagacitas, sapientia vere christiana! ut non tam argutando dixeris eum intellexisse, quid scripserint auctores sacri, quam, impetu interno ductum, quid senserint, ipsum sensisse; ita in expositionibus nihil deest, nihil superest, nihil claudicat; cardinem rei acu quasi tetigit feriitque, ut veritate tibi persuasum, pietate te commotum, simplicitate delectatum sentias.

AUGUSTINE'S

EXPOSITION
OF
THE SERMON ON THE MOUNT.

EXPOSITION,

ETC.

ST. MATTHEW, CHAP. V.

VER. 1. '*And seeing the multitudes, He went up into a mountain; and when He was set, his disciples came unto Him.*'—Augustine expresses himself with no great decision on a question which has always occupied and divided harmonists—namely, whether the Sermon on the Mount, as reported by St. Matthew, is the same discourse as that which St. Luke records (vi. 20–49). Against their identity, he finds this to have been spoken on a mountain (ver. 1), that in the plain (Luke vi. 17); while yet, on the other hand, the strong internal resemblance, with the fact that the same miracle, the healing of the centurion's servant, follows upon both, speaks for the identity of the two. He suggests, as a reconciliation of all difficulties, that the Lord may perhaps, first, on some higher eminence of the mountain have spoken the discourse to his disciples which St. Matthew records; and then, coming down to the foot of the mountain, have repeated the same to the multitude, in a briefer form, and one more suitable to them: and that of this repetition we have the record in St. Luke. Yet, before leaving the question, he allows that this difference, of one discourse having been spoken on a mountain, the other in the plain, does not imperatively demand such a scheme; which, as it must be owned, has something forced and unlikely about it. The two statements are capable of reconciliation: our Lord may have 'stood' (Luke vi. 17) on some more level space upon the slope of the mountain, capable of conveniently receiving the multitude, and then, when they were assembled, have sat down (Matt, v. 1), and spoken once for all that one discourse which both Evangelists relate.[1] And this is, no doubt, the truer and more natural explanation; from which the inner differences, as Augustine himself affirms, need move us as little as the outer. One Evangelist does not contradict another, when, as St. Luke here, he relates more succinctly what the other had related more at length; or again, when he finds place in his narrative for some portions of a discourse, which the other, though reporting parts of it more fully, has omitted.

Ver. 2, 3. '*And He opened his mouth, and taught them, saying, Blessed are the poor in spirit: for theirs is the kingdom of heaven.*'—There is an emphasis, acknowledged by all later interpreters, in the words, '*He opened his mouth,*' which are not merely another way of

---

[1] *De Cons. Evang.* ii. 19; Quanquam etiam illud possit occurrere, in aliquâ excelsiore parte montis primo cum solis discipulis Dominum fuisse, quando ex eis illos duodecim elegit; deinde cum eis descendisse, non de monte, sed de ipsâ montis celsitudine in campestrem locum, id est, in aliquam æqualitatem quæ in latere montis erat, et multas turbas capere poterat; atque ibi stetisse, donec ad eum turbæ congregarentur; ac postea cum sedisset, accepisse propinquius discipulos ejus, atque ita illis cæterisque turbis præsentibus unum habuisse sermonem, quem Matthæus Lucasque narrarunt, diverso narrandi modo, sed eâdem veritate rerum et sententiarum, quos ambo dixerunt.

saying, He began to teach, but signify that He was now beginning a discourse more than commonly weighty and full (cf. Job iii. 1; xxii. 20; Acts viii. 35; x. 34). Augustine has not let this go unobserved, although he finds exclusively an indication of *the length* of the discourse introduced with this preface, and not also of its weight and solemnity.[1] It is not, indeed, that he does not rate at its proper height the significance of this discourse. He claims for it, on the contrary, to be a complete body of Christian divinity; which he who has mastered and taken in will be furnished with all things necessary for the perfect life. He urges its closing words in proof that nothing less than this was the divine speaker's intention.

In this first beatitude much, indeed everything, turns on the interpretation which the words '*in spirit*' obtain. '*Poor in spirit*' Augustine explains as poor in their own spirits, and so rich in the Spirit of God; being thus as the valleys, filled with the waters which roll off from the high and barren hills.[2] Yet while this is, no doubt, in the main the true meaning, he lays on the words '*in spirit*' not exactly their right stress. He would have it, Blessed are they that have not an elated spirit; taking '*spirit*' altogether in an evil sense,[3] as that in man which lifts

---

[1] *De Serm. Dom. in Mon.* i. 1: Ista circumlocutio quâ scribitur, Et aperiens os suum, fortassis ipsâ morâ commendat aliquanto longiorem futurum esse sermonem.

[2] *Enarr. in Ps.* cxli. 4: Beati pauperes spiritu suo, divites Spiritu Dei. Omnis enim homo qui spiritum suum sequitur, superbus est, Subdat spiritum suum, ut capiat Spiritum Dei. Ibat in culmen, residat in valle. Si ierit in culmen, denatat ab illo aqua, si in valle resederit, implebitur ex eâ.

[3] Thus *De Serm. Dom. in Mon.* i. 1: Non habentes inflantem spiritum, and *Enarr. in Ps.* cxliii. 7; and *in Ps.* ciii, 30; Noluerunt

itself up against God, and so hinders the reception of any of his gifts or blessings. But what our Lord would say is this, Blessed are they that are poor in the spirit of their minds; the term '*poor*' excluding the false riches of pride and self-sufficiency, while '*in spirit*' marks the region in which this poverty should find place; that He is not now speaking of worldly riches or worldly poverty, not of the things outside of a man, but of those which are within. It is as much as to say, Blessed are they that are inwardly poor, who in their hearts and spirits have a sense of need, of emptiness, and poverty.

His explanation, it will be seen, though capable of gaining slightly in accuracy, yet effectually excludes the Roman Catholic interpretation, that it is any outward poverty or riches of which Christ is speaking, that, for example, He is foreannouncing here any Mendicant Orders, with some singular beatitude which should be theirs.[1] Augustine had far too deep an insight into Christian truth to limit and explain Christ's saying here by the other form in which St. Luke records it, namely, 'Blessed be ye poor.' So far from this, He evermore interprets that by this, completing the briefer by the fuller, not cutting down (which were absurd) the fuller to suit with the briefer. For he that was so faithful a monitor to the rich of this world, warning them of the dangers especially theirs, hardness of heart, self-indulgence, pride, and notably the last—for as every fruit has its worm, so wealth has this[2]—was no less faithful to the poor; did not fall

---

habere spiritum suum; habebunt Spiritum Dei; see also the preceding note.

[1] Many Roman Catholic interpreters make πτωχοὶ τῷ πνεύματι, the *voluntarily* poor.

[2] *Serm.* lxi. 9: Omne pomum, omne granum, omne frumentum, omne lignum, habet vermem suum. Vermis divitiarum, superbia.

into the other extreme, which is equally a temptation (Lev. xix. 15), of flattering or favouring them; would not let them believe that their outward poverty did itself constitute humility, however it might be a help to it, or that they were necessarily '*poor in spirit*,' because poor in worldly goods. He often tells them they were not to take for granted that every beggar was a Lazarus;[1] while on the other side there were Abrahams and Jobs, who were adorned with this true poverty, even in the midst of their worldly abundance.[2] This poverty of spirit being the condition of every blessing, therefore to it is attached the promise of '*the kingdom of heaven*,' which is inclusive of all blessings; for all the beatitudes which follow are but, as he observes, the unfolding of this first one. The phrase itself, '*kingdom of heaven*,' so often recurring in St. Matthew (in the other New Testament Scriptures it is '*kingdom of God*,' as sometimes with him), he claims

[1] *Enarr. in Ps.* cxxxi. 15: Pauper Dei in animo est, non in sacculo. Procedit aliquando homo habens plenam domum, uberes terras; . . . . novit quia in ipsis non est presumendum; humiliat se Deo, facit inde bene; ita cor ipsius erigitur ad Deum, ut noverit quia non solum nihil illi prosunt divitiæ ipsæ, sed et impediunt pedes ipsius, nisi Ille regat et Ille subveniat: et numeratur inter pauperes, qui saturantur panibus. Invenis alium mendicum inflatum, aut ideo non inflatum, quia nihil habet, quærentem tamen unde infletur. Non attendit Deus facultatem, sed cupiditatem; et judicat eum secundum cupiditatem, quia inhiat rebus temporalibus, non secundum facultatem, quam non ei contigit adipisci. And *Enarr. in Ps.* lxxxv. 1: Resistit Deus superbis, et holosericatis et pannosis: humilibus autem dat gratiam, et habentibus aliquam substantiam hujus seculi et non habentibus. Cf. *Enarr. in Ps.* xciii. 1; and *Serm.* clxxvii., where he seeks especially to bring out the force of St. Paul's words: Qui *volunt* divites fieri (1 Tim. vi. 5).

[2] *Enarr. in Ps.* lxxi. 2: Quâ paupertate etiam beatus Job pauper fuit, et antequam magnas illas terrenas divitias amisisset. Quod ideo commemorandum putavi, quoniam sunt quidam qui facilius omnia sua pauperibus distribuunt, quam ipsi pauperes Dei fiant.

as belonging exclusively to the New Covenant; so that
while all else was in the Old, even life eternal and the
resurrection of the dead, yet this name is never found
there, being reserved for his lips who should be at once a
King to rule, and a Priest to sanctify, his people.[1] This
is not perfectly correct; '*kingdom of God*,' occurs once
in a remarkable passage in the Apocrypha (Wisd. x. 10).
When Jacob saw the ladder reaching to heaven, and angels
ascending and descending on it (Gen. xxviii. 12), he saw,
we are there told, 'the kingdom of God.'

Ver. 4. '*Blessed are the meek: for they shall inherit
the earth.*'—Augustine shares with the Vulgate the better
arrangement of the beatitudes which places this immediately after the first, reversing the position of this and
of that which in our Bibles has precedence of it, but
which, for the truer logical coherence, should follow; and
which in the best modern critical editions, as in Lach-
mann's and Tischendorf's, does follow. He rightly explains this meekness as having immediate reference to
our bearing, not toward God, but toward our fellow-men.[2]
And then comes out the appropriateness of the blessing:
men count that in a world of violence and wrong, the
meek will inevitably make themselves a prey; that an
Isaac, who gives up the well again and again rather than
contend for it, will at length have nothing left him which

[1] *Con. Faust.* xix. 31: Regnum cælorum . . . . ori ejus nomi-
nandum servabatur, quem Regem ad regendos et Sacerdotem ad
sanctificandos fideles suos universus ille apparatus veteris Instrumenti
in generationibus, factis, dictis, sacrificiis, observationibus, festivita-
tibus, omnibusque eloquiorum præconiis, et rebus gestis et rerum
figuris parturiebat esse venturum.

[2] *De Serm. Dom. in Mon.* i. 2: Mites sunt qui cedunt improbitati-
bus et non resistunt malo, sed vincunt in bono malum.

he may call his own (Gen. xxvi. 20). But it is not so. Wonderful under God is the strength and power of meekness; with it is ever the victory at the last: in the words of the eastern proverb, 'The one staff of Moses breaks in shivers the ten thousand spears of Pharaoh.' These '*meek*' shall in the end inherit all things, even this '*earth*,' from which it seemed at the outset as if they would be thrust out altogether.[1] Here, too, we have one of Augustine's striking antithetic sayings: 'Dost thou wish to possess the earth? beware then lest thou be possessed by it.'[2]—There is a designed emphasis in the shape which the promise assumes, '*for they shall inherit the earth*,'—and that in more ways than one,—'*the earth*,' possession in land always remaining the surest of earthly possessions,—and '*inherit*,' possession by inheritance in the orderly succession of father and son being ever counted to have the strongest promise and pledge of continuance.[3]

Ver. 5. '*Blessed are they that mourn; for they shall be comforted.*'—There is, Augustine often takes occasion

---

[1] *Serm.* liii. 8 : He observes how in each case congrua congruentibus apposita sint; and on this: Quia mites homines facile excluduntur de terrâ suâ, Beati, inquit, mites, quoniam ipsi hæreditate possidebunt terram. It shall be theirs, not merely as a future benefit, but a present, according to those profound words of his (*Ep.* cliii. 6) : Omne quod male possidetur, alienum est: male autem possidet, qui male utitur; and again (*ibid.*): Fidelis hominis totus mundus divitiarum est: infidelis autem nec obolus. So that he does not in fact contradict that meaning which looks at it as a future inheritance, when (*Ep.* cxlix.) he explains '*the earth*' spoken of here as, Ecclesiam hæreditatemque fidelium atque sanctorum, quæ dicitur terra viventium.

[2] *Serm.* liii. 2 : Vis possidere terram? vide ne possidearis a terrâ.

[3] *De Serm. Dom. in Mon.* i. 2 : Significat quandam soliditatem et stabilitatem hæreditatis perpetuæ.

to remark, a mourning which has no compensating blessing attached to it; there is misery enough among men, which yet has no blessing, for it leads to no repentance, or at best is only a 'sorrow of this world.' One is groaning for one thing, one for another—for this temporal loss, for that worldly tribulation; for the hail that has laid waste his vineyard, for the death that has entered into his dwelling, for the powerful foes that are seeking his harm: and if perchance the groaning of the faithful man reaches to the ears of the world, the world lays his sorrowing to the same account. Men say he has suffered this loss or that; for they know not of a mourning which springs from a higher source, a mourning for our own sins, for the sins of others, out of a sense of our exile here, of our separation from the true home of our spirits, out of a longing for the eternal Sabbath.[1] And yet it is only this nobler grief that has the promise linked to it, that shall be followed by any true consolation. To be thus miserable is indeed to be happy; while, on the contrary, he that is altogether without this mourning gives too sure an augury that there is reserved for him a mourning of another kind, and which

---

[1] On the words of the Psalmist, Rugiebam a gemitu cordis mei (*Enarr. in Ps.* xxxvii. 6), he has these beautiful remarks: Propterea rugiebam, inquit, a gemitu cordis mei, quia homines si quando audiunt gemitum hominis, plerumque gemitum carnis audiunt, gementem à gemitu cordis non audiunt. Abstulit nescio quis res hujus, rugiebat, sed non a gemitu cordis: alius, quia extulit filium; alius quia uxorem; alius quia grandinata est vinea, quia cuppa acuit, quia diripuit jumentum ipsius nescio quis, alius quia damnum aliquod passus est, alius quia timet hominem inimicum; omnes isti a gemitu carnis rugiunt et vero servus Dei, quia ex recordatione, sabbati rugit, ubi est regnum Dei, quod caro et sanguis non possidebunt: Rugiebam, inquit, a gemitu cordis mei.

shall not be exchanged, as shall this, for the consolations of the kingdom of heaven.[1]

Ver. 6. '*Blessed are they which do hunger and thirst after righteousness; for they shall be filled.*'—It is not that the hunger and thirst are in themselves the blessing, but only as they create a longing for the heavenly aliment, which except for this hunger would be slighted or loathed.[2] Very beautifully Augustine draws from John vi. 26–65 a commentary on this text, making '*righteousness*' here equivalent with 'bread from heaven' there, and urging that in both passages we should understand nothing short of Christ Himself. This is at once evident of the 'bread from heaven,' and Augustine cites the words of St. Paul (1 Cor. i. 30), 'Christ Jesus . . . made unto us righteousness,' in proof that '*righteousness*' here is equally exchangeable for Him in whom the righteousness is contained; the hungering and thirsting after which is no desiring merely a moral amelioration, but a longing after Christ, and the being clothed with his righteousness, and satisfied out of his fulness.[3] The Jews, he says, were in the con-

---

[1] *Enarr. in Ps.* xxxvii. 1: Felix est qui sic miser est; . . . immo miser esset si lugens non esset: and again (*Enarr. in Ps.* cxlviii. 1): Qui non gemit peregrinus, non gaudebit civis. *Ep.* ccxlviii.: Pia est ista tristitia, et, si dici potest, beata miseria, vitiis alienis tribulari, non implicari; mœrere, non hærere; dolore contrahi, non amore attrahi. Hæc est persequutio quam patiuntur omnes qui volunt in Christo pie vivere, secundum apostolicam mordacem veracemque sententiam (2 Tim. iii. 12). Quid enim hic sic persequitur vitam bonorum, quam vita iniquorum? And again, *De Serm. Dom. in Mon.* v. 5: Non parvus est ad beatitudinem accessus, cognitio infelicitatis suæ.

[2] *Serm.* lxi. 6: Præcedat saturitatem fames, ne fastidium non perveniat ad panes.

[3] Thus, too, he exchanges with a true feeling of the sense,

dition of mind directly opposed to that which here has the blessing attached to it, when, going about to establish their own righteousness, they would not submit themselves to the righteousness of God (Rom. x. 3); as no less were those who disputed with the Lord concerning the bread of God that came down from heaven (John vi.), which He would have given them, but which they scornfully put back: for they had not the spiritual hunger, the sense of emptiness, which alone would have interpreted his words, or imparted a value to his offer.[1] Augustine cannot find the entire fulfilment of the appended promise, '*for they shall be filled,*' in the present life; for now our lips are but sprinkled, as it were, with a few drops from that river of joy, whereof then we shall drink to the full: yet the longing now is needful, if there is to be a satisfying of the longing hereafter; and the more longing, the ampler satisfaction, for this longing is itself the dilating of the vessel that it may contain the more.[2]

'*righteousness*' for '*God*,' in some allusions to this passage: *Enarr. in Ps.* cxlv. 18.

[1] *In Ev. Joh. Tract.* xxvi.: Isti a pane de cælo longe erant, nec eum esurire noverant. Fauces cordis languidas habebant.... Panis quippe iste interioris hominis quærit esuriem: unde alio loco dicit, Beati qui esuriunt et sitiunt justitiam, quoniam ipsi saturabuntur. Justitiam vero nobis esse Christum, Paulus Apostolus dicit. Ac per hoc qui esurit hunc panem, esuriat justitiam; sed justitiam quæ de cælo descendit, justitiam quam dat Deus, non quam sibi facit homo. And then he justly explains the 'righteousness of God' (Rom. i. 17), not as the righteousness with which God is righteous in Himself, but the righteousness which He gives to his people.

[2] *De Util. Jejun.* I: Pertinet ergo ad homines hanc vitam mortalem gerentes, esurire ac sitire justitiam: impleri autem justitiâ, ad aliam vitam pertinet. Hoc pane, hoc cibo pleni sunt Angeli: homines autem dum esuriunt, extendunt se; dum se extendunt, dilitantur; dum dilatantur, capaces fiunt; capaces facti, suo tempore replebuntur. Quid ergo, hic nihil inde capiunt qui esuriunt et sitiunt

Ver. 7. '*Blessed are the merciful, for they shall obtain mercy.*'—This mercifulness Augustine is sometimes disposed to restrict to the relief of the temporal needs of our brethren; yet is it a pitifulness which is evidently of a wider reach, embracing the whole outcomings of a Christian's heart, whether in inward sympathies or outward acts, in relation to the sorrows and sufferings of his brethren. And here the blessed retaliations of the kingdom of God shall find place; upon which he expresses himself thus: 'Do, and it shall be done. Do with another, that it may be done with thee: for thou aboundest, and thou lackest. Thou aboundest in things temporal, thou lackest things eternal. A beggar is at thy gate, thou art thyself a beggar at God's gate. Thou art sought, and thou seekest. As thou dealest with *thy* seeker, even so God will deal with his. Thou art both empty and full. Fill thou the empty out of thy fulness, that out of the fulness of God thine emptiness may be filled.'[1]

Ver. 8. '*Blessed are the pure in heart, for they shall see God.*'—The '*pure heart*' Augustine explains rightly as the single heart, the heart without folds; and this, with the promise of seeing God which is annexed, causes him to connect this passage with others wherein our Lord speaks of the single eye, that eye of the soul (Matt. vi. 22,

justitiam ? Capiunt plane, sed aliud est cum quærimus de refectione iter agentium, et aliud cum quærimus de perfectione beatorum. And *Enarr. in Ps.* cxxii. 4: Quantacumque justitia in nobis fuerit, ros est nescio quis ad illum fontem, ad saginam illam tantam stillicidia quædam sunt, quæ vitam nostram molliant, et duram iniquitatem solvant. *Enarr. in Ps.* xxxv. 10: Quis est fons vitæ nisi Christus? Venit ad te in carne, ut irroraret fauces tuas sitientes: satiabit sperantem, qui irroravit sitientem.

[1] *Serm.* liii 5.

23; Luke xi. 34), which, only when healthy, is receptive of divine light, and the channel of light to the whole interior man; that declaration being identical with this, that only the pure in heart shall see God.[1] But *how* this seeing of God should be—for he will not explain away the words into a mere figure of a general felicity—is a question which occupied him greatly; yet one, as he truly said at the beginning of a long Epistle on the subject, in which holy living will help infinitely more than subtle speculation.[2] And as this question occupied him, so did another which grew out of it, namely, *when* this should be? a question which must mainly depend for the answer it receives on the answer given to the first. *What* the seeing of God is must decide *when* this seeing shall be, whether in this life or in the life to come? or whether, like so many other promises, it shall have a partial and inchoate fulfilment now, a complete fulfilment hereafter? To arrive at a satisfactory answer it will be needful to put together, from his different writings, the results at which upon these points he arrives. He most truly takes his first stand upon this; that the seeing of God at all involves, and itself rests upon, the divine constitution of man, his original creation in the divine image; and hence, to use an image of the later Platonists, as, because the eye is soliform ($\dot{\eta}\lambda\iota o\varepsilon\iota\delta\eta s$), it therefore can see the sun, so

---

[1] Beati mundicordes, as he commonly expresses it with a word of his own; but the Vulgate, Beati mundo corde;—mundum cor = simplex (i.e. sine plicâ) cor = $\dot{o}\phi\theta a\lambda\mu\dot{o}s$ $\dot{a}\pi\lambda o\hat{v}s$ (Luke xi. 34). Perhaps sincerus (= infucatus) would be nearer to the Greek $\kappa a\theta a\rho\dot{o}s$, since they both rest on the image of immunity from foreign admixtures—this of colours, that (according at least to one etymology), of honey from the wax that would impair its perfect purity.

[2] *Ep.* cxlvii.: Primum mihi videtur plus valere in hâc inquisitione vivendi quam loquendi modum.

man, because made in a divine image, is therefore capable of knowing and seeing God.[1] But this image of God in which man was first created is not outward but inward— 'created after God in righteousness and true holiness' (Ephes. iv. 24). The seeing then which rests upon this must be an inward seeing; not, as some said, whom Augustine earnestly rebukes, with these eyes of flesh, but it must be through the restoration of the effaced likeness of God in the soul that the forfeited capability of seeing Him must be restored. The enlightened eyes of the understanding, the heart purified by faith—these, and no bodily eyes, are the organs by which God is seen. In proportion as we are unlike to Him, we are incapable of seeing Him; in proportion as we grow in likeness to Him, as we are 'renewed in knowledge after the image of Him that created' us, we grow in the power of this vision.[2]

Here, then, is the answer to the other question: *When shall it be, in this life, or in the coming?* Plainly in both. For, since this renewal is begun here, the vision must begin here also; though it be now but a seeing 'through a glass darkly;' while its consummation will be there,

---

[1] *Serm.* lxxxviii. 6: Fecit autem te Deus, o homo, ad imaginem suam. Daretne tibi unde videres solem quem fecit, et non tibi daret unde videres eum qui te fecit, cum te ad imaginem suam fecerit?

[2] Thus *Ep.* xcii. 3 (with allusion to 1 John v. 2): In tantum ergo videbimus, in quantum similes ei erimus, quia nunc in tantum non videmus, in quantum dissimiles sumus. Inde igitur videbimus, unde similes erimus. Quis autem dementissimus dixerit, corpore nos vel esse vel futuros esse similes Deo? The whole Epistle is directed against those who thought the corporeal eye would be the organ with which God would be seen; yet elsewhere (*Ep.* cxi.; and *De Civ. Dei*, xxii. 29) he expresses himself more doubtfully, as being unable to say what accessions of power the spiritual body may receive.

where it will be 'face to face.' For this most earnestly he affirms, that it will be a seeing which shall be intuitive and immediate, a seeing 'Him as He is;' no mere theophany, such as were the apparitions of God to the saints in the Old Testament; no taking, upon his part, of a form in which to make Himself apparent to men; but a revelation of God in his own most proper essence, from which will follow a seeing Him *as He is*. This was denied to Moses once; no man, while yet flesh and blood, could so see God and live (Exod. xxxiii. 20), but it shall be granted to all the faithful in the world to come. And here, Augustine observes, is the reconciliation of those passages, some of which say, that 'no man hath seen God at any time' (John i. 18), that no man hath seen Him, nor can see (1 Tim. vi. 16); while others speak of men being introduced into his presence, beholding Him, and speaking with Him (Gen. xviii. 1; Isai. vi. 1).[1] It is to the attaining of this pure heart, this purged eye of the soul, that all helps and appliances of grace are tending.[2] This is the great meaning and purpose of them all—of sacraments, of preaching, of Scripture—to prepare and fit us for this, for a time when we shall be enabled to see the

---

[1] See his beautiful letter to Paulina, *Ep.* cxlvii. 6–8: Ipse ergo erat in eâ specie quâ apparere voluerat, non autem ipse apparêbat in naturâ propriâ, quam Moses videre cupiebat. Ea quippe promittitur sanctis in aliâ vitâ . . . . Multi viderunt, sed quod voluntas elegit non quod natura formavit.

[2] *Serm.* lxxxviii. 5: Tota igitur opera nostra, fratres, in hâc vitâ est, sanare oculum cordis unde videtur Deus. Ad hoc sacrosancta mysteria celebrantur, ad hoc sermo Dei prædicatur, ad hoc agunt quidquid agunt divinæ sanctæque literæ, ut purgetur illud interius ab eâ re quæ nos impedit ab aspectu Dei. In this and the following chapters is much more that is admirable on the purging the inward eye.

Seer:[1] for in that seeing all blessedness is included; without it there were no heaven, with it there could be no hell.[2]

Ver. 9. '*Blessed are the peacemakers, for they shall be called the children of God.*'—Augustine sometimes understands by '*peacemakers*' those that have made peace in the little world of their own hearts, in whom the spirit is ruling and the flesh serving; who, submitting themselves to God, are able to submit their own lower nature to their higher; who thus being content to be ruled, are able in their turn to rule:[3] but generally he takes a wider range, for this is evidently too narrow. It is true that the Latin *pacifici*,[4] which he has in common with the Vulgate, and which is rather 'the peaceable' than '*the peacemakers*,' encourages a narrower view; as indeed it confounds in a great measure this beatitude with the second, for the '*meek*' and the 'peaceable' will be nearly the same. But the naming of '*peacemakers*' introduces a new thought. The Christian is not merely himself quiet in the land, quiet in his own heart, but he is a diffuser of peace around him—the peace of this world, but more than this, the peace also of God; knowing the blessedness of that peace himself, he says also by word and deed to his brethren, 'Be ye reconciled with God.'[5]

---

[1] Videre Videntem, as in one place he calls it.

[2] Visio Dei est tota vita æterna. Si mali Dei faciem viderent, pœnis caderent.

[3] So *De Serm. Dom. in Mon.* i. 2.

[4] Pacifici = εἰρηνικοί (βουλόμενοι εἰρήνην, Prov. xii. 20), as opposed to those who are ἐξ ἐριθείας (Rom. ii. 8); but the word here is εἰρηνοποιοί.

[5] Thus Augustine, with allusion to Luke x. 5: Quo pleni sunt, fundunt.

Too many expositors look exclusively to that other and lower peace, those especially who prize Christianity rather as a healer of the outward sores of the world, than as that which alone stanches the deep inner hurts of men's souls. Not that the peace of this world is excluded:[1] the Gospel does bring this peace, but only by the way: it is aiming at a higher peace, and one for the sake of which, as being the only true peace, the Christian is willing for a season to forego and sacrifice the other, to be called a troubler, and one who turns the world upside down, a bringer in of the sword of division, rather than one knitting anew the bands of a broken love. Thus it is, he observes, with the truth of Christ even in the individual man; for in one sense there is in the redeemed man not peace but war—a war which this very redemption has brought about: in him the flesh lusteth against the spirit, and the spirit against the flesh; yet thus is he on the way to that peace which alone deserves the name. And so also must it be in a sinful world (2 Tim. iv. 2).[2]

Ver. 10–12. '*Blessed are they which are persecuted for righteousness' sake: for theirs is the kingdom of heaven. Blessed are ye, when men shall revile you, and persecute you, and shall say all manner of evil against you falsely, for my sake. Rejoice, and be exceeding glad: for great is your reward in heaven: for so persecuted they the prophets which were before you.*'—Augustine oftentimes very graphically describes the new forms

---

[1] Thus Augustine himself, writing to a soldier, says (*Ep.* clxxxix., *ad Bonifac.*): Esto ergo etiam bellando pacificus, ut eos quos expugnas ad pacis utilitatem vincendo perducas. Beati enim pacifici, ait Dominus.

[2] *Con. Lit. Petil.* ii. 69.

which persecution assumes, though remaining in its essence still the same, when now it is no longer the persecution which heathens direct against Christians, but that which bad Christians direct against good; and we learn from him by the way some of the shapes which in his time the scoffings of the ungodly against the true servants of God assumed.[1] But further, he has need frequently to urge that it is, according to the Lord's own express limitation, a suffering '*for righteousness' sake*,' and that alone, which has the promise; in other words, that it is the cause which makes the martyr. This he had need to affirm against the Donatists, who, because they were suffering, on account of their schism, many things at the hands of the civil power, claimed on the score of their suffering, and without further question this blessing as their own; appealing to these sufferings of theirs as a satisfying evidence of the righteousness of their cause. Now, not to say that many of their sufferings were self-inflicted,[2] many the just punishment of civil crimes, even those which they bore for their faith's sake gave them no right to assume this, till another question had been settled in their favour. For, without in the least seeking to justify all the means which the temporal power used, and Augustine, with the rest of the Church in Africa, in part though not wholly approved, for the

---

[1] *Enarr. in Ps.* xc. 3: Dicunt, Magnus tu, justus, tu es Elias, tu es Petrus, de cælo venisti.

[2] *Con. Gaudent.* i. 28: Genus hominum .... crudelissimum in mortibus alienis, vilissimum in suis. See the almost incredible details of this fury of self-destruction which possessed them, in his letter to Count Boniface (*Ep.* clxxxv. 3). Yet the actual facts do not altogether bear him out, when of one of them he asks (*Con. Gaudent.* i. 21), Quam persecutionem patimini, nisi a vobis?

forcible reducing of them to unity, in this he plainly had right, when he entirely denied their claim, merely on the strength of these sufferings, to be the rightful inheritors of this blessing.[1] Another point had first to be proved, namely that it was for Christ's sake, as witnesses for Christ's truth, and as the true representatives of Christ's body, that they suffered what they did. They could not, in arguing with the Catholics, who entirely denied this, bring these sufferings in proof that they, because they suffered these things, were the true Church of Christ. Else by the same proofs, as he keenly retorts, the priests of Baal were martyrs, when Elijah slew them; and so far as a cross went, the malefactors had that in common with the Lord.[2] If the Donatists found in these persecutions the evidence that they were Christ's Church, by the same right the pagans who still survived in the Roman Empire might appeal to the forbidding of their worship, the closing of their temples, the pains and penalties which attended an adherence to their superstitions, as so many evidences of their truth. Once grant that suffer-

[1] Thus Gaudentius, a Donatist, writes: Nostram caussam solæ nobis istæ persecutiones gravissimam reddunt, and proceeds to quote these verses; Augustine replies (*Con. Gaudent.* i. 20): Recte ista dicerentur a vobis quærentibus martyrum gloriam, si haberetis martyrum caussam. Non enim felices ait Dominus, qui mala ista patiuntur, sed qui propter filium hominis patiuntur, qui est Christus Jesus. Vos autem non propter ipsum patimini, sed contra ipsum. And again: Non ex passione certa justitia, sed ex justitiâ passio gloriosa est. Ideoque Dominus . . . , non generaliter ait, Beati qui persecutionem patiuntur, sed addit magnam differentiam quâ vera a sacrilegio pietas secernatur. Ait enim, Beati qui persecutionem patiuntur propter justitiam. Cf. *Con. Lit. Petil.* ii. 71; *Con. Crescon.* iv. 46; *Ep.* xliv. 2, 4.

[2] *Ep.* clxxxv. 2: Et ipse Dominus cum latronibus crucifixus est, sed quos passio jungebat, caussa separabat. Cf. *Serm.* cccxxxi. 3.

ings of themselves constituted martyrs, and every mine would be full of them; no criminal who perished by the sword of justice but would be the rightful claimant of a crown.[1]

Augustine, with reference to the promise here, enlarges often on the sustaining power of Christian hope, and of an eye directed to this '*great reward.*'[2] At the same time on this word '*reward*' he is very distinct, and carefully guards against all claims which, on the strength of it, the proud heart of man might make. The '*reward in heaven*' does, indeed, bear a relation to that which is done or suffered for Christ's sake on earth, yet is it a relation of grace, and not of debt. God has chosen, and of his own free will and unmerited bounty appointed, that there should be such a relation, and now 'He is faithful that promised.' The doctrine of preventing grace, legitimately carried out, must for ever exclude the notion of any claim, as of merit properly so called; not that there are not merits, or rather graces, which will hereafter be recognized, but that these merits are them-

---

[1] *Enarr. in Ps.* xxxiv. 23: Martyres non facit pœna, sed caussa. Nam si pœna martyres faceret, omnia metalla martyribus plena essent, omnes catenæ martyres traherent; omnes qui gladio feriuntur, coronarentur. Nemo ergo dicat, Quia patior justus sum. Quia ipse qui primo passus est, pro justitiâ passus est, ideo magnam exceptionem addidit, Beati qui persecutionem patiuntur *propter justitiam* . . . . Nemo ergo dicat, Persecutionem patior; non ventilet pœnam, sed probet caussam. *Enarr. in Ps.* cxlv. 7: Quidquid jure pateris, non est injuria. Latrones multa patiuntur, sed non injuriam. Scelerati, malefici, effractores, adulteri, corruptores, omnes patiuntur multa mala, sed nulla est injuria. Cf. *Con. Lit. Petil.* ii. 19; *Serm.* cccxxxvii. 1, 2; cccxxviii. 4.

[2] *Enarr. in Ps.* xxxvi. 23: Attende mercedem, si vis sustinere laborem.

selves gifts of God,[1] so that eternal life will be but the adding of one more, one crowning gift, to all that preceded.[2] It will be but 'grace for grace.'[3]

Augustine contemplating this heptad of beatitudes no longer singly, but as a whole, suggests more than once, that perhaps they may stand in some relation to the sevenfold operations of the Holy Spirit whereof Isaiah (ch. xi.) speaks; though it can hardly be said that he very successfully traces the correspondencies of each to each. He notes how the eighth beatitude returns upon the first, having the same promise, '*the kingdom of heaven*,'[4] which, in the intermediate ones, has not been forsaken, for that one comprehends all the others, but has

[1] *Ep.* cxciv.: Ipsa vita æterna gratia nuncupatur, nec ideo quia non meritis datur, sed quia data sunt et ipsa merita quibus datur. And again (*De Grat. et Lib. Arb.* 8): Si vita bona nostra nihil aliud est quam Dei gratia, sine dubio et vita æterna, quæ bonæ vitæ redditur, Dei gratia est; et ipsa enim gratis datur, quia gratis data est illa, cui datur.

[2] *Ep.* cxciv.: Cum Deus coronat merita nostra, nihil aliud coronat, quam munera sua. *Enarr. in Ps.* lxx.: Tua peccata sunt, merita Dei sunt. Supplicium tibi debetur, et cum præmium venerit, sua dona coronabit, non merita tua. And see his anti-Pelagian treatises, *passim*.

[3] *Ep.* cxciv.: Nunc vero de plenitudine ejus accepimus non solum gratiam quâ nunc juste in laboribus usque ad finem vivimus, sed etiam gratiam pro hâc gratiâ, ut in requie postea sine fine vivamus. Augustine has here given the hint, at least, of the right explanation, which so many even now miss, of that difficult χάριν ἀντὶ χάριτος (John i. 16), that it means one grace heaped upon, and as a better grace coming in some sort *in the room of* (ἀντί), a preceding (so Theognis, ἀντ' ἀνιῶν ἀνίας, troubles upon troubles). It is scarcely, however, probable that St. John meant, as he implies, by the first χάρις, the grace of this life, and by the second, the grace of eternal life, but, rather by the two together, the uninterrupted stream of God's gifts in Christ, which are ever succeeding, and, so to speak, *replacing* one another.

[4] *De Serm. Dom. in Mon.* i. 4; and *Serm.* cccxlviii.

been broken up, or rather contemplated successively in its various aspects; and how this return indicates that now the perfect and complete man has on all his sides been declared.[1] For these, as he says most truly, are not different persons that will be differently blest; it is not that one, being pure in heart, will see God; another, being merciful, will obtain mercy; and a third who, hungering and thirsting after righteousness, will be filled. But these are different sides of the same Christian character, with the capacities of blessedness which are linked to each; so that, while it is true that, because the man is '*pure in heart,*' and not because he is '*merciful,*' or '*meek,*' or a '*peacemaker,*' he will '*see God*;' and again, because he is '*merciful,*' and not because he is '*pure in heart,*' that he will '*obtain mercy,*' and so with the rest, yet it is the same person throughout to whom all the promises belong. Just as, were it said, 'Happy are they that have feet, for they can walk; happy are they that have tongues, for they can speak;' we should not think of one man having a tongue, another feet, but only to each limb attribute its appropriate function.[2] It is true, indeed, that these graces, like grapes of the same cluster, may ripen some earlier than others, may be some of them finer and fuller than others, yet do they not the less all hang upon the same stalk; and the same process of

---

[1] *De Serm. Dom. in Mon.* i. 3: Octava tanquam ad caput redit: quia consummatum perfectumque ostendit et probat.

[2] *Serm.* liii. 9: Sic tanquam spiritalia membra componens, docuit quid ad quid pertineat. Apta est humilitas ad habendum regnum cælorum, apta mansuetudo ad possidendum terram, aptus luctus ad consolationem, apta fames et sitis justitiæ ad saturitatem, apta misericordia ad impetrandam misericordiam, aptum mundum cor ad videndum Deum.

ripening is going forward in them all. He might have added, perhaps, that in these beatitudes thus distinguished from one another, there is an implicit summons to seek to complete the Christian character in all its aspects; to polish the diamond on all its sides, that so on every side it may be capable of reflecting that light of heaven which on that side also will fall upon it.

Ver. 13. '*Ye are the salt of the earth: but if the salt have lost his savour, wherewith shall it be salted? it is thenceforth good for nothing, but to be cast out, and to be trodden under foot of men.*'—The transition from that which went before is easy: '*Ye are the salt*;' as such intended to communicate a savour of life unto others; to hinder the world from becoming a putrefying mass of corruption. Beware then lest you yourselves, through fear of worldly incommodities and persecutions, lose this your seasoning power, for there are none other to impart grace to you, since it is you that are appointed to impart this to the rest of the world.[1] And the salt which has thus '*lost his savour*,'[2] what will it be good for, '*but to be cast out and to be trodden under foot of men*'? Augustine

---

[1] *De Serm. Dom. in Mon.* i. 6: Si vos per quos condiendi sunt quodammodo populi, metu persecutionum temporalium amiseritis regna cælorum, qui erunt homines per quos a vobis error auferatur, cum vos elegerit Deus, per quos errorem auferat cæterorum?

[2] Here, as there is occasion not unfrequently to notice, the earlier Latin translation which Augustine uses has a better word than that substituted in the Vulgate. In the latter, μωρανθῇ is rendered evanuerit, which is not indeed incorrect, as Tholuck (*Ausleg. d. Bergpredigt*, p. 121) asserts, for we have in Cicero, Salsamenta vetustate evanescunt: but the old *infatuerit* was singularly happy; fatuus = μωρός, the man saltless, insipid. We have no such happy word for it as the French *fade*.

makes here the beautiful observation, that they are not truly thus '*trodden under foot*,' who suffer persecution without shrinking, but they who through fear of persecution become vile, abandoning their faith; for undermost although he may *seem*, yet he is not truly so, who, whatever he may be suffering below on earth, has his heart fixed above in heaven.[1]

Ver. 14. '*Ye are the light of the world. A city that is set on an hill cannot be hid.*'—They, the Apostles, are '*light*,' yet not in themselves, but 'light in the Lord;' rays darted forth from the sun, but not the sun itself. In themselves, even as all others, they were 'sometimes darkness' (Ephes. v. 8), and, receding from the true light, would become darkness again. For no man is a true light, having light in himself, but is as a candle or a lamp, which has been kindled and may be quenched again; having ever need to exclaim with the Psalmist, 'The Lord is my light.'[2] By this '*hill*' on which the city is set, Augustine understands Christ Himself, the foundation upon which the Church is built, the stone cut out without hands, which growing into a mountain fills the world.[3] Yet the Lord may perhaps mean no more than that the

---

[1] *De Serm. Dom. in Mon.* i. 6: Non itaque calcatur ab hominibus, qui patitur persecutionem, sed qui persecutionem timendo infatuatur. Calcari enim non potest nisi inferior, sed inferior non est qui quamvis corpore multa in terrâ sustineat, corde tamen fixus in cælo est.

[2] *Enarr. in Ps.* cxviii. 105: Nulla quippe creatura, quamvis rationalis et intellectualis, a seipsâ illuminatur, sed participatione sempiternæ veritatis accenditur.

[3] *Serm.* cccxxxviii. 1: Ipse est mons, qui ex parvo lapide crevit, et totum orbem crescendo implevit. And *Con. Faust.* xvi. 17: Se scilicet montem, fideles autem suos in sui nominis gloriâ fundatos asserens civitatem.

Church can no more escape the notice of the world, than a city set on an eminence the eyes of men.

Ver. 15. '*Neither do men light a candle and put it under a bushel, but on a candlestick; and it giveth light to all that are in the house.*'—To find, as Augustine does, in this '*bushel*' a particular allusion to worldly cares, or worldly lusts, which we may not suffer to darken the light of the spirit, putting that uppermost which ought to be undermost, and *vice versâ*, certainly seems far-fetched.[1] What the Lord would say is this: You were not given such rare gifts, to let them rust in idleness. It is a statement at once of God's intention concerning them, and a warning that they do not defeat that intention. That salt which is yours was intended to season, see then that it grow not savourless; this city was meant to be visible, beware lest it lose the power of drawing men's eyes to it; this light which is kindled in you was meant to shine and to give light to all that are in the house, that is, in the Church, or, as he rather inclines to interpret it, in the world; see then that you suffer not this light to be obscured in you; it was imparted for a very different end.

Ver. 16. '*Let your light so shine before men, that they may see your good works, and glorify your Father which*

---

[1] *De Serm. Dom. in Mon.* i. 6. And yet it is impossible to deny the beauty of his further explanation of this passage, where concerning the candlestick on which the candle is to be set he says (*Serm.* ccxcvi. 6): Crux Christi est magnum candelabrum. Qui vult lucere, non erubescat de ligneo candelabro. . . . Audi ergo Paulum Apostolum, audi lucernam in candelabro exsultantem, Mihi autem absit gloriari, nisi in cruce Domini nostri Jesu Christi (Gal. vi. 14).

is in heaven.'—There will be an opportunity of entering into Augustine's explanation of this passage, when we come to his reconciliation of the command here given, '*Let your light shine before men,*' with the warning given in this same discourse against doing any of our righteousness '*before men, to be seen of them*' (vi. 1–18). For the present it will suffice to observe, that he suggests the difficulty, and in this way solves it: the Lord says not here, '*Let your light so shine before men, that they may glorify you;*' but, '*that they may glorify your Father which is in heaven,*'—this his glory, and not your own, is to be the end and aim of your efforts;[1] and the later prohibition will not be found to be a prohibition of the doing of good deeds before others, but of the doing them with the purpose that those others may exalt and glorify *us*.

Ver. 17, 18. '*Think not that I am come to destroy the law, or the prophets. I am not come to destroy, but to fulfil. For verily I say unto you, Till heaven and earth pass, one jot or one tittle shall in no wise pass from the law, till all be fulfilled.*'—To the question, all important for the right understanding of this discourse, and indeed for any true apprehension of the relation in which the newer legislation of Christ stood to the older of Moses, namely, in what way Christ was come, '*not to destroy the law, but to fulfil,*' Augustine gives apparently many answers; yet not in fact many, being all at the root

---

[1] *Serm.* cccxxxviii. 3: Non autem Dominus jussit bona opera abscondi, sed in bonis operibus laudem humanam non cogitare. Cf. *Serm.* cxlix. 13: Hoc si quæris, ut glorificetur Deus, noli timere ne videaris ab hominibus. Etiam sic intus est eleemosyna tua in abscondito: ubi solus ille, cujus gloriam quæris, te videt hoc quærere.

but one. First, he says, Christ fulfilled the law by Himself perfectly keeping it. Secondly, He fulfilled it, by shedding abroad that love in the hearts of his people, out of which and out of which alone, it is truly fulfilled[1] (Rom. xiii. 9, 10); and where, through the weakness of the flesh, and the remains of old corruptions, men yet came short, Himself fulfilling it in their room, and so having a right to appear as an Advocate in their behalf.[2] Thirdly, He fulfilled it, when in Him whatsoever was shadowed out in the types of the old law found a completion; whatsoever was prophesied and promised, became in Him Yea and Amen[3] (2 Cor. i. 20). And lastly, He fulfilled it, by unfolding how much it contained, showing how, beside the letter which they deemed so easy to satisfy, it had also an inner spirit: that it had a kernel as well as an outer husk; and he oftentimes quotes as a true parallel to this saying, the words of the Baptist: 'The law was given by Moses, but grace and truth came by Jesus Christ'[4] (John i. 17); this 'grace' that was given by Christ being the power of fulfilling that law, which was before only a threatening and killing letter;[5] this 'truth' being not opposed to

---

[1] *Serm.* cxxv.: Quia venit dare caritatem, et caritas perficit legem; merito dixit, Non veni legem solvere, sed implere. *Ep.* clxvii. 6: Lex libertatis, lex caritatis est.

[2] *Con. Faust.* xix. 17: Deinde quia, etiam sub gratiâ positis, in hâc mortali vitâ difficile est omni modo implere quod in lege scriptum est, Non concupisces: ille per carnis suæ sacrificium Sacerdos effectus, impetrat nobis indulgentiam, etiam hinc adimplens legem; ut quod per nostram infirmitatem minus possumus, per illius perfectionem recuperetur, cujus capitis membra effecti sumus (1 Joh. ii. 1).

[3] *Con. Faust.* xix. 8.   [4] *Ibid.* xvii. 16.

[5] *Serm.* cliv. 1: Concupiscentiam terruit, non exstinxit; terruit, non oppressit; fecit timorem pœnæ, non amorem justitiæ.

untruth,[1] but truth in the sense of reality or body, opposed to shadow or outline ; so that those words of St. John's, and these of our Lord's, he would make exactly to answer to that declaration of St. Paul, where, speaking of the distinction between clean and unclean meats, and of holidays, new moons, and sabbaths, he says; 'which are a *shadow* of things to come, but the *body* is of Christ' (Col. ii. 17 ; cf. Heb. x. 1). All these explanations run into one ; since in Christ's law-fulfilling walk in the flesh, as the promised Man, and in the consequences of that life of perfect holiness, in his resurrection and ascension, power was first given to humanity to keep the law ; even as by that was first revealed to men all which the law of love was, and all the blessed demands which it made upon them ; and no less the quarter in which they were to find help for all their shortcomings therein, of which shortcomings they had now become conscious as they had never been before.

By these answers it will at once be seen how little Augustine consents with them, Manichæans of old, Quakers in modern times, who affirm that in the new legislation of Christ there is any abrogation of, or withdrawing of, or casting a slight upon, any part of the old.[2] He had on this matter the same conflict to maintain with the Manichæans, which Irenæus, Tertullian, and others in earlier times, had maintained with the Gnostics. These, as those, eagerly snatched at such passages as Matt. v. 31, 32, 43, 44 ; they urged them as plain proofs that Christ had come,

---

[1] Not ἀλήθεια, opposed to ψεῦδος, but ἀλήθεια (= εἰκών, Heb. x. 1 = σῶμα, Col. ii. 17) to σκιά, or ὑπόδειγμα, Heb. ix. 23. Cf. *Enarr. in Ps.* lxxiii. 1.

[2] As he well says: Qui addit quod minus habet, non utique solvit quod invenit, sed magis perficiendo confirmat.

according to his own avowal, to repeal the Mosaic code; they affirmed that whatever of that code He sanctioned and allowed to stand fast, was not peculiar to Moses, but belonged to the universal morality, while everything distinctive of Moses was by Him disallowed and cast aside. Now Augustine, in reply to these enemies of the Old Testament, does not avail himself of the timid gloss of some modern commentators, and admit that there is such a repealing; but then plead that it is only the Pharisaical additions to the law, or perversions of it, which thus are repealed. Rather he denies the repealing altogether; and this verse, he affirms, gives us the key-note of the Sermon on the Mount, at least to the end of its first chapter.[1] He declares that in each case the old stands fast, however there may be a new unfolded from it. This verse, as may well be supposed, was a hard saying to the adversaries. They had *many* ways of escape from it, having no good one. Sometimes they denied that the words were Christ's at all, urging that they are only recorded by St. Matthew, who was not called till a later period of our Lord's ministry than that at which he reports them to have been spoken, and whose witness they claimed therefore the liberty of

[1] *Con. Faust.* xix. 26: Si Christus ubi quibusdam antiquis sententiis propositis adjunxit, Ego autem dico vobis, neque primorum hominum legem hoc verborum additamento adimplevit, neque illam quæ per Mosem data est quasi contrariorum oppositione destruxit; sed potius omnia ex Hebræorum lege commemorata ita commendavit, ut quidquid ex personâ suâ insuper loqueretur, vel ad expositionem requirendam valeret, si quid illa obscure posuisset, vel ad tutius conservandum quod illa voluisset. Vides quam sit aliter intelligendum, quod ait. Non se venisse legem solvere, sed adimplere; scilicet, ut non quasi semiplena istis verbis integraretur, sed ut quod literâ jubente propter superborum præsumtionem non poterat, suadente gratiâ propter humilium confessionem impleretur, opere factorum, non adjectione verborum.

putting by.[1] Or allowing these words to be the Lord's, they replied, that He did not mean the Jewish law (however He might be willing that the Jews should understand Him so to speak, and thus lay aside a part of their bitter enmity against Him), but quite a different thing; that the law which He came to fulfil was the natural law written on men's hearts.[2] And then, with an attempt to shift the ground of controversy, they would retort on the Catholics, that as little could *they* understand Him as here speaking of that law which was given by Moses; for neither did they themselves act as though Christ had come to fulfil and confirm that, but, on the contrary, had suffered a great part of its enactments, its feasts and its sacrifices, its circumcision and its sabbaths, its differences of meats, and a thousand other legal observances, to fall out of use; and would now earnestly oppose their revival. The Catholics, they said, not less than themselves, did by their practice plainly imply that Christ had dissolved and abrogated the law which He found in force at his coming.[3]

This charge against the Church, that it too was a dissolver of the law, and could not therefore hold to these words in any sense which would give it a right to accuse others for utterly rejecting them, was, of course, one well worthy of an answer, and Augustine girds himself to the answering it fully. He replies that, in the Church, nothing which there was in the synagogue is abrogated, but rather everything confirmed,—inasmuch as in Christ the type has passed into the reality, the flower into the

---

[1] *Con. Faust.* xvii. 3.   [2] *Ibid.* xix. 1.
[3] *Con. Faust.* xviii. 1, 2. Faustus, the Manichæan, says, Nec tu id credis, de quo me solum incusas.

fruit, the prophecy into the fulfilment, and in that is to stand fast for ever. Had those that were Christ's continued after his coming to cling to the type and the prophecy, had they abode among the outlines and the shadows, refusing the substantial realities which now in Him and in his Incarnation were made theirs, *then*, indeed, there would have been, on their part, a dissolving of the law and the prophets, inasmuch as it would have seemed that nothing of all which these had foretold or prefigured had come to pass; that all was promise, and nothing fulfilment. But now, whatever they let go in the letter, they did, in the very letting go, declare to be for them spiritually fulfilled.[1] They did not practise now the circumcision of the flesh, but only because Christ had given them the true circumcision of the Spirit, and so caused the shadow to give place to the substance. They kept not the feast of unleavened bread, for in Christ whatever that feast had foreshadowed was accomplished; He had purged out the old leaven from men's life, causing them to be unleavened in Him;[2] nor kill the passover, now that the true Lamb of God, indeed without blemish, was slain. They observed not the sabbath, which, indeed, was only such in a figure; for now the true sabbaths, those to which the others pointed, were come; seeing that He was come, in whom is the true rest and sabbath-keeping for men's spirits, He who could say, 'Come unto Me, all ye that labour and are heavy laden, and I will

---

[1] *Con. Faust.* xviii. 4. And again: Ideo ablata quia impleta.

[2] *Con. Faust.* xix. 10: Cum quæris, Cur azyma sicut Judæi non observet Christianus, si Christus non venit legem solvere sed implere? Respondeo, immo propterea magis hoc non observat Christianus, quia quod illâ figurâ prophetabatur, expurgato veteris vitæ fermento, novam vitam demonstrans, Christus implevit.

give you rest.'[1] In this way Christ fulfilled, and did not dissolve, the ceremonial part of Moses' law,—even as the moral precepts, by the new light which He cast upon them, by the added grace that He gave, enabling men to observe them.[2] But to this subject there will be frequent necessity of returning.

Ver. 19, 20. '*Whosoever therefore shall break one of these least commandments, and shall teach men so, he shall be called the least in the kingdom of heaven: but whosoever shall do and teach them, the same shall be called great in the kingdom of heaven. For I say unto you, That except your righteousness shall exceed the righteousness of the scribes and Pharisees, ye shall in no case enter into the kingdom of heaven.*'—What is this being '*least in the kingdom of heaven,*' which is here threatened? Augustine starts with taking certainly for granted that the doer and teacher of transgression,[3] whom Christ is speaking of here, even though it be only the transgression of '*one of these least commandments,*' cannot be one who will ultimately have any part with

[1] Con. Faust. xix. 19. Cf. Con. Adimant. 16.
[2] *Con. Faust.* xix. 18: Hæc præcepta sunt morum; illa sacramenta sunt promissorum: hæc implentur per adjuvantem gratiam, illa per redditam veritatem; utraque per Christum, et illam semper gratiam donantem, nunc etiam revelantem, et hanc veritatem tunc promittentem, nunc exhibentem.
[3] He, however, does not understand the words exactly thus—but of one who does ill, while he teaches well, making this a parallel phrase to Matt. xxiii. 3, 'they say and do not.' (Beza, in modern times, has the same construction, making καὶ διδάξῃ = κἂν διδάξῃ, and referring οὕτω to the ποιεῖν, and not to the λύειν.) Thus, *In Ev. Joh. Tract.*; cxxii. 9: Denique ut ostenderet istos minimos reprobos esse, qui docent bona loquendo, quæ solvunt male vivendo, nec quasi minimos in vitâ æternâ futuros, sed omnino ibi non futuros . . . continuo subjecit, Dico enim vobis, nisi, &c. Cf. *Serm.* cclii. 3.

Him. There are two explanations, then, of the finding a place at all assigned to him in Christ's kingdom: for on the face of the words, he that is '*least in the kingdom*' has a place in that kingdom, albeit that place is the lowest. The one is to understand '*the kingdom of heaven*' as the Church militant, the kingdom in the present earlier state of its development, in which false teachers and evil workers are mingled with the doers and teachers of the truth, and to say, that in this he shall have a place, though, in God's estimate, the lowest place, and one from which, as an unworthy occupant, he shall hereafter be thrust out altogether. In this way Augustine oftentimes explains the passage, referring in proof of such use of the term, '*kingdom of heaven*,' to such passages as Matt. xiii. 47.[1] Sometimes, however, he has another solution; he takes '*the kingdom of heaven*' as the perfected kingdom of glory, that into which nothing unholy shall enter; and then he understands the announcement that he shall be '*least*' there, as one of those mitigated forms of expression, in which oftentimes threatening is more awfully concentrated than in many a loudest menace; to say that he '*shall be least*' there, being but another way of saying that he shall not be found there at all.[2] The net now has fish of all kinds and all sizes, but then it shall only contain '*great fishes*'[3] (John xxi. 11) in it, and such as

---

[1] Thus *Serm.* cclii. 3: Minimus vocabitur in regno cælorum. Sed in quo regno cælorum? In ecclesiâ quæ modo est. . . . Ibi erit, sed minimus. Cf. *De Civ. Dei*, xx. 9.

[2] ’Ελάχιστος = novissimus *et nullus*.

[3] *In Ev. Joh. Tract.* cxxii. For the full understanding his allusion here, it would be needful to enter into the allegorical signification which he finds in the miraculous draught of fishes after the Resurrection; see my *Notes on the Miracles*, 11th edit. pp. 497, sqq.

are '*least*' shall not be found in it at all. It will at once be seen that these two explanations do not contradict one another; he shall be least in the kingdom now, and excluded from it altogether hereafter.

It seems, I confess, improbable to me that the '*least in the kingdom of heaven*' can mean one excluded from it altogether, especially as our Lord has used elsewhere the selfsame phrase in so very different a sense (Matt. xi. 11). We may more naturally understand Him to be speaking here of some, who out of a false freedom taught, and themselves practised, an exemption from certain special Christian precepts, dealing with them as though they were annulled and abrogated; and who yet, despite of this, did in the inmost centre of their life belong to Christ. Such should be '*least in the kingdom of God*' —in it, being saved by their faith; but '*least*' in it, as having taken so false and one-sided a view of its enactments—'*least*' now in the judgment of God, and in the work which from that false standing point they should be able to accomplish—'*least*' hereafter in the place that should be assigned them. And Augustine's argument, drawn from ver. 20,—which he makes only to be the stronger and yet more emphatic repetition of ver. 19,— and so '*least in the kingdom*,' in the former verse, to be identical with the having no entrance into that kingdom in the latter,—appears to me an erroneous one, drawn from a wrong view of the relation in which the verses stand to one another. The second does not say over again what the first had said, but rather there is progress and a climax in the verses. Such a relaxing for yourselves and for others of the commandments will *set you low* in the true kingdom of obedience and holiness (ver.

19); but this of having a righteousness so utterly false and hollow as that of the Scribes and Pharisees, will not merely set you low, but will exclude you from that kingdom altogether (ver. 20); for while that marks an *impaired* spiritual vision, this marks a vision utterly darkened and destroyed.

Ver. 21, 22. '*Ye have heard that it was said by them of old time,*[1] *Thou shalt not kill; and whosoever shall kill shall be in danger of the judgment: But I say unto you, That whosoever is angry with his brother without a cause shall be in danger of the judgment: and whosoever shall say to his brother, Raca, shall be in danger of the council: but whosoever shall say, Thou fool, shall be in danger of hell-fire.*'—On the words, '*Whosoever is angry with his brother without a cause,*' Augustine observes, that in the Greek MSS. the last words find no place, and it is simply and with no qualification, '*Whosoever is angry with his brother shall be in danger of the judgment.*' This, however, is not the fact with the larger number of existing MSS., in which, as in Fathers of the second century, and also in most of the early Versions, εἰκῆ is to be found. He must himself naturally have desired it there; for he sides in this matter, and rightly, with the Peripatetic rather than the Stoic, everywhere recognizing the possibility of a holy anger; and he ingeniously shows, that even should it be right to omit '*without a cause,*' the prohibition of anger will still not be absolute, nor without its qualifications; since it is with thy brother, not

---

[1] Grammatically, it would be quite possible to render τοῖς ἀρχαίοις, as the Authorized Version has done, 'by them of old time' (v. 27; v. 33); but '*to* them of old time' is better, and is preferred by Augustine.

with thy brother's sin, that thou art forbidden to be angry.[1] Anger itself may be a holy passion; it is attributed to Christ (Mark iii. 5), and to God; the possibility of its being sinless in man is expressly recognized in those words of the Apostle, 'Be ye angry, and sin not' (Ephes. iv. 26). For it is not, he says, itself hatred, though when it is cherished long it is evermore in danger of degenerating into hatred; as wine too long kept, of turning into vinegar: and therefore is it to be gotten rid of, to be emptied out from the vessel of the heart, without delay: 'Let not the sun go down upon your wrath.'[2]

Augustine tells us, that he learned from a Jew whom he had questioned about the word '*Racha*,' that it is one with no distinct significance, being rather an interjection, the vague exclamation of an indignant mind.[3] And accepting this account of the word, he finds a natural and

[1] *Retract.* i. 19: Non fratri irascitur, qui peccato fratris irascitur. It is here that he notes εἰκῆ to be wanting in the Greek MSS.; in his Exposition of the discourse itself he reads it. Among the leading MSS. the Codex Vaticanus is the only one that now has it not. A and C have unfortunately *lacunæ* exactly here.

[2] *Ep.* xxxviii.: Nulli irascenti ira sua videtur injusta [εἰκῆ]. Ita enim inveterascens ira fit odium, dum quasi justi doloris admixta dulcedo, diutius eam in vase detinet, donec totum acescat, vasque corrumpat. Quapropter multo melius nec juste cuiquam irascimur, quam velut juste irascendo in alicujus odium iræ occultâ facilitate delabimur. In recipiendis enim hospitibus ignotis, solemus dicere, multo esse melius malum hominem perpeti, quam forsitan per ignorantiam excludi bonum, dum cavemus ne recipiatur malus. Sed in affectibus animi contra est. Nam incomparabiliter salubrius est etiam iræ juste pulsanti non aperire penetrale cordis, quam admittere non facile recessuram, et perventuram de surculo ad trabem.

[3] *De Serm. Dom. in Mon.* i. 9: Dixit enim esse vocem non significantem aliquid, sed indignantis animi motum exprimentem; *in Joh. Tract.* li. 2. Meyer (*in loco*) is in error when he ascribes to Augustine a derivation of 'Racha' from the Greek ῥάκος, a rag. Augustine names this, but only to reject it as inadmissible.

easy climax here. The first grade of the sin is, when a man feels the emotion of a causeless anger in his heart, which yet he so represses, that it does not find any utterance without. In the second it breaks forth into utterances of passion, such as this ' *Racha*,' which, however, having no fixed meaning attached to them, are not words of settled scorn and contempt. That is the third degree of the sin, when it is indeed no longer merely anger, for it has ripened into hate. He is no doubt perfectly right in affirming that degrees of guilt are intended to be signified here; although it is impossible to acquiesce in the interpretation of his Jew. ' *Racha* ' is no such mere exclamation, but a term of reproach, not indeed very severe, but having a fixed meaning, and that very nearly equivalent to our English, Oh vain man! [1]

And as ascending degrees of guilt are involved in those different outcomings of anger, so also degrees of penalty are expressed by the '*judgment*,' the ' *council*,' and the ' *hell-fire* ' or Gehenna; but all of them penalties divine, not human: with the deeper guilt there goes along the deeper damnation. For it is a strange mar-

[1] Racha = ὦ ἄνθρωπε κενέ, Jam. ii. 20. The use by St. James of this very term, and our Lord's own use of that very μωρός, which He here forbids (Matt. xxiii. 17), are proofs, if any were needed, that these terms are instanced but as signs of inward states of enmity and scorn: else might a new Pharisaism develop itself out of this very teaching of Christ's; which, as avoiding certain expressly forbidden utterances of outrage and ill will, should count itself free to use any other. But, even as these, where love is, may be righteously and holily used, and Christ and his servants spake the keenest things in love (*De Civ. Dei*, xxi. 27: Non dicit fratri suo, Fatue, qui, cum hoc dicit, non ipsi fraternitati, sed peccato ejus infensus est), so where love is not, the guilt of ' *Racha*,' and ' *Thou fool*,' will be incurred not merely where other words are substituted for these, but where no word at all escapes from the lips.

ring and misunderstanding of our Lord's words on the part of some,—one from which Augustine, as will be seen by the next quotation, is altogether free,—to make the two earlier, the *'judgment'* and the *'council,'* expressions of penalties inflicted by earthly tribunals; and only the third, or *'Gehenna,'* that which comes directly from the sentence of God. On the contrary, they are all earthly forms under which the different degrees of loss and injury for the spirit of man, reaching at last to its total loss and perdition,—set forth by the casting out into the place appointed for the burning of the offal of Jerusalem,—are described. It is scarcely possible to imagine a more entire missing of the meaning, a more complete perplexing of the whole passage, than is theirs, who find here any allusion to earthly judgment-seats or human councils, save as the shadows under which the things heavenly, in themselves unutterable, are portrayed.[1] Therefore our translation ' *hell-fire* ' is not happy, as somewhat countenancing the confusion; not that the eternal loss is not indicated here, but since that has twice before been mentioned under forms of things earthly, so should it still have been here. The valley of Hinnom, profaned by the idolatrous worship of Moloch (2 Kin. xxiii. 10 ; Jer. vii. 31), and thereafter the place where every abomination was flung forth, the offal and the carcases, to be gnawed by the worm, and from time to time consumed by the fire, is the ' *Gehenna* ' here. And our Lord is saying exactly the contrary to that which they who so interpret will then be making Him to say. He is

---

[1] *De Serm. Dom. in Mon.* i. 9 : Videntur ergo aliqui gradus in peccatis et in reatu, sed quibus modis invisibiliter exhibeantur meritis animarum, quis potest dicere ?

saying, Moses gave you a law for the outer man; he told you that if you killed, you should die. That is well; but there is another region which that precept could not reach, which nothing that Moses had to impart could reach, a region with which earthly tribunals do not meddle, but over which I am Lord; and I tell you that you must learn to look at the least germs of evil will to your brother, the faintest rudiments of hate, as having in them the nature of deadliest sin, as implicit murder,[1] to be checked in the very outset; since each successive growth of this indulged evil will bring you under greater and greater condemnation, till at last it will bring on a total and final separation of your souls from the one fountain of grace and love : so that, being entirely reprobate, ye shall be cast out to that fearful place, of which the valley of Hinnom, with its worm and its fire, is the nearest, though indeed only the faint, earthly representation.

Ver. 23, 24. '*Therefore if thou bring thy gift to the altar, and there rememberest that thy brother hath ought against thee; leave there thy gift before the altar, and go thy way; first be reconciled to thy brother, and then come and offer thy gift.*'—In this way Augustine traces the connexion with what precedes : If thou mayest not be angry with thy brother, much less mayest thou retain in thine heart a deep-seated and lasting alienation

---

[1] Augustine quotes, exactly to the point, 1 John iii. 15. And *Serm.* lviii. 7 : Gladium non eduxisti, non vulnus in carne fecisti, non corpus plagâ aliquâ trucidâsti. Cogitatio sola odii in corde tuo est, et teneris homicida. . . . Quantum ad te pertinet, occidisti quem odisti. Emenda te, corrige te. Si in domibus vestris scorpiones essent aut aspides, quantum laboraretis, ut domus vestras purgaretis, et securi habitare possetis ? Irascimini, et inveterantur iræ in cordibus vestris, fiunt tot odia, tot trabes, tot scorpii, tot serpentes ; et domum Dei, cor vestrum, purgare non vultis ?

from him: or elsewhere, with a slight difference: Thou hast heard the awful consequences of a sin against thy brother, how it separates thee not merely from him, but from God: hear now also the remedy,[1] how thou mayest restore thy disturbed relations with thy God; for thy present condition unfits thee for communion with Him, deprives thee of the privilege of offering to Him any gift, seeing that thou must *thyself* be an offering, before any meaner thing which thou bringest can be welcome as such.[2]

But how obey the command to '*go*,' to our brother? The half-completed sacrifice will hardly endure so long a delay. It may be that we are ignorant where now to seek him; or, if we know, that lands and seas lie between him and us. This going then must be most often a going in heart, a hastening with the swift affections of love, not with the tardy motion of the feet.[3] And the '*altar*' and the '*offering*' must in like manner be spiritually understood. We offer our gift, when we bring any sacrifice of praise or prayer; we offer it on God's altar when we bring it aright: heretics, as Augustine observes, offer not *on the altar*, they rather cast their unaccepted gifts on the ground. From all this it is plain that he does not see

---

[1] *Serm.* lxxxii. 3: Ecce ille reatus gehennæ quam cito solutus est. Nondum reconciliatus, eras gehennæ reus: reconciliatus, securus offers munus tuum ad altare.

[2] *Serm.* lxxxii. 3: Offers munus tuum, et tu non es munus Dei.

[3] *De Serm. Dom. in Mon.* i. 10: Pergendum est ergo . . . non pedibus corporis, sed motibus animi, ut te humili affectu prosternas fratri ad quem carâ cogitatione cucurreris, in conspectu ejus, cui munus oblaturus es. Ita enim etiamsi præsens sit, poteris eum non simulato nimo lenire, atque in gratiam revocare, veniam postulando; si hoc prius coram Deo feceris, pergens ad eum non pigro motu corporis, sed celerrimo dilectionis affectu.

any immediate nor any direct reference here to the Holy Eucharist; though, indeed, in that, as being the culminating act of self-oblation unto God, there must be on the part of the offerer a perfect charity, if his highest gift, to wit, that of himself, is to be graciously received. Speaking at a time when the Jewish temple-worship was not yet overthrown, nor its service abolished, our Lord clothes an eternal truth in language borrowed from that 'worldly sanctuary;' and to find direct allusion to any thing but this in these terms '*altar*' and '*gift*'[1] is highly unnatural; and certainly, as far as I know, is not countenanced by Augustine.[2]

But there still remains to consider what these words, '*have ought against thee*,' may mean. Is the offerer of the gift to be regarded as the injured person or the injurious? Is he to hasten and *bestow* forgiveness for a wrong that has been done him? or to *sue* forgiveness for a wrong that he has done? The words, as Augustine rightly observes,[3]

---

[1] The most important passage in Augustine on the spiritual sacrifices which the faithful are evermore to offer unto God, and the relation in which they stand to the abrogated sacrifices of the law, is to be found *De Civ. Dei*, x. 3-6. Thus, c. 3: Cum ad illum sursum est, ejus est altare cor nostrum: ejus Unigenito eum sacerdote placamus: ei cruentas victimas cædimus, quando usque ad sanguinem pro ejus veritate certamus: ei suavissimum adolemus incensum, cum in ejus conspectu pio sanctoque amore flagramus: ei dona ejus in nobis, nosque ipsos vovemus, et reddimus; ei beneficiorum ejus solemnitatibus festis et diebus statutis dicamus sacramusque memoriam, ne volumine temporum ingrata subrepat oblivio: ei sacrificamus hostiam humilitatis et laudis in arâ cordis igne fervidæ caritatis.

[2] Yet there must be some passage of the kind, as Johnson, in his *Unbloody Sacrifice*, numbers him among those who have so interpreted the '*altar*' here, but he does not give any especial reference.

[3] *De Serm. Dom. in Mon.* i. 10: Si in mentem venerit quod aliquid habeat adversum nos frater: id est, si nos eum in aliquo læsimus, tunc enim ipse habet adversum nos: nam nos adversus

clearly point out the latter to be the meaning. If our brother had wronged us, *we* should have something against *him*, not he against us. It would be no duty then to seek him, or to ask his pardon; but only to be willing to be sought by him, and to bestow pardon on him; only where we have been the wronger, can we *seek* it. This done, '*then come and offer thy gift,*' that is, this being accomplished in spirit, go forward in the sacrifice of worship, or praise, or supplication, or whatsoever else it was, whereof thou hadst commenced the offering to thy God.[1]

Ver. 25, 26. '*Agree with thine adversary quickly, whiles thou art in the way with him; lest at any time the adversary deliver thee to the judge, and the judge deliver thee to the officer, and thou be cast into prison. Verily I say unto thee, Thou shalt by no means come out thence, till thou hast paid the uttermost farthing.*'— Augustine's interpretation of the precept, '*Agree with thine adversary quickly,*' is remarkable, though it requires some modification before it can claim entire assent. That other explanation seems weak and trivial, though supported by considerable authorities, which finds nothing here but a counsel of worldly prudence, amounting to this, Seeing that the issue of every pleading before a judge is uncertain, be not stiff and stern in refusing terms of peace and reconciliation, lest unexpectedly judgment be given against thee, and afterwards thou rue bitterly thine

---

illum habemus, si ille nos læsit: ubi non opus est pergere ad reconciliationem: non enim veniam postulabis ab eo qui tibi fecit injuriam, sed tantum dimittes. A comparison with Mark xi. 25; Rev. ii. 4, 14, 20, confirms this as the true meaning of ἔχειν τι κατά τινος.

[1] *De Serm. Dom. in Mon.* i. 10: Atque inde veniens, id est, intentionem revocans ad id quod agere cœperas, offers munus tuum.

obstinacy and thine implacable mind. But since counsels of a merely worldly prudence do not and cannot find place in our Lord's teaching, it is nothing strange that Augustine, not so much as noticing this literal explanation, at once looks for a spiritual, and inquires, who is this '*adversary*' with whom we are bidden to '*agree*.' It cannot, he observes, be the devil, for however the term '*adversary*' (ὁ ἀντίδικος, cf. 1 Pet. v. 8) would suit him, yet our part is not to consent, but to proclaim and maintain never ceasing warfare, with him.[1] Nor can it be the flesh, though that too is an adversary warring against the soul; for men are only too willing to consent with it, and the true course is not so to do, but rather to make it consent with us.[2] Nor can it, he affirms, be any fellow-man whatever; for what power would such a one have to deliver us over to an eternal doom?[3] As little can the '*adversary*' be exactly God, though He too might well be termed an adversary of the sinner, since then the image would be disturbed, and God would be at once the accusing party, and the judge before whom the two parties are going. Therefore, Augustine concludes, though that last explanation was not far from the truth, it will be better to see in this adversary the Law—an adversary indeed, so long as for the past it condemns us, and for the present commands us one thing while we do and love

---

[1] *De Serm. Dom. in Mon.* i. 11: Neque concordare cum illo expedit, cui semel renunciando, bellum indiximus, et quo victo coronabimur: neque consentire illi jam oportet, cui si nunquam consensissemus, nunquam in istas incidissemus miserias.

[2] *De Serm. Dom. in Mon.* i. 11: Qui eam servituti subjiciunt, non ipsi ei consentiunt, sed eam sibi consentire cogunt.

[3] *Ibid.* i. 11: Quomodo judici traditurus est, qui ante judicem pariter exhibebitur?

another: and every step of our lives which we take with this adversary unreconciled, is a drawing nearer to the judgment-seat, and to a certain condemnation there.[1] But when we love the thing which the law commands, as in Christ we are enabled to do, and the righteousness of the law is fulfilled in us, then we are reconciled with it. It is a law, indeed, still, but a law of liberty.[2] For the past also we are reconciled with it, inasmuch as through Christ Jesus and faith in his blood it has lost its accusing power; we have learned to accuse ourselves, and have thus taken from the law its desire of accusing us any more. And this is to be done '*quickly*,' because we know not how soon for us '*the way*' may be ended, and we may find ourselves suddenly in the presence of the Judge.[3]

Such is the explanation of the passage offered by Augustine. It can hardly be accepted without certain

---

[1] *Serm.* ccli. 8: Quis est adversarius tuus? Sermo legis. Quæ est via? vita ista. Quomodo est ille adversarius? Dicit, Non mœchaberis, et tu vis mœchari. Dicit, Non concupiscas rem proximi tui; et tu vis rapere res alienas. . . . Quando vides quia ille sermo aliud jubet, et tu aliud facis, est adversarius tuus. . . . Compone, dum es cum illo in viâ. Adest Deus qui vos concordet. Quomodo vos concordat Deus? Donando peccata et inspirando justitiam ut fiant opera bona. Cf. *Serm.* cix. 3, 4: Adversarius est voluntatis tuæ, donec fiat auctor salutis tuæ. . . . Adversarius est nobis, quamdiu sumus et ipsi nobis. . . . Si cum eo consenseris, pro judice invenies patrem, pro ministro sævo angelum tollentem in sinum Abrahæ, pro carcere paradisum. Cf. *Serm.* ix. 3, and *Serm.* ccclxxxvii.

[2] The redeemed man is not any more, according to Augustine's profound distinction (*In Ev. Joh. Tract.* iii.), *sub* lege, but *cum* lege and *in* lege—not *under* the law (qui enim sub lege est, non implet legem, sed premitur a lege: *Enarr. in Ps.* cxliii. 1), but yet neither ἄνομος, because ἔννομος Χριστῷ (1 Cor. ix. 21), because every loosing from the old is in its very nature an attaching to the new (Rom. vii. 1-4).

[3] *De Serm. Dom. in Mon.* i. 11.

modifications. It is most true, as he affirms, that the outraged law of God is the real '*adversary*,' but yet that law is here contemplated, according to the whole connexion of the passage, as embodied and finding its mouthpiece in the brother who has something against us. And his objection to understanding by the adversary a fellow-man at all—for how, he asks, could such have power to deliver us to the heavenly judgment?—is capable of an easy dilution. An injured brother's appeals to the All-seeing and All-searching against our continued enmity, our determined refusals to walk in love, will be, whether he desire it or not, a delivering of us to the judge; as further he will deliver us, compelled as he will be to appear against us and to be our accuser at the last day.[1]

Dealing with the minor details of this parabolic saying, and the distribution of its several parts, by '*the judge*,' Augustine understands not the Father, but Christ, since 'the Father judgeth no man, but hath committed all judgment unto the Son;'—by '*the officer*,' an angel, since He will come with all his holy angels to judge both the quick and the dead;—by the '*prison*,' the outer darkness, the place of lost spirits; not purgatory, as some in modern times, who see in the words, '*till thou hast paid the uttermost farthing*,' a limit defined, after which there would be deliverance from this prison. That such an interpretation was stirring in Augustine's time we learn from his own words. It was one, as he owns, to which he would most gladly have himself consented, but that he found the Scriptures on the other side too clear and too

---

[1] It is remarkable that Hilary had already anticipated this objection and difficulty, and answered it: Adversario tradente nos judici, quia manens in eum simultatis nostræ ira nos arguit.

strong. He asks with truth, How can any paying of this debt come to pass in that world where there is no place for amendment or repentance?[1] and is compelled to find here the expression of an everlasting doom.[2]

Ver. 27, 28. '*Ye have heard that it was said by them of old time, Thou shalt not commit adultery: But I say unto you, That whosoever looketh on a woman to lust after her hath committed adultery with her already in his heart.*'—Here Augustine makes an accurate and important distinction; that it is not, namely, the looking at a woman, out of which, unawares to the beholder, there rises up in his heart the suggestion of an unholy desire, which constitutes a man guilty of adultery; but the looking *with the intention and purpose* of thereby feeding desire;[3] though, indeed, it is only a practical

---

[1] *De Serm. Dom. in Mon.* i. 11 : Unde enim solvitur illud debitum, ubi jam non datur pœnitendi et correctius vivendi locus? And again : Semper solvit novissimum quadrantem, dum sempiternas pœnas terrenorum peccatorum luit. At the same time in this very passage he adds some words of caution, which show that the mystery of the doom of impenitent sinners was one not fully thought out by him: Neque ita hoc dixerim ut tractationem diligentiorem videar ademisse de pœnis peccatorum quomodo in Scripturis dicantur æternæ, quanquam quolibet modo vitandæ sunt potius quam sciendæ.

[2] *De Octo Dulc. Quæst.* qu. 1 : Illud enim quod dicitur, quandoque, etsi post plurimum temporis, eos qui in catholicâ communione moriuntur, quamvis usque in finem vitæ hujus flagitiosissime et sceleratissime vixerint, de pœnis ultricibus exituros familiarius meum tangit affectum. But he goes on to say, such passages as 1 Cor. vi. 9, 10; Ephes. v. 5, 6, are too strong on the other side.

[3] *De Serm. Dom. in Mon.* i. 12 : Non dixit, Omnis qui concupiverit mulierem, sed qui viderit mulierem ad concupiscendum eam: id est, hoc fine et hoc animo attenderit, ut eam concupiscat. And again, *Con. Julian.* iv. 14: Illud [videre] Deus condidit, instruendo corpus humanum; illud [videre ad concupiscendum] diabolus seminavit, persuadendo peccatum. This distinction has been often

Pelagianism, which would deny the concupiscence itself, whether stirred by a distinct act of the will or not, to be of the nature of sin. Still it is not this which Christ is here denouncing, but rather the deliberate fomenting and feeding of lust through the fuel of impure looks. He that so doth, '*hath committed adultery already in his heart,*' and this, even though from one cause or another sin be not 'finished' in act, as well as in desire.

Ver. 29, 30. '*And if thy right eye offend thee, pluck it out, and cast it from thee: for it is profitable for thee that one of thy members should perish, and not that thy whole body should be cast into hell. And if thy right hand offend thee, cut it off, and cast it from thee: for it is profitable for thee that one of thy members should perish, and not that thy whole body should be cast into hell.*'—He questions whether this '*right eye*' which must be plucked out, and this '*right hand*' which must be cut off, shall be understood generally of anything that is eminently dear to us,[1] or whether we shall attach to them a more special signification. He determines for the latter, and will have the '*right eye*' to mean some beloved friend, our counsellor and guide in divine things, whom yet we must cast off if he would lead us into heresies and errors,[2] even as by the '*right hand*' is meant our active

overlooked; yet lies in the words themselves. Πρὸς τὸ (eo ut) is not = εἰς τὸ (ita ut). In the first, which stands here, is involved not merely the event, but also the intention.

[1] *De Serm. Dom. in Mon.* i. 13: Quidquid namque est quod significat oculus, sine dubio tale est quod vehementer diligitur. Solet enim et ab iis qui vehementer volunt exprimere dilectionem suam, ita dici, Diligo eum ut oculos meos, aut etiam plus quam oculos meos.

[2] *Serm.* lxxxi. He instances, as an example of what he means, our Lord's conduct with Peter, and his words to him, 'Get thee

helper and minister in the same, whom in like manner, under the like circumstances, at whatever cost and pain to ourselves, we must reject and cut off. They are therefore called the '*right* eye' and the '*right* hand,' that is, those of most price and esteem, because they are guides and helpers in things of greatest moment, to wit, in things spiritual. And in this he notes that another consequence is included: for if even such must be cast off, how much more the *left* eye and the *left* hand, the helpers not in spiritual but in worldly things, if they would put a stumbling block in our way.

The only objection to this interpretation is its narrowness; that it does not and cannot exhaust the meaning of the words: though it is important to hold fast what in it is involved, namely, that these are not sins, but *occasions of sin*, which are to be cut off without pity. Christ is not here telling us that our sinful lusts are to be renounced, for that is of course; but that what is harmless in itself, yea, in its subordinate position useful and comely, and thus likened to the hand and the eye, even this, if through any peculiarity of our temperament or condition, through any temptation in which it entangles us, it hinders the main work of our salvation, is to be offered up to that, as the less to the greater, as a part to the whole. Thus suppose one felt that the love of art threatened to kill in him the love of God, he would have no choice but to count as an enemy that which in itself might be well worthy of honour, and to deal with it as such.

behind Me, Satan ' (Matt. xvi. 23), when he would have placed a stumbling block in his way; though in that case it did not come to the actual casting off, the rebuke being effectual to bring back Peter to his true position.

Ver. 31, 32. '*It hath been said, Whosoever shall put away his wife, let him give her a writing of divorcement: But I say unto you, That whosoever shall put away his wife, saving for the cause of fornication, causeth her to commit adultery: and whosoever shall marry her that is divorced committeth adultery.*'—Here, too, the Manichæans found a contradiction between the teaching of Moses and of Christ; Moses giving facilities for divorce; '*Whosoever will put away his wife, let him give her a writing of divorcement;*' but Christ throwing every hindrance in the way of it, declaring that marriage, '*saving for the cause of fornication,*' was indissoluble. It is true that in this they involved themselves in a contradiction which did not escape the keenness of the adversary with whom they had to do; since Moses, whom they spake against, was yet here, according to their own principles, worthiest of praise, in helping to dissolve the bands of an institution, which they traced up to the devil,[1] and which, as they affirmed, contributed to the detaining of the divine principle in a material prison. But presently leaving this, which was only by the way, Augustine answered triumphantly, that the legislation of Moses and of Christ, so far from being opposed to one another, were in fact both in the same line. When Moses said, '*Whosoever shall put away his wife, let him give her a writing of divorcement,*'[2] this was not spoken to

[1] *Con. Faust.* xix. 26 : Verumtamen quæro cur displiceat dimittere uxorem, quam non ad matrimonii fidem, sed ad concupiscentiæ crimen, habendum esse censetis ? Eo modo enim putatis partem Dei vestri etiam carnis compedibus colligari.

[2] *De Serm. Dom. in Mon.* i. 14 : Qui dimiserit, det illi libellum repudii : ut iracundiam temerariam projicientis uxorem libelli cogitatio temperaret. Qui ergo dimittendi moram quæsivit, significavit quantum potuit duris hominibus se nolle disscidium.

encourage divorces, but, on the contrary, to throw impediments in their way. A man could not at every light motion of caprice or anger dismiss his wife, but was thus compelled to have resort to a legal process, and to the Scribe, who alone could draw out the necessary instrument, and who might be assumed, from his position and education, to be a wise and a prudent man; able, therefore, and willing, if that were possible, to remove misunderstandings and offences, to knit again the bands of a broken love between the two parties; and who, only when every such attempt had failed, would give the bill of divorce which the husband required.[1] This much the law did; why it did not more the Lord Himself tells us elsewhere; 'Moses, because of the hardness of your hearts, *suffered* you to put away your wives (Mat. xix. 8);'[2] but the legislation of Moses is in the same direction with that of Christ, the one a lower, the other a higher, witness for the sanctity of marriage; in each there was alike a declaration that the Lord 'hateth putting away,' though Moses did not impose upon them who were yet living in the oldness of the letter, the higher precept, or introduce them into the fuller blessings which they only were capable of receiving who were walking in the newness of the Spirit.

---

[1] *Con. Faust.* xix. 26 : Præsertim quia, ut perhibent apud Hebræos scribere literas Hebræas nulli fas erat nisi scribis solis. . . . Ad hos igitur quos oporteret esse prudentes legis interpretes et justos disscidii dissuasores, lex mittere voluit eum, quem jussit libellum repudii dare, si dimisisset uxorem. Non enim ei poterat scribi libellus, nisi ab ipsis qui per hanc occasionem ex necessitate venientem quodammodo in manus suas bono consilio regerent, atque inter ipsum et uxorem pacifice agendo dilectionem concordiamque suaderent.

[2] *Con. Faust.* xix. 29.

Is the sin, Augustine stops here to inquire, which the Lord recognizes as a justifying cause of divorce, to be taken in its literal sense, and to be limited to that? or shall we rather receive it according to its wider spiritual significance, and by this '*fornication*' understand every graver sin which corrupts and defiles the soul, according to that profound symbolism of Scripture, which evermore speaks of all grievous departures of all kinds from God under this image of the breaking faith by a wife with her husband? His determination, in which however he disagrees with most of the Fathers of the Church, is in favour of the latter interpretation.[1] Yet one cannot doubt that the literal is the true sense of the passage. There is no cogency in his argument, that there are other sins of a deeper dye even than this; and, therefore, if this justifies a separation, by so much the more will those others. It is enough to reply that those other sins, if indeed they be graver, yet do not contradict the very idea of marriage, do not assail it at its very heart and centre; so little do they do so, that if only this faith be kept, marriage may exist as truly between the unregenerate as the faithful, the wicked as the godly, though of course it will not be to them the type and figure of so great a mystery. Nor is it to be supposed that our Lord, uttering here, as He knew He was uttering, a word which should be in all ages as a sharp sword, piercing even to the dividing asunder of relations the closest, would yet have

---

[1] *De Serm. Dom. in Mon.* i. 16: Ex quo intelligitur quod propter illicitas concupiscentias, non tantum quæ in stupris . . . committantur, sed omnino quaslibet, quæ animam corpore male utentem a lege Dei aberrare faciunt, et perniciose turpiterque corrumpi, possit sine crimine et vir uxorem dimittere et uxor virum. Cf. c. 12, and *Quæst.* lxxxviii. qu. 83.

left it in such vagueness and uncertainty, exposed to such cruel abuses, as it must needs be, if the literal meaning of the words be once abandoned, and that which is thus proposed accepted in its stead.[1]

But there is another question, in the matter of which the judgment of Augustine has certainly had a most powerful influence, first, on the interpretation of the words of Scripture, and through this on the determinations of the Church;—I mean the lawfulness of the marriage of the innocent and injured party, after separation on account of a breach of the marriage vow on the other side. It is well known that while the Greek Church allows adultery as a sufficient ground for the dissolution of marriage, the Western Church, and ourselves as a branch of it, pronounces the marriage bond indissoluble, except by the death of one or other of the contracting parties, and forbids the innocent party no less than the guilty to enter into another union. And this remains the law of the Church, however by recent legislation the civil law has been put in antagonism with it. As often as the matter has been brought into debate, Augustine's authority has been appealed to in support of the decision at which the Western Church has arrived; and his weight is no doubt thrown very decidedly into this scale.[2] He does not,

[1] Augustine himself, in his *Retractations*, i. 19, acknowledges that the whole matter—latebrosissima quæstio, as he terms it—deserves to be considered anew, and though he does not withdraw, yet speaks with no confidence of, the decision to which he has arrived. Sed quam velit Dominus intelligi fornicationem, propter quam liceat dimittere uxorem, utrum eam quæ damnatur in stupris, an illam de quâ dicitur, Perdidisti omnem qui fornicatur abs te (Ps. lxxii. 27), in quâ utique et ista est, . . . etiam atque etiam cogitandum est atque requirendum.

[2] Thus *Serm*. cccxcii. 2: Solius fornicationis causâ licet uxorem

however, profess to see his way in the matter with perfect clearness, and acknowledges at the last [1] how little satisfied he is with his own endeavours to bring the Scriptures bearing on the matter into manifest harmony with one another; so great indeed for him is the obscurity which hangs over the whole question, that in a work written late in life he does not shrink from affirming that, whichever interpretation be the right one, he who shall adopt the other cannot be said more than venially to err.[2]

His arguments in proof that there can be no permission here of marriage in any case after divorce (the divorced party still living), are chiefly these. Such an interpretation of this passage cannot be the right one, for so this Scripture will be brought into contradiction with 1 Cor. vii. 10, 11, 'Let not the wife depart from her husband. But and if she depart, let her remain unmarried, or be reconciled to her husband.' The steps of his argument are these: Our Lord declares one only ground which will justify a wife departing from her husband, that is, his adultery. St. Paul therefore here could not have contemplated any other. Contemplating, then, as he must have done, this, he did yet enjoin, 'Let her remain unmarried,' unless she be reconciled to him.[3]

To this it has been replied that St. Paul *did* con-

adulteram dimittere, sed illâ vivente non licet alteram ducere. . . . Adulteria sunt, non conjugia.

[1] *Retract.* ii. 57: Scripsi duos libros . . . cupiens solvere difficillimam quæstionem. Quod utrum enodatissime fecerim, nescio: immo vero non me pervenisse ad hujus rei perfectionem sentio.

[2] *De Fide et Oper.* 19: In ipsis divinis sententiis ita obscurum est utrum et iste, cui quidem sine dubio adulteram licet dimittere, adulter tamen habeatur si alteram duxerit, ut quantum existimo venialiter ibi quisque fallatur.

[3] *De Conjug. Adulter.* i. 1–7.

template other grounds of separation, not indeed as finding place in the highest Christian state, where clearly there would be no room for them, but yet as not entirely inconsistent with a true Christian profession; and this provisional bearing with a more imperfect state of things, and this moderation in dealing with the perplexities which sprang from the first growing up of a Christian Church out of a heathen world, is part, they say, of the wonderful wisdom of the great Gentile Apostle. But while he bears with such things, he yet declares at the same time the higher law; and with this toleration of *separations*, will yet in no case allow an infringement of the Lord's precept, which forbids *divorces* on all lower grounds, and so forbids a new marriage upon either side, saving where the adultery of the other party has, *de facto*, dissolved the union, having annulled its essential condition; '*They two* shall be one flesh.' But this view is altogether strange to Augustine. When he is pressed, as he is by Pollentius, whom he answers at length, with the Lord's own words here, and at Matt. xix. 9, he forsakes the canon[1] which he has himself elsewhere laid down, namely, that the shorter and more incomplete passage is to receive the law of its interpretation from the longer and fuller; and reversing this rule he finds the limitation of these passages of St. Matthew in the parallel ones of St. Mark (x. 11), and St. Luke (xvi. 18).[2] And then, to bring these sayings into agreement with those, he affirms, that by the ex-

---

[1] Pauciora exponi debent secundum plura, et regula generalis per exceptionem alibi traditam est limitanda.

[2] *De Conjug. Adult.* i. 11, 22 : Quod subobscure apud Matthæum positum est, quoniam totum a parte significatum est, expositum est apud alios, qui totum generaliter expresserunt, sicut legitur apud Marcum (x. 11); et apud Lucam (xvi. 18).

ception, '*saving for the cause of fornication*,' the Lord intended, that it would be a *greater* sin to dismiss her without this provocation, not that it would be *no* sin with this provocation to do it, and to marry another; for, he says, the Lord pronounced it adultery in either case, although in one of a worse kind than in the other.[1]

Another argument which Augustine finds against understanding the words as involving such a permission, is that so a reconciliation with the guilty party becomes impossible; while yet he believes that under the new covenant of grace such, where there is repentance, ought to find place; for he argues that as God receives back the souls that have departed from Him, and defiled themselves, into his favour and grace, if only penitent and believing, reunites them to Himself, this should be the pattern and example for his people; there should not be a sterner severity and remembrance of sin on man's part; there should not be in any case a casting off for ever.[2] But the analogy does not hold good; he should have taken the sins not merely which are inconsistent with, but that *which directly contradicts*, the idea of the relations between God and man, and shown that there is forgiveness for that. Now there

---

[1] *De Conjug. Adult.* i. 9 : Cur ergo, inquis, interposuit Dominus causam fornicationis, et non potius generaliter ait, Quicunque dimiserit uxorem suam et aliam duxerit, mœchatur ? . . . . Credo, quia illud quod majus est, hoc Dominus commemorare voluit. Majus enim adulterium esse quis negat, uxore non fornicante dimissâ alteram ducere, quam si fornicantem quisque dimiserit, et tunc alteram duxerit ? Non quia et hoc adulterium non est, sed quia minus est.

[2] *Ibid.* ii. 6: Hæc crimina in Vetere Dei Lege nullis sacrificiis mundabantur, quæ Novi Testamenti sanguine sine dubitatione mundantur; et ideo tunc omnimodo prohibitum est ab alio contaminatam viro recipere uxorem. . . . Nunc autem postea quam Christus ait adulteræ, Nec ego te damnabo, vade, deinceps noli peccare; quis non intelligat debere ignoscere maritum, quod videt ignovisse Dominum amborum.

is only one such sin, and that we know is irremissible, the sin against the Holy Ghost. If there is to be an argument from this analogy, here and here only would it be fairly drawn. Other blemishes in the conduct of the married one to another, as harshness or unkindness, disturb the relation, but do not, as does this sin, contradict and deny its fundamental idea. Moreover, one cannot help feeling, that while this recommendation, that the innocent party should receive back the guilty, *may* spring from a deep sense of the forgiveness which sinners, who have themselves been forgiven, should extend one to another, yet often it does spring from an unworthy apprehension of marriage, from a slight sense of the reality of the wrong that has been inflicted, of the sanctity that has been violated.

While I thus venture to criticize the arguments by which Augustine justifies the conclusions at which he has arrived, I do not dispute his conclusions themselves; but the much which can be urged backward and forward on the Scriptures by which one determination of this question is supported and the other, makes it, I think, plain that it is not by appeal to this text or that, that the Church must justify the position which in this matter she has taken. The real justification of her position is, that it is most in harmony with that idea of marriage which Christ has brought into the world, and which He has set his Church to maintain and uphold against all those influences which are ever at work in a sinful world to lower and debase it.

Ver. 33–37. '*Again, ye have heard that it hath been said by them of old time, Thou shalt not forswear thy-*

self, but shalt perform unto the Lord thine oaths : but I say unto you, Swear not at all ; neither by heaven ; for it is God's throne : nor by the earth ; for it is his footstool : neither by Jerusalem ; for it is the city of the great King. Neither shalt thou swear by thy head, because thou canst not make one hair white or black. But let your communication be, Yea, yea ; Nay, nay : for whatsoever is more than these cometh of evil.'—This prohibition, apparently absolute, of all swearing perplexed Augustine not a little, and this he takes occasion more than once to confess.[1] He feels that it cannot be as absolute as it seems ; that the oath, or calling upon God to be a witness of the truth, or an avenger of the falsehood spoken, cannot in itself be sinful, since rather it is a religious act, the testimony of faith in a righteous and living God. Moreover he finds that God Himself swears ;[2] as at Ps. cix. 4 ; Gen. xxii. 16 ; Num. xiv. 28 ;[3] many, too, of his servants, and in some of the holiest moments of their lives (thus St. Paul, Rom. i. 9 ; 1 Cor. xv. 31 ; 2 Cor. i. 23 ; Gal. i. 20) ; and these oaths cannot be transgressions on their parts.[4] He himself, when he

---

[1] *Serm.* clxxx. 4 : Scio difficilem questionem, et caritati vestræ fateor, semper illam vitavi.

[2] Sometimes however, as *Enarr. in Ps.* lxxxviii. 4, he denies that this is in point, saying : Deus solus securus jurat, quia falli non potest. But since the perjury is in the intention, not in the mere sounds that proceed from the lips, the man who does not wish to deceive might in this respect just as securely swear as God, who is not able to be deceived.

[3] He might have added the σὺ εἶπας of our Lord (Matt. xxvi. 64), which is in the strictest sense an oath : since according to the Hebrew manner, it was the proposer, and not the taker of the oath, who repeated its words.

[4] *De Mendac.* 15 : Præcepti violati reum Paulum, præsertim in

found that an oath would give strength to the words which he spoke, and charity made him earnestly to desire that they should be implicitly believed, was in the habit of confirming them by an appeal to the present and all-seeing God;[1] and though, as he says, he did this ever with a solemn awe, yet his moral sense told him he was not sinning herein.

But what then does our Lord mean by this '*Swear not at all*'? He is often content to answer, that it is a counsel of prudence. He who swears often *may* escape falling into perjury, but he who swears never cannot fall into it; as you *may be* delivered from falling over a precipice, even though you walk on its very edge; but you come into no possible danger of this fall, if you put an ample space between yourself and it.[2]

It is not wonderful that Augustine should feel little content with a reply such as this, which indeed could satisfy nobody. But surely this would be a truer point of view from which to contemplate the words,— a view, as will be seen by the two or three next quotations, not altogether strange to Augustine, though he has not wrought it consistently out. There were, we know, whole worlds of mischief at work among our Lord's hearers and

Epistolis conscriptis atque editis ad spiritalem vitam salutemque populorum, nefas est dicere.

[1] *Serm.* clxxx. 9.

[2] *Serm.* clxxx.; *Ep.* clvii. 5; *De Serm. Dom. in Mon.* i. 17: Sicut enim falsum loqui non potest, qui non loquitur; sic pejerare non potest, qui non jurat. *Serm.* cccvii. 3: Non est peccatum, verum jurare, sed quia grande peccatum est, falsum jurare, longe est a peccato falsum jurandi, qui omnino non jurat: propinquat falsæ jurationi, qui vel verum jurat. Dominus ergo, qui prohibuit jurare, supra ripam te noluit ambulare, ne pes tuus in angusto labatur, et cadas. Compare *De Mendac.* 28.

contemporaries in the matter of oaths : as first, that some were regarded as more binding than others; that those made in the name of God must indeed be performed, while of those by the altar and the gift on the altar, by the temple and the gold in the temple, some obliged, while others were of no force at all; and the spiritual rulers of the people, blind leaders of the blind, had made a scale of the obligation of these several oaths on the consciences of men (Matt. xxiii. 16–22). Then, too, men had learnt to think that if only God's *Name* were avoided, there was no irreverence in the frequent oaths, '*by heaven,*' '*by the earth,*' '*by Jerusalem,*' by their own heads—and in these introduced on the slightest need, or on no need whatsoever; just as now-a-days men who would not be wholly profane will substitute for the Name of God sounds that nearly resemble, but are not exactly it, or the name, it may be, of some heathen deity; and this out of a lingering respect for that Holy Name.

Our Lord then, with all this before his eyes, addresses that listening crowd, not abolishing, but here too filling out and completing, the commandment given by Moses. You have heard, He would say, long ago the sanctity of the judicial oath, and of that taken upon solemn occasions, and in the express Name of God. Moses forbade all rash and all false swearing by that awful Name. But I forbid light irreverent adjurations of every kind, and at every time—adjurations so lightly spoken and so lightly broken. I banish them altogether, and from every region of your life.[1] The '*at all*' which perplexes Augustine so much,

[1] *Serm.* clxxx. 10 : Istam ergo consuetudinem quotidianam, crebram, sine causâ, nullo extorquente, nullo de tuis verbis dubitante, jurandi, avertite a vobis, amputate a linguis vestris, circumcidite ab ore vestro.

and has perplexed so many, is doubtless to be interpreted and limited by what immediately follows. *All these kinds of oaths*, which I specify, are forbidden you. You do not, by using them, really avoid taking God's name in vain. For why have these oaths anything binding? It is God's presence in these created things which gives them any hold over your consciences. If you swear by heaven, you have not escaped the swearing by his Name, for heaven is his throne—if by the earth, it is his footstool—by Jerusalem, it is the city of the great King—if by your head, as supposing that there at least you are swearing by something which is your own, yet it is not so; that is God's workmanship, you could not of your own power make one hair of it black or white.[1] So that every oath is an awful thing, and in its ultimate ground rests upon God, though the lightness and frivolity of men cause them willingly to conceal this fact from themselves.

And then He opens to them the deep mystery of the oath, that it is a consequence of sin; not itself evil, but '*of evil*;'[2] so that in the highest idea of intercourse, as between unfallen beings, angels with angels, it could find no place: it would be utterly inconceivable. Only where the tree of life has been forsaken for the mournful yet wondrous teaching of the tree of the knowledge of good and evil, only where the lie has come forth, could there be any

---

[1] *De Serm. Dom. in Mon.* i. 17 : Quid enim poterat quisque magis an se pertinere arbitrari quam caput suum? Sed quomodo nostrum est, ubi potestatem faciendi unius capilli albi aut nigri non habemus?

[2] *De Mendacio,* 18: A malo alterius, cui non aliter videtur persuaderi posse quod dicitur, nisi jurando fides fiat, aut ab illo malo nostro, quod hujus mortalitatis adhuc pellibus involuti cor nostrum non valemus ostendere: quod utique si valeremus, juratione opus non esset.

word to designate the truth. Were all speech the exact outcoming of the inner life, were there never any gulf between that and this, there could be no form of speech which would carry fuller assurance than another. He that demands an oath recognizes the untruthfulness of man; he does not indeed affirm that the other of whom he demands it would now speak falsehood without it; but only that in him, and in himself, and in every man, is that which, except for the ever newly-awakened sense of a standing in the presence of God, the all-seeing and the all-avenging, would lead to untruth; that only God, and the awful sense of God's presence among them, can keep men true; so that in this respect the oath is a deeply religious act, a confession that God is true, and only in God can any man be other than a liar. Yet not the less it '*cometh of evil*,' since men ought not to need, and but for their first great departure from God would not need, thus continually to be brought back into his presence in whose presence they ought continually to abide. And the oath disappears, wherever there is any near approximation to this dwelling in the Divine presence. The true ideal of Christian conversation, that toward which the Church is continually striving, that to which multitudes of God's saints have already arrived in all their intercourse one with another, is one in which the oath *has* become superfluous, in which the simplest Yea and Nay are all that are ever offered or asked, each having entire confidence that the other is always speaking as though God heard him. After this sincerity, this entire truthfulness of conversation one with another, the Lord would have his disciples strive, and to this attain. Let guile and deceit cease from among you, and the oath will cease also; for it is '*of evil*,' of *your* evil; and it is only that evil which renders it so frequently offered, and so frequently required.

Ver. 38, 39. '*Ye have heard that it hath been said, An eye for an eye, and a tooth for a tooth: but I say unto you, that ye resist not evil: but whosoever shall smite thee on thy right cheek, turn to him the other also.*'—Here is again the apparent difficulty of harmonizing the new and old; the appearance as though Christ did not intend to harmonize them, did not mean to put his legislation in connexion with, but rather in opposition to, the legislation of Moses; and with this difficulty, the temptation to forsake the true explanation for the easy one—for that, I mean, which seems easy at first, but which yet will presently involve him that snatches at it in infinite perplexities and contradictions. Augustine's dispute with the Manichæans must have brought him early to a consciousness of this. They, of course, gladly seized on this passage,[1] as another proof of the manner in which Christ sought to disconnect and dissociate his teaching from the teaching of the Old Testament; as if He were here saying, They of old time taught one thing, but I teach another: they encouraged retaliation; but I denounce it, and in its place require the extreme forgiveness of injuries. The true explanation however is, that the different precepts belong to different domains of man's life; and Christ is bringing the inner domain of man's life under *his* law, while Moses had been satisfied with bringing the outward under the dominion of his. But that outward is not abolished in one jot or tittle of it by the new law of love. It is still '*an*

[1] See *Con. Adim.* 8.

eye for an eye, a tooth for a tooth,' not indeed always in this form exactly, but the *spirit* of all law which is exercised in a Christian State is retributive and avenging, and approximating more or less to this. Neither does it herein sink or obscure its character as a *Christian* State, but rather asserts it the more. The civil magistrate is ' a revenger to execute justice.' God has appointed him to be such; and without such a witness, all sense of righteousness and of judgment would quickly perish from the world.

Moreover, as Augustine observes,[1] it is monstrous to adduce this precept, ' *an eye for an eye, and a tooth for a tooth,*' as fostering revenge, that is, private animosity and hate. For, he asks, is the natural man, is the enraged savage, satisfied with inflicting on his foe *as much* as he has suffered ? No; his desire is ever to inflict *more*; to return two, twenty, a hundredfold it may be, for the one which he has received; thus a second time disturbing the balance of equity, though in the other scale,—and so

[1] *Con. Faust.* xix. 25: Quandoquidem et illud antiquum ad reprimendas flammas odiorum, sævientiumque immoderatos animos refrenandos, ita præceptum est. Quis enim tantundem facile contentus est reponere vindictæ, quantum accepit injuriæ ? Nonne videmus homines leviter læsos moliri cædem, sitire sanguinem, vixque invenire in malis inimici unde satientur ? Quis pugno percussus non aut judicia concitat in damnationem ejus qui percusserit, aut si ipse repercutere velit, totum hominem, si non etiam telo aliquo arrepto, pugnis calcibusque contundit ? Huic igitur immoderatæ ac per hoc injustæ ultioni, lex justum modum figens, pœnam talionis instituit; hoc est, ut qualem quisque intulit injuriam, tale supplicium pendant. Proinde, Oculum pro oculo, dentem pro dente, non fomes sed limes furoris est ; non ut id quod sopitum erat, inde accenderetur, sed ne id quod ardebat, ultra extenderetur, impositus. Est enim quædam justa vindicta, justeque debetur ei qui fuerit passus injuriam : unde utique cum ignoscimus, de nostro quodammodo jure largimur. Cf. *De Serm. Dom. in Mon.* i .19.

himself losing, and causing his adversary, under the sense of an unmerited amount of injury, to lose, the sense of a righteous government in the world, according to which every transgression of law will recoil on the transgressor, and receive a just recompense of reward. This law then of Moses, which took the execution of the vengeance out of his hands who might so easily be tempted to mar it, by overdoing it, or by doing it in hatred and personal enmity, was not a fostering, but a checking, and in its measure a subduing, of the evil of man's heart. It did not indeed implant there a principle of love, nor yet certainly secure that they who availed themselves of it should be pure from all motives of private hate, and inspired only by a zeal for God's outraged justice, and a desire to make an offending brother recognize the law against which he had been sinning. It might be only, as in one place he terms it, a righteousness of the unrighteous.[1] But still (as a preparation at least), it was working in this line, until a higher Lawgiver should come, and teach that besides this law of righteousness, there was a law of love which He would write in the hearts of his people, and which would teach them that, where only selfish interests were perilled, every thing was to be forgiven, every thing to be foregone—a law of love not unknown to saints of the elder covenant (1 Sam. xxiv. 4; Ps. vii. 4)—even as this same law would teach them the harder lesson yet of carrying out, where need was, the justice, at once retributive and corrective, of God,[2]—and

---

[1] *Enarr. in Ps.* cviii. 4: Quæ, si dici potest, injustorum justitia est.
[2] *De Serm. Dom. in Mon.* i. 20: Neque hic ea vindicta prohibetur, quæ ad correctionem valet: etiam ipsa enim pertinet ad misericordiam . . . . 'Sed huic vindictæ referendæ non est idoneus, nisi qui odium quo solent flagrare qui se vindicare desiderant, dilectionis magnitudine

this, apart from the slightest feeling that herein they were suspending the law of love, or rendering to the man evil for his evil; on the contrary it would be still good for his evil, inasmuch as it would be justice for his injustice, right for his wrong. Truly a hard thing, yet not an impossible, rightly to carry out.

The command which Christ has here given to '*resist not evil*,' and the others of like import which are scattered through the Gospels, but which lie the closest in this discourse, are open to abuse upon two sides. There is, first, the abuse of the Quaker, who demands that there should be throughout a cleaving to the letter, and who affirms that it is nothing but cowardice and a shrinking from the strictness of Christ's law, and from the painfulness of the demands which it makes upon us, which prevents these precepts of his from being literally interpreted and obeyed. Augustine meets this assertion, first historically, showing that neither did the Lord Himself, nor yet his Apostles, who must be held as authoritative interpreters of his word, hold themselves bound in every case to the letter of these commandments. For instance, when the servant of the High Priest struck our blessed Lord with the palm of his hand, He did not offer Himself to be stricken again, but firmly, though mildly, rebuked the smiter (John xviii. 22, 23). And St. Paul spake a yet sterner word to that judge who unrighteously bade *him* to be stricken; 'God shall smite *thee*, thou whited wall' (Acts xxiii. 3).[1] Then,

---

superaverit. *Enarr. in Ps.* cviii. 5: [Deus] autem etiam cum vindicat, non reddit malum pro malo, quoniam justum reddit injusto. Quod autem justum est, utique bonum est. Punit ergo non delectatione alienæ miseriæ, quod est, malum pro malo; sed dilectione justitiæ, quod est, bonum pro malo.

[1] *De Mendac.* 15; *De Serm. Dom. in Mon.* i. 19.

further, he refutes this interpretation by showing how such a cleaving to the letter of this and similar precepts, will continually issue in a violation of the spirit of Christ's commandments. Thus, in his case who dared to lift up his hand against the Lord, to have offered him the other cheek would have been no love, for it would have been a tempting of him to repeat his fearful offence.[1] Again, because it is said, 'Give to every man that asketh of thee' (Luke vi. 30), am I therefore to give an open knife to an infant,—a drawn sword to a madman or a murderer,— money to him who, as I well know, will surely spend it to his own hurt in riot and excess? Because it is said, '*Resist not evil*,' are therefore the merciless and the destroyers to be allowed to tread the world under their feet, and the righteous, though they may possess the power, to do nothing to restrain them?

No; it is clear this cannot be the meaning. Our Lord can be legislating here only for the inward spirit of man.[2]

---

[1] *In Ev. Joh. Tract.* cxiii. 4: Hic dicet aliquis, Cur non fecit quod ipse præcepit? Percutienti enim non sic respondere, sed maxillam debuit alteram præbere. Quid quod et veraciter mansuete justeque respondit, et non solum alteram maxillam iterum percussuro, sed totum corpus figendum præparavit in ligno? Et hinc potius demonstravit, quod demonstrandum fuit, sua scilicet magna illa præcepta patientiæ, non ostentatione corporis, sed cordis præparatione facienda. Fieri enim potest ut alteram maxillam visibiliter præbeat homo, et iratus. Quanto ergo melius et respondet vere placatus, et ad perferenda graviora tranquillo animo fit paratus?

[2] *Ep.* cxxxviii. 2: Denique ista præcepta magis ad præparationem cordis, quæ intus est, pertinere, quam ad opus quod in aperto fit; ut teneatur in secreto animi patientia cum benevolentiâ in manifesto autem id fiat quod eis videtur prodesse posse, quibus bene velle debemus, hinc liquido ostenditur, quod ipse Dominus Jesus, exemplum singulare patientiæ, cum percuteretur in faciem, respondit, Si male dixi, exprobra de malo: si autem bene, quid me cædis? Nequaquam igitur præceptum suum, si verba intueamur, implevit . . . et tamen

This offering of the other cheek *may be* done outwardly; but only inwardly can it be a rule of action, *always* right; being as it is the meekness of the spirit under wrong, the preparedness of heart to bear as much as has been already inflicted or more, if so any good may come to the injurious person. But Christian love and prudence are in each case to decide whether it is also a precept for the outward conduct. It may be so; it will be so often; for instance, if thou thinkest that thy offending brother will be won by thy Christian patience, and his evil overcome by this exhibition of thy good, then it will be thy duty, if he has done thee one wrong, to lay thyself open to a second: if thou hopest thus to teach him the worthlessness of the things after which he is striving, to let him spoil thee again.[1] Deal with him as a prudent keeper will sometimes deal with a madman in his charge, giving way to and humouring him in part; or as a compassionate physician, that contradicts not his patient in the delirium of his fever.[2] But if thou countest that his evil will grow with impunity, that he will strengthen himself in his sin, and therefore in his misery, through thy forbearance, then it is thy duty to turn to him thy love on its severer side, to repress the outcomings of his evil,[3] though it will be

paratus venerat, non solum in faciem percuti, verum etiam pro his quoque a quibus hæc patiebatur crucifixus occidi, pro quibus ait in cruce pendens, Pater, ignosce illis, quia nesciunt quid faciant.

[1] *Ep.* cxxxviii. 2: Qui ergo vincit bono malum, patienter amittit temporalia commoda, ut doceat quam pro fide atque justitiâ contemnenda sint, quæ ille nimis amando fit malus.

[2] *De Serm. Dom. in Mon.* i. 19.

[3] *Ep.* cxxxviii. 2: Cui licentia iniquitatis eripitur, utiliter vincitur: quoniam nihil est infelicius felicitate peccantium, quâ pœnalis nutritur impunitas, et mala voluntas velut hostis interior roboratur. *De Serm. Dom. in Mon.* i. 20: Posse peccatum amore potius vindicari, quam impunitum relinqui.

the same love that dictates this line of conduct or the other.[1] Thus in a State which is really Christian, war itself will be no violation of charity, but will be carried on in the spirit of love, that those against whom it is waged may not be allowed to make miserable themselves and others, that henceforth it may be more happily consulted for them, than they would else have consented to consult for themselves.[2] Nor indeed are God's sharpest punishments of men, so long at least as their state of trial lasts, other than such outcomings of his infinite pity, which would fain chasten now and for a little, that it may not be obliged to condemn hereafter and for ever.[3]

From all this it will appear, that while Augustine denies that the literal, or what calls itself the literal, scheme of interpretation, is to be painfully cleaved to, yet it is not because this is too high, too loving, and too large, but because it oftentimes would not be high, or large, or loving enough. Thus, for instance, a sparing might oftentimes be no true mercy, nor grow out of any root of love, but might only be an indulgence of our own indolence, or sloth, or cowardice.[4] So that in thus interpreting he in no way

---

[1] *Enchir. de Fide, Spe, et Car.*: Qui emendat verbere in quem potestas datur, vel coercet aliquâ disciplinâ; et tamen peccatum ejus, quo ab illo læsus aut offensus est, dimittit ex corde, vel orat ut ei dimittatur, non solum in eo quod dimittit atque orat, verum etiam in eo quod corripit, et aliquâ emendatoriâ poenâ plectit, eleemosynam dat, quia misericordiam dat. Multa enim bona præstantur invitis, quando eorum consulitur utilitati, non voluntati.

[2] *Ep.* cxxxviii. 2: Si terrena ista respublica præcepta Christiana custodiat, et ipsa bella sine benevolentiâ non gerentur, ut ad pietatis justitiæque pacatam societatem victis facilius consulatur.

[3] *Serm.* clxxi. 4.

[4] *Ep.* cliii.: Plurimum interest quo animo quisque parcat. Sicut enim est aliquando misericordia puniens, ita et crudelitas parcens. And he proceeds to give examples of this. Cf. *Con. Petil.* ii. 67:

favours, but goes directly against, the glosses which the world makes on these sayings of our Saviour, and which it willingly believes to be the only alternatives, if the literal interpretation be forsaken. What the world says, or, when it dares not say, what it thinks in its heart, is very nearly as follows:—This all is very fine morality, only it is unhappily *super*fine, and quite unfit for every-day work and wear;—these precepts are evidently pitched at too high a key for practical use; and must be a good deal taken down before they will actually serve the needs of men. It could never be meant that we are to be *so* meek, *so* forgiving, *so* ready to impart as this; that were only to make ourselves a prey. These are extreme sayings; and it will be enough, if we make some approximation, nearer or more remote, to the behaviour here enjoined.—But no: it is not thus: the commands are to stand fast evermore in all their breadth and fulness: their only limitation is this, that love and the Spirit of God are in each case to be their interpreters, to apply them to the emergent necessity. Where this love and this Spirit are wanting, the precept *must* be interpreted wrongly: if in the letter, it will be in a loveless form; or, if that be forsaken, then there will be a sinning against the letter and the spirit alike.

Ver. 40, 41. '*And if any man will sue thee at the law, and take away thy coat, let him have thy cloak also. And whosoever shall compel thee to go a mile, go with him twain.*'—These verses Augustine brings into comparison with the precept of St. Paul, 'redeeming the time, because

Sicut est plerumque crudelis fallax adulatio, sic semper misericors justa correptio. Cf. *In* 1 *Ep. Joh. Tract.* vii.

the days are evil' (Ephes. v. 16), that is, as he understands it, *purchasing* time, with all its precious advantages, at the cost of meaner things. Give up those meaner things, even though they be thine by right; give thy coat, and thy cloak too, rather than lose thy time, time lent thee for working out thy salvation, in too eagerly seeking to regain them.[1] To enter into the meaning of that difficult passage would be alien to the present purpose; yet, as few or none would now affirm that this is exactly its meaning, there is no true parallel here. That may be, and indeed certainly is, a counsel of Christian *prudence*, but this is not so. Rather we have here, in the form of an outward precept, a law for the inward spirit of a Christian man; and one, as Augustine has himself so often and so distinctly declared, to be, or not to be, embodied by him in act, according to the varying moral and spiritual necessities of the brother that may sin against him. It may be thou canst teach him the higher lesson by letting him have the thing he is unduly snatching at: let him have it then: count his soul more precious than thy worldly goods. But the precept does not necessarily exclude the other dealing of love. It may be that what now he most needs to learn is, that unrighteousness is not to carry the day unchecked, that even in this present evil time 'the way of the transgressors is hard.' Then thou art bound by the same law of love to resist him, and to make him feel that there is a divine order even in the midst of this disordered world; an order which he cannot violate at will; which, though it appear so weak, is indeed mighty; which if he infringe, it will surely

---

[1] *Serm.* clxvii. 4: Judicio vult tecum contendere, ... vult avocare te litibus a Deo tuo. . . . Quantum ergo melius est ut nummum amittas, et tempus redimas.

assert and avenge itself. For as God dealt with men by Law and by Gospel, and the same love was in each, as the Law punished and the Gospel forgave, each for the bringing about an end beyond itself, and the same end, even the righteousness and thus the salvation of the sinner, though they sought it by ways so different, so will there be counterparts to both in the wise and loving conduct of a Christian man toward his offending brother.[1] The everlasting rule is, that thou render good for thy brother's evil: the shape in which thou shalt render it, love — which means something higher than a mere unwillingness to inflict present pain—shall prescribe.

Exactly so, too, will it be in a Christian State. The judge, indeed, being the representative but of one side of the Divine character, of the Divine justice, does not pardon, but only acquits or condemns. The king, however, is a larger mirror of the Divine perfections, of grace no less than of justice: he, therefore, after the condemnation, is free to pardon. It was this, the *kingly* function, which our Lord exercised when He bade the woman taken in adultery to go free (John viii. 11). He did not thereby act against his own law, given by Moses, which had said that such should be stoned: He only completed it.[2] The idea upon which her pardon, upon which every pardon pronounced by the monarch as the fountain

---

[1] In this matter it is not possible beforehand to give any other rule than that which Augustine himself gives, when he says, Dilige, et fac quod voles.

[2] *Enarr. in Ps.* v.: Numquid Christus fecit contra legem suam? . . . . Non ergo Deus contra legem suam, quia nec imperator contra leges suas facit, quando confessis dat indulgentiam. Moÿses minister legis, Christus promulgator legis; Moÿses lapidat ut judex, Christus indulget ut rex.

of grace in the land, properly rests, is that this will bring about in him who is its object a truer righteousness than the payment of the extreme penalty would have done, that there is something in him which promises that the end which punishment should reach will more surely be attained by the method of grace. Were it otherwise, the true love would be to suffer the punishment to take its course. So that here, too, justice and grace appear as identical—as love, manifesting itself now at its one pole, now at the other. It is true, indeed, that the grace comes out less frequently in the Christian State than in the Christian Church, that in the former it is ever the exception. For the State stands in many respects in relation to the Church, as the legal economy to the evangelical, an outer court of the same temple; and as in that earlier economy the side of grace came out less prominently than that of severe justice, so fares it in the State also, which yet knows, as that knew, of the one no less than of the other.[1]

Ver. 42. '*Give to him that asketh thee, and from him that would borrow of thee turn not thou away.*'—Hitherto, Augustine observes, it has been the more negative virtues of not injuring, and being patient under the injuries of others, which the Lord has urged on his disciples. But this were little, unless the more active and communicative graces were added also; and so follows the precept, '*Give to him that asketh thee.*' But can this, he inquires, mean,

[1] A long letter of Augustine's to a civil ruler (*Ep.* cliii. *ad Macedon.*), justifying the Church in its frequent pleadings for the pardon of criminals, is full of matter of the deepest interest on these relations of the Church and State, and of the love whereof punishment no less than pardon is, according to its true idea, the utterance.

that no request is ever to be denied? Was Joseph, then, to give to the wife of Potiphar what she asked? or Susannah to the Jewish elders? Shall I give money to a man to help him in oppressing the innocent? or which I know that he will spend upon his fleshly lusts?[1] It is plain that a thousand other monstrous cases of the kind might be cited, down to that of the Carpocratians, who justified indulgence in all carnal appetites by these words, saying, Whatever the flesh asked, they were bound to give it.

Clearly, then, the command must have its limitation somewhere. Augustine finds the limitation in the words themselves:—Give *to every man*; yes, but not *every thing*.[2] If you send a lazy loitering mendicant away with a lecture upon idleness, you have sent him 'not empty away.' You have given to him, although not the exact thing which he sought. Here, too, he observes, we have the Lord's own interpretation of his words. When that suitor cried to Him from the crowd, ' Master, speak to my brother, that he divide the inheritance with me' (Luke xii. 14), and the Lord made answer, ' Man, who made Me a judge or a divider over you?'—might it not appear that He forgot his own precept, refusing even this easily granted request which was made to Him? But it was not so; He gave the man, not indeed what he asked, but something far better, a medicine for the hurt of his soul, in that warning word: ' Take heed and beware of covetousness'[3] (Luke xii. 13, 15). So, too, Joseph gave, but it was

---

[1] *De Serm. Dom. in Mon.* i. 20.

[2] *Serm.* ccclix.: Omni petenti te da. Non est dictum, *Omnia petenti te da*: Prorsus da; et si non quod petit, tu tamen aliquid da: malum petit, tu bona da.

[3] *Serm.* ccclix.: Non dedit Dominus hoc, nec tamen nihil dedit. Minus negavit, sed quod plus est donavit . . . Ergo hanc regulam

a counsel of chastity; for when he made answer, How shall I, a servant, betray the confidence of my lord (Gen. xxxix. 8, 9)? in that was implicitly involved an exhortation to her, How then wilt thou, a wife, betray the yet higher confidence of thine husband? The command then, '*Give*,' as interpreted by the life of Him who uttered it, is ever to stand fast, but it is, Give that which will make the receiver truly richer; and often in this sense a seeming denial will be the most real giving,[1] as on the other side there are gifts which are no gifts, which as it was wrong to ask, so would it be far better never to have received. He who gives these does not really give; and while he seems to be keeping the letter of this, is indeed violating the spirit of all Christ's commandments.

So much on the general interpretation which this precept should receive. On its details Augustine does not yield us much; yet he notes how the Lord has instanced, as examples of the things whereof a disciple of his shall patiently, where need is, endure the loss, some that are most necessary, the cloak and the coat, that so He may implicitly involve all others; for if these, how much more readily the superfluous, shall be forgone.[2]

tenete. Date quando petimini, etsi non hoc quod petimini. Hoc fecit Dominus. Petebat ille. Quid? Divisionem hæreditatis. Dedit Dominus. Quid? Peremptionem cupiditatis ... Numquid petitorem inanem dimisit, et non potius veritate implevit?

[1] *Enchir. de Fide, Spe, et Car.* 72: Non solum ergo qui dat esurienti cibum, sitienti potum, nudo vestimentum, et quod cuique necessarium est indigenti, verum etiam qui emendat verbere in quem potestas datur, vel coërcet aliquâ disciplinâ, et tamen peccatum ejus, quo ab illo læsus et offensus est, dimittit ex corde, vel orat ut ei dimittatur, non solum in eo quod dimittit atque orat, verum etiam in eo quod corripit, et aliquâ emendatoriâ pœnâ plectit, eleëmosynam dat, quia misericordiam præstat.

[2] *De Serm. Dom. in Mon.* i. 19: Si enim de necessariis hoc imperatum est, quanto magis superflua contemnere convenit?

Ver. 43-45. '*Ye have heard that it hath been said, Thou shalt love thy neighbour, and hate thine enemy: But I say unto you, Love your enemies, bless them that curse you, do good to them that hate you, and pray for them which despitefully use you, and persecute you; That ye may be the children of your Father which is in heaven: for He maketh his sun to rise on the evil and on the good, and sendeth rain on the just and on the unjust.*'—Here also Augustine has seized with a firm grasp that which can alone be the right interpretation of these words. Having to do with the saying, '*Thou shalt hate thine enemy*,' he does not, to withdraw it from Manichæan calumnies, betake himself to the poor evasion, that because the exact words are nowhere found in the Old Testament, therefore the Lord has here in his mind not an Old Testament precept, but a Pharisaical abuse of such, denouncing some addition to it which the Scribes had falsely made. Be the words in the Old Testament or no, they express the spirit of it; and no one need shrink from allowing this, if only he will keep in mind that they were addressed to Israel solely as the theocratic people, as having therefore no enemies but those who also were God's enemies,[1]—whom

[1] *Con. Faust.* xix. 24: Unusquisque iniquus homo, in quantum iniquus est, odio habendus est; in quantum autem homo est, diligendus est; ut illud quod in eo recte odimus arguamus, id est, vitium, quo possit illud quod in eo recte diligimus, id est, humana natura ipsa, emendato vitio, liberari ... Audito igitur et non intellecto quod antiquis dictum erat, Oderis inimicum tuum, ferebantur homines in hominis odium, cum deberent non odisse nisi vitium. Hos corrigit Dominus, dicendo, Diligite inimicos vestros, ut, qui jam dixerat, Non veni legem solvere, sed adimplere, ideoque de odio inimici quod scriptum est in lege, non solveret, præcipiendo utique ut diligamus inimicos, cogeret nos intelligere quonam modo possemus unum eumdemque hominem et odisse propter culpam, et diligere propter naturam.

therefore they should hate, but only as God hated,—hating, that is, the evil in them, and not any thing besides. The precept was no concession to man's weakness,[1] but a summons to holiness, to a keeping themselves unspotted from the world that surrounded them. Let us understand this, and then we shall see that the Divine legislator of the New Covenant does not intend to repeal this any more than the preceding commandments of Moses. '*Thou shalt hate thine enemy*' still stands fast,—'*thine enemy*,' because God's enemy; there shall be in thee the abhorrence of evil, the holy hatred of sin; though now He adds out of the rich treasure-house of his grace another power, that of loving the man, even while we hate the evil that is in him;—all which Augustine illustrates by the example of the physician, who of the very good will that he bears to the sick man the more hates and makes the more earnest war against the sickness by which he is holden.[2]

He often takes occasion to remark how side by side with these passages, which they who misinterpreted, wilfully or otherwise, denounced as encouraging hatred, and countenancing revenge, there were innumerable others, even in the Old Testament (dawn-streaks of the coming day), which breathed the very spirit of these new precepts of Christ; however the strength to fulfil them may have been for the most wanting, till He came to give it.[3] Thus

---

[1] Even Augustine himself does not always hold fast to this the one right exposition; as, for instance, when, *De Serm. Dom. in Mon.* i. 21, he says: Nec quod in lege dictum est, Oderis inimicum tuum, vox jubentis justo accipienda est, sed permittentis infirmo.

[2] *Serm.* cclxxii. (*Appendix*): Quod cum sancto et pio animo feceris, vices cælestis Medici agis, odio habens morbum, et diligens ægrotum. *Enarr. in Ps.* xxxvii. 10: Non ergo hoc orent [homines] ut moriantur inimici; sed hoc orent, ut corrigantur, et mortui erunt inimici.

[3] *Con. Faust.* xix. 28-30: Omnia vel pæne omnia, quæ monuit seu præcepit ubi adjungebat, Ego autem dico vobis, inveniuntur

he compares with the restraint upon anger (Matt. v. 22), the words at Prov. xvi. 34. The adultery *of the heart* which the Lord denounces (Matt. v. 28) is equally met and forbidden in the Old Testament, which has not merely its seventh, but its tenth commandment: 'Thou shalt not *covet* thy neighbour's wife.' The love of enemies is enjoined, Prov. xxv. 21; and in the law itself, where it is written: 'If thou meet thine enemy's ox or his ass going astray, thou shalt surely bring it back to him again' (Exod. xxiii. 4, 5); while some of God's chosen saints, a Joseph and a David (1 Sam. xxiv. 5; Ps. vii. 4), give noble examples of it in their lives. The ground and motive of this love being the goodness of God to all, has its parallel, Wisd. xii. 1. The indissolubility of marriage is declared, Gen. ii. 24, of which words we know the use made by the Lord Himself (Matt. xix. 4). When the Manichæans fastened upon sayings like this, '*He maketh his sun to rise on the evil and on the good*,' and argued that He who said this, or of whom this might be said, could never be the same God whose severity in word and act comes so fearfully out in the Old Testament, Augustine answers, that neither is the Old Testament without its frequent declarations of God's inexhaustible mercy, his patience, his love, nor yet the New without abundant announcements and instances of his severity and anger; he quotes in proof Matt. x. 28; xxii. 13; xxv. 41; Rom. i. 24; ii. 5; Heb. xii. 29; Luke xix. 27; 2 Cor. v. 3; Acts v. 5.[1]

et in illis veteribus libris. It is worth while to compare Tertullian (*Adv. Marc.* iv. 14-17), who is dealing with the same great question, and asserting against the Gnostics, as Augustine against the Manichæans, the one spirit which pervades the Old Testament and the New.

[1] *Con. Adim.* 7: Ex quo facile apparet et in eâ patientiâ quæ invitat ad pœnitentiam; et in eâ indulgentiâ, quæ ignoscit pœniten-

It was true that there was more of fear in the Old Testament, and more of love in the New,[1] yet was there each in each; and it was only by a directing of the attention of the simple exclusively to the one side or the other, that they could be set in contrary lights, and thus played off against each other.[2]

Then too, whatever difficulty may spring from passages in which the saints and servants of God appear to be seeking and longing after vengeance upon their enemies, such difficulty belongs quite as much to the New Testament as to the Old. How, for instance, shall we understand Rev. vi. 9, where the souls under the altar exclaim, 'How long, O Lord, holy and true, dost Thou not judge and avenge our blood on them that dwell on the earth?' Augustine is perplexed by this and similar utterances. But who, he concludes, shall presume to say that this is not a prayer against the kingdom of sin, under which they suffered such things; which kingdom the very charity that now is theirs, makes them so to desire and pray that it may be

tibus; et in eâ justitiâ quæ punit eos qui corrigi nolunt, utrumque Testamentum convenire atque congruere, tanquam ab uno Deo utrumque conscriptum. Cf. *Con. Adv. Leg. et Proph.* i. 16-18.

[1] *Con. Adim.* 22 : Sicut enim tempore caritatis bonitas, sic tempore timoris severitas Dei maxime commendatur. *De Mor. Eccles.* 28: Quanquam enim utrumque in utroque sit, prævalet tamen in Vetere timor, amor in Novo.

[2] *Con. Adv. Leg. et Proph.* i. 17 : Vaniloqui et mentis seductores adversantes litteris sacris, quas intelligere nolunt, eligunt ex eis aspera quæ ibi leguntur ad commendandam severitatem Dei, et de litteris Evangelicis atque Apostolicis lenia quæ ibi leguntur ad commendandam bonitatem Dei; et apud homines imperitos hinc ingerunt horrorem, inde quærunt favorem; quasi difficile sit, ut quisquam similiter blasphemus atque impius, eo modo adversetur Novo Testamento, quo isti Veteri, carpens de Vetere quibus ibi commendatur Dei bonitas, et e contrario de Novo quibus ibi commendatur Dei severitas.

overthrown.[1] Again, there is St. Paul's motive for doing good to an enemy, 'For in so doing thou shalt heap coals of fire on his head' (Rom. xii. 20); which at first sight, and as some have understood it,[2] seems to contain the precept not so much of love as rather of a subtler hatred. The image has been explained thus : Do thine enemy good, for thus thou wilt draw down on him, supposing him to continue in his enmity, a more signal vengeance from heaven. But this would not be, as South well and wittily remarks, loving our enemy, but only hating him more artificially. Or else thus: Do thine enemy good, for so thou wilt bring upon him the smart of a livelier pain, of a stronger self-rebuke, of a deeper self-scorn. This last explanation is on the way to the right one, but, stopping here, is equally with the other opposed as much to the universal spirit, as to the present argument, of St. Paul; and Augustine, vindicating with a righteous earnestness the passage from any such covert malice, shows that the benefits are to be imparted, not with the purpose of aggravating an enemy's punishment, but for the bringing about in him of that true repentance, which shall, if it may be, avert the punishment altogether; that the 'coals of fire' heaped upon the head are the image of a pain inflicted indeed, but yet inflicted in love, and for the burning out

---

[1] *De Serm. Dom. in Mon.* i. 22 : Nam ipsa est sincera et plena justitiæ et misericordiæ vindicta martyrum, ut evertatur regnum peccati, quo regnante tanta perpessi sunt.

[2] Some in his time did so abuse the passage: thus *Enarr. in Ps.* lviii. 10, he observes : [Malevolus] malitiose sapit quod scriptum est, Hoc enim faciens, carbones ignis congeres super caput ejus. Agit enim ut amplius aggravet et ei excitet indignationem Dei, quam carbonibus ignis significare putat, non intelligens illum ignem esse pœnitentiæ urentem dolorem, quousque caput erectum superbiâ beneficiis inimici ad humilitatem salubrem deponitur.

of the malice in the man,¹ a present smart which is to issue in a lasting cure. For fear of a mistake, and intending for ever to exclude one, the Apostle, he observes, was careful to add, himself interpreting what he just had spoken, 'Be not overcome of evil, but overcome evil with good.'²

Augustine pauses to inquire whether this '*sun*' which God makes to rise on the evil as on the good, this '*rain*' which He sends on the unjust no less than the just, are to be taken literally,—a declaration of the natural bounties and blessings whereof all are partakers; or not rather the '*rain*' of his grace, the '*sun*' of his righteousness (Mal. iv. 2), wherewith he visits the hearts of all, though some are as soil which refuses to be softened by the one (Heb. vi. 7, 8), or warmed by the other. But he decides, and doubtless rightly, in favour of the former explanation;³ for they are not '*evil*' upon whom the spiritual Sun has risen, but through his rising upon them have passed into the number of the '*good*;' nor they '*unjust*' upon whom this rain comes down, but are now the '*just*' through its fertilizing and refreshing powers. Rather this '*sun*' and

¹ *Serm.* cxlix. 18 : Ipsa vero ustio, pœnitentia est, quæ tanquam carbones ignis, inimicitias ejus malitiasque consumit. Umbreit in a valuable note on Prov. xxv. 22, takes quite the same ethical view of the command, but explains the image a little differently : Thou shalt make him *to glow with shame*; and Augustine, too, in one place, says that the enemy under this treatment *blushes* (erubescit).

² *Enarr. in Ps.* lxxviii. 10 : Quomodo autem potest vincere in bono malum, in superficie bonus, et in alto malus, qui opere parcit, et corde sævit, manu mitis, voluntate crudelis? Cf. *De Doct. Christ.* iii. 16.

³ *Serm.* lviii. 6; *De Serm. Dom. in Mon.* ii. 23. In this view he brings out rightly the meaning of '*his sun*': Addidit *suum*, id est, quem ipse fecit atque constituit, et a nullo aliquid sumsit ut faceret.

'*rain*' are the common mercies of which all are partakers,[1] even those that 'walk in their own ways,' from whom He does not withhold 'rain from heaven, and fruitful seasons, filling their hearts with food and gladness' (Acts xiv. 16, 17). And this same unstinted bounty of God, this love which comprehends all, according to the measure in which they are capable of being comprehended by it, supplies the measure in which those who would indeed show themselves '*the children of their Father which is in heaven*,' are to exercise love, the pattern they are to set before themselves for imitation.

Ver. 46, 47. '*For if ye love them which love you, what reward have ye? do not even the publicans the same? And if ye salute your brethren only, what do ye more than others? do not even the publicans so?*'— There are three manners of returns, as Augustine sometimes observes, which men may make one to another. There is, first, the returning of good for good, and evil for evil, being the principle which the world recognizes, and on which it acts: '*Do not even the publicans the same?*'[2] This is the rule of the natural man. But beneath this there is the returning of evil for good, which is devilish; while above it there is the returning of good for evil, which is divine, which is God's principle of action; and to this the children of God are summoned here.[3]

---

[1] *Enarr. in Ps.* xxxv. 6.
[2] *In* 1 *Ep. Joh. Tract.* viii.: Extende dilectionem in proximos, nec voces illam extensionem. Prope enim te diligis, qui eos diligis, qui tibi adhærent. Extende ad ignotos, qui tibi nihil mali fecerunt. Transcende et ipsos, perveni ut diligas inimicos. *Serm.* cclxxiii. (*Appendix*): Amas amantes te, filios et parentes. Amat et latro, amat et draco, amant et lupi, amant et ursi.
[3] This is drawn out somewhat differently, *Enarr. in Ps.* cviii. 2.

Ver. 48.—'*Be ye therefore perfect, even as your Father which is in heaven is perfect.*'—This was a favourite text of the Pelagians, adduced by them in proof that men might live here altogether without sin. God, they said, would not have commanded what was impossible; if perfection had been unattainable, Christ would not have required it. But Augustine answers that we must know what this '*perfect*' means.[1] It is not necessarily, complete and having attained its ultimate end in everything; but that may be 'perfect' in one respect which is not perfect in another: or again, a man may be '*perfect*,' as having every grace and lacking none, and yet imperfect, in that he has them not in that intensity which the immutable law of truth requires. And here both these limitations find place. It is on an especial point the Lord is speaking: '*Be ye perfect:*' Love, He says, not merely your friends, but your enemies; stop not short at that easier love, but go on to the harder, fulfilling the course set before you; and do this because God does it. But he who asserts this to mean, Do all this in the measure in which God does it,—and who believes this possible, declares, not that he has a high apprehension of what man's love ought to be, but that he has most poor and unworthy apprehensions of what God's love is. It was not that Augustine desired to cast a slight on any true strivings after added measures of Christian grace;[2] but only on those theories of a sinless

---

[1] *De Pecc. Mer. et Rem.* ii. 15. It may be seen, also, how he dealt with this and passages of the like kind such as Deut. xviii. 13; 2 Cor. xiii. 11; Col. i. 28; Phil. ii. 14, in his treatise *De Perfect. Justit.* 8, 9; he says of most of them: Ipsum finem commemorant, quo currendo pertendant.

[2] Rather his language is such as this (*Serm.* clxix. 15): Semper tibi displiceat quod es, si vis pervenire ad id quod nondum es. Nam

perfection, as detecting plainly the false root out of which they grew, that the Pelagian spoke of this perfection as within man's reach, not out of his stronger faith in the power of the grace which would bring it about, but out of his weaker sense of the extent and malignity of the evil which was opposed to its attainment. His talk about this state of a perfect health was not an extolling of the medicine, but an extenuating, and more or less a denying, of the malignity of the disease—an all-important distinction!

In the life to come, undoubtedly, this command would be literally and in all its extent fulfilled. God's people will be perfect, even as He is perfect: and yet not so, that the distinction between the nature of God and the nature of man will be abolished, as some appeared to Augustine to affirm, but man will reach the perfection of his nature, as God has ever subsisted in the perfection of his.[1]

ubi tibi placuisti, ibi remansisti. Si autem dixeris, Sufficit; et peristi. Semper adde, semper ambula, semper profice.

[1] *Con. Maxim.* i. 12: Ipse secundum naturam suam, nos secundum nostram. *Quæst. in Deut.* v. qu. 9: Neque enim quia dictum est Estote perfecti, sicut Pater vester cælestis perfectus est, ideo æqualitatem Patris sperare debemus: quamvis non defuerunt qui et hoc futurum putaverunt; nisi forte quid dicant parum intelligimus. Cf. *Enarr. in Ps.* xciv. 1. Feeling strongly, he often expresses himself strongly on the mischief which these perfectionists did, first to themselves and then to others. Thus, *De Civ. Dei*, xiv. 9: Nunc satis bene vivitur si sine crimine. Sine peccato autem qui se vivere existimat, non id agit ut peccatum non habeat, sed ut veniam non accipiat.

ST. MATTHEW, CHAP. VI.

VER. 1–4. '*Take heed that ye do not your alms before men, to be seen of them: otherwise ye have no reward of your Father which is in heaven. Therefore when thou doest thine alms, do not sound a trumpet before thee, as the hypocrites do in the synagogues and in the streets, that they may have glory of men. Verily I say unto you, They have their reward. But when thou doest alms, let not thy left hand know what thy right hand doeth: that thine alms may be in secret: and thy Father, which seeth in secret, Himself shall reward thee openly.*'—The connexion of that portion of the Sermon on which we now are entering, with the preceding, Augustine traces thus. Hitherto the Lord has taught his disciples *what* they were to do; He now proceeds to teach them *how* they shall do it, with what simplicity and singleness of eye.[1] And this teaching, he observes, is never super-

---

[1] *In* 1 *Ep. Joh. Tract.* viii.: Videte quanta opera faciat superbia. Ponite in corde, quam similia faciat et quasi paria caritati. Pascit esurientem caritas, pascit et superbia; caritas ut Deus laudetur, superbia ut ipsa laudetur. Vestit nudum caritas, vestit et superbia. Jejunat caritas, jejunat et superbia. Ergo Scriptura divina intro nos revocat, a jactatione hujus faciei forinsecus. Redi ad conscientiam tuam, ipsam interroga. Noli attendere quod floret foris, sed quæ radix est interna. Radicata est cupiditas? species potest esse bonorum factorum: vere opera bona esse non possunt. Radicata est caritas? securus esto, nihil mali procedere potest. Blanditur

fluous; for even after the eye is in the main purged to see God, yet it is ever hard to prevent the creeping in of harmful influences, even where least suspected, and this from the very accompaniments of our good actions;[1] as, for instance, from the praises of men, which these will draw after them. And very usefully he brings out how, quite apart from the mere and utter hypocrite, who has no motive in any thing which he does but his own glory, there are many in whom there is a large admixture of motives, whose good deeds have two sources, one pure and one sullied; for whom, indeed, God and the pleasing of God is first; yet the intention does not remain altogether in its simplicity; there is also an eye turned askant to some meaner reward.[2]

At the same time it is important to observe, and he often observes, that the warning is throughout not against *having* the praise of men, but against the doing of anything *that we may have* their praise, instead of doing it with a single eye to God's glory. It is not, Take heed that ye be not seen in your alms; but, '*Take heed that you do not your alms before men, to be seen of them*,' that is, with this object and aim. For in some sort we are bound in charity to desire men's praises; that is, if there be good wrought by us, we are bound in love to desire there may be a recognition of that good on their part: since their failing to recognize it would mark a wrong condition in them. We are bound to desire that our conversation may

superbia; sævit amor: accipitur magis plaga caritatis, quam eleëmosyna superbiæ.

[1] *De Serm. Dom. in Mon.* ii. 1: Oculo magnâ ex parte mundato difficile est non subrepere sordes aliquas de his rebus, quæ ipsas bonas nostras actiones comitari solent, veluti est laus humana.

[2] *Ibid.* ii. 2.

be attractive, for we may thus sometimes at the same moment do a double alms, ministering to the rich man the example, to the poor the help, that he needs.¹ If our conscience tells us that God's glory, and not pride or ostentation, is the mainspring of our actions, let us be fearless in this matter, and not dread or even shun to be seen, only taking care that this shall not be the final scope of our deeds.² And here, he says, lies the reconciliation of such declarations as that of St. Paul, 'I please all men in all things' (1 Cor. x. 33), and that other in which he says, 'If I yet pleased men, I should not be the servant of Christ' (Gal. i. 10). 'I please men as a mean to an end, for the winning of them to the truth : I do not make the pleasing of them itself my end ; on the contrary, this is something which I utterly forego, whenever higher interests of God's truth are at stake.' Yet his own affecting words in his '*Confessions*,'³ concerning the difficulty which he found when praised, in distinguishing whether the pleasure he felt was a pleasure that others should be glorifying God for the good which they saw in him, or a pleasure in being thus himself extolled and glorified, and the deep heart-searchings into which this doubt brought him, will not easily be forgotten by those who once have

¹ *In* 1 *Ep. Joh. Tract.* viii.: Si enim abscondis ab oculis hominis, abscondis ab imitatione hominis. Duo sunt quibus eleëmosynam facis: duo esuriunt, unus panem, alter justitiam. . . . Ille enim quærit quod manducet, ille quærit quod imitetur. Pascis istum, præbes te isti: ambobus dedisti eleëmosynam. Cf. *De Civ. Dei*, v. 14; and *Serm.* clix. 10–13.

² *Enarr. in Ps.* lxv. 2 ; *in Ps.* cxviii.: Admonuit ne aliquid propter gloriam hominum fiat, non quia ipsa laus humana culpanda est, nam quid tam optandum est hominibus, quam ut eis placeant quæ debent imitari? sed propter ipsam laudem bene operari, hoc est vanitatem in suis operibus intueri.

³ *Conf.* x. 37.

read them. He notes the peculiar difficulty which besets the faithful man here. In other matters he may avoid that which would prove the occasion of sin in him; he may put the temptation far from him; but he cannot here; for we must not get away from goodness, so to get away from the praises which follow it, and the temptations which follow those praises.

He continually finds an illustration of the warning here conveyed, lest snatching at an earthly we forfeit a heavenly reward, in the doom of the foolish virgins of the parable (Matt. xxv. 11–13). In them he beholds the image of persons, who like those noted here, are working for, and living on, the praises of men. These praises were as the oil actually present in the virgins' lamps; and so long as the supply of this oil lasted, they were adorned with apparent good works. But when these praises fail, as at the last day they must fail, then for them everything will have failed; all wherein they found their impulses to good will have ceased; and the good itself, such as it was, will cease likewise. Meanwhile for the past they will have already received and already exhausted their reward;[1] what they laboured for they got; and now there will remain for them nothing but that sentence, 'I know you not,' uttered from his lips with whom no work avails which is not wrought out of love to Him.[2] He very wittily likens these boasters of their good deeds, who are

---

[1] *Enarr. in Ps.* cxviii.: Perceperunt mercedem suam, vani vanam.

[2] *Serm.* xciii. 9: Non sunt fraudati laudibus humanis: quæsierunt laudes humanas, habuerunt. Istæ laudes humanæ in die judicii non eos adjuvant. *Enarr. in Ps.* cxlvii. 13: Non inveniunt tunc faventes, non inveniunt tunc laudantes, a quibus solebant laudari et quasi excitari ad bona opera, non robore bonæ conscientiæ, sed incitamento linguæ alienæ.

thus losers of all true reward, to the hen, which has no sooner laid its egg, than by its cackling it calls some one to take it away.

Augustine has a laborious, and, as I cannot but think, an unnecessary discussion concerning what the '*left hand*' may mean, which is not to be permitted to know what the '*right hand*' does. It were better to recognize this as one of those vigorous popular sayings, which are not to be required to give an account of themselves in detail. They cannot do this, and it is in the very contradictions which would arise if they were pressed to attempt it, that their strength lies. Thus it is true that, so far as knowledge can be attributed to the hands at all, it is impossible that the left hand should not know what the right hand gave, since both are organs of one and the same will; but this impossibility must not make us quit the meaning which the words at first obviously suggest. Rather we are to see in this very impossibility which lies on the surface of the precept, an exhortation involved to the utmost possible secrecy, or I should rather say, simplicity, in almsgiving;—for the secrecy is an accident, such as in the nature of things must often be wanting; but the simplicity, the suppression as far as possible of all reflex consciousness of the work and dwelling on it, ought always to be there. After rejecting many explanations as untenable, he ends by explaining the '*left hand*' as the carnal desire, manifesting itself in the look turned askant to the human praise and reward, whereas by the '*right hand*' is meant the single purpose of fulfilling the divine commands;[1] and he makes the entire precept to amount

---

[1] *Serm.* cxlix. 14: Sinistra est animi cupiditas carnalis, dextera est animi caritas spiritalis. [Elsewhere, the left, the ipsa delectatio

to this, Let not meaner motives mingle with and defile your higher. That such a lesson underlies the whole teaching of Christ with which we now have to do, is plain; but assuredly He is giving here to his disciples rather an *example* of what He would have them do, than the *principle* on which they are to do it: Since you are looking for a higher reward than the praises of men, let your alms be given in secret,—and this He then clothes in a strong gnomic saying,—so secretly that, if that were possible, no part of yourselves save that actually engaged in the giving should know of the gift—no, not even the brother-hand.

Ver. 5, 6. '*And when thou prayest, thou shalt not be as the hypocrites are: for they love to pray standing in the synagogues and in the corners of the streets, that they may be seen of men. Verily I say unto you, They have their reward. But thou, when thou prayest, enter into thy closet, and when thou hast shut thy door, pray to thy Father which is in secret; and thy Father which seeth in secret shall reward thee openly.*'—To these words, '*Enter into thy closet, and shut thy door,*' Augustine, without excluding the literal sense, and the warning against prayers made to be seen,[1] gives also a mystical meaning. This '*closet,*' or chamber, is the heart of man; '*the door*' the avenues of sense by which disturbing and defiling thoughts of this world would fain enter in; a '*door*' at which the Tempter is ever knocking; who yet

laudis—the right, the intentio implendi divina præcepta.] Si ergo cum quisque facit eleëmosynam, miscet cupiditatem temporalium commodorum, ut in opere illo aliquid tale conquirat, miscet sinistræ conscientiam operibus dextræ. Cf. *Enarr. in Ps.* cxxxvi. 5.

[1] *Enarr. in Ps.* cxli. 3: Si homines reddituri sunt, effunde ante homines precem tuam: si Deus redditurus est, effunde ante eum precem tuam.

passes on and leaves us, if he finds it resolutely closed against him.¹ Then, he says, we fulfil the apostolic commandment, 'Give no place to the devil,' when we diligently close the heart's door against him, and against the crowd of distracting thoughts with which he is ever seeking to mar and spoil our prayers. On the shutting of the door in this sense he is often urgent, yet not more urgent than the immense importance of the subject would warrant. Thus in one place he says, Wert thou speaking with me, and that, not as one asking a favour, but as with thine equal, and shouldst thou suddenly break off and give a message to thy servant, could I esteem it otherwise than an affront? Yet this is what thou doest daily with thy God.² And in another popular exposition ³ he inquires

---

¹ *De Serm. Dom. in Mon.* ii. 3: Parum est intrare in cubicula, si ostium pateat importunis, per quod ostium ea quæ foris sunt improbe se immergunt, et interiora nostra appetunt. Foris autem diximus esse omnia temporalia et visibilia, quæ per ostium, id est, per carnalem sensum in cogitationes nostras penetrant, et turbâ vanorum phantasmatum orantibus obstrepunt. And elsewhere: Clauso ostio, id est, exclusâ phantasmatum turbâ. Cf. *Enarr. in Ps.* cxli. 3, 4: Tentator non cessat pulsare ut irrumpat; si clausum invenerit, transit. Quid est autem claudere ostium? Hoc ostium tanquam duas habet valvas, cupiditatis et timoris; aut cupis aliquid terrenum, et hoc intrat; aut times aliquid terrenum, et hoc intrat. Timoris ergo et cupiditatis januam claude contra diabolum, aperi ad Christum.

² *Enarr. in Ps.* cxl. 5: Quid facis de cogitationibus tuis? quid facis de tumultu et catervâ rebellantium desideriorum . . . Confiteris peccata, Deum adoras: video corpus ubi jaceat, quæro ubi volitet animus. Modo si mecum loquereris, et subito averteres te ad servum tuum, et dimitteres me, non dico a quo aliquid petebas, sed cum quo ex æquo loquebaris, non mihi injuriam factam deputarem? Ecce quid facis quotidie Deo. *Enarr. in Ps.* lxxxv. 4: Et tolerat Deus tot corda precantium, et diversas res cogitantium; omitto dicere et noxias, omitto dicere aliquando perversas et inimicas Deo; ipsas superfluas cogitare, injuria est ejus, cum quo loqui cœperas.

³ *Enarr. in Ps.* xxxiii. 5: Attendat sanctitas vestra: Quomodo

why men are so reluctant to obey this command,—why they so seldom turn in upon the solitude of their own hearts,—why they so much prefer to be abroad than at home. And then he likens them to such as have discomfortable households, and so are unwilling to return to their homes, knowing full well that only wretchedness and strife await them there. It would be otherwise if their hearts were pure, if their consciences were at peace; they would not then find every thing driving them abroad, but rather every thing attracting them home.

Ver. 7, 8. '*But when ye pray, use not vain repetitions, as the heathen do: for they think that they shall be heard for their much speaking. Be not ye therefore like unto them: for your Father knoweth what things ye have need of, before ye ask Him.*'—In his exquisitely beautiful letter upon prayer, addressed to the noble widow Proba, Augustine distinguishes between the '*much speaking*,' which is here rebuked, and the much praying, which elsewhere the Lord has so earnestly commanded. He who said, '*Seek*,

nolunt intrare domos suas qui habent malas uxores: quomodo exeunt ad forum et gaudent. Cœpit hora esse, quâ intrent in domum suam; contristantur. Intraturi sunt enim ad tædia, ad murmura, ad amaritudines, ad eversiones. Si ergo miseri sunt qui cum redeunt ad parietes suos, timent ne aliquibus suorum perturbationibus evertantur, quanto sunt miseriores, qui ad conscientiam suam redire nolunt, ne ibi litibus peccatorum evertantur? Ergo ut possis libens redire ad cor tuum, munda illud. Aufer inde cupiditatum sordes, aufer labem avaritiæ, aufer tabem superstitionum, aufer ista omnia; intra in cor tuum, et gaudebis ibi. Cum ibi cœperis gaudere, ipsa munditia cordis tui delectabit te, et faciet orare: quomodo si venias ad aliquem locum, silentium est ibi, forte quies est ibi, mundus est locus. Oremus hic, dicis, et delectat te compositio loci, et credis quod ibi te exaudiat Deus. Si ergo loci visibilis te delectat munditia, quare te non offendit immunditia cordis tui?

and ye shall find,' and spake a parable 'that men ought always to pray and not to faint,' who Himself passed whole nights in prayer, must be as far as possible from finding fault with prayer which is long drawn out, if only it *be* prayer indeed. He can only condemn that, in which, while it retains the name of prayer, an endless tumult and hubbub of words is substituted for all deeper, and oftentimes in words unspeakable, utterances of the spirit; or which, having begun aright, has yet degenerated so far, that the words have now survived the feeling with which the prayer was commenced.[1]

And why not this '*much speaking?*' Because that which we need is known already to Him from whom we ask it. But might it not seem that this rebuke reached much further than to the condemnation of wordy unmeaning prayers? For if it be thus, argued some, if He thus knows before we ask, what necessity to ask at all? And, first, what need to express any petition in words, to tell Him aught, who knows every thing already? But these words, Augustine replies, are only the accidental clothing of our prayers, in which we array them for our own sakes, and not for his;—so entirely accidental, that very often our prayer exists without them. They were

[1] *Ep.* cxxx. 10: Neque enim, ut nonnulli putant, hoc est orare in multiloquio, si diutius oretur. Aliud est sermo multus, aliud diuturnus affectus; nam de ipso Domino scriptum est quod pernoctaverit in orando, et quod prolixius oraverit: ubi quid aliud quam nobis præbebat exemplum, in tempore precator opportunus, cum Patre exauditor æternus? Absit ab oratione multa locutio; sed non desit multa precatio, si fervens perseverat intentio. Nam multum loqui est in orando rem necessariam superfluis agere verbis; multum autem precari est ad eum quem precamur diuturnâ et piâ cordis excitatione pulsare. Nam plerumque hoc negotium plus gemitibus quam sermonibus agitur, plus fletu quam affatu.

given us at first as helps to memory, instructing us in the things which we ought to desire or deprecate either with words or without them.[1] But then the more real question remains: What need to pray at all, either in words or in unuttered desires? Will not He who is altogether good, give unasked what his earthly children need? But the prayer, Augustine makes answer, is the preparation and the enlargement of the heart for the receiving of the divine gift; which indeed God is always prepared to give, but we are not always prepared to receive.[2] In the act of prayer there is a purging of the spiritual eye, which thus is averted from the things earthly that darken it, and becomes receptive of the divine light,— able not to endure only the brightness of that light, but to rejoice in it with

---

[1] *De Serm. Dom. in Mon.* ii. 3; *De Trin.* xv. 13.

[2] *De Serm. Dom. in Mon.* ii. 3: Ipsa orationis intentio cor nostrum serenat et purgat, capaciusque efficit ad accipienda divina munera, quæ spiritaliter nobis infundantur. Non enim ambitione precum nos exaudit Deus, qui semper paratus est dare suam lucem nobis; non visibilem, sed intelligibilem et spiritalem ; sed nos non semper parati sumus accipere, cum inclinamur in alia, et rerum temporalium cupiditate tenebramur. Fit ergo in oratione conversio cordis ad eum qui semper dare paratus est, si nos capiamus quod dederit; et in ipsâ conversione purgatio interioris oculi, cum excluduntur ea, quæ temporaliter cupiebantur, ut acies cordis simplicis ferre possit simplicem lucem, divinitus sine ullo occasu aut immutatione fulgentem ; nec solum ferre, sed etiam manere in illâ; non tantum sine molestiâ, sed etiam cum ineffabili gaudio, quo vere ac sinceriter beata vita perficitur. And on this that God should command men to pray, he says elsewhere (*Ep.* cxxx. 8): Quod quare faciat qui novit quid nobis necessarium sit, prius quam petamus ab eo, movere animum potest, nisi intelligamus quod Dominus et Deus noster non voluntatem nostram sibi velit innotescere, quam non potest ignorare, sed exerceri in orationibus desiderium nostrum, quo possimus capere, quod præparat dare. Illud enim valde magnum est, sed nos ad capiendum parvi et angusti sumus. And elsewhere: Tam largo fonti vas inane admovendum est.

an ineffable joy. In the earnest asking is the enlargement of the heart for the abundant receiving; even as in it is also the needful preparation for the receiving with a due thankfulness; while, on the contrary, the good which came unsought would too often remain the unacknowledged also.[1]

Ver. 9. '*After this manner therefore pray ye: Our Father which art in heaven, Hallowed be thy name.*'—On the Prayer itself Augustine first notes how we nowhere read of them of the Old Covenant as instructed to say '*Our Father.*' Their word was rather, Master,[2] as their relation was a servile one. Not, indeed, that they were altogether without hints that the filial relation was the true one, and that into which God designed to bring his people. There were glimpses of this in the Old Testament (Deut. xxxii. 6; Exod. iv. 22; Ps. lxxxii. 6; Isai. i. 2; lxiii. 16; lxiv. 8; Mal. i. 6); yet Israel at best was but as the heir, who, 'as long as he is a child, differeth nothing from a servant.' The spirit of adoption, ' whereby we cry Abba Father,' was not theirs: for this is the exclusive prerogative of the New Covenant, the gift of the Son, and the fruit of the Incarnation;[3] to as many as believe on Him He gives power to become the sons of God (John i. 12). Most fitting, he remarks, is this address with which to begin our supplication, for by words like

---

[1] *Serm.* lvi. 3: Ideo voluit ut ores, ut desideranti det, ne vilescat quod dederit: quia et ipsum desiderium ipse insinuavit.

[2] *De Serm. Dom. in Mon.* ii. 4: Multa enim dicta sunt in laudem Dei quæ per omnes sanctas scripturas varie lateque diffusa poterit quisque considerare, cum legit: nusquam tamen invenitur præceptum populo Israel ut diceret, Pater noster, aut ut oraret Patrem Deum: sed Dominus eis insinuatus est, tanquam servientibus, id est, secundum carnem adhuc viventibus.

[3] Ut homines nascerentur ex Deo, primo ex ipsis natus est Deus.

these our love is kindled; since what should be dearer to children than a Father?—and no less our devout affection, that such as we should be permitted thus, and on these relations, to hold converse with God. Nor less is herein involved and expressed our confidence that we shall not ask in vain, when, before asking, we have already received this greatest gift of all, the adoption of sons.[1] Hereby too are we prompted to the study of sanctity, that we prove not altogether unworthy of so high a descent. Moreover, he observes, it is not '*My Father*,' but '*Our Father*,' for this is the prayer of brethren that in Christ are knit together into one mystical body, adopted in Him into one and the same spiritual family upon earth.[2]

'*Which art in heaven*,'—not, he observes, as though God were locally in the higher regions of the world, having by comparison forsaken the other; for, if it were thus, they would be nearer Him who dwell on the mountains than those in the plains, and the birds of the air, as nearer yet, would be more fortunate and happier than either.[3] But he understands by '*heaven*' the hearts of the faithful, and the words to mean, Who dwellest in them as in a temple, as in thy chosen habitation;—and, of course, when the language here used is once transferred from

---

[1] *De Serm. Dom. in Mon.* ii. 4: Quo nomine et caritas excitatur, ... et quædam impetrandi præsumtio, quæ petituri sumus; cum prius quam aliquid peteremus tam magnum donum accepimus, ut sinamur dicere, Pater noster, Deo. Quid enim jam non det filiis petentibus, cum hoc ipsum ante dederit, ut filii essent?

[2] *Ibid.*, and *Serm.* lxiv. (*Appendix*): Oratio fraterna est; non dicit, Pater meus, tanquam pro se tantum orans, sed, Pater noster, omnes videlicet unâ oratione complectens, qui se in Christo fratres esse cognoscunt.

[3] *De Serm. Dom. in Mon.* ii. 5.

the material to the moral world, there is no difficulty in speaking of God as dwelling, and delighting to dwell, rather in one place than another.[1] But the words '*which art in heaven*' are capable of a simpler explanation, and do not require that we betake ourselves to an allegory to justify their use. For while it is quite true that the local heavens are no more the habitation of God than any other place (1 Kin. viii. 27),—that, since God is a Spirit, all place is out of place when we are thinking of Him, —yet this attribution of the pure immeasurable spaces of the ether above us—the regions lifted high 'above the smoke and stir of this dim spot'—to God for his habitation, is part of the unconscious symbolism which is common to all ages and all people, and in no respect a denial of his declaration, 'I fill heaven *and earth*.' The introduction of these words into the beginning of this prayer rests on this universal symbolism; they are, as it were, a *Sursum corda*, they remind us that now we have lifted up our hearts from earth and things earthly to another and a higher world.

But this is not their only value; we have in them a protest against all pantheistic notions about prayer, all such as rest on an assumption of the identity of our spirit and the Spirit of God. We are thus bidden to look for God, not in, but out of and above, ourselves. Prayer is not to be an act of introversion, the sinking in of the spirit upon itself, but the struggling up of our spirit toward another Spirit, higher and holier than our own, one with which our spirit

---

[1] *Ep.* clxxxvii.: Fatendum est ubique esse Deum per divinitatis præsentiam, sed non ubique per habitationis gratiam. This whole letter is on the presence of God, and how far it may be attributed to one place more than another.

is indeed allied, but yet with which it is not one and the same; 'the Spirit beareth witness with our spirit.' The Mohammedan Sufies, and other pantheistic devotees of the East, in the deepest abstraction of their devotions, are indeed worshippers of no other God but self, inasmuch as they have lost or denied this distinction; for which the words here, no less than the recognition of a relation implying difference and distinction in the address, '*Our Father*,' are a standing witness.

'*Hallowed be thy Name.*' What is this? Augustine asks; can God be holier than He is already? Not in Himself; that Name in itself remains always the same, '*hallowed*' for evermore; but in us its sanctification is capable of increase, and in this petition we are asking for this increase of its sanctity in ourselves and in others, that God, in fact, may be more known and honoured and feared among men as the Holy One.[1] While then there must not be such an emptying of the phrase '*Name* of God,' as would leave it nothing more than the awful title by which we designate Him, for then in this petition there would be little more than a desire that blasphemous speeches might cease out of the world; so, on the other hand, we must not take the 'Name of God' as identical with God Himself, as

[1] *Serm.* lvii. 4: Pro nobis rogamus, non pro Deo. . . . Quod semper sanctum est, sanctificetur in nobis. *Serm.* lvi. 4: Quid est sanctificetur? sanctum habeatur, non contemnatur. *Enarr. in Ps.* ciii. 1: Quid ergo rogamus? Ut illis hominibus, qui per infidelitatem nondum habent, nomen Dei sanctum sit, quibus nondum est ille sanctus, qui per se et in se et in sanctis suis sanctus est. Rogamus pro genere humano, rogamus pro orbe terrarum, pro omnibus gentibus, quotidie sedentibus et disputantibus, quia non est rectus Deus, et non recte judicat Deus; ut aliquando ipsi se corrigant, et rectum cor ad illius rectitudinem ducant; et adhærentes ei, directi ad rectum, non jam vituperent, sed placeat rectis rectus.

is evident from the fact that we could not desire that God might be '*hallowed*,' or holier than He already is. But his Name we can; for it is that whereby He has revealed Himself to men; it is all of Himself, which, not being ineffable, He has uttered and declared;—the coming out of all which may be known of Him from the unfathomable abyss of being (Exod. iii. 13, 14).[1] As long as there is room either for ourselves or for others to love this Name, this revelation of his perfections, more, so long this prayer must find utterance from our lips, and so long cannot altogether give place to the 'Holy, Holy, Holy,' which is not prayer and petition, but purely and solely adoration and praise.

Ver. 10. '*Thy kingdom come. Thy will be done in earth, as it is in heaven.*'—This is not as though his kingdom were not already among us; but even as the present light is absent to the blind and to them who wilfully close their eyes, so that kingdom, though it be ever with us, is yet now absent from them who refuse to know of it.[2] But all must know it then, when it shall not merely be spiritually but visibly set up; and it is this we ask, that the kingdom may so come to us now, that we may be found in it then.[3] '*Thy will be done*,'—that is, Let it be

[1] *Enarr. in Ps.* ci. 25.
[2] *De Serm. Dom. in Mon.* ii. 6: Quemadmodum enim etiam præsens lux absens est cæcis et eis qui oculos claudunt, ita Dei regnum quamvis numquam discedat de terris, tamen absens est ignorantibus. And *In Ev. Joh. Tract.* lxviii. (on the words, Tunc justi fulgebunt sicut sol in regno Patris sui: Matt. xiii. 43): Regnum fulgebit in regno, cum regno venerit regnum, quod nunc oramus et dicimus, Veniat regnum tuum. Sed nondum regnat hoc regnum.
[3] *Serm.* lvi. 4: Ut in nobis veniat, optamus; ut in illo inveniamur, optamus.

done here according to thy will; for Augustine denies, what at first sight might seem to lie in the words, that the end and consummation here prayed for is the absorption of all other wills in the will of God, so that in this sense his will shall be everywhere the only one done. Rather is it the bringing all the lesser circles of the wills of God's creatures to have the same centre as the great circle of God's all-embracing will. God's will is not that his creatures should not will, but that they should will only what is good and true: it is not that their wills should be annihilated, but brought back into harmony with his will, the will of perfect goodness. This may seem at first a distinction hardly worth making, yet the whole Monothelite controversy was a witness to the deep importance which the Church attached to the maintaining of the reality of a human will in Christ, and thus in them who are Christ's, which should be subordinated indeed to the divine will, yet not abolished by it.[1] And this is his practical exposition of the words: Grant that we may never seek to warp the straight to the crooked, thy will to ours, but always to correct the crooked by the straight, our will by thine.[2] And this '*in earth as it is in*

---

[1] *De Serm. Dom. in Mon.* ii. 6: Qui ergo faciunt voluntatem Dei, in illis utique fit voluntas Dei; non quia ipsi faciunt ut velit Deus, sed quia faciunt quod ille vult; id est, faciunt secundum voluntatem ejus.

[2] *Enarr. in Ps.* xxxi. 11: Duæ voluntates sunt, sed voluntas tua corrigatur ad voluntatem Dei, non voluntas Dei detorqueatur ad tuam. Prava est enim tua, regula est illa, regula, ut quod pravum est, ad regulam corrigatur. And presently before: Quomodo distortum lignum etsi ponas in pavimento æquali, non collocatur, non compaginatur, nec adjungitur, semper agitatur et nutat, non quia inæquale est ubi posuisti, sed quia distortum est quod posuisti: ita et cor tuum, quamdiu pravum est et distortum, non potest colliniari rectitudini Dei, et non potest in illo collocari, ut hæreat illi. *Enarr. in Ps.* cxlvi. § 7:

heaven;' as by the angels there, by us also here.[1] This is the simple explanation, not, as he sometimes throws out, that '*heaven*' may be the Church, and '*earth*' the world. For this is a prayer for perfection and completion; and since that will is only imperfectly done even in the Church, such could not be the ultimate longing of the souls of the faithful, nor that in which they would find their final rest. And this same objection is fatal to all other explanations of the like kind.[2]

Ver. 11. '*Give us this day our daily bread.*'—The things eternal having been thus asked for, the petitions which remain have to do with this life of our pilgrimage.[3] Augustine objects to the narrowing of this petition to any one thing; either, as some did, to the Holy Eucharist, or as others, who gave it somewhat a wider meaning, to all spiritual refection; or, again, as others, going into quite the other extreme, to the nourishment of the body exclusively.[4] This '*bread*' is rather the whole aliment of body and of spirit; of the body, as food, with whatever else is necessary for our earthly life; and of the spirit no less; so that the frequent communions, the daily worship, the study of the Scriptures, the hymns we hear and sing, these all will appertain to, and be included in, the '*daily bread*'

Distortum cor, parum est quod non se corrigit ad Deum: et Deum vult distorquere ad se.

[1] *Serm.* lvii. 6: Quomodo te non offendunt Angeli tui, sic te non offendamus et nos.

[2] Such are to be found *De Serm. Dom. in Mon.* ii. 10; *Serm.* lvi. 5, and lvii. 6.

[3] *Serm.* lvii. 7: Restant petitiones pro istâ vitâ peregrinationis nostræ.

[4] *De Serm. Dom. in Mon.* ii. 7.

which we ask.¹ He does not fail to remark the silent rebuke that there is here for the worshipper, who takes these words in his mouth, while he is allowing himself in anxious and far-looking cares, while he is making luxurious provision for the flesh and for its lusts. It is but '*bread*' which with his lips he asks, and that for the day.² This prayer is the answer of the faithful to the admonition of the Apostle, 'Having food and raiment, let us be therewith content' (1 Tim. vi. 8).³

Ver. 12. '*And forgive us our debts, as we forgive our debtors.*'—This petition Augustine does not refer to the great forgiveness, which is assumed as a thing already past, already in baptism possessed, and out of faith in which, and in the adoption that went with it, the entire Prayer proceeds. He refers this rather to the daily sins of infirmity, in which even he who watches the most will yet be entangled; and without which a life in the flesh can scarcely be led:⁴ hardly without some of the world's dust

---

¹ *Serm.* lvii. 7 : Da æterna, da temporalia. Promisisti regnum, noli negare subsidium. Dabis apud te sempiternum ornamentum, da in terrâ temporale alimentum. *Serm.* lviii. 4 : Quicquid animæ nostræ et carni nostræ in hâc vitâ necessarium est, quotidiano pane concluditur.

² The difficult question of the meaning of ἐπιούσιος does not trouble him much. He is in general satisfied with quotidianus ; or, if he uses Jerome's correction, supersubstantialis—and the only passage in which I have found it is in a sermon which his Benedictine editors have dismissed to the *Appendix* (*Serm.* lxiv.),—he does not more than refer the word to Christ, the bread of life, qui omnem *superat substantiam.*

³ *Serm.* lviii. 4 : Pereat avaritia, et dives est natura.

⁴ *Con. Ep. Parmen.* ii. 10 : Quod utique non de illis peccatis dicitur, quæ in baptismi regeneratione dimissa sunt, sed de iis quæ quotidie de seculi amarissimus fructibus humanæ vitæ infirmitas contrahit. *Ep.* cclxv. § 8 : Est etiam pœnitentia bonorum et humilium

adhering to him[1] will even the faithful man walk through the world's paths. But in this prayer there is, so to say, the shaking off this dust before it has settled upon him and hardened into a crust.[2] Herein is the daily washing *of the feet*, for them that are already partakers of the great washing which was from head to foot and once for all (John xiii. 10).[3] The daily sins of a Christian man may be small, yet are not therefore to be despised; for if despised, then, though not else, they become indeed dangerous. And feeling the importance of this matter, he illustrates it with manifold comparisons. It is of little drops that mighty rivers, yea ruinous and wide-wasting inundations, are made up. The leak may be trifling, yet if waters are always coming in, and are not as constantly pumped out, they will in the end sink the ship. A mountain of minute grains of sand will as effectually crush out the life, as the same bulk of solid lead.[4] Little venomous

---

fidelium pene quotidiana, in quâ pectora tundimus, dicentes, Dimitte nobis debita nostra, sicut nos dimittimus debitoribus nostris. Neque enim ea nobis dimitti volumus, quæ dimissa non dubitamus in baptismo, sed illa utique quæ humanæ fragilitati, quamvis parva, tamen crebra subrepunt; quæ si collecta contra nos fuerint, ita nos gravabunt et oppriment, sicut unum aliquod grande peccatum. Quid enim interest ad naufragium, utrum uno grandi fluctu navis operiatur et obruatur, an paulatim subrepens aqua in sentinam et per negligentiam derelicta atque contemta impleat navem atque submergat? Cf. *Ep.* liv.: *De Civ. Dei*, xxi. 27: Quid est ergo *peccata vestra*, nisi peccata, sine quibus nec vos eritis, qui justificati et sanctificati estis?

[1] Vix sine pulvere, as more than once he expresses it.
[2] *Serm.* cccli. § 4-6.
[3] *In Ev. Joh. Tract.* lvi.: Quotidie pedes lavat nobis, qui interpellat pro nobis; et quotidie nos opus habere ut pedes lavemus . . . in ipsâ Oratione Dominicâ confitemur, cum dicimus, Dimitte nobis. Cf. *Serm.* cccli. 3; *Enchir. de Fide, Spe, et Car.* 71.
[4] *Serm.* lviii. 9: Non potes hic vivere sine ipsis [sc. peccatis], vel minuta sint, vel levia sint. Sed ipsa levia et minuta non contem-

insects, if only there are enough of them, will kill a man with their multitudinous bites, as certainly as some wild beast with its single one.¹ But in this prayer there is for the man that faithfully uses it, the pledge and power of a daily cleansing, the medicine of hurts, which may be slight, but which are hurts notwithstanding.²

Augustine uses the testimony of this prayer against all proud Pelagian notions of an absolutely sinless life and conversation in this present time.³ He loves to entrench himself here;⁴ he recurs often to the fact that it was to the Apostles themselves that this prayer was first given; they were to acknowledge in these words their own sinfulness,⁵ and

nantur. De minutis guttis, flumina implentur. Non contemnantur vel minora. Per angustas rimulas navis insudat aquâ; impletur sentina: et si contemnatur sentina, mergitur navis. Cf. *Enarr. in Ps.* cxxix. § 5 ; *Serm.* lvi. 9 : Quid interest, utrum te plumbum premat, an arena? plumbum una massa est, arena minuta grana sunt, sed copiâ te premunt.

¹ *Serm.* cclxxviii. 12, 13 : Magnæ bestiæ uno morsu occidunt hominem : minutæ autem cum fuerint multæ congregatæ, plerumque interimunt : et talem perniciem inferunt, ut pœnis hujusmodi gens superba Pharaonis judicari meruerit.

² *De Pecc. Mer. et Rem.* iii. 13 ; *Ep.* clxvii. 6 : Quoniam in multis offendimus omnes, suggerit Dominicam tanquam quotidianam quotidianis, etsi levioribus, tamen vulneribus, medicinam.

³ Of such a perfect state he says, *De Pecc. Mer. et Rem.* iii. 13 : Optandum est ut fiat, conandum est ut fiat, supplicandum est ut fiat; non tamen quasi factum fuerit, confitendum.

⁴ *Ep.* clxxvi. § 2 : Nova quippe hæresis et nimium perniciosa tentat assurgere inimicorum gratiæ Christi, qui nobis etiam Dominicam Orationem impiis disputationibus conantur auferre. Cum enim Dominus docuerit ut dicamus, Dimitte nobis debita nostra, isti dicunt posse hominem in hâc vitâ, præceptis Dei cognitis, ad tantam perfectionem justitiæ sine adjutorio gratiæ Salvatoris, per solum liberum voluntatis arbitrium pervenire, ut ei non sit jam necessarium dicere, Dimitte nobis debita nostra.

⁵ *Ep.* clvii. 2 : Omnibus enim necessaria est Oratio Dominica, quam etiam ipsis arietibus gregis, id est, apostolis suis Dominus dedit,

shall any other assume themselves more exempt from imperfection than they, and therefore to have outgrown its use? And if not, if it was intended, as it plainly was, for all, and for these at all periods of their Christian life, it cannot be admitted for an instant that Christ would put a lie into the mouth of any; which yet He would do, if any who were without sin were still at his bidding to pray this prayer, asking forgiveness for sins of which they were not, and knew they were not, guilty. The Pelagians had two or three escapes from this conclusion. One was this, that a perfect man might yet pray this prayer out of humility—a lying humility, which Augustine more justly characterizes as itself an awful sacrilege, such as would constitute him a sinner, had he been none before.[1] Or again, they replied that this prayer was given to the Apostles while they were yet carnal, and suited them then, but not afterwards.[2] This plea he refutes by comparison of other passages, as 1 John i. 8, where no such subterfuge is possible. Somewhat more plausibly than this, they affirmed that the sinless man would merge himself, and his own separate life, in the life of the whole body of the Church, and could therefore honestly use this prayer, inasmuch as in the body to which he belonged there still

---

ut unusquisque Deo dicat, Dimitte nobis debita nostra. *De Civ. Dei*, xiv. 9: Non enim qualiumcunque hominum vox est; sed maxime piorum, multumque justorum atque sanctorum. Cf. *Serm.* clxiii. 9; *De Sanctâ Virginitate*, § 51.

[1] *Con. Ep. Parmen.* ii. 10: Quod si hoc in oratione ficte et non veraciter dicunt, putantes se non habere quod eis dimittat Deus, id ipsum est inexpiabile sacrilegium. Cf. *Serm.* clxxxi. 3: Justus es, sine peccato es; sed propter humilitatem te dicis peccatorem. Non accipit Deus mendacem humilitatem tuam.

[2] *Serm.* cxxxv. 7.

was sin, though not in himself.[1] Augustine answers them at length, and observes how one at least of their favourite examples of such a sinless man, that is, Daniel, has left them no opportunity for such an evasion; for he expressly distinguishes the two, his own sin and the congregation's (Dan. ix. 20), 'While I was confessing my sin, and the sin of my people.' He rightly concludes that for the spiritual priesthood of the New Covenant this prayer contains the same confession of sin as under the Old did the offerings which the priests made first for themselves, before ever they made them for the sins of the people. As those offerings implicitly convinced them (Heb. vii. 27), so this prayer explicitly convinces us of sin.[2]

This remission of our debts being not so much as asked except on a condition, '*as we forgive our debtors,*' causes Augustine often to remark how terrible a prayer this may become. If we pray it, keeping an unforgiving temper, we shall be ourselves blocking up the way by which our prayers should have ascended, not merely failing to extricate ourselves from the bands of our sins, but with our own hands drawing the cords of them more closely round us

---

[1] *De Pecc. Mer. et Rem.* ii. 10. These are their words: Sancti et perfecti jam Apostoli dicebant, Dimitte nobis debita nostra, . . . ut per hoc quod dicerent *nostra*, in uno esse corpore demonstrarent et illos adhuc habentes peccata, et seipsos qui jam carebant omni ex parte peccato. Very different indeed are Augustine's own words on the justification of sinners, and on the witness which this Prayer offers of the grounds on which this justification must rest (*De Civ. Dei*, 19. 27): Ipsa nostra justitia, quamvis vera sit, propter veri boni finem ad quem refertur, tanta tamen est, ut potius peccatorum remissione constet, quam perfectione virtutum. Testis est oratio totius Civitatis Dei quæ peregrinatur in terris. Per omnia quippe membra sua clamat ad Deum, Dimitte nobis debita nostra.

[2] *Serm.* cxxxv.: Sacrificia convincebant sacerdotes . . . Non attendo quod loqueris, sed quid offeras. Victima tua convincit te.

than before.¹ It will little profit to do as some do, who, conscious of this, when they approach this petition, avoid it, and pass on to the next: like a debtor who, seeing his creditor at a distance, turns into some side alley out of the way in which before he was going. For whom is it that we seek to shun? a creditor who, so long as we keep this temper, will meet us everywhere, and whom it is impossible to evade² (Ps. cxxxvi. 7).

Ver. 13. '*And lead us not into temptation, but deliver us from evil: for thine is the kingdom, and the power, and the glory, for ever. Amen.*'—Augustine traces a connexion with the last petition: Forgive us what we have done: grant that we do not the same any more.³ He mentions that it was read in numerous Latin copies, though he had never found it in the Greek,—and that many of the faithful in his time were wont to pray, '*Suffer us not to be led into temptation*';⁴ it seeming

---

¹ *Serm.* clxxxi. 6: Hoc tibi dicit Deus, Debitor meus es, habes et tu debitorem. Debitor meus es, quia peccâsti in me; habes debitorem fratrem, quia peccavit in te. Quod feceris cum debitore tuo, facio et ego cum meo; id est, si dimittis, dimitto; si tenes, teneo. Tu contra te tenes, qui altero non dimittis. *Serm.* lviii. 6: Qui vult dicere efficaciter, Dimitte, oportet ut dicat veraciter, Sicut et nos dimittimus. *Serm.* cccxv. 7: Ibi illa inimica [ira] stat contra te. Sepit viam orationis tuæ, murum erigit, et non est quâ transeas.

² *Serm.* ccclii. 2: Quomodo quisque in vico cum occurrerit ei, cui aliquid debet, si ad manum est diverticulum, dimittit quo ibat, et it per aliam partem, ne faciem videat creditoris. Hoc tu in isto versu te fecisse arbitratus es. Devitâsti dicere, Dimitte sicut ego dimisi, ne sic dimitteret, id est, non dimitteret, quia non dimittis. Quem devitas? quis devitas? Quo ibis, ubi tu esse possis, et ille non esse?

³ *Serm.* xlviii. 8: Dimitte quæ fecimus, et da ut alia non committamus.

⁴ *De Don. Persev.* 6.

to them that an actual leading of men into temptation
might not by any means be attributed to God (Jam.
i. 13). But he often shows that none need shrink from
the words, or seek to rob them of their force, by any such
additions either secretly or openly made. God does
tempt, quite as truly as the devil tempts: all the difference lies in the end and aim with which they severally do
it,[1]—the one tempting to deceive, the other to approve;
Satan to bring out men's evil to their ruin, God to bring
out, and through the conflict to strengthen, their good to
their everlasting gain; or if to bring out their sin, yet this
only as a process of transition to a higher good, that so,
discovering their sin and recovering from it, they may
walk henceforward more humbly, more circumspectly; that
knowing better the evil which is in them, they may take
up arms the more earnestly against it. He adduces oftentimes St. Peter, and his permitted fall, as an instance of
what he means. *He* too had said, like the Psalmist, 'I
shall never be moved.'[2] How good was it for him that
the temptation came, and that through it he should find

---

[1] *In Ev. Joh. Tract.* xliii.: Intelligimus duas esse tentationes,
unam quæ decipit, alteram quæ probat: secundum eam quæ decipit, Deus neminem tentat: secundum eam quæ probat, tentat vos
Dominus Deus vester, ut sciat si diligitis eum; . . . non ergo Deus
nescit, sed dictum est, ut sciat, quod est, ut scire vos faciat. Cf.
Serm. ii. 3: Non enim sibi homo ita notus est, ut Creatori; nec sic
æger sibi notus est, ut medico. . . . Si Deus cessat tentare, magister
cessat docere. Cf. *Serm.* lvii. 9.

[2] *De Corrept. et Grat.* 9: Hæc vox et apostoli Petri esse potuit:
dixerat quippe et ipse in abundantiâ suâ, Animam meam pro te
ponam; sibi festinando tribuens, quod ei fuerat a Domino postea
largiendum. . . . Sed quia didicit non de seipso fidere, etiam hoc ei
profecit in bonum, faciente illo qui diligentibus eum omnia co-operatur
in bonum.

out the secret of his weakness, and thus also the secret of his strength.[1]

But this question being set at rest, there arises another; for, seeing that a temptation may come, and often does come, from God, it becomes the more needful to explain why we should here be bidden to deprecate temptation; how, too, such a deprecation will agree with those Scriptures, in which we are invited to count it all joy when we fall into divers temptations (Jam. i. 2). Augustine, in reply, draws a distinction between the being *led into* temptation, and the being tempted.[2] The first is the coming under the power of a temptation greater than we can bear, and *this* we deprecate,[3] saying, 'Lead us not into temptation,' but not the other, for we acknowledge that other to be the sad but needful condition of our life in the flesh. And many both in ancient and modern times have taken the same line: they have understood these words to imply, Lead us not so far *into* temptation, that a way back shall be impossible; suffer us not to be so inextricably entangled in it, that there shall be no means of escape; but with the temptation make ever the way of deliverance. Now though it is most true that

---

[1] *Serm.* lxxvi. 4: Multos impedit a firmitate, præsumtio firmitatis. Cf. *Serm.* cclxxxvi. 3; *Enarr. in Ps.* xxxvi. 1.
[2] *De Serm. Dom. in Mon.* ii. 9: Aliud est induci in tentationem, aliud tentari. . . . Inducimur enim si tales acciderint, quas ferre non possumus. *Ep.* cxxx. 11: [Petimus] ne deserti ejus adjutorio alicui tentationi vel consentiamus decepti, vel cedamus afflicti. Cf. *Ep.* clxxvii. § 4: where may be seen as well the use which Augustine makes of this petition also in his controversy with the Pelagians.
[3] *De Serm. Dom. in Mon.* ii. 9: Tanquam si quispiam cui necesse sit igne examinari, non oret ut igne non contingatur, sed ut non exuratur.

this will always be the prayer of the faithful,[1] yet such a distinction cannot be maintained as lying in the words. '*Lead us not into temptation*' is indeed what it seems at first sight, a prayer that we may not be tempted; yet not as declining to meet temptation when it comes, not as denying the blessing with which it may be charged; while yet out of a deep sense of our own infirmity, and of the uncertainty and hazard of the issue, we pray that it may be averted, however willing we may be manfully to encounter it, yea, to count it all joy, if in God's gracious dealings with us it should arrive.[2]

On the question whether the words which follow, '*But deliver us from evil*,' constitute a distinct petition, and so the number of petitions in the Lord's Prayer be seven and not six, Augustine rather wavers. In one place[3] he makes seven petitions, and finds a meaning and a mystery in the number, drawing a parallel between the seven and the seven beatitudes out of which the whole discourse unfolds itself; and he then refers '*Lead us not into temptation*' to evil threatening in the future, '*But deliver us from evil*' to evil which already is around and about us.[4] And seeing that throughout all Scripture seven is the covenant number, the number of sacrifice and the number of prayer, the signature of all meetings between God and man, there

---

[1] See Tholuck, *Auslegung der Bergpredigt*, p. 430.

[2] *Ep.* cxxx. 14: In his ergo tribulationibus quæ possunt et prodesse et nocere, . . . quia dura, quia molesta, quia contra sensum nostræ infirmitatis sunt, universali humanâ voluntate ut a nobis hæc auferantur, oramus.

[3] *De Serm. Dom. in Mon.* ii. 11; *Serm.* lviii. 10.

[4] *De Serm. Dom. in Mon.* ii. 9: Ultima et septima petitio est, Sed libera nos a malo. Orandum est enim ut non solum non inducamur in malum quo caremus, quod sexto loco petitur; sed ab illo etiam liberemur, quo jam inducti sumus.

can be no doubt that the number of petitions here is seven, and not six. Yet he himself sometimes departs from this truer view, and expressly unites these two last as forming parts of the same petition.¹ When, too, as has just been noticed, he makes '*Lead us not into temptation*' to refer to the future, and '*Deliver us from evil*' to the present, he has reversed the true order, and that which the very sequence of the petitions indicates. '*Lead us not into temptation*' is a prayer that we may be kept from the evil which may be now alluring and threatening to ensnare us: '*Deliver us from evil*' is the cry for an entire deliverance, for the redemption of the body, for the coming of that time when, to speak his own language, all that is as yet only *in spe* shall be also *in re*; so that we have here, in these three concluding petitions, a past, a present, and a future; and this the true order he has himself elsewhere implicitly indicated.² That this deliverance from evil is first and chiefly a deliverance from our evil selves, that this is the deliverance which more than any other we need, he often most truly and most profoundly brings out.³

¹ *Serm.* lvii. 10: Ideo addidit *sed*: ut ostenderet hoc totum ad unam sententiam pertinere. . . . Liberando nos a malo non nos infert in tentationem: non nos inferendo in tentationem, liberat nos a malo. Presently after he speaks of them as *sex vel septem* petitiones. Cf. *Enchir. ad Laurent.* 116.

² *Con. Julian.* vi. 14: Quâ [scil. gratiâ] *liberor*, ut sciam ne intrem in tentationem, a concupiscentiâ meâ abstractus et illectus, . . . quâ *liberabor*, ut spero, in æternum, ubi jam nulla lex in membris meis repugnet legi mentis meæ—this last *liberabor* being evidently in his mind the answer to the prayer, '*Deliver us from evil*,' as the *liberor* to the prayer, '*Lead us not into temptation.*' This the right meaning he has spoken out, *De Pecc. Mer. et Rem.* ii. 4: Deinde addimus quod perficietur in fine, cum absorbebitur mortale a vitâ: Sed libera nos a malo.

³ Libera me a me. And again, *Serm.* xliv. 3: Libera me ab

Augustine knows nothing of the doxology, as neither do the other principal Fathers of the Latin Church; nor yet, commenting on the Sermon on the Mount, does he notice the '*Amen,*' though elsewhere he gives well what its meaning is on the lips of the faithful, that it is their seal and consent and adstipulation to all that has been spoken.[1]

Ver. 14, 15. '*For if ye forgive men their trespasses, your heavenly Father will also forgive you: but if ye forgive not men their trespasses, neither will your Father forgive your trespasses.*'—Augustine has oftentimes solemn observations on the fact that our Lord should return back upon this condition of our obtaining forgiveness, and upon this only, among all the matters of which the Prayer had treated; here giving one blow more to the die, so to make the impression sharper and deeper on the minds of all.[2] And this He does, because of the fearful consequence of a failure here; for to retain our anger or our malice is not merely to retain one sin, but in the retaining of that one to retain also every other; it is not merely to shut one door, but in that one to shut every door, by which the grace of God might enter into our souls.[3]

homine malo, a meipso. *Serm.* lvii. 9: Te vince, et mundus est victus.

[1] In a fragment of a sermon, vol. v. p. 1510: Fratres mei, Amen vestrum subscriptio vestra est, consensio vestra est, adstipulatio vestra est.

[2] *Enchir. de Fide, Spe, et Car.* 74: Ad tam magnum tonitruum qui non expergiscitur, non dormit sed mortuus est.

[3] *Serm.* lvii. 11, 12: Unde accepturus enim veniam fueras pro cæteris delictis, hoc perdis. Si quid aliis sensibus, aliis cupiditatibus peccaveras, hinc erat sanandum quia dicturus eras, Dimitte, sicut et

On the plan and inner coherence of the Prayer he notes how the first three petitions contain, as we have seen that the last three contain, a beginning, a middle, and an end. God's '*Name*,' at his coming in the flesh, began to be '*hallowed*;' since that his '*kingdom*' has been ever coming, as it is in part '*come*;' hereafter it will be a perfected kingdom, at his second advent, from which time his '*will*' will '*be done*' here as perfectly as '*in heaven*.' So too, he observes, as the eternal things are first in dignity, they are here placed first in order. We are asking in the first three petitions things which, though having for us a beginning in time, will yet stand fast through eternity; the Name will be hallowed, the kingdom established, and the will accomplished for ever. But the other and later petitions relate to things transitory: the daily bread will not be needed by them who are nourished on the beatific vision of God; nor the forgiveness of trespasses by them that henceforth shall sin no more; nor exemption from temptation, where there is nothing any longer within or without to tempt; nor deliverance from evil, where all evil shall have ended.[1]

This Prayer, as he often takes pains to show, is the mould into which our desires should be cast,[2] a groundplan given us, which we may fill in, and on which we may build at large; while yet there will be no necessity

nos dimittimus. . . . Illo perdito cuncta tenebuntur; omnino nihil dimittitur.

[1] *De Serm. Dom. in Mon.* ii. 10; *Serm.* lviii. 10: Tres ergo petitiones superiores æternæ sunt; quatuor autem sequentes ad istam vitam pertinent.

[2] *Serm.* lvi. 3: Verba quæ Dominus noster Jesus Christus in Oratione docuit, forma est desideriorum. Compare *De Perfect. Just.* 8: Oratione insinuans omnes regulas sancti desiderii.

of going beyond it, being as it is regulative for all other prayers; for there is not, he affirms, any possible request that a faithful man ought to make, which cannot be reduced under one or other rubric of this Prayer, which is not an unfolding of something shut up in the Lord's Prayer. It is only such a request as ought never to have been made, something that we 'ask amiss,' which will not range itself under one or other of these petitions.[1]

Ver. 16–18. '*Moreover when ye fast, be not, as the hypocrites, of a sad countenance: for they disfigure their faces, that they may appear unto men to fast. Verily I say unto you, They have their reward. But thou, when thou fastest, anoint thine head, and wash thy face; that thou appear not unto men to fast, but unto thy Father which is in secret: and thy Father, which seeth in secret, shall reward thee openly.*'—Here is another precept, Augustine observes, on purity of intention, which is now altogether the matter in hand, a warning that no ostentation or desire of human praise be allowed to mingle with actions which ought to be done simply before God, with an eye to a heavenly and not an earthly reward.[2] All the precepts in this part of the

---

[1] *Ep.* cxxx. 12 : Si per omnia precationum sanctarum verba discurras, quantum existimo, nihil invenies quod in istâ Dominicâ non contineatur et concludatur Oratione. . . . Qui autem dicit in oratione, verbi gratiâ, Domine, multiplica divitias meas; aut, Da mihi quantas illi vel illi dedisti; aut, Honores meos auge; aut, Fac me in hoc seculo præpotentem atque clarentem; . . . puto eum non invenire in Oratione Dominicâ quo possit hæc vota coaptare.

[2] *De Serm. Dom. in Mon.* ii. 12: Manifestum est his præceptis omnem nostram intentionem in interiora gaudia dirigi, ne foris quærentes mercedem huic seculo conformemur, et amittamus pro-

discourse warn us, how it is not merely in the pomp and splendour of worldly things that pride may display itself, but that also it may lurk under rags and in sackcloth, being then a pride the more perilous as being the more veiled. For he who seeks eagerly to outdo others in the adorning of his body, and in the magnificence of his surroundings, deceives nobody with a fraudulent appearance of sanctity, being at once convinced as a lover of the vanities of this world.[1] But he who draws men's eyes upon himself by an unusual squalor and self-neglect, when he assumes this of choice and not endures it of necessity, must be judged by the rest of his conversation, whether through contempt of superfluous ornament, or with some sinister aim he has done it; for the Lord Himself has warned us to beware of wolves in sheep's clothing, and to know men not by their appearance, but by their fruits. This knowledge we may presently arrive at; for, if we give heed, there will not want for tokens whereby we shall be able to judge whether such a one be indeed a wolf in sheep's clothing, or a sheep in its own. Yet, he adds, a faithful man should not therefore flatter the eyes of men with a superfluous adorning, on the plea that there

missionem tanto solidioris atque firmioris, quanto interioris beatitudinis.

[1] *De Serm. Dom. in Mon.* ii. 12: In hoc autem capitulo maxime animadvertendum est, non in solo rerum corporearum nitore atque pompâ, sed etiam in ipsis sordibus luctuosis esse posse jactantiam, et eo periculosiorem quo sub nomine servitutis Dei decipit. Qui ergo immoderato cultu corporis atque vestitûs, vel cæterarum rerum nitore præfulget, facile convincitur rebus ipsis, pomparum seculi esse sectator, neque quenquam fallit dolosâ imagine sanctitatis. Qui autem inusitato squalore ac sordibus intentos in se oculos hominum facit, . . . cæteris ejus operibus potest conjici utrum hoc contemtu superflui cultûs, an ambitione aliquâ faciat.

T

are those who wear the rough garment to deceive; the sheep should not lay aside their own clothing, because sometimes the wolves cover themselves with the like.[1]

But with this clear insight into the whole purpose of the passage, it is singular that Augustine should have found a difficulty in the words, 'Anoint thine head;' which he does, from the fact of such anointing in times of fasting or indeed at any time having altogether disappeared when he wrote: he therefore interprets the precept mystically of the inward gladness of the spirit before the Lord.[2] Yet surely here, as in so many other places, we are to see the permanent and the universal embodied and presented to us in the forms of the transitory and local; and we shall interpret these words according to their true spirit and intention, when we substitute for this of anointing the head any other forms of outward seemliness and decent adorning, which are in use in our own time, and the omission of which would attract a peculiar observation. These forms shall not be thus omitted; there is no such proclamation to be made to all the world of what the Christian man may be doing. It hardly needs to add that this, ' When ye fast,' Augustine interprets everywhere as a command. It was reserved for others to turn ' When ye fast,' into the more convenient, 'If ye choose to fast.' He notices other ways besides this of ostentatious demonstration in which fasting may be defeated of any accompanying good; as when it goes together with any indulged sin, when, abstaining from

---

[1] *De Serm. Dom. in Mon.* ii. 24: Non ideo debent oves odisse vestimentum suum, quia plerumque illo se occultant lupi.

[2] *Ibid.* ii. 12: Intelligendum est hoc præceptum unguendi caput . . . ad interiorem hominem pertinere.

things which are sometimes allowable, we do not abstain from those which are always unlawful ;¹ or again, when it is a mere *varying* of our luxuries, and not an *abridging* of them:² and he draws a picture, evidently from the life, in more places than one, of a luxurious 'fool-fasting,' as our Reformers happily named it, which had already sprung up in his time; and which, keeping the name, had entirely evaded the reality of fasting, being in truth no mortifying of the appetite, but only a pampering of it in new forms and by novel devices; or again, when that which thereby is spared, is not spared for the poor but for ourselves;³ in all which cases it shall not be seen, he says, by our heavenly Father with any pleasure, nor bring any blessing with it.

Ver. 19, 20. '*Lay not up for yourselves treasures upon earth, where moth and rust doth corrupt, and where thieves break through and steal: but lay up for yourselves treasures in heaven, where neither moth nor rust doth corrupt, and where thieves do not break through nor steal.*'—In his work especially dedicated to the elucidation of this discourse, Augustine hastens rapidly over these verses; though in other places he has loved to enlarge upon them much: yet not so rapidly even there, but that he seeks to trace their connexion with what went

¹ *Serm.* cxliii. (*Appendix*): Quid enim prodest pallidum esse jejuniis, si odio et invidiâ livescas ? Quid enim prodest vinum non bibere, et iracundiæ veneno inebriari ?
² *Serm.* ccx. 8, 9: Tanquam non sit Quadragesima piæ humilitatis observatio, sed novæ voluptatis occasio. And again, *Serm.* ccv. 2 : Nemo sub abstinentiæ specie mutare affectet potius quam resecare delitias.
³ *Serm.* cxliv. (*Appendix*): Jejunium tuum te castiget, sed lætificet alterum.

before and what follows, a connexion which others have despaired of finding. He finds the following: Give with no unworthy aim, with no by-ends and outlooks for thine own advantage—that were to '*lay up treasures on earth*;' but do good for the love of God, for the pure love of thy brother—that is to '*lay up treasures in heaven*:' and then he points to the following verses (22, 23) in proof that it is singleness and purity of intention upon which the Lord is still dwelling. But this is scarcely tenable; for while it is most true that all which is done out of an unworthy motive perishes, yet the specifying of the '*moth*' and '*rust*'[1] and '*thieves*,' as the instruments of destruction, points to the more obvious interpretation, namely, that this laying up of treasures upon earth is not, as he would have us to understand, a laying out of the temporal mammon seemingly for God, though indeed with unworthy selfish aims; but the not laying it out for Him at all, nor even appearing so to do, but rather only and evidently for ourselves.

If there be a connexion, it might perhaps be rather

---

[1] For βρῶσις Augustine has, with the old Italic, *comestura*; the Vulgate, *ærugo*. Here again the change was for the worse, seeing that βρῶσις has not the special significance, so given it, of *rust*, but refers generally to the eating tooth of time, to the consumption, by whatever means, of the things which are on earth. Not here only, but in other passages as well, the earlier Latin Versions were more accurate than the Vulgate which in the end superseded them. Thus the Vulgate translates κατασκηνώσεις (Matt. viii. 20) *nidos*, which we have followed, 'nests' (*A. V.*), but the earlier translation more correctly, *diversoria* (AUGUSTINE, *Con. Faust.* xxii. 48); or *tabernacula* (Augustine, *Quæst.* xvii. *in Matt.*, qu. 5). So, too, Heb. vi. 7, the Vulgate renders δι' οὓς γεωργεῖται, *a quibus* colitur; and has again drawn us along with its error: '*by whom* it is dressed' (*A. V.*); but the old Italic: *propter quos* colitur (TERTULLIAN, *De Pudic.* 20); and our Revised Version, 'for whose sake it is tilled.'

traced thus: Prefer the unseen and eternal before the seen and transitory; as I have bidden you to do this in other things, to count the praise of God better than the praise of men,—this being hollow and transient, that real and enduring,—so also and for the same reasons count it better to have treasure in heaven than on earth. Count it a blessed thing that by giving to God you can set the seal of endurance upon that which is in its nature so transitory, that you can transport beyond mortal decay and evil chance, that which of itself is so obvious to these. And this is a language which Augustine himself often uses: Lift up, he says, your fruits to a higher floor, where they will not be exposed to the same inevitable danger of corrupting and spoiling as threatens them on the lower.[1] For He who gave, desires that we should not lose even his lower gifts, but should keep them for ever; and therefore yields counsels such as this, offering to take into his own secure keeping that which we in no other way can retain: to send it before us, to that world whither we are certainly going, that we may find it there.[2] You

---

[1] *Enarr. in Ps.* xlviii. 9: Modo si amicus tuus intraret in domum tuam, et inveniret te in loco humido frumenta posuisse, qui forte sciret naturam corruptionis frumentorum, quam tu nescires, daret tibi hujusmodi consilium, dicens, Frater, perdis quod cum magno labore collegisti: in loco humido posuisti; paucis diebus ista putrescunt. Et quid facio, frater? Leva in superiora. Audires amicum suggerentem, ut frumenta levares de inferioribus ad superiora, et non audis Christum monentem, ut thesaurum tuum leves de terrâ ad cælum. Cf. *Serm.* lx. 7.

[2] See his beautiful words, *Enarr. in Ps.* xxxviii. 7, where, among other things, he says: Quare ibi ponis ubi possis amittere, ubi, si non amittas, ibi permanere perpetuo non potes? Est alius locus quo te transferam. Præcedat te quod habes, noli timere ne perdas: dator ego eram, custos ego ero. And again, of what is offered to God he says, *Serm.* xlii. 2: Non dico, Hoc non perit, sed dico, Hoc solum

trust *in* God, will you not then trust Him? you believe *in* Him, will you not then believe Him, and that He has secret channels of communication between this world and the other, so that all what is committed to these channels will there be found?[1] Beware, he sometimes adds, lest you be of the number of them, the men of the earth, who have slept their sleep, even the sleep of a vain worldly existence, and when they awaken to a world of realities their hands are empty; they 'have found nothing,' and this because they placed nothing in the hand of Christ, which in each one of his poor was stretched out to them.[2] And he often uses the gathering distresses and troubles of his time, the barbarian invasions, which having already wasted Italy, were fast advancing upon Africa, and which were bringing an evident insecurity on all things temporal, as an additional motive for heartily obeying this com-

non perit. And in a sermon, *De Contemptu Mundi* (vol. v. p. 713): Si amas divitias, præmitte, easque sequaris; ne cum amas in terrâ, aut vivus eas amittas aut mortuus.

[1] *Enarr. in Ps.* xxxviii. 7: Si haberet quispiam amicus tuus quosdam locos vel cisternas, et quæque receptacula fabricarum ad servandum aliquem liquorem vel vini vel olei quæreres, et diceret tibi; Ego tibi servo: haberetque ad illa receptacula occultos canales quosdam transitusque, ut per hos clanculo iret quod palam funderetur, et diceret tibi, Quod habes, hic funde: videres autem tu non esse illum locum ubi ponere cogitabas, et timeres fundere; ille qui sciret machinamenta quædam occulta locorum suorum non tibi diceret, Funde securus, hinc illuc pervenit; non vides quâ, sed crede mihi qui fabricavi? Fabricavit enim per quem facta sunt omnia mansiones omnibus nobis: illuc vult præcedere quod habemus, ne hoc in terrâ perdamus.

[2] *Enarr. in Ps.* lxxv. 6: Dormierunt somnum suum viri divitiarum, et nihil invenerunt in manibus suis. . . . Nihil inveniunt in manibus suis, quia nihil posuerunt in manu Christi. Vis aliquid invenire in manibus tuis postea? Noli contemnere modo manum pauperis, et respice manus inanes, si vis habere manus plenas.

mand;[1] since apart from the inevitable quitting at death, it seemed likely that many would be compelled to loosen their grasp of their possessions long before. Thus, writing to the clergy and people of Hippo, who in his absence had omitted, under the pressure of their worldly calamities, some customary bounties to the poor, he reminds them, that if indeed the weak fabric of this world was about to fall, what more urgent reason and motive could there be than this, why they should quickly transfer whatsoever of their treasure they could to that City more strongly built, which alone would survive the shock.[2] And to some who were already stripped of their worldly possessions he addresses himself thus: The enemy has invaded your house; would he have invaded heaven? He has slain the servant that watched your goods; would he have slain the Lord who was willing to have kept them, there where no thief approaches, neither moth corrupts?[3] You have ransomed your life from the barbarians at the cost of all that you had. And how did this necessity arise? Because you would not render a portion of that all unto Christ. You

[1] *Serm.* lx. 6: Non surgitur, non proceditur, nisi ut unâ voce dicatur ab omnibus: Væ nobis, ruit mundus. Si ruit, quare non migras? Si tibi architectus diceret, Ruituram domum tuam; nonne prius migrares quam murmurares? Structor mundi tibi dicit, Ruiturum mundum, et non credis? Cf. *Serm.* xxxviii. 5–7.

[2] *Ep.* cxxii.: Sicut enim ad loca munitiora festinantius migrant, qui ruinam domûs vident contritis parietibus imminere; sic corda Christiana quanto magis sentiunt mundi hujus ruinam crebrescentibus tribulationibus propinquare, tanto magis debent bona quæ in terrâ recondere disponebant, in thesaurum cælestem impigrâ celeritate transferre; ut si aliquis humanus casus acciderit, gaudeat qui de loco ruinoso emigravit.

[3] *Serm.* lx. 8: Invasit hostis domum, numquid invaderet cælum? Occidit servum custodem, numquid occideret Dominum servatorem quo fur non accedit, neque tinea corrumpit?

would not *give*, and therefore He *took*; and took, not as He was once prepared to receive at your hands, but took, and left no blessing behind.[1] That which comes from his people at the gentle pressure of his simple bidding, comes as the fine and sweet and golden-coloured olive-oil which runs freely from the fruit, almost before ever the press has touched them. This is as the lees, as the thick and vile *amurca*, which is wrung out by the force of a harsh constraint at the last.[2]

Ver. 21. '*For where your treasure is, there will your heart be also.*'—This is the reason, he says, why Christ desires his people to lay up store in heaven, namely, that they may have a heart in heaven; this is why He bids them to lift up their goods, that they may lift up their souls as well. For it is the power which the '*treasure*' has inevitably to draw after it the heart, the fact that it is the loadstar to which the needle *must* point, which makes it of such consequence *where* this treasure is stored.[3] For him that has his treasure in earth, it is vain when he hears the stirring summons of the Church, Lift up your hearts, to make answer, We lift them up unto the Lord. He does not, he cannot do so; his heart is of

---

[1] *Serm. de Contemptu Mundi*, vol. v. p. 713 : Christo modicum non dedisti, et barbaris totum quod habuisti, dedisti. . . . Christus rogat, et non accipit. Ille torquet, et totum aufert.

[2] Mundus est torcular; abundant pressuræ ejus, oleum esto tu, non amurca.

[3] *Enarr. in Ps.* xc. 16: Quare autem vult [Christus] ut locum mutes thesauro tuo, nisi ut locum mutes cordi tuo ? Nemo enim cogitat nisi de thesauro suo. Quam multi hic sunt qui me modo audiunt, et non est cor eorum nisi in saccellis suis. In terrâ estis quia in terrâ est quod amatis; mittatur in cælum, et erit ibi cor vestrum.

necessity where his treasure, that which he esteems his best good, is,—in the earth, and not in heaven; and so long as his treasure is there, his heart must remain there as well.[1]

Ver. 22, 23. '*The light of the body is the eye: if therefore thine eye be single, thy whole body shall be full of light. But if thine eye be evil, thy whole body shall be full of darkness. If therefore the light that is in thee be darkness, how great is that darkness.*'—Augustine understands '*the eye*' here as the intention with which our works are performed,—'*the body*' the sum total of these works themselves. '*If thine eye be single,*' if the intention, that is, be right and pure, directed to God and to the pleasing of God, all the works which are wrought according to that intention, which in other words are wrought in faith,[2] will be right and pure also; they will be illuminated as well. '*But if thine eye be evil,*' if thine intention is defiled and blinded by the appetite of things carnal and temporal, all the works that spring out of that impure motive shall be sharers in the darkness.[3]

[1] *Serm.* cccxlv.: Si autem in terrâ obruis cor tuum, erubesce, quia mentiris cum respondes, quando audis, Sursum corda. Nam dicitur, Sursum corda; et continuo respondes, Habemus ad Dominum. Deo mentiris. In terrâ obrutum cor habes, quia ubi fuerit thesaurus tuus ibi erit et cor tuum.

[2] *Con. Julian.* iv. 3: Hunc oculum agnosce intentionem, quâ facit quisque quod facit; et per hoc disce eum qui non facit opera bona intentione fidei bonæ, hoc est, ejus quæ per dilectionem operatur, totum quasi corpus, quod illis, velut membris, operibus constat, tenebrosum esse, hoc est plenum nigredine peccatorum.

[3] *De Serm. Dom. in Mon.* ii. 13; *Enarr. in Ps.* cxviii. 37: Proinde magni interest cum aliquid bonum facimus, cujus rei contemplatione faciamus; . . . ut scilicet non tantum si bonum est quod facimus, sed præcipue si bonum est propter quod facimus, cogitemus.

There are two explanations of what follows: '*If therefore the light that is in thee be darkness, how great is that darkness*'—one, which makes the second '*darkness*' to be the darkness *which shall then ensue* in the body, or, to leave the image, in the whole domain of man's spiritual life; if the avenues of light are stopped, what an absolute darkness will ensue through that whole region of man's soul! According to the other meaning, which indeed includes this, but also something more, the second '*darkness*' is the darkness *before existing* (τὸ σκότος, with the article) in that region; and then we must understand our Lord as contemplating the whole region of man's passions and propensities as itself '*darkness.*' This obscure and confused chaos was to have been lighted up by the rays of heavenly light received through the eye of the soul; but if even this eye is obscured, if that which was light and the channel of light becomes darkness, how will it fare with that *which of its own nature is darkness*; not, as our Version has it, '*that darkness*,' but '*the darkness*;' being, as that is, now cut off, by the obstruction of its one avenue of light, from the only illumination which could have reached it? I cannot doubt that this deeper, is also the truer, meaning. Tholuck [1] affirms that Augustine has embraced it; yet certainly not in his exposition of this discourse; where his meaning, though hard to catch, is certainly not this, nor have I been able to find any other passage to justify the assertion.[2]

---

[1] *Auslegung der Bergpredigt*, p. 452.

[2] It is evidently implied in the translation of the Vulgate, *Ipsæ* tenebræ quantæ erunt (but for this Augustine has, Tenebræ quantæ!); and by Jerome, Ipsa caligo quantis tenebris obvolvetur; by Chrysostom

Ver. 24. '*No man can serve two masters: for either he will hate the one, and love the other; or else he will hold to the one, and despise the other. Ye cannot serve God and mammon.*'—Augustine has a subtle remark, noting the nice selection of the words here, and clearing this passage even from the appearance of an unnecessary repetition. In the first clause, the '*master*' whom the man will '*hate*' is Satan, the '*master*' whom he will '*love*' is God, and this the faithful man will both do and profess to do. But no man actually and openly professes to hate God and love the devil; and therefore in the second clause, when the Lord is putting the converse case, He changes both words, which would be no longer the most appropriate; the sinner '*holds to*' Satan, when he follows his rewards; he practically '*despises*' God when he heeds not his promises and his threatenings; however little he may acknowledge to himself or to others that he is doing either this or the other.[1] Augustine does not commit the mistake, which is a modern one, of making '*mammon*' a proper name, and an actual title of ' the god of this world;' but, on the contrary, explains it rightly, though at the same time he says with truth, that *its* service is *his* service.[2]

Ver. 25, 26. '*Therefore I say unto you, Take no thought for your life, what ye shall eat, or what ye shall

also, and most of the ancients, though the other is in modern times the more frequent explanation.

[1] *Quæst. Evang.* ii. 36: Non dixit, Odiet, sed contemnet: sicut solent minas ejus postponere cupiditatibus suis, qui de bonitate ejus ad impunitatem sibi blandiuntur.

[2] *De Serm. Dom. in Mon.* ii. 14: Lucrum Punice mammon dicitur. Sed qui servit mammonæ, illi utique servit, qui rebus istis terrenis merito suæ perversitatis præpositus, magistratus hujus seculi a Domino dicitur.

drink; nor yet for your body, what ye shall put on. Is not the life more than meat, and the body than raiment? Behold the fowls of the air: for they sow not, neither do they reap, nor gather into barns; yet your heavenly Father feedeth them. Are ye not much better than they?'
—While there cannot be a single eye (ver. 22), so long as we propose a double object for our striving, and while under the pretext that we are only providing things necessary, the whole inordinate care and servitude to mammon may again come in, abstain, Christ would say, from all excessive anxiety; for, as Augustine traces the argument in the latter clause of the verse, will not He who gave the more excellent thing, the breath of life, give also the meaner thing, the meat by which that life is sustained? He who fashioned your marvellous bodies, cannot and will not He furnish the raiment which they need?[1]

Ver. 27. *'Which of you by taking thought can add one cubit unto his stature?'*—Augustine connects this verse with the first clause of the verse following. He who has determined your bodies shall be just what they are, which is evidently God, for ye yourselves are powerless to change any thing in them, cannot He clothe them as well?[2] But Maldonatus acutely remarks, that this cannot

---

[1] *De Serm. Dom. in Mon.* ii. 15: Dominus admonet, ut meminerimus multo amplius nobis Deum dedisse, quod nos fecit et composuit ex animâ et corpore, quam est alimentum atque tegumentum; ... qui dedit animam multo facilius escam esse daturum. He rightly remarks that ψυχή here is to be translated '*life*' and not soul, as at Matt. x. 39: 'He that findeth his life (ψυχὴν) shall lose it.'

[2] *De Serm. Dom. in Mon.* ii. 15: Cujus potestate atque dominatu factum est, ut ad hanc staturam corpus vestrum perduceretur, ejus providentiâ etiam vestiri potest.

be the true connexion, as is clear from a comparison with the parallel passage in St. Luke (xii. 25-27), where the interposition of ver. 26 makes it impossible that such can be the line of thought. Nor has he himself the right explanation, which, as I am persuaded, is only attained when the word by us translated 'stature' (ἡλικία) is accepted rather in its other sense, as 'term of life' (John ix. 21-23).[1] Much may be urged against our present translation. In the first place, had our Lord desired to show that a man could not do '*that thing which is least*' (Luke xii. 26)[2] for his body, we should rather expect, '*Which of you by taking thought can add one inch*,' or, He might have put it yet more strongly, '*one hair's breadth unto his stature?*' So large a measure as a cubit is, according to the laws of a natural rhetoric, altogether out of place. We shall feel this more vividly if we substitute some nearly corresponding measure for cubit, which last not being a measure familiar to us, we fail to realize how large an augmentation to the stature this would prove. But, suppose it were asked, 'Which of you with all his caring can make himself *a foot* taller?' should we not feel at once that the foot was an excessive measure to have here employed, and that the meaning of the question must be sought elsewhere? And then there is this objection, which reaches deeper, namely, that increase of stature is not a matter about which men are wont to take anxious thought; it can scarcely be said for one in ten thousand

---

[1] This was first, I believe, suggested by Erasmus. Hammond has brought well together the arguments in its favour.

[2] Augustine feels that adding a cubit to the body can hardly be called '*that which is least*,' and seeks to help the interpretation thus (*Quæst. Evang.* ii. 28): Minimum est enim hoc, sed Deo corpora operanti.

to be an object of desire. It is otherwise with added length of days (1 Kin. iii. 11; Prov. iii. 16). If then we substitute '*length of life*' or '*age*,' which our Revisers propose as an alternative reading, in the place of '*stature*,' our Saviour's argument will be as follows: To what profit is all this solicitude about that which is to sustain life, when after all it can effect so little? with all your carking and caring you cannot make the most trifling addition, not so much as a single cubit, to the length of your life:[1] God brings in the day that terminates your course, whensoever He will (Luke xii. 10). He contemplates life here as a course (see Job ix. 25; 2 Tim. iv. 7; Ps. xxxix. 5, 'Thou hast made my life as an handbreadth'), and the cubit, which is much in the stature of a man, that rarely consisting of more than four cubits in all, will be exceedingly little, and therefore most appropriate, in the length of this.

Ver. 28–32. '*And why take ye thought for raiment? Consider the lilies of the field, how they grow: they toil not, neither do they spin: and yet I say unto you, That even Solomon in all his glory was not arrayed like one of these. Wherefore, if God so clothe the grass of the field, which to day is, and to morrow is cast into the oven, shall He not much more clothe you, O ye of little faith? Therefore take no thought, saying, What shall we eat? or, What shall we drink? or, Wherewithal shall we be clothed? (For after all these things do the Gentiles seek:) for your heavenly Father knoweth that ye have need of all these*

[1] Attempts thus to add to it are not without example in the East. Von Hammer, in his *Fundgruben des Orients*, gives a copy of a regularly executed document of the kind, in which an inferior formally makes over to his patron a certain number, I think fifteen, of the years of his life.

things.'—These sayings, with some which went before, might appear to cast a slight upon *all* labour and *all* providence on man's part; nor have they altogether escaped this abusive interpretation. The Manichæans, for instance,[1] in their eager quest for discrepancies between the Old Testament and the New, if so they might find help for their assertion, that the Old had a different author from the New, since it taught another doctrine, found in this passage a contradiction to Solomon's exhortation, ' Go to the ant, thou sluggard, &c.' (Prov. vi. 6-8). Nor were they the sole abusers of Christ's words; for the idle vagabond monks, who bore, after the Church had cast them out, the name of Euchites,[2] or The Praying People, affirmed not merely the lawfulness of living without labour, but on the plea of what is here taught, regarded as a point of perfection the abstaining from all toil; since thus they came closest to this command of Christ, feeding like the birds out of God's hand, and living on his free bounty, without any carefulness for to-morrow.[3] But

[1] *Con. Adimant.* 24. See another contradiction that they found between this passage and Gen. iv. 10, in this same treatise, c. 4, with Augustine's admirable answer. To the passage from the Proverbs (vi. 6) he gives it altogether a spiritual significance. The time of outward prosperity is our summer, in which we must lay up of the Word of God, of the lessons of his truth, and all that which shall secretly nourish and feed us when the winter of tribulation and sorrow shall arrive. See his excellent words, *Enarr. in Ps.* lxvi. 2, and *in Ps.* xxxvii. 20.

[2] *Liber de Hæres.* 57 ; *Retract.* ii. 21.

[3] *De Op. Monach.* 3 : Evangelica præcepta, de quibus nonnulli non solum pigritiam sed etiam arrogantiam suam fovent. And c. 30 : Quis ferat homines contumaces saluberrimis apostoli monitis resistentes, non sicut infirmiores tolerari, sed sicut etiam sanctiores prædicari, ut monasteria doctrinâ saniore fundata, geminâ illecebrâ corrumpantur, et dissolutâ licentiâ vacationis, et falso nomine sanctitatis?

Augustine set himself with a strong earnestness against this perversion of Christ's words, and the spreading evil which from this had infected many,—dedicating an especial treatise to this object. It cannot be, he says, that abstaining from labour is a point of perfection, for the blessed Apostle St. Paul himself, with reasons abundant to justify his releasing himself from toil, laboured with his own hands, and gave the same commandment in the Churches, 'that if any would not work, neither should he eat' (2 Thess. iii. 8-11; cf. Acts xviii. 1; xx. 33). And forethought and preparation for the coming day can as little be forbidden; for the Lord Himself with his disciples had a purse, from which things needful were purchased (John xii. 6); the fragments that remained over of the loaves were at his bidding carefully gathered up, evidently to be reserved for another occasion. How far looking was the Apostle Paul in the matter of the collection for the poor saints at Jerusalem (1 Cor. xvi. 1; Acts xi. 27); how much pleased at its largeness (2 Cor. ix. 15);[1] how provident in all his arrangements concerning the different members of the Church (1 Tim. v. 16). Were the not making of any provision for the morrow the point of perfection, then the savage who wastes what he cannot immediately consume, who lives only for and in the present moment, would have attained the highest condition of all.[2]

---

[1] *De Op. Monach.* 16: Quantâ pinguedine sanctæ lætitiæ perfusus apostolus, dum loquitur de alterno supplemento indigentiæ militum et provincialium Christi. Cf. *De Mendac.* 15.

[2] *Con. Adimant.* 24: Si hoc [Matt. vi. 24] ideo dictum est ut non servetur panis in crastinum, magis hoc implent vagi Romanorum, quos Passivos appellant, qui annonâ quotidianâ satiato ventre, aut donant statim quod restat aut projiciunt; quam vel Domini discipuli,

Augustine turns upon these idle mendicant monks, who by his account made no very edifying use of the leisure which by this interpretation they had acquired— wandering about the country, vending now the relics of martyrs, if indeed of martyrs—now phylacteries and amulets—professing now to be on a journey to visit their kindred, whom they had heard to be alive in some distant land, and everywhere seeking the profits of a gainful poverty, the rewards of a simulated holiness;[1] and addresses to them such remonstrances as this, If you determine to take this Scripture in the letter, you must at least be consistent, and carry your interpretation through. It is true you neither sow nor reap; you understand Christ literally, where toil is to be escaped; by the same reason you should have no barns; but you have such, in which you make no scruple about storing the labours of others. If you will be as the birds, what means the preparation of your food, your grinding and your baking? what your reserving of a part for to-morrow?[2] And then he draws a lively picture of a flock of ravenous monks, such as they would be, if indeed they adhered to the letter of this

qui etiam cum ipso Domino cæli et terræ in terrâ ambulantes loculos habebant: vel Paulus apostolus, qui omnium terrenorum contemptor sic tamen gubernavit ea quæ præsenti vitæ erant necessaria, ut etiam de viduis præceperit (1 Tim. v. 16).—*Passivus*, in this passage, is a word of African origin, and was applied to persons who led an idle, tramping, gipsy-like kind of life (Du Cange).

[1] Sumptus lucrosæ egestatis, aut simulatæ pretium sanctitatis.

[2] *De Op. Monach.* 23 : Cur ergo isti manus otiosas et plena repositoria volunt habere? Cur ea quæ sumunt ex laboribus aliorum, recondunt et servant unde quotidie proferatur? Cur denique molunt et coquunt? Hoc enim aves non faciunt. And 24: Cur volatilia cæli non vobis sunt exemplo ad nihil reservandum, et vultis ut sint exemplo ad nihil operandum?

precept; he imagines them lighting on a field, and gathering what they needed for the moment of its produce, which they must consume raw as they find it.

But who is it that really lives according to the spirit of the precepts which his Saviour has given to him here? He, Augustine replies, who dares to believe that if by infirmity or other cause he is cut off from his work, he shall indeed be fed without his toil, as the birds are, shall be clothed, as the lilies are; but with health and strength and opportunity, knows that these are God's appointed means whereby he shall acquire things needful for the body;[1] who knows that it is the anxiety, and not the labour (for that is God's appointment), which is excluded;[2] the doubt whether God could, if need were, provide for him in any other way, which is forbidden; with the sense that it is none save only He who ever under any circumstances, whether we labour or whether we are hindered from labour, does in fact provide.

Ver. 33, 34. *But seek ye first the kingdom of God, and his righteousness; and all these things shall be added unto you. Take therefore no thought for the morrow: for the morrow shall take thought for the things of itself. Sufficient unto the day is the evil thereof.*'—Augustine does not take the exhortation here, as actually excluding

---

[1] *De Op. Monach.* 27: Si et nos per aliquam vel infirmitatem vel occupationem non possimus operari, sic ille nos pascet et vestiet, quemadmodum aves et lilia, quæ nihil operantur hujuscemodi: cum autem possumus, non debemus tentare Deum nostrum, quia et hoc quod possumus, ejus munere possumus, et cum hinc vivimus, illo largiente vivimus, qui largitus est ut possimus.

[2] *De Mendac.* 15 : Satis elucet ista præcepta sic intelligenda ut nihil operis nostri temporalium adipiscendorum amore, vel timore egestatis, tanquam ex necessitate faciamus.

prayer for these lower things; only they shall not be the objects of our first, our foremost, our most earnest desires. The great things of the kingdom are to claim these; but in subordination to those greater we may ask for health of body, peace in our times, things sufficient for our earthly life, with the other conditions of an outward prosperity;[1] we may believe that in the measure in which they will profit us, these will be added to us. Thus he imagines some finding fault with the course which Peter pursued, when after the resurrection he returned to his boat and his nets (John xxi. 3); as demanding whether there were not herein a lack of faith in this promise of his Lord. Having sought first the kingdom of God, should he not have trusted that all things else would be added to him? But were they otherwise than added to him, Augustine asks, when the Lord guided that multitude of fishes into his net? Was not God as truly the giver of those as of the other fish which presently the Apostles found prepared upon the shore (ver. 9)?[2]

The last clause of ver. 34 is not without its difficulty, but Augustine passes it over very lightly in his Exposition of this Discourse; while even the little which he has there said about its interpretation, he at a later day with-

---

[1] *Serm.* lxiii. (*Appendix*): Nec hoc sic dicimus, ut pro rebus temporalibus Deum non oremus, id est, pro sanitate corporis, aut pro pace temporum, aut pro abundantiâ fructuum. Debemus et ista a Deo petere, sed secundo et tertio loco, ut primas partes in omni intentione nostræ orationis amor animæ et desiderium vitæ æternæ obtineat. *Serm.* clxxvii. § 2: Sint hæc ad necessitatis usum, non ad caritatis affectum; sint tanquam stabulum viatoris, non tanquam prædium possessoris. Refice et transi.

[2] *In Ev. Joh. Tract.* cxxii. 4: Num quis alius pisces qui caperentur apposuit.

draws,¹ and this without offering any explanation in the room of that which he disallows; nor do I remember to have met elsewhere in his writings any help to its understanding.² One would gladly know what exact significance he ascribed to the word which we have translated ' *evil* ' (κακία). That there is room for much difference of opinion about it is sufficiently indicated by the fact that Wicliff has rendered it ' *malice*,' following in this the Vulgate, which has *malitia* ; but Tertullian better, *vexatio* ; while Tyndale renders it '*trouble*,' Cranmer's Bible '*travail*,' and the Geneva '*grief*;' the Rheims Version agrees with our own.

¹ *Retract.* i. 19.
² Such explanations as that which occurs *Conf.* x. 31, varying little or nothing as they do from that which in his *Retractations* he explicitly withdraws, must be considered as withdrawn with it.

ST. MATTHEW, CHAP. VII.

VER. 1, 2. '*Judge not, that ye be not judged. For with what judgment ye judge, ye shall be judged: and with what measure ye mete, it shall be measured to you again.*'—These words, Augustine observes, must not be understood as though the Christian man were altogether to abdicate the right of discerning between good and evil; for the Lord Himself bids us to know men by their fruits, that is, to judge by the outward evidence which they give us of what spirit they are; and says again, 'Judge righteous judgment' (John vii. 24); and his Apostle, 'Do not ye judge them that are within' (1 Cor. v. 12)? And this judgment may fitly find place; for there are some sins which are manifest; actions which cannot be done with a right intention, but which are 'open beforehand, going before to judgment' (1 Tim. v. 24). On these a Christian *must* pass a judgment; though even here he will refrain from judging what will be the final condition of him who does these things, since it will be always possible that he may repent and be saved. But this '*Judge not*' chiefly refers to those acts which are capable of a double interpretation;[1] such are ever to have the judgment of charity. He gives for examples the following:

[1] *De Serm. Dom. in Mon.* ii. 18: Sunt quædam facta media quæ ignoramus quo animo fiant, quia et bono et malo fieri possunt, de quibus temerarium est judicare, maxime ut condemnemus.

If a man, on the plea of bodily weakness, should decline to keep the fasts of the Church, and others should give no credit to his plea, regarding it as only an excuse for self-indulgence, an unwillingness to mortify the flesh, this were to transgress the commandment, and to be 'judges of evil thoughts.' Or a man rules his house, as it seems to us, with too severe a strictness; yet let us not therefore conclude him harsh and cruel, since he may very possibly do this out of a zeal for righteousness, and the love of holy discipline.[1] In these, and all similar cases, that word will apply, ' Who art thou that judgest another man's servant? to his own master he standeth or falleth ' (Rom. xiv. 4); and that other word, 'Judge nothing before the time' (1 Cor. iv. 5); and our Lord's precept here, '*Judge not, that ye be not judged.*' Nor is it things questionable alone, and acts capable of a double interpretation, on which men are tempted to exercise uncharitable judgments. But the evil of their own hearts, the sad consciousness of their own mingled, and oftentimes impure motives, makes them prompt to suspect the same in others, and to think that even deeds evidently good so far as the appearance reaches, do yet grow out of some evil root.[2] Against all this, he reminds us, the seeking of that charity which ' thinketh no evil,' is the only remedy that will avail.

[1] *Serm.* lxvi. (*Appendix*) : De illis vero quæ aperta sunt et publica mala judicare et arguere, cum caritate tamen et amore, et possumus et debemus, odio habentes non hominem sed peccatum, non vitiosum sed vitium ; detestantes morbum potius quam ægrotum.

[2] Thus *Enarr. in Ps.* cxviii. 39, with a mournful, yet most true heart-knowledge, he says: Hoc enim proclivius homo suspicatur in alio, quod sentit in seipso. Compare our own proverb, Ill doers are ill deemers.

But how, he enquires, shall the promise or threat, for it may be the one quite as much as the other, '*with what judgment ye judge, ye shall be judged*,' be fulfilled? It cannot mean that if we judge rashly of others, God will judge rashly of us; or, if we measure unjustly to them, it will in turn be measured unjustly to us.[1] He answers that it is not the *temerity* of the sinner's judgment which God will imitate, but the *severity* of it: 'with the froward Thou wilt show Thyself froward' (Ps. xviii. 26). Nor in the moral world can the retaliation, whether it come directly from God, or from those that are his vicegerents on earth, be considered as a new act of injustice, being rather the restoration of the disturbed balances of righteousness,[2] by the throwing of a counter-weight into the scale opposite to that into which the offender had thrown his weight. Punishment is the recoil of crime, and the force of the backstroke is in proportion to the force of the original blow.

Some, as we learn, found in the concluding words of ver. 2 an argument against the everlasting duration of the punishment of the wicked. These argued, that as men sinned within limits of time, so within limits of time their punishment must be restrained, according to this phrase, '*With what measure ye mete, it shall be measured to you again*,' and according to that general equity, which demands that the sin which is temporal shall receive punishment which is temporal as well. But their

---

[1] *De Serm. Dom. in Mon.* ii. 18.
[2] So, speaking of Dives and Lazarus, with reference to this verse, he says, *Serm.* ccclxvii.: Pensantur . . . . pro purpurâ flamma, refectio pro nuditate, *ut salva sit æquitas stateræ.* Cf. *De Civ. Dei*, xxi. 11.

sin, he replies, though accidentally confined within limits of time and space, had its true seat and root in that which is subject to no such limitations, in their will, in that latent eternity which is in every man.[1] Sin, though coming outwardly to pass under conditions of time and of space, yet in its essence lies out of these altogether,— is eternal as the woe it brings.[2]

[1] *Ep.* cii. qu. 4: In eâdem igitur mensurâ, quamvis non æternorum malefactorum, æterna supplicia remetiuntur, ut quia æternam voluit haberi peccati perfruitionem, æternam vindictæ inveniat severitatem. See, too, his argument from the analogy of human punishments (*De Civ. Dei*, xxi. 11). The chapter is remarkable, as anticipating so much of Bishop Butler's argument, in the chapter of *The Analogy*, 'On the Government of God by Rewards and Punishments.' Among other things he says : Jam vero damnum, ignominia, exsilium, servitus, cum plerumque sic infligantur ut nullâ veniâ relaxentur, nonne pro hujus vitæ modo similia pœnis videntur æternis? Ideo quippe æterna esse non possunt, quia nec ipsa vita quæ his plectitur porrigitur in æternum: et tamen peccata quæ vindicantur longissimi temporis pœnis, brevissimo tempore perpetrantur, nec quispiam exstitit qui censeret tam cito nocentium finienda esse tormenta, quam cito factum est vel homicidium, vel adulterium, vel sacrilegium, vel quidlibet aliud scelus, non temporis longitudine, sed iniquitatis et impietatis magnitudine metiendum.

[2] Against those who would fain persuade themselves and others that all the dread announcements of the final doom of impenitent sinners are, as he describes it, minaciter potius quam veraciter dicta, he urges, what many have urged since, the dread antithesis (at Matt xxv.) of the αἰώνιος κόλασις and the αἰώνιος ζωή. *De Civ. Dei*, xxi. 23: Deinde quale est æternum supplicium pro igne diuturni temporis existimare, et vitam æternam credere sine fine, cum Christus eodem ipso loco, in unâ eâdemque sententiâ dixerit, utrumque complexus, Sic ibunt isti in supplicium æternum, justi autem in vitam æternam ? Si utrumque æternum, profecto aut utrumque cum fine diuturnum, aut utrumque sine fine perpetuum debet intelligi. Par pari enim relata sunt, hinc supplicium æternum, inde vita æterna. Dicere autem in hoc uno eodemque sensu, Vita æterna sine fine erit, supplicium æternum finem habebit, multum absurdum est. Unde quia vita æterna sanctorum sine fine erit, supplicium quoque æternum quibus erit, finem procul dubio non habebit.

Ver. 3–5. '*And why beholdest thou the mote that is in thy brother's eye, but considerest not the beam that is in thine own eye? Or how wilt thou say to thy brother, Let me pull out the mote out of thine eye; and, behold, a beam is in thine own eye? Thou hypocrite, first cast out the beam out of thine own eye; and then shalt thou see clearly to cast out the mote out of thy brother's eye.*'— In his excellent commentary on David's great penitential Psalm (the 51st, with him the 50th) Augustine illustrates this forwardness to pull out the mote from a brother's eye combined with unconsciousness of a beam in our own, from the history of David; who in the time of his own worst sin blazed up in a righteous indignation, for such no doubt he deemed it, against one whose offence, as set before him by the prophet, was infinitesimally small if compared with his own (2 Sam. xii. 5); and he justly traces up the severity of the sentence which David pronounces against the wrong-doer, not to the sense of righteousness which he still possessed, but to his present blindness in respect of the character of his own transgression.[1]

As examples of what the Lord means severally by '*the mote*' and '*the beam*,' Augustine often instances anger and hate: transient anger is a mote, disturbing indeed, but not destroying, the spiritual vision; while hatred, which is anger grown inveterate,[2] the mote now swollen into a beam,[3] quite destroys that vision, causing a man

---

[1] *Enarr. in Ps.* l. 5.
[2] *De Serm. Dom. in Mon.* ii. 19: Odium est ira inveterata.
[3] *Serm.* lxxxii. 1: Festuca initium trabis est. Nam trabes quando nascitur, prius festuca est. Rigando festucam, perducis ad trabem: alendo iram malis suspicionibus, perducis ad odium.

to walk altogether in darkness (1 John ii. 11).[1] He who in his heart nourishes hatred to his brother, with what front shall he condemn and rebuke his brother for the passing anger which may find place in his? At times he is willing to restrict the application to this single case, but elsewhere perceives rightly that this would be too narrow an interpretation, and makes '*the mote*' and '*the beam*' to be respectively any smaller and greater sins: '*the mote*' such a one as injures, but is still consistent with, a state of grace, an impaired but not a destroyed vision of God; '*the beam*' involving absolute blindness, and for the time at least a total suspension of spiritual vision.

He is very earnest in warning that we do not understand this precept and prohibition,—which in our cowardice and sloth we might easily be tempted to do,— as though all fraternal correction and rebuke were hereby pronounced to be unlawful. The warning is only directed against the rebuking in a wrong spirit, without earnest endeavours at self-amendment, without the recognition of a sinfulness common to all,[2] without the remembrance that we also have been 'foolish, disobedient;' and thus a rebuking, not in the spirit of meekness and of love, but in that of arrogance or scorn, or with an evil pleasure in the humiliation of a brother.[3] So far from all Christian

[1] *Serm.* lvi. (*Appendix*): Cordis oculum festuca turbat, trabes excæcat. . . . Per subitaneam iracundiam cordis oculus turbatur, per odium lumen caritatis exstinguitur.

[2] On this '*Judge not*,' he asks, *Serm.* ccclxxxvii.: Ergo tacebimus et neminem omnino corripiemus? Corripiamus plane, sed prius nos. Proximum vis corripere: nihil est tibi te ipso propinquius.

[3] *De Serm. Dom. in Mon.* ii. 19: See also much that is most admirable on this matter of Christian rebuke, *Exp. Ep. ad Gal.* vi. 1, where among other things he says: Nunquam alieni peccati objur-

rebuke being here condemned, there is implicitly a command to exercise this difficult grace,[1] only at the right time and in the right temper; '*then*,' after we have in ourselves sought the removal of all that is hindering our own vision of God, and unfitting us from giving true counsel to our brother, '*shalt thou see clearly to cast out the mote out of thy brother's eye*;'[2] and it is not to love, but to hate our brother,[3] under the plea of charity to refrain from the exercise of this rebuke, when it is needed. He observes often with what sharp correction love will sometimes be armed, while indifference or hatred will either keep silence, or else flatter, and by this flattery strengthen and confirm in evil.[4]

gandi suscipiendum est negotium, nisi cum internis interrogationibus examinantes nostram conscientiam liquido nobis coram Deo responderimus, dilectione nos facere.

[1] *Exp. Ep. ad Gal.* vi. 1 : Nihil autem sic probat spiritalem virum, quam peccati alieni tractatio, cum liberationem ejus potius quam insultationem, potiusque auxilia quam convicia meditatur.

[2] *Serm.* lxxxii. 2 : Lumen quod in te est, non te permittit negligere lumen fratris. Very excellent, too, is what he says on the peril which lies so near to the exercise of this rebuke, and that this may err in quantity or in quality, and that thus through our fault a brother may perish. Thus *Ep.* xcv. § 3 : Quis enim sit vindicandi modus non solum pro qualitate vel quantitate culparum, verum etiam pro quibusdam viribus animarum quid quisque sufferat, quid recuset, ne non solum non proficiat, sed etiam deficiat, quam profundum et latebrosum est. And then he further goes on to complain of the difficulty of bringing into perfect harmony such passages as Matt. xviii. 15 and 1 Tim. v. 20.

[3] *Ibid.* : Tua patientia, illius mors est.

[4] *In* 1 *Ep. Joh. Tract.* vii. : Si qui forte vultis servare caritatem, fratres, ante omnia ne putetis abjectam et desidiosam. . . . Non putes tunc te amare servum tuum, quando eum non cædis; aut tunc te amare filium tuum, quando ei non das disciplinam ; aut tunc te amare vicinum tuum, quando eum non corripis. Non est ista caritas, sed languor.

Ver. 6. '*Give not that which is holy unto the dogs, neither cast ye your pearls before swine, lest they trample them under their feet, and turn again and rend you.*'—Augustine is at pains to distinguish between the '*holy*' and the '*pearls*: ' he allows them indeed ultimately to mean the same, yet the same contemplated upon different sides. '*That which is holy*' is the truth as it may not be spoiled or corrupted, or, if in itself inviolable, as it may not be laid open to profane attempts of this kind. The '*pearls*' are the same mysteries of the faith, as they are too precious to be exposed to slights and a careless contempt.[1] So also he distinguishes between the '*dogs*' and the '*swine*: ' the '*dogs*' are for him the active opposers of God's truth (the rabiosa canis, see Acts xiii. 45); the '*swine*' the more passive despisers[2] (the amica luto sus); somewhat as we have in the parable of the marriage of the king's son, some who killed the king's messengers, and some who were content with despising his message (Matt. xxii. 5, 6). And then he distributes the two outbreaks of hostility, ascribing the contemptuous trampling under foot to the swine, the turning again and rending to the dogs.[3]

---

[1] *De Serm. Dom. in Mon.* ii. 20 : Sanctum ex eo quod non debet corrumpi, margarita ex eo quod non debet contemni.

[2] *Ibid.* ii. 20 : Canes ergo pro oppugnatoribus veritatis, porcos pro contemptoribus positos non incongrue accipimus. And he assumes the same, *Enarr. in Ps.* ix. 15, where of these two kinds of opposers he says : Qui malunt pertinaciter latrare, quam studiose quærere, aut qui nec latrare nec quærere, sed in suarum voluptatum cœno volutari.

[3] *Ibid.* ii. 20 : Porci quamvis non ita ut canes morsu appetant, passim tamen calcando coinquinant. It may be seen in Hammond what can be said in defence of this distribution ; it is in itself most harsh, connecting the first and fourth clauses, the second and the third, instead of the first and third, the second and fourth. Cer-

Yet this assuredly is an erroneous distribution, and both belong to the swine, so that there might well be a semicolon after 'Give not that which is holy unto the dogs;'[1] for the treading under foot is as little characteristic of these animals as the other outbreak of enmity, the turning again and rending: while this and that are alike the most graphic and exactest delineations of the bearing of the enraged swine; which we must of course here consider, not as the domesticated creature, but as the hog in the ferocity of its savage state.[2] The warning in fact is this, You will at once expose the truth to insult and yourselves to injury.[3] It will follow that, if we are to find here two different classes of bestial opposers, the 'dogs' will be the unclean, the utterly and shamelessly sunken in impure lusts (Rev. xxii. 15; the canis immundus of Horace); the 'swine' the fierce and bitter opponents of the truth of God (Ps. lxxx. 13: 'The wild boar out of the wood doth root it out'). Among the enemies of the truth the first would be the Heliogabalus, the second the Galerius.[4]

tainly the connecting particle would not be καὶ but ἤ, were this the meaning.

[1] In Bishop Lloyd's New Testament there is a punctuation equivalent to this, but it is not common.

[2] The στραφέντες will express the quick sharp *turn* of the boar, with which the wound is inflicted (Horace: Verres *obliquum* meditans ictum. Ovid: *Obliquo* dente timendus aper); and the ῥήξωσι, the nature of the wound, which is formidable not so much from its depth as from being a long tearing or ripping up, or, as we have it, '*rending.*' For the swine's treading under foot see Plautus, *Trucul.* ii. 2. 13.

[3] *Serm.* lxxvii. 6: Ne forte, &c. . . ., id est, post contemptum margaritarum vestrarum etiam molesti sint vobis.

[4] An accurate fixing of the meaning of τὸ ἅγιον confirms this view. We translate it vaguely, '*that which is holy,*' but rather 'the holy thing,' i.e. the altar flesh (see Lev. xxii. 6-16, LXX., where that is several times called τὰ ἅγια, which no unclean person might eat; Jer. xi. 15; Hagg. ii. 12). It is not that the dogs would not eat it,

Ver. 7, 8. '*Ask, and it shall be given you; seek, and ye shall find; knock, and it shall be opened unto you: for every one that asketh receiveth; and he that seeketh findeth; and to him that knocketh it shall be opened.*'— The following, according to Augustine, is the connexion between these verses and those that went before. Some one, hearing those last words, might be tempted to say in his heart, 'But what pearls have I, which I am even in danger of losing, by casting them before the unworthy? I hardly seem to have such for myself.' In answer to this thought, rising out of a sense of spiritual poverty, opportunely follows a suggestion of the effectual way whereby this poverty may be removed. I should prefer to assume mere juxtaposition, rather than a connexion so forced and artificial as this. In his *Retractations* Augustine disallows the distinction which in his Exposition of this Discourse he had drawn between these three; which, being thus recalled, it will be needless to examine; and he recognizes in all three, exhortations to an instancy of earnest prayer.[1] He finds in ver. 11 a proof that this is

for it would be welcome to them; but that it would be a profanation to make it a σκύβαλον (Exod. xxii. 31). Such '*dogs*' are they who would turn the grace of God into lasciviousness. This, the true interpretation of τὸ ἅγιον, was preserved in the ancient Church, in the cry of the deacons to those about to communicate, τὰ ἅγια τοῖς ἁγίοις, which did not mean generally, holy things for holy persons, but the holy flesh for the holy persons, for the kingdom of priests; with allusion to those Levitical ordinances, now transmuted and glorified, referred to above. So, too, there is a singular propriety in the image of the pearls; selected, as Maldonatus suggests, for a certain remote likeness to acorns which they bear; and the fury of the swine is excited by discovering that they are not these, but something which, though infinitely more precious, they have no desire for.

[1] L. i. 19: Operose quidem tria ista quid inter se differant expo-

so; where 'ask' evidently stands for and represents not merely the 'ask' of ver. 7, but resumes and gathers up in itself the 'seek' and 'knock' of that earlier verse as well. In his popular homiletic use of these words he very frequently brings into comparison the two parables of the Unjust Judge (Luke xviii. 1), and the Friend at midnight (Luke xi. 5).[1] The image of the knocking, with the final opening of the door, gives to the latter parallel a peculiar fitness. An objection to all which is here promised might be urged, namely, that notwithstanding this and like promises in Scriptures (as John xiv. 13; xv. 16; xvi. 23; 1 John iii. 22), the saints do *not* always obtain their petitions, do *not* invariably 'ask' and 'receive.' Scripture itself asserts no less: St. Paul asked, earnestly and often, for the removal of the thorn in his flesh, whatever that may have been, and it was not only not removed, but his petition expressly denied him (2 Cor. xii. 7–9). Augustine takes up this very example in proof that God's servants *are* always heard; Paul himself on this very instance was heard, not indeed to his present desire, but to his lasting spiritual health, seeing that by that temptation and through those buffetings of Satan he was perfected as he could not have been without them.[2] God dealt with him as the faithful physician deals with his patient, from whom he withdraws not the

---

nendum putavi, sed longe melius ad instantissimam petitionem omnia referuntur. So *Enarr. in Ps.* cxviii. 48.

[1] *Serm.* lxi. 4: Ecce paterfamilias et magnus dives, divitiarum scilicet spiritualium et æternarum, hortatur et dicit tibi, Pete, quære, pulsa. Hortatur ut petas, negabit quod petis? Attende a contrario similitudinem. And he quotes Luke xviii. 1. Cf. *Ep.* cxxx. 8.

[2] *In* 1 *Ep. Joh. Tract.* vi.: Deus etsi voluntati nostræ non dat, saluti dat.

knife and the cautery, for all his urgency of crying; he knows how far the hurt reaches, will search and tent it to the bottom, and so make a perfect cure: he knows too that the patient will thank him for this in the end; and thus he hears him for his lasting desire, which is health; not for his momentary wish, which is release from present pain. It is thus that God hears his servants for the abiding desire of their souls, which is holiness; not for the immediate craving, which may be ease.[1] Augustine brings out, moreover, the other side of this truth, namely that as a petition may be refused in love, so also it may be granted in anger. Granted in this sense was that of the devils, who were permitted to enter into the swine; but who thereby hastened for themselves the doom which most they feared (Matt. viii. 41, 42). It did not fare otherwise with those in the wilderness who impatiently asked for quails, and perished while the meat was yet in their

---

[1] *Serm.* cclxxxvi. 6: Ne contristemini quando petitis et non accipitis, et arbitremini quod ante oculos vos non habeat Deus, si ad tempus non exaudiat voluntatem vestram. Non enim semper ægrum exaudit medicus ad voluntatem, quamvis ejus sine dubio procuret atque appetat sanitatem. Non dat, quod petit; sed quod non petit, hoc procurat. Petit frigidam, non dat. Crudelis factus est, qui venit sanare? Artis est, non crudelitatis. Non dat ad horam quod delectat: ut sanus possit omnia, nondum sano negantur aliqua. *In* 1 *Ep. Joh. Tract.* vi.: [Deus] secare vult, urere vult. Tu si clamas et non exaudiris, in sectione, in ustione, et tribulatione, novit ille quousque putre est. Tu jam vis revocet manus, et ille vulneris sinum attendit; scit quousque perveniat: non te exaudit ad voluntatem, sed exaudit ad sanitatem. *Serm.* cccliv. 7: Petit æger ut quod ad salutem apponit medicus, cum voluerit ægrotus, auferatur. Medicus dicit, Non: mordet, sed sanat. Tu dicis, Tolle quod mordet. Medicus dicit, Non tollo, quia sanat. Tu ad medicum quare venisti? Sanari, an molestiam non pati? Non ergo exaudivit Dominus Paulum ad voluntatem, quia exaudivit ad sanitatem. Cf. *Enarr. in Ps.* cxxx. 1; *Enarr.* 2ª *in Ps.* xc. § 6.

mouths (Ps. lxxviii. 29-31). On the other hand, a petition may be refused in love; in which case it is not really refused, but rather granted in a higher shape than that contemplated by the asker.[1] There is a beautiful passage in Augustine's *Confessions*, where, concerning some prayers of his mother Monica's, he says, God gave heed to the *hinge* of her desire, that on which all her prayer turned, though He did not yield her the boon exactly in the way by which she sought it. Her desire and her earnest prayer was that her son might not sail for Italy, so did she dread for him the temptations which would meet him there: he sailed notwithstanding, and it was there at length that he found Christ.[2]

Ver. 9-11. '*Or what man is there of you, whom if his son ask bread, will he give him a stone? Or if he ask a fish, will he give him a serpent? If ye then, being evil, know how to give good gifts unto your children, how*

---

[1] *Enarr.* 2ª *in Ps.* xxvi. 4: Vere felix est non qui id habeat quod amat, sed qui id amet quod amandum est. Multi enim miseri magis habendo quod amant, quam carendo. Amando enim res noxias miseri, habendo sunt miseriores. Et propitius Deus, quum male amamus, negat quod amamus; iratus autem dat amanti quod male amat.

[2] *Conf.* v. 15: Quid a te petebat, Deus meus, tantis lacrimis, nisi ut navigare me non sineres? Sed tu alte consulens, et exaudiens *cardinem desiderii ejus*, non curasti quod tunc petebat, ut in me faceres quod semper petebat. We may compare *Serm.* lxxx.: Qualis est apud te filius tuus nesciens res humanas, talis es et tu apud Dominum, nesciens res divinas. Ecce ante te filius tuus totâ die plorans, ut des illi cultrum, id est gladium: negas te dare, non das, contemnis flentem, ne plangas morientem. Ploret, affligat se, collidat se, ut leves eum in equum: non facis, quia non potest eum regere; elidet et occidet illum. Cui negas partem, totum illi servas. Sed ut crescat, et totum possideat secure, non das illi modicum periculosum.

much more shall your Father which is in heaven give good things to them that ask him?'—The very ingenious allegories which Augustine discovers in the '*bread*' and the '*stone*,' the '*fish*' and the '*serpent*,' and not less in the '*egg*' and the '*scorpion*,' mentioned by St. Luke (xi. 12), but not by our Evangelist, may be seen by any who cares to follow up the references below.[1] For myself, I cannot believe that '*bread*' and '*fish*' are selected for any other reason than as the most familiar objects of wholesome nourishment which a father would give to his children. The allusions indeed are drawn from the daily life of Galilæan fishermen (Mark viii. 6, 7; John xxi. 9), such as many of Christ's hearers were; and in each case the antithesis rests on a felt resemblance between what is asked, and what *might* be given in its stead: '*a stone*' has some likeness to '*bread*' (Matt. iv. 3), '*a serpent*' to '*a fish*,' and a scorpion, when coiled up, to an egg. Such allegories as Augustine here proposes should pass for what they are worth, as the harmless, oftentimes edifying and graceful, plays and scintillations of a religious fancy;[2] meant very often for nothing more by those who offer them; but which assume a different aspect, when they are by others fixed and hardened into permanent expositions of Scripture truth: then they often

---

[1] *Ep.* cxxx. 8; *Quæst. Evang.* ii. 22.

[2] This was Augustine's own feeling about them, however sometimes he may lay on them a greater weight than they can well bear, and may play with them overmuch. Thus *In Rom. Inchoat. Exp.* § 13, having fallen on one of these correspondencies between things natural and things spiritual, and followed it up a little, he checks himself with this observation: Sed hæc verborum consonantia, sive provenerit sive provisa sit, non pugnaciter agendum est ut ei quisque consentiat, sed quantum interpretantis elegantiam hilaritas audientis admittit.

degenerate into an unworthy trifling with the Word of God.

Those here addressed as '*being evil*' are the very same, Augustine observes, into whose mouths the Lord has so lately put that word, '*Our Father*;'[1] to whom He has made the promise, '*Ask, and it shall be given you*:' so that every faithful man has a double aspect—he is '*evil*' through his old nature; he is good through participation with Him who is the highest good, who is in some sense the alone good (Matt. xix. 17), the good in Himself, while others are good only through Him, and as they are sharers in his goodness.[2] He has thus seized the true force of this '*being evil*,'[3] which they fail to catch who take '*evil*,' not as a designation of all men, of human nature in general (Gen. viii. 21), as it is opposed to the goodness and holiness of God, but of some particular men sunken deeper in corruption than the rest;[4] as if Christ would say, Even the worst among you (even the '*evil*') do not extend their malignity to their children, but in their relations to them show themselves bountiful and good. But the other is the truer and deeper explanation, which embraces the whole race of men under this charge of '*being evil*;' and yet, being such, He would say, you

---

[1] *Ep.* cliii. 5: Num igitur Deus Pater malorum est? Absit. Quomodo dicitur, Pater vester cælestis, quibus dicitur, Cum sitis mali: nisi quia utrumque Veritas monstrat, quid simus Dei bono, quid humano vitio, hoc commendans, illud emendans? Cf. *Serm.* xc.: Pater ergo malorum, sed non relinquendorum, quia medicus sanandorum.

[2] *Con. duas Ep. Pelag.* iii. 3: Inde mali, unde adhuc filii sæculi, jam tamen filii Dei facti pignore Spiritûs Sancti.

[3] *Con. Adv. Leg. et Proph.* i. 22.

[4] So Augustine himself at times, as *De Serm. Dom. in Mon.* ii. 21: Malos appellat dilectores adhuc seculi hujus et peccatores.

still have natural affections, the yearnings of a parent's heart toward your children, and, according to your ability and knowledge, impart unto them '*good gifts*,' such as, if not in the highest sense '*good*,' are yet good for the necessities of this present life. How much more certainly will a Heavenly Father impart to his children the true riches of his kingdom; for it is such riches that the Lord has predominantly in his eye, as is evident from a comparison with the parallel passage in St. Luke (xi. 13), where instead of '*good things*,' it is his 'Holy Spirit' which is promised to them that ask it.[1] As He will not deny his children, altogether withholding what they ask (ver. 7, 8), so neither will He deceive his children, giving to them a useless or a noxious thing instead of a good (ver. 9, 10). He observes that here again it is the same argument as finds place in the parable of the Unjust Judge (Luke xviii. 2–8), an argument from the worse to the better.

Ver. 12. '*Therefore all things whatsoever ye would that men should do to you, do ye even so to them: for this is the Law and the Prophets.*'—Some will perhaps remember in Gibbon's *Memoirs* the sneer which this precept calls out, namely that, extolled as it has been, he had read the same in a book written four hundred years before Christ announced it in the Gospel. In proof of this assertion he adduces a passage from Isocrates,—which by the way is no anticipation of it at all, for it is merely the

[1] *Enarr. in Ps.* cxviii. 48: Alius porro Evangelista non ait, Dabit *bona* petentibus se, quæ multipliciter possunt intelligi, vel corporalia vel spiritalia; sed circumcidit inde alia, satisque diligenter expressit quid nos vehementer atque instanter voluerit poscere Dominus, et ait, Quanto magis Pater vester dabit Spiritum bonum petentibus se?

negative injunction of not doing to others what we are unwilling to suffer from them, a rule of selfish prudence very far removed from Christ's law of an active love. The same precept, but only in this the negative form, occurs, Job iv. 15. But Augustine, so far from being afraid of the charge that the precepts of the Gospel are old, or that others uttered them before Christ, counts it the glory of the written and spoken law, that it is the transcript of that which was from the first, and not merely as old as this man or that, but as the creation itself, a reproduction of that obscured and well-nigh forgotten law written at the beginning by the finger of God on the hearts of all men. When therefore heathen sages or poets proclaimed any part of this, they had not, so doing, anticipated Christ;[1] they had only deciphered some fragment of that law, which He gave at the beginning; and which, when men, exiles and fugitives from themselves and from the knowledge of their own hearts, had lost the power of reading, He came in the flesh to read to them anew,[2] and to bring out the well-nigh obliterated characters afresh.

He notes that in the Latin copies it was not, '*All things*,' but '*All good things whatsoever ye would that*

---

[1] *Enarr. in Ps.* cxl. 6: Dixit hoc Pythagoras, dixit hoc Plato. ... Propterea si inventus fuerit aliquis eorum hoc dixisse quod dixit et Christus, gratulamur illi, non sequimur illum. Sed prior fuit ille quam Christus? Si quis vera loquitur, prior est quam ipsa Veritas? O homo, attende Christum, non quando ad te venerit, sed quando te fecerit.

[2] *Enarr. in Ps.* lvii. 2 : Quia homines appetentes ea quæ foris sunt, etiam a seipsis exules facti sunt, data est etiam conscripta lex : non quia in cordibus scripta non erat; sed quia tu fugitivus eras cordis tui, ab illo qui ubique est, comprehenderis, et ad teipsum intro revocaris.

men should do to you, do ye even so to them.' He however rejects this '*good*,' which indeed has no place in the Vulgate, as clearly an interpolation, not being found in any Greek MSS., and suggests the manner in which it probably crept into the text. It had occurred to some one reading or transcribing this passage, But what if a man should desire sinful things of another, as to be invited of him to a drunken revel, and should proceed himself first to invite the other to the like, that he might be requited in kind, this could not surely be a fulfilling of the Lord's command. And so to escape a consequence, which to the reader or transcriber seem involved in the words, he guarded and qualified '*all things*' by inserting this '*good*.'[1] Augustine, however, will admit no such difficulty here; for he says we do not *will* other than *good* things; we *desire* bad things.[2] 'To will,' it is true, may

[1] *De Civ. Dei*, xiv. 8: Cavendum enim putaverunt, ne quisquam inhonesta velit sibi fieri ab hominibus, ut de turpioribus taceam, certe luxuriosa convivia in quibus se, si et ipse illis faciat similia, hoc præceptum existimet impleturum. Cf. *De Serm. Dom. in Mon.* ii. 22.

[2] *De Serm. Dom. in Mon.* ii. 22: Id enim quod dictum est, Quæcunque vultis, non usitate ac passim, sed proprie dictum accipi oportet. Voluntas namque non est nisi in bonis. Nam in malis flagitiosisque factis, cupiditas proprie dicitur, non voluntas. Cf. *De Civ. Dei*, xiv. 8. To the unregenerate belongs indeed the liberum *arbitrium*, that is, in each individual case a choice is possible to them: the libera *voluntas* pertains only to the regenerate; this is their redemption, that they have the will set free in Christ. And there is a higher yet, as Augustine teaches, even than this libera voluntas, namely, the *libertas*, the beata necessitas boni, which may be ascribed only to God and to his holy Angels; as at the other extreme there is the misera *necessitas* peccandi, the condition of devils, and that into which evil men are every day more and more coming. Tertullian's method of guarding this passage from abuse (*Adv. Marc.* iv. 16) appears at first sight different from Augustine's, but essentially agrees with it.

be sometimes used in a laxer and lower sense; but this does not hinder, where need is, the restricting it to the higher, in which sense we must accept it here. This is not so artificial a solution of the difficulty, a difficulty lying merely on the surface, as at first it seems. Still it would be simpler to say that this precept is addressed to the regenerate man; who, *as such*, can only desire from others that which would be good and profitable, being done by himself to them.—'*For this is the law and the prophets*,' not, '*all* the law and the prophets,' as Christ expresses Himself elsewhere (Matt. xxii. 40), for there He has been giving the two commandments, love to God, and love to our neighbour, so that He could thus speak; but the commandment here in its utmost latitude includes only the love to our brother.

Ver. 13, 14. '*Enter ye in at the strait gate: for wide is the gate, and broad is the way, that leadeth to destruction, and many there be which go in thereat. Because strait is the gate, and narrow is the way, which leadeth unto life, and few there be that find it.*'—What is it, Augustine asks, which makes this gate so strait to us, and this way so narrow? It is not so much '*strait*' in itself, as that we make it strait for ourselves, by the swellings of our pride;—and then, vexed that we cannot enter, chafing and impatient at the hindrances we meet with, we become more and more unable to pass through. But where is the remedy? how shall these swollen places of our souls be brought down? By accepting and drinking of the cup, wholesome though it may be distasteful, of humility; by listening to and learning of Him, who having said, '*Enter ye in at the strait gate*,' does to them who enquire, 'How shall we enter in?' reply, 'By Me;' 'I am the Way;' 'I am the Door.'[1]

We may here adduce an example of the rich symbolic significance which of old men loved to trace in many of the ways and works of the lower creation; most, it is true, of these having been discovered by us with our more accurate knowledge to be mythical, yet which may still in their higher application survive for us. Thus Augustine, dealing with this precept, refers to the artifice by which the serpent is believed to get rid of its old skin, namely, by forcing itself through some narrow aperture, and so leaving behind that old, and coming out in all the freshness and splendour of its new. And wouldst thou, he asks, according to the bidding of the Apostle, put off the old man and put on the new, there is but one way to affect this. Thou must not be afraid of the straitness of this gate; it is only by forcing thyself through it, that thou canst leave behind thee the *exuviæ* of the old man.[2] And if processes like

---

[1] *Serm.* cxlii. 5: Clamat ille qui factus est Via; Intrate per angustam portam. Conatur ingredi, impedit tumor: et tanto magis perniciose conatur, quanto magis impedit tumor. Tumidum autem vexat angustia, vexatus autem amplius tumebit. Amplius tumens quando intrabit? Ergo detumescat. . . . Accipiat humilitatis medicamentum, bibat contra tumorem poculum amarum sed salubre, bibat poculum humilitatis. Quid se arctat? Non sinit moles, non magna, sed tumida. Magnitudo enim soliditatem habet, tumor inflationem.

[2] *Enarr. in Ps.* lvii. 5: Et quomodo exuo, inquis, veterem hominem? Imitare astutiam serpentis. Quid enim facit serpens, ut exuat se veterem tunicam? Coarctat se per foramen angustum. Et ubi, inquis, invenio hoc foramen angustum? Audi. Arcta et angusta est via quæ ducit ad vitam. . . . Ibi ponenda est vetus tunica, et alibi poni non potest. Aut si vis vetustate impediri, gravari, premi, noli ire per angustam. Cf. *Serm.* lxiv. 2; *De Doct. Christ.* ii. 16; *Quæst.* 17 *in Matt.* qu. 8. Augustine is very fond of these adaptations from the natural history, or oftener from the

these be painful, yet still remember the present time is the time of cure, not of enjoyment.¹—And on the '*many*'

natural mythology, of animals; makes frequent allusion to curious legends about them, in which he finds reflexes of spiritual truths; as here of the mystery of the regeneration. In the story of the pelican killing its callow young, and then wounding its own bosom, and revivifying them on the third day with the blood from thence, he finds a natural type of Him who says, 'I kill and I make alive' (*Enarr. in Ps.* ci. § 8). A part of the wisdom of the serpent which the faithful shall imitate is this, that when threatened it offers its *body* to the assailant, but at all hazards protects its *head*. Christ is every man's head: let the persecutor wound thee anywhere, in thy goods, in thy person, but not in thy faith, not in Him (*Enarr. in Ps.* lvii. § 10; *Serm.* lxiv. 2). The legend of which a record is kept in our word 'treacle,' that namely of the serpent's flesh as the only antidote to the serpent's bite, he naturally does not miss, nor fail to make use of (*Con. duas Epist. Pelag.* iii. 7). 'Bear ye one another's burdens' he illustrates by this legend of a custom among stags (*Enarr. in Ps.* cxxix. § 4): Dicuntur cervi quando transeunt in proximas insulas pascuæ gratiâ, capita super se invicem ponere; et unus qui ante est solus portat caput, et non ponit super alterum: sed cum et ipse defecerit, tollit se ab anteriore parte, et redit posterius, ut et ipse in altero requiescat: et sic portant omnes onera sua, et perveniunt ad quod desiderant; et non patiuntur naufragium, quia quasi navis est illis caritas; cf. *Enarr. in Ps.* xli. § 4. Plutarch has somewhere ascribed the same device to cranes in their long flights. For other properties of the stag see *Enarr. in Ps.* xli. § 3. The fact that the hen droops and sickens, loses all the freshness and brightness of her plumage while she is nursing her young, reminds him often of Him who in the days of his flesh wept over Jerusalem, whose children He would fain have gathered together, even as a hen gathers her chickens under her wings, and they would not (Matt. xxiii. 37); thus (*Enarr.* Iᵃ *in Ps.* lviii. § 10): Infirmatus est usque ad mortem, et assumsit infirmitatis carnem, ut pullos Jerusalem colligeret sub alas suas, tanquam gallina infirmata cum parvulis. Certe notam rem dico, quæ in conspectu nostro quotidie versatur: quomodo raucescit vox, quomodo fit hispidum totum corpus? deponuntur alæ, laxantur plumæ, et vides circa pullos nescio quid ægrotum, et ea est materna caritas quæ invenitur infirmitas; cf. *Enarr.* Iᵃ *in Ps.* xc. § 5; *Serm.* cv. § 8; cclxiv. 1. He has a singular legend of the manner in which the eagle renews its youth (Ps. ciii. 5); of which in like manner he makes spiritual application (*Enarr. in Ps.* cii. § 9).

¹ *Serm.* lxxxvii. 11: Sanitatis tempus est, non voluptatis.

and the '*few*,' Be not led away, he says, by the numbers of those, nor abashed by the fewness of these; for when thou comparest, do not *number*, but *weigh* them; and in a just balance note how few grains are enough to overbalance whole armsful of chaff.[1]

Ver. 15–20. '*Beware of false prophets, which come to you in sheep's clothing, but inwardly they are ravening wolves. Ye shall know them by their fruits. Do men gather grapes of thorns, or figs of thistles? Even so every good tree bringeth forth good fruit: but a corrupt tree bringeth forth evil fruit. A good tree cannot bring forth evil fruit, neither can a corrupt tree bring forth good fruit. Every tree that bringeth not forth good fruit is hewn down, and cast into the fire. Wherefore by their fruits ye shall know them.*'—Our Lord has said just before that there are few who find this way of life, and now there is danger lest heretics, who commonly glory in their fewness,[2] as though it marked them especially as the '*little flock*' for whom the kingdom was reserved, should snatch at these words, and boast themselves as the finders of the way, and the leaders in it. Therefore follows immediately the caution, '*Beware of false prophets.*' This is the connexion which Augustine traces. On the '*good fruit*,' the not having of which, and the having of the contrary to which, will reveal these false prophets for what they are, he has something to say. These 'fruits,' it is clear, cannot be such more prominent works of an outward piety—prayer, fasting, alms—as have

---

[1] *Enarr. in Ps.* cccix. 4: Noli numerare, sed appende: stateram affer æquam. . . . Vide contra pauca grana quantam paleam leves.

[2] *De Serm. Dom. in Mon.* ii. 23: Hæretici, qui se plerumque paucitate commendant.

been mentioned before ; for they are the '*clothing*' which at first meets the eye; the true and natural clothing in the case of the sheep; the adventitious and false in that of the wolves. But the '*fruits*' which they ought to have, and have not, having rather their evil contraries, he explains by a reference to Gal. v. 22, and to the 'fruit of the Spirit' enumerated there.[1] He does not deny that there may be in bad men imitations also of these, but the simple eye will most often detect them; and here is the explanation of all which, before these cautions are given, has been said concerning the keeping of the eye single, since the single eye will alone be able to profit by them.[2] This is not the usual explanation of the early Church, in which the '*fruits*' that shall reveal the true character of these deceitful workers are generally taken as false doctrines, by their bringing forward of which, false teachers, who may wear an outward appearance of sanctity, shall sooner or later be detected. Yet any explanation to be satisfying must combine both of these ; seeing that it is impossible to draw a line of separation between false doctrines and sinful acts. The one is as much a work as the other, and just as really the utterance of the inner man and the fruit which he bears.

The impossibility of the actual outcoming from evil being other than evil, the certainty therefore that sooner or later it will display itself in its true nature, this the Lord illustrates and sets forth by the analogy of trees, which have no choice but to bear each after its kind. Yet here

---

[1] So *Enarr. in Ps.* cxlix. 1 : Non enim fructus ostenditur nisi in factis. . . . Quærimus fructus caritatis, invenimus spinas dissentionis. Ex fructibus eorum cognoscetis eos.
[2] *De Serm. Dom. in Mon.* ii. 24.

Augustine notes how the error of the Manichæans is carefully to be guarded against. They, while they arbitrarily rejected so much of Christ's teaching, exalted greatly the Sermon on the Mount, calling it the 'divine discourse,'[1] mainly on account of these verses 17 and 18, in which they professed to find a support for their scheme of two original principles[2]—one good, from which all good proceeded, and one evil, from which all evil; and of two races of men, having severally their descent from the one and from the other. But he shows plainly that what went before and what comes after (see Luke vi. 43-45), alike require another interpretation; that only when forcibly rent away from the context, can the words give even a semblable support to such a doctrine. There is no assertion here of a Manichæan dualism; neither does Christ say of men, that there is aught irrevocably fixed in their natures, so that some can never become good, and others never evil; but only that *so long as a man is as an evil tree*, he cannot bring forth good fruits, that if he would *do* good he must first *be* good.[3] To support the other interpretation,

[1] See the words of Faustus in Augustine's treatise, *Con. Faust.* xxxii. 7: Credimus . . . cunctum Sermonem deificum, qui maxime duarum præferens naturarum discretionem, ipsius esse non venit in dubium.

[2] *De Serm. Dom. in Mon.* ii. 24: Illorum error maxime cavendum est, qui de ipsis duabus arboribus duas naturas opinantur esse, quarum una sit Dei, altera vero neque Dei, neque ex Deo.

[3] *Con. Adimant.* 26: Mala ergo arbor fructus bonos facere non potest; sed ex malâ fieri bona potest, ut bonos fructus ferat. And again, Muta cor et mutabitur opus. Cf. *De Act. c. Fel. Manich.* ii. 2, 4; *Con. Fortunat. Disput.* 2. He is scarcely correct, however, when he explains 'Make the tree good' (Matt. xii. 33), as though it were an admonition; for how then explain 'Make the tree corrupt,' which follows? But '*Make*' here answers to our English, Suppose; to the Latin *Fac* or *Pone*; Grant or suppose a corrupt tree, give me such by way of argument, and I say the fruit will be corrupt also.

as he justly observes, it ought to have been said, A good tree cannot become a bad one, nor a bad tree good. There is indeed, he affirms, a difference in men, as they are natural, or regenerate, as they belong to the stock of the wild olive (the *oleaster*), or have been engrafted anew on the good olive tree, as they pertain to Adam or to Christ. But then the wild olive is not of a different kind from the good, being only a degeneration of that good.[1] This degeneration took place at the Fall; then, that which was a good tree became a wild and bitter stock, and as such it filled the world with its suckers;—incapable of restoring *itself* to its first and nobler condition, yet capable of *being* restored, if only grafted anew upon one of that stock from which it originally fell away, and becoming through this re-engrafting partaker of its better life. The first Adam, the head of the fallen race, is this wild olive, but only having become such at his fall; the second Adam, the head of the restored race, is the good olive, in whom are laid up the possibilities of renewal and restoration for all.

But Augustine, as he had, on the one side, to deny, against the Manichæans, an evil creation coming from the hands of a God of perfect goodness,—to deny that there were any men the original foundations of whose being were laid in evil, trees which could not become good, and which therefore could not bring forth good fruit,—so also had he, on the other side, to deny, against the Pelagians, that the degenerate tree was capable of restoring *itself*,

---

[1] Augustine is very earnest on this, of evil having no independent subsistence, but being only a degeneration of good; so that in one place dealing with this matter at large, he says (*Enchir. de Fide, Spe, et Car.* xii. 13) : Quid est malus homo, nisi malum bonum ?

and bringing forth good fruit, by its own unaided powers :[1] and as he needed to rescue this verse from Manichæan abuses, so too it furnished him with weapons against the shallow Pelagian scheme which was fain to regard men's deeds apart from the living root in the man out of which they grew. When he, awfully conscious of God as the one fountain of all goodness, laid down the great principle, No act is good, if it be not of faith,[2] that is, if the man who did it stood not in a living connexion with the one source of goodness, they sought to embarrass him with the splendid deeds of heathens and unbaptized men,—with the chastity of Scipio, the fortitude of Regulus, the incorruptibility of Fabricius : they demanded, whether he would deny these to be good ? To this he made answer, that they had no right as moralists to take isolated acts, and ask a judgment upon them. For the true question is this, Was he who wrought these acts a righteous man ? was the tree good ? since if not, He who is Himself the Truth had declared that the fruit could not be good. We may feel that the truest application of his principle to Pelagian objectors would have been one, which should not thus make these

---

[1] The statement of Pelagius (*De Grat. Christi*, i. 18) is so exactly that of a Pelagian world now and at all times, that it is worth quoting : Habemus autem possibilitatem utriusque partis a Deo insitam, velut quandam, ut ita dicam, radicem fructiferam atque fœcundam, quæ ex voluntate hominis diversâ gignat et pariat, et quæ possit ad proprii cultoris arbitrium vel nitere flore virtutum, vel sentibus horrere vitiorum. It is at once evident that this theory of human nature is at the bottom of all our modern schemes of education, which proceed on the plan of cultivating the old stock, rather than engrafting on a new.

[2] *Enarr.* 2ᵃ *in Ps.* xxxi.: Laudo fructum boni operis, sed in fide agnosco radicem. There is here in the introduction to this Psalm a large discussion, in the most popular form, on the relation of faith and works, the tree and its fruits, and one full of interest.

lofty deeds to have been wholly false, only 'more splendid sins,' as Augustine is reported to call them, though I have never traced the passage; but rather to have replied, that among these also many were of faith; that wherever by any man a deed was wrought lofty or pure or true, that also was of *his* inspiration from whom all good things come, and who left not Himself anywhere without a witness. Yet, however we may thus feel that the 'faith without which it is impossible to please God,' might have been made by Augustine of larger reach, and to embrace some whom he excludes, his principle stands fast. He was here asserting the foundation of all morals, namely, that the condition of the man determines the value of the deed,[1] that the motive *is* the deed,[2]—and of all religion, namely, that it is only the man in relation with God who can do righteous acts; or in forms of speech which this Scripture supplies, and which he often uses, The good tree only can bring forth good fruit; and in this world that tree only is good, which has been engrafted on a nobler stock, and made partaker of a better and nobler life than its own.[3]

Ver. 21, 22. '*Not every one that saith unto me, Lord,*

[1] *Serm.* clxxviii. 11 : Deus enim cor interrogat, non manum. *Serm.* ccxcii. 7 : Qualis homo est, tales actus habet.

[2] One of the chief obligations of Christian Ethics to Augustine and to his influence, is that he nowhere deals with, but everywhere attacks at the root, what one might not unfitly call *quantitative* morality,—I mean a morality which has room for such questions as this, which I take from a Roman Catholic book of casuistry lately published in Italy : '*How many* scudi must a man steal to constitute a mortal sin?' The light has indeed become darkness, when it could propose to the conscience such questions as this.

[3] The largest use of this passage, in its bearing on the Pelagian controversy, is to be found in his treatise *Con. Julian.* iv. 3.

Lord, shall enter into the kingdom of heaven; but he that doeth the will of my Father which is in heaven. Many will say to me in that day, Lord, Lord, have we not prophesied in thy name? and in thy name have cast out devils? and in thy name done many wonderful works?'
—How, Augustine enquires, are these words of the Lord to be reconciled with those other of his Apostle, 'No man can say that Jesus is the Lord but by the Holy Ghost' (1 Cor. xii. 3)? for here are some who 'say that Jesus is the Lord,' whom yet He denies ever to have been his, who therefore could never have said this in the power of the Holy Ghost.[1] But he easily sets the two passages at one. The '*saying* that Jesus is the Lord,' is there that *saying* which is the genuine outcoming and utterance of the innermost conviction, even as all speech should be, and would have been, if sin had not made every man more or less a liar, his word not seldom now being contrary to his thought. Yet those who so speak, as Augustine urges, rather seem to say,[2] than say; while in that highest sense of saying, in which saying is the expression of being, no man *says* ' that Jesus is the Lord but by the Holy Ghost;' no man, for it comes to this, believes it in his heart but by the Holy Ghost. This is the statement of St. Paul;[3] while our Lord, employing words as men are commonly

---

[1] The apparent opposition comes out in the double *dicit* of the Latin (here, Non omnis qui *dicit* mihi Domine, and there, Nemo potest, *dicere* Dominus Jesus), more than either in the Greek or English, which both have different words in the two places.

[2] *De Serm. Dom. in Mon.* ii. 25: *Videtur* enim *dicere* etiam ille qui nec vult nec intelligit quod dicit: sed ille proprie *dicit*, qui voluntatem ac mentem suam sono vocis enuntiat.

[3] Exactly in the same way, when he declares, ' Whosoever shall *call* upon the name of the Lord shall be saved ' (Rom. x. 13), the word ' call ' is to be taken in the same pregnant sense.

wont to employ them, who do not deny even to falsehoods the title of speech, declares there will be some who will have said, 'Lord, Lord,' but not out of a true heart; whose saying therefore will profit them nothing. By help of this same important distinction Augustine elsewhere delivers our Saviour's declaration, 'Whosoever speaketh against the Holy Ghost, it shall not be forgiven him' (Matt. xii. 32), from shallow, and yet mischievous, interpretations,[1] as though any mere words, —even such as a man in the wildest and guiltiest moments of his blasphemy might have spoken,—could be here intended, or indeed anything intended short of the entire and final alienation of the heart and will and life from everything divine, the contradiction of the whole man to all of God's which testifies of grace and mercy and truth and holiness; a sin therefore, in its very nature, excluding forgiveness;[2] while it excludes the conditions under which alone forgiveness could be obtained.

Will these who plead, '*Have we not prophesied in thy name? and in thy name have cast out devils?*' herein be speaking truly, or will this be a crowning untruth, added

---

[1] *Exp. Ep. ad Rom.*: Verbum enim dicere non ita videtur hîc positum, ut tantummodo illud intelligatur quod per linguam fabricamus, sed quod corde conceptum etiam opere exprimimus. Thus on the parallel, Rom. x. 10, 'With the mouth confession is made unto salvation,' he observes (*In Ev. Joh. Tract.* xxvi.): De radice cordis surgit ista confessio. Aliquando audis confitentem, et nescis credentem. Sed nec debes vocare confitentem, quem judicas non credentem. . . . Si aliud in corde habes, aliud dicis; loqueris, non confiteris. Here, it will be noted, he makes 'confess' to be the pregnant word.

[2] *Exp. Ep. ad Rom.*: Qui hoc verbum, quod sine veniâ vult intelligi Dominus, in Spiritum Sanctum dicit, hoc est, qui desperans de gratiâ et pace quam donat, in peccatis suis perseverandum sibi esse dicit, *dicere* intelligendus in factis.

to all that have gone before in their lives? Some, Augustine replies, might be tempted to understand it in the latter sense, that in this also they are liars, from finding a difficulty in attributing the actual performance of miracles or wonderful works to ungodly men, to any who should at last hear that terrible 'Depart from Me,' from the lips of the Saviour. But there is no difficulty here. The Egyptian magicians, Saul,[1] Balaam, with many more,[2] were most really partakers of a spiritual power, though they used it for their own harm; nor will it be otherwise, according to our Lord's own declaration, with the false prophets of the last days (Matt. xxii. 24). And, suggested by this and like passages, he has many instructive words and warnings on the nothingness of all gifts, even up to the greatest gift of working all miracles, if charity be wanting. These all are no proofs of holiness, without which holiness we cannot see God (Heb. xii. 14); while without these gifts we may very well have a place in his kingdom. And he often refers to the return of the Seventy. Not the gifts which they had in common with a few, not the fact that the devils were subject to them, were true subjects of rejoicing for them; but rather, as their Lord reminded them, that which they had in common with all believers, namely, that their names were written in Heaven (Luke x. 17–20).[3] And he has many warnings, drawn from the

[1] *Enarr. in Ps.* ciii. 3.
[2] *Ad Simplicianum,* ii. qu. 1 : Non enim eos mentientes putamus ista dicturos in illo judicio, ubi nullus erit fallendi locus, aut ullam vocem talium legimus, dicentium, Dileximus te. Cf. *Serm.* cxxxviii. 3.
[3] *Enarr. in Ps.* cxxx. 1 : Non omnes Christiani boni dæmones ejiciunt, omnium tamen nomina scripta sunt in cælo. Non eos voluit gaudere ex eo quod proprium habebant, sed ex eo quod cum cæteris salutem tenebant. Cf. *Serm.* cxliii. 7.

declaration here,[1] against wishing to be signalized in the Church for gifts, which always bring with them a danger of puffing up the possessor, rather than for graces, which will keep him humble. Better, in this mystical body, to be a little finger which is sound, than an eye which is bleared and winking;[2] though one be a member of such slight account, the other the noblest in the body.

Ver. 23. '*And then will I profess unto them, I never knew you: depart from Me, ye that work iniquity.*'— This, '*I never knew you*,' must be accepted according to that deeper meaning of *knowing*, which includes also loving—a knowing which, in its essence, is reciprocal, he only being known who also knows; so that Augustine has all right when he affirms, '*I never knew you*,' to be but another way of saying, Ye never knew Me. Not to be known of the Lord is never to have known Him, and is therefore itself the condemnation.[3] And hereupon follows that terrible sentence of doom, that everlasting separation from the presence of God,[4] wherein everything that is

[1] *Enarr. in Ps.* ciii. 3: Videant qualem rationem habituri sunt cum Deo qui sanctis non sancte utuntur.
[2] *Enarr. in Ps.* cxxx. 1: Tutior est enim in corpore digitus sanus, quam lippiens oculus. . . . Non ergo quærat quisque in corpore Christi nisi sanitatem.
[3] *Enarr. in Ps.* cxli. 4: Non novi nos. Non inde gaudeant et dicant, Non puniemur, quia non novit nos Judex. Jam puniti sunt, si eos non novit Judex.
[4] *Enarr. in Ps.* xlix. 3: Si enim possemus facere, fratres, ut dies judicii non veniret, puto quia nec sic erat male vivendum. Si non veniret ignis die judicii, et sola peccatoribus immineret separatio a facie Dei, in quâlibet essent affluentiâ deliciarum, non videntes a quo creati sunt, et separati ab illâ dulcedine ineffabilis vultûs ejus, in quâlibet æternitate et impunitate peccati, plangere se deberent. Sed quid loquar, aut quibus loquar ? Hæc amantibus pœna est, non contemnentibus. Qui dulcedinem sapientiæ et veritatis utcunque sentire cœperunt, noverunt quod dico, quanta pœna sit tantummodo a facie

fearful is contained. Augustine often brings out that the terribleness of that 'Depart from Me' presents itself unto men under very different aspects, as they are or are not the true servants and children of God. For the faithful man, for him who has been saying, 'One thing have I desired of the Lord, to behold the beauty of the Lord, and to enquire in his temple,' it is dreadful for this, even that it is exclusion from the face of the Beloved; he is not therefore one of the 'workers of iniquity,' lest he should thus lose the light of God's countenance.[1] But for the ungodly these words are dreadful, not for this exclusion, but only for the after pains and penalties which on this exclusion will follow; and if hindered from sinning, it is not the fear of displeasing that Lord, and so of being bidden to depart from Him, that hinders them; on the contrary, if they could ensure to themselves an eternal impunity of sinning, they would choose to sin on for ever. Not fear of this loss of his favour, of this separation from his presence, but the dread of what in his anger He could do to them, restrains them.[2] And he often presses each man to judge of him-

Dei separari: qui autem illam dulcedinem non gustaverunt, si nondum desiderant Dei faciem, timeant vel ignem; supplicia terreant, quem præmia non invitant. Cf. *Enarr.* 2ᵃ *in Ps.* xxvi. 9.

[1] Gratis amans, non puniri timens ab eo quem tremit, sed separari ab eo quem diligit.

[2] He has an instructive passage, *In* 1 *Ep. Joh. Tract.* ix. on the subject, where he likens souls in these two conditions to two wives; the one purely loving her absent husband, the other adulteress in will, though not daring to be also in deed; each *fearing* her husband. Et quomodo discernuntur duo ista timores? Timet illa, timet et illa; ... Jam ergo interrogentur, Quare? Illa dicit, Timeo virum, ne veniat: illa dicit, Timeo virum, ne discedat. Illa dicit, Timeo ne damner: illa dicit, Timeo, ne deserar. Yet the servile fear has its subordinate value; it may be keeping a place and making room for the holy fear, though the latter cannot enter till the first go out; to

self, and of his state, whether he be a lover of God or only a fearer of hell, by asking himself what is the truly terrible which this 'Depart from Me,' contains for him.[1]

Ver. 24–27. 'Therefore whosoever heareth these sayings of mine, and doeth them, I will liken him unto a wise man, which built his house upon a rock: and the rain descended, and the floods came, and the winds blew, and beat upon that house; and it fell not: for it was founded upon a rock. And every one that heareth these sayings of mine, and doeth them not, shall be likened unto a folish man, which built his house upon the sand: and the rain descended, and the floods came, and the winds blew, and beat upon that house; and it fell: and great was the fall of it.'—There is a solemn awfulness in this conclusion, which Augustine bids us specially to note; namely that neither by the one nor the other of these two classes, not by those who are swept away any more than by those who stand, can the open despisers of the truth be signified.[2] For in both cases there is a readiness to hear the word, a certain good-will therefore towards the truth. But this is not enough. In one way only does that which is heard win a stable foundation in the soul, that is, through passing into action, when the heard is also the obeyed. Christ, as in so many other places of Scripture, is Himself the 'rock;' that man builds on the rock, who does the things which he hears and learns of Christ. Augustine use his own illustration, Sicut videmus per setam introduci linum quando aliquid suitur, seta prius intrat, sed nisi exeat, non succedit linum.

[1] *Serm.* clxxviii. 10.
[2] *Ep.* cxxvii. 7: Dominus enim Jesus non ab iis qui non audiunt, sed eos inter se auditores verborum suorum, latissimo limite non tenui distinctione discrevit.

distinguishes, but not in a way calling for especial note, three forms of trial and temptation, as severally set forth under '*the winds,*' '*the rain,*' and '*the floods*;'[1] and in one place asks: If it be thus to have built insecurely, what will it be not to have built at all? Some indeed might say, Better not to build at all, if such is the doom of building insecurely. But will it be a more tolerable doom to be swept away naked, than to be swept away among and together with the ruins of thy fallen house?[2] That were not to hear at all, to have built nothing; this is to hear and not do, to have built weakly and insecurely. It remains as the only prudent thing,—to hear, and what we hear to do; being doers of the word, and not hearers only, deceiving our own selves (Jam. i. 22).

[1] Thus *Annot. in Job*, xxxviii. 25.
[2] *Serm.* clxxix. 9: Venit pluvia, veniunt flumina. Numquid ideo tutus, quia raperis nudus? *Enarr. in Ps.* cii. 21: Audire et non facere, in arenâ ædificare est; audire et facere, in petrâ ædificare est; nec audire, nec facere, nihil ædificare est. Si in arenâ ædificas, ruinam ædificas: si nihil ædificas, expositus pluviis, fluminibus, ventis, ante rapieris quam steteris. Ergo non est cessandum, sed ædificandum; nec sic ædificandum, ut ruina ædificetur; sed in petrâ ædificandum, ut tentatio non evertat.

The ample treasures of St. Augustine's writings have more than once suggested books not unlike this in plan. Thus there is a *Catena* on the Epistles of St. Paul drawn altogether from his works, which is commonly ascribed to Bede as its author; Baronius doubts whether correctly, but apparently on no sufficient grounds. There is a *Commentary on St. Luke*, collected by Jacobus a Logenhagen, Antverp., 1574; also, from an anonymous author, *Augustinus in Vetus et Novum Testamentum*, Basileæ, 1542. This last is slightly and negligently done: the obvious passages which one might lay hands on at once are given, but little care is used in collecting what is scattered up and down, and it abounds with large and needless gaps. The books of moral and theological *Loci Communes* which have been

SERMON ON THE MOUNT. 327

formed exclusively from his writings, have a remoter resemblance. Of such there are several, as *D. Aurelii Augustini Millelogium Veritatis*, a F. Bartholomæo de Urbino, Lugdunum, 1555, alphabetically arranged under several heads. Another commonplace book of his most notable sayings, by Johannes Piscatorius Lithopolitanus, Augustæ Vindelicorum, 1537, has not an alphabetical but a dogmatic arrangement. And of more importance than either of these is Reiser, *S. Augustinus Veritatis Evangelico-Catholicæ Testis et Confessor*, Francof., 1678; in this the chief passages of his writings are brought together in which he witnesses for the Reformed as against the Roman Catholic theology.

www.ingramcontent.com/pod-product-compliance
Lightning Source LLC
Chambersburg PA
CBHW070229230426
43664CB00014B/2251